Quality Lesson Plans for Outdoor Education

Kevin Redmond

Andrew Foran

Sean Dwyer

Human Kinetics

Library of Congress Cataloging-in-Publication Data

Redmond, Kevin.
    Quality lesson plans for outdoor education / Kevin Redmond, Andrew Foran, Sean Dwyer.
        p. cm.
    Includes bibliographical references.
    ISBN-13: 978-0-7360-7131-4 (soft cover)
    ISBN-10: 0-7360-7131-8 (soft cover)
    1. Recreation leaders--Training of--Handbooks, manuals, etc. 2. Outdoor recreation--Study and teaching--Handbooks, manuals, etc. 3. Outdoor education--Study and teaching--Handbooks, manuals, etc. 4. Experiential learning--Study and teaching--Handbooks, manuals, etc. I. Foran, Andrew. II. Dwyer, Sean, 1972- III. Title.
    GV181.35.R44 2010
    796.507--dc22

                2009035783

ISBN-10: 0-7360-7131-8
ISBN-13: 978-0-7360-7131-4

The Web addresses cited in this text were current as of August 2009, unless otherwise noted.

Acquisitions Editor: Gayle Kassing, PhD; **Developmental Editor:** Ray Vallese; **Assistant Editor:** Derek Campbell; **Copyeditor:** Alisha Jeddeloh; **Permission Manager:** Dalene Reeder; **Graphic Designer:** Bob Reuther; **Graphic Artist:** Denise Lowry; **Cover Designer:** Keith Blomberg; **Photographer (cover):** Kevin Redmond; **Photographer (interior):** Photos courtesy of the following, unless otherwise noted: Andrew Foran (introduction; units 1, 3, 11, and 12), Kevin Redmond (units 2, 4, 7-9, and 13-16), Darlene Thomasina Pidgeon (unit 5), Amanda Stanec (unit 6), Sean Dwyer (unit 10), Tara Marshall (unit 17), Matthew Ngo (unit 18), Janel Swain (unit 19), Blair Doyle (unit 20), and Zacchari Crouse (unit 21); **Photo Asset Manager:** Laura Fitch; **Visual Production Assistant:** Joyce Brumfield; **Photo Production Manager:** Jason Allen; **Art Manager:** Kelly Hendren; **Associate Art Manager:** Alan L. Wilborn; **Illustrators:** Argosy, unless otherwise noted; art on p. 53 by Keri Evans; figure 8.18 on p. 285 by Alan L. Wilborn; **Printer:** Versa Press

Printed in the United States of America   10   9   8   7   6   5   4   3   2   1

The paper in this book is certified under a sustainable forestry program.

Human Kinetics
Web site: www.HumanKinetics.com

United States: Human Kinetics, P.O. Box 5076, Champaign, IL 61825-5076
800-747-4457
e-mail: humank@hkusa.com

Canada: Human Kinetics, 475 Devonshire Road Unit 100, Windsor, ON N8Y 2L5
800-465-7301 (in Canada only)
e-mail: info@hkcanada.com

Europe: Human Kinetics, 107 Bradford Road, Stanningley, Leeds LS28 6AT, United Kingdom
+44 (0) 113 255 5665
e-mail: hk@hkeurope.com

Australia: Human Kinetics, 57A Price Avenue, Lower Mitcham, South Australia 5062
08 8372 0999
e-mail: info@hkaustralia.com

New Zealand: Human Kinetics, P.O. Box 80, Torrens Park, South Australia 5062
0800 222 062
e-mail: info@hknewzealand.com

To all those who get outside and embrace the world;
who lead others to follow and share in the abundance of life;
and who feel, smell, taste, hear, see, explore, and find adventure
in all things natural. For Len Rich, an outdoor enthusiast
whose time in this world has passed, but whose lessons will
live on in this book and in the curiosity of those who
cast their lines into the great unknown of the world.

Contents

CD-ROM Contents

Preface

T.A. Loeffler

Several summers ago, Kevin Redmond and I sat together in my office to flesh out a book proposal. We sacrificed a rare sunny June day to draft our ideas for a book that we both wanted and needed on our professional bookshelves but that no one had written yet. Both of us, busy outdoor educators, longed for a comprehensive resource to use in preparing our classes.

Kevin teaches outdoor education in his high school physical education classes, and I teach outdoor education to physical education students at the university level. Both of us juggle heavy teaching loads, family commitments, and personal outdoor dreams. We wanted a resource that would speed and guide our class preparations. We looked at what was available and couldn't find anything that gave us the detailed lesson plans we desired.

Three years later, I am thrilled to have on my bookshelf the asset that Kevin and I imagined that day. I would like thank Kevin, Andrew, and their team for their obvious hard work and attention to detail in the preparation of *Quality Lesson Plans for Outdoor Education.* I now have a wide-ranging resource, packaged into 13 book units and 8 CD-ROM units, that covers all of the major activities and knowledge areas I teach in my outdoor activity classes.

The book begins with an introduction to outdoor education. The authors use a thorough exploration of outdoor teaching strategy, philosophy, and technique to lead, inform, and inspire readers to improve their teaching. Following this, the book is organized into units that deliver detailed lesson plans for 13 outdoor activities.

As most outdoor programs would, the authors lead with a unit covering core camping skills. This unit provides excellent lesson plans for the development of foundational camping skills that every outdoor student needs. Units relating to navigation and environmental ethics round out the fundamental curricular skills and ensure that the reader is well prepared to teach students

how to stay warm, dry, and found while at the same time care for the environments in which they learn and travel.

The book contains six units devoted to land-based activities (hiking and backpacking, rock climbing, mountain biking, Nordic skiing, snowshoeing, and archery) and four units covering water-based activities (flatwater canoeing, whitewater canoeing, sea kayaking, and fly casting and fly fishing).

The CD-ROM bound into the book delivers eight additional units that cover whitewater kayaking, alpine skiing, telemark skiing, spin-cast fishing, weather, staying safe and comfortable, risk management, and leadership and group development. These units are available in PDF format so that outdoor leaders can easily print the lessons they want to carry into the field. In addition, the CD-ROM also contains PDF versions of the 13 units found in the book. Thus, all 21 units are available in electronic format for convenient searching and printing. This valuable feature saves both time and energy.

Another way that *Quality Lesson Plans for Outdoor Education* assists the reader is by presenting all of the units in the same format. Each unit begins with an introduction to the activity, equipment needed, site selection, social skills and etiquette, risk management, unit description, and short descriptions of the lessons. This enables the outdoor educator to rapidly move between units without having to navigate new terrain each time.

Similarly, within each unit, each lesson plan follows the same format. Beginning with an overview and learning objectives, the lesson plans highlight activities including both skill cues and teaching cues.

- Skill cues cover the important points for the educator to emphasize when teaching an outdoor skill (for example, care of canoe paddles).

- Teaching cues relate to how an instructor can teach particular skills (for example, demonstrating how to size a canoe paddle).

Lesson plans conclude with closure activities to facilitate reflection and integrate learning.

Quality Lesson Plans for Outdoor Education is a unique and groundbreaking resource for both outdoor educators and outdoor education students. In one comprehensive package, the authors deliver more than 140 lesson plans for teaching a variety of outdoor skills and knowledge. I am so grateful that Kevin and I forewent a day of sunshine to give birth to the idea that eventually led to this book. Having this tremendous resource will enable me to spend much more time outside having fun and less time inside planning classes. This book makes a substantial contribution to the field of outdoor education.

Warning: Extreme risks exist in outdoor activities, and serious injury or death can result. Although outdoor activities are enjoyable and the potential of injury or death can be minimized, the activities demand formal and competent training from a professional. Whether you are camping, rock climbing, mountain biking, canoeing, skiing, or participating in any of the other activities in this book, outdoor activities require a continuous skill base, repetition of sound practices, and numerous field experiences. Safety is the most important concern in any outdoor endeavor. This book is to be used as a reference tool only. It is not to replace or substitute professional training and field experiences. As the reader, you assume full responsibility for your own safety, and you assume the risks associated with outdoor activities. Be responsible: Get training, stay current on products and techniques, and know your limitations.

Acknowledgments

We would like to acknowledge the following people for their contribution in the completion of this book.

- Sophia, Thomas, Susan, and Jacquelyn Redmond; and Alec, Zachary, and Janice Foran for their support and willingness to model at a moment's notice
- Janice and Amy Dwyer for their support and understanding throughout the completion of this project
- The Nova Scotia Department of Education for their support in developing outdoor education curriculum
- Leo Van Ulden of Wallnuts Climbing Gym
- John Elkins, physical education itinerant with Eastern School District (igloo lesson)
- Sarah Skotty, Tiffany Hayne, and Patrick Duggan, physical education teachers

- Fred Carberry, retired physical education teacher, for his generous support with lesson plan materials and guidance over the years
- Mark Jones, former physical education specialist with NL Department of Education
- Richard J.R. Mandville (strike indicator)
- Joan Wulff of Fly-O fly casting progressions
- T.A. Loeffler of Memorial University of Newfoundland and Labrador—your collaboration in the original proposal for this book and continued support are reflected in the final product. Thank you!

Gayle Kassing, Ray Vallese, Derek Campbell, Kate Kaput, and the rest of the team at Human Kinetics—your expertise, professionalism, and solution-oriented approach have made this monumental project manageable and pleasurable. Thank you for your hard work, continued guidance, and support.

Introduction

▼ Andrew Foran ▼

For many people, life seems to be drawing a strong divide between outside and inside. Many of us have forgotten that the outdoors can be inhabited as a classroom, a valuable learning site. However, teaching in the outdoors is different from teaching in a classroom or gymnasium. The outdoors is a place where participants have the opportunity to actualize and expand their understanding of content and abstract curriculum. They discover personal growth insights as they form positive community relations. Many skills can be realized in the outdoors beyond the skills of various outdoor pursuits, including communication, cooperation, problem solving, decision making, citizenship, and critical thinking.

Being outdoors is a sensual experience. The big-picture visual, the body caressed by the elements, the natural scents of local flora and fauna—all of these contribute to a teaching environment that is potentially more distracting while at the same time all the more rewarding than an indoor classroom. Participating in activities under these conditions has the potential to elevate the intensity of the experience—to create an adventure in education.

Outdoor education uses the natural environment to help participants learn experientially, and direct experience is the foundation for the lessons in this text. As outdoor leaders coordinating these learning experiences, we will always position practitioners as reflective and seeking opportunities to strengthen their outdoor practices to improve the quality of the learning experience for their participants. The outdoor classroom is a paradox, limitless for instructional purposes but challenging in establishing safe yet effective boundaries for learning. The quality of the outdoor learning experience is significant for helping participants experience personal success, realize an intense

focus on their self-esteem as active and engaged people, and develop an authentic connection to natural wonders. Engaging in active learning with others has the ability to fill the senses to the point of creating a life-changing event. The outdoor classroom frequently brings learning beyond the cerebral to touch the hearts of participants whereby they become advocates of environmental awareness and protection.

Learning and growth require time for reflection.

The power of the outdoor experience is further manifested in testimonials of those who have participated in an outdoor activity program. Oftentimes the skills taught are forgotten, but the experience is the catalyst for lifelong personal growth and pleasure by interacting with the natural world through outdoor activities.

Philosophy and Strategy

The most important consideration when teaching outdoors is to provide an experience that lures participants into the activity and provides a positive experience, leaving the participants with the desire to do it again. Activities in this book are to be delivered using an experiential approach to teaching and learning. The objective is to learn by doing and to reflect on the activities with guidance from the outdoor leader to ensure connections to the intended outcome were made. The goal of the outdoor leader is to provide participants with a positive experience and to allow the lesson to occur in the intended environment, resulting in authenticity for the participant. The expectation is for outdoor leaders to teach these activities in the environment they were intended for, to use the related equipment as it was intended, to adhere to set standards within each of the pursuits to ensure safety, and to impart the subtleties of related etiquette.

Experiential education is concerned with enhancing the lesson content through interaction between learner and educator, learner and environment, and learner and other learners. Experiential education develops the competency of the learner to integrate what is being taught with the actions that are required for each skill. The outdoor leader is responsible for establishing the learning environment, placing boundaries on the learning objectives, sharing appropriate information to support the learning, and facilitating the learning in general. It is essential for participants to be actively engaged in cocreating the educational process and aware of their learning within the activities, which require careful guidance of the outdoor leader.

Outdoor leaders need to be knowledgeable, skilled, and able to relate to their participants in order to provide constructive feedback on their developing competencies in a given outdoor pursuit. Therefore, the outdoor leader has to engage in a process of learning that contains a knowledge component, a doing component, and a valuing component that is based on an outcome-focused reflection connected to learning activities that appropriately sequence the transfer of learning. Furthermore, it is important to bring attention to two learning orientations that tend to result in outdoor activities: personal growth and the growth of the group as a learning community. The outdoor leader has to balance the individual experience and the group experience; both contribute to a positive learning experience. Additionally, a peak experience for some may not be the highlight for a group. Everyone is different; thus the value that is garnered from the activities will be within degrees.

Quite simply, outdoor education is leading participants through carefully selected activities that challenge them to consciously apply their knowledge and skills. We advocate activities that integrate and involve the following:

- Any combination of senses: touch, smell, hearing, sight, taste
- Appropriate, positive release and reason for emotions: pleasure, excitement, anxiety, fear, hurt, empathy, attachment
- Appropriate level of challenge for the physical conditions: environmental conditions, strength, energy level
- Cognition based on reflection: constructing knowledge, establishing beliefs, solving problems

Outdoor education has the potential to be holistic as multiple domains of learning are built into the learning process, contributing to physical, emotional, spiritual, and social beings. Guided by the outdoor leader, participants become aware of their ability and see the value of the shared experience with others—the emergence of a learning community outdoors. As well, the outdoor leader is not disconnected from the learning process; being active in the learning process allows the outdoor leader to share in the process of learning. Teachers learn from teaching outside and from the generated learning of their group.

A critical understanding for the outdoor leader is that learning does not happen only because you do something! We advocate hands-on and minds-on learning; thus, reflection must lead participants to their performance within the intended outcome of each activity. Genuine, constructive feedback must be offered to participants, showing them where they have to grow for proficiency. The outdoor leader must be willing to assess the growth of participants, both formally and informally, and connect this assessment to the domains of learning—mental, physical, and emotional. Therefore, for outdoor education the stance is personal and group development resulting from the ability of participants to set goals, constructively build on previous experience, experiment with introduced knowledge and skills to see what works and how it works for them as learners, and revise their goals and knowledge based on their experience. This text has outdoor leaders focus on the areas of creative problem solving, communication, cooperation, decision making, critical thinking, team building, conflict resolution, and fun. These skills are central in our desire to lead people in outdoor education programs.

Skills Enriching the Experience

Outdoor education is a specialized body of instruction. It would be rare for any one outdoor leader to possess competencies related to all possible outdoor pursuits. Additionally, it is often sound practice to begin with the experiences, curiosities, and questions of those engaged in the experience. When programming with integrity, the outdoor leader approaches each activity with the appropriate skill level, equipment, critical thinking focused on detecting and correcting areas for skill improvement, ability to dialogue with participants, and ability to assess participants to further challenge and refine their ability. However, the participants have a responsibility as well. They must ask questions of themselves and link themselves to their learning communities, supporting others in their learning experiences and ensuring positive learning based on sound decisions and meaningful action.

As with any type of education, outdoor education can be done well or badly, with or without attention and care. The outdoor leader must never take the position that the experience is the only teacher; this could lead to the perception that experiential education is not a rigorous or beneficial learning experience. Outdoor leaders cannot shrug off their instructional responsibilities and allow the outdoor experience to run its course, placing more responsibility on the shoulders of their participants. The onus of responsibility for any learning is on the participant, but all responsibility for teaching rests on the outdoor leader. There is no place for an apathetic person, whether participant or outdoor leader, to hide when it is that person's responsibility to actively construct new knowledge and skill.

The goal in outdoor education is holistic learning. The goal of the outdoor leader is to help participants become aware of the world, their skill level in a pursuit, their contribution to their learning community, and the inevitable interaction between the environment and learning. If anything, outdoor education demands that outdoor leaders pay even greater attention to the quality of the lesson by asking the following: What did participants know before the experience, what do they know because of the experience, and how can I challenge them to grow?

When we turn to the question of why we should engage in outdoor education as a form of experiential learning, many outdoor leaders can attest to the richness of being in the field and that the more active our learning is, the more we seem to retain. Indeed, for some it is only the opportunity to participate in hands-on learning experiences that commits them to the learning process. By insisting that abstract intellectual exchange is the only way to demonstrate academic ability, we may be preventing numerous people from both discovering and demonstrating their potential. When it comes to learning style, concrete, socially contextual learning is often the preferred mode.

The following is a list of essential skill areas for the outdoor leader:

- Skill development in every outdoor pursuit is an essential component of any outdoor educational experience.
- When skill is essential to safety (e.g., belaying and climbing), learning the skills is nonnegotiable and a primary focus of the program.
- When skill enriches the experience, skill development may occur at a more relaxed pace based on individual readiness to learn (e.g., strokes to keep the canoe going straight).
- Give participants enough information and practice with a skill that they can feed themselves with more after the session because of curiosity and simple enjoyment of the outdoor activity.
- A cross-curricular approach helps make connections to related areas in learning and life, allowing for greater diversity of learning opportunities, teachable moments, and ultimately a broader experience.

Tips for Teaching in the Outdoors

The educational philosophy of experiential education first developed in the late 19th century and has since been articulated in a variety of fields, including cooperative education, outdoor education, organizational development and training, and service learning. The essence of experiential education is the notion that experiential moments—doing as part of the learning process—can result in meaningful learning. Effective teaching requires that the outdoor leader take an active role in constructing the learning with participants—learning is not to be left to chance, nor is the meaning of the experience for the participants assumed to be the intended learning. No one can argue that experience happens—it is unavoidable—but learning is a delicate process as the outdoor leader helps the participant make sense out of a communal process.

Teaching in natural spaces can enhance the learning experience—the place makes it more meaningful.

The challenge for outdoor leaders and participants is how to make meaning out of an experience: how to begin with raw experience and then process the intentional learning into working knowledge. An assumption of experiential education is that it is intended to be holistic and integrative, based on the process of making meaning out of experience. The idea that experience, learning, and development are interconnected has provided a jumping-off point for various forms of outdoor programs.

Natural Spaces as Natural Classrooms
- Use natural divides such as trees, foliage, and rivers to create an effective outdoor classroom.
- Natural spaces help provide a sense of authenticity for the learning. Go beyond the notion of "If you can teach it outside, do it" to teach the skills in the environment that was intended.

Risk Assessment of Site
- The teaching site should be free of residual risk and with clearly established boundaries.
- Where risks exist, they should be highlighted to the group and management strategies should be in effect.

Large-Group Management
- Large groups should be broken into smaller groups or stations.
- You should be able to observe all groups from a central area, though the groups may be somewhat separated by natural divides.

Natural Teaching Aids
- Use what is accessible to aid your delivery, such as using hands and knuckles to demonstrate topography or a canoe as a chalkboard.
- You need to develop strategies to help your participants learn: visual cues (diagrams, checklists), analogies related to the topic, appropriate personal stories that depict learning moments that participants can relate to, focused group discussions that draw out participant knowledge, skill demonstrations, stop–start techniques to break complex skill sets down for learners, and so on. These are only a few examples of instructional strategies.

Sun
- The sun should be in your eyes, making it easy for participants to see you.

- In cold climates, select a site where sun shines on participants' backs for a warming effect.
- In hot climates, avoid the sun if possible by moving to a shaded area.

Wind

- Wind should carry sound to participants; it should be moving from you toward participants.
- In cold climates, avoid windy teaching sites because of the cooling effect of wind.
- In hot climates, wind may help cool participants, making them more comfortable.

Water In, Water Out and Thermoregulation

- Adequate water-in, water-out breaks should be provided, allowing participants to maintain healthy hydration and thermoregulation.
- Check participants to make sure they are dry, and if they are damp, insist on changes of clothing.

Safety

- The activity must be delivered in a manner that is safe and that participants perceive as safe.
- This assessment depends on the group's maturity and skill level, the terrain, and the technical challenge of the outdoor lesson.

Skill

- You should only place a primary emphasis on skill development when the skill is essential to the safety of the participants.
- Skill is to be developed to the minimum required for completing the tasks essential to achieving the experience. The ultimate goal is for participants to leave with a positive outdoor experience. When appropriate, challenge learners to stretch and expand their skill abilities by leading extension activities.
- Further skill development may be necessary to elevate participants' technical expertise. For example, when paddling a river, participants may navigate a rapid by running straight through without stopping; learning skills such as eddy turns, ferries, and surfing will elevate the experience for participants as the novelty of the primary experience wears off.

Specific Strategies for Teaching in the Outdoor Classroom

- Teach in outside places that are authentic to the lesson.

- Participants have expectations for the activity; do not lose sight of the doing as a means for authentic learning.
- The outdoors is a natural classroom where teaching and learning can be different than in the indoor classroom. Take steps to preserve your instructional space for future lessons.
- Participant interests can be sparked through firsthand experience, a necessary aspect of the experiential process; be sure to match the activity challenge to the age of the participants.
- Participants require outdoor leaders who are knowledgeable, informed, interested, and attentive—show enthusiasm during the session regardless of the weather!
- Develop a sense of community, a safe, fun, friendly environment for learning and practicing new skills.
- Move the focus from competitive aspects to skill performance; focus on progression with positive support by providing constructive feedback.
- Know the outcomes for each activity. This will allow detection (what is not quite right) and correction (skill adjustments to improve performance).
- Be prepared for each lesson: Have safety checks in place, reminders for updating participants, equipment inspected, and the instructional site confirmed and inspected.
- Participant engagement is essential; keep it fun but in a structured format to maximize learning time in the field.
- Use visuals and a hands-on approach for demonstrations—promote a sense of doing.
- Participants pay less attention to long speeches. Use simple words and phrases in discussions.

Facilitation

On the surface, experiential education can look somewhat chaotic. It appears messy and nonlinear and can require participants to experiment, practice, fail, and reassess before they find success in an outdoor activity. Learning connections in outdoor activities depend on your ability to assess the learning and help the participant apply meaning to the experience—this is a nonlinear, recursive process. You must be in tune with what is here and now.

Keep participants' focus in the moment. Learning outside may not take a linear route; therefore, facilitation is essential.

- The essence of experiential learning is that it is participant centered, not educator centered.
- An outdoor leader must be connected to the participants, alive with all the senses to feel where the participants are with the experience.
- Outdoor leaders cannot merely toe their own line during the experience and push their own agenda in spite of the participants' skill and comfort levels in the outdoor pursuit.
- Outdoor leaders must remain as human as anyone else; thus, they must be in touch with three levels of participation: their own experience, the participant's experience, and the group's experience.
- Facilitation is more about asking the right questions than about giving the right answers.
- In outdoor activities, there is a constructed reality due to direct-learning experiences; thus, each participant has an experienced reality. The outdoor leader should be able to glimpse and respect the experienced reality of each group member.

Effective outdoor leaders are able to focus on the learning of each participant by centering the intended outcome with the following:

- Articulate the unarticulated—help participants articulate and connect to their understanding and performance within a particular skill. Do not say it for them; it's not your experience but theirs.
- Make the invisible visible—show the participants what they were doing and able to do. Build on the positive to motivate them to challenge themselves within the activity.
- Own the disowned—help participants take ownership of weaknesses and set goals that allow them to perform to the ability they strive for in a particular activity.
- Allow for engaged doing—help participants to drop their inhibitions and express thoughts, ideas, and feelings with spontaneity in a trusting and supportive environment.
- Honest facilitation allows outdoor leaders to model integrity by incorporating their expertise in a way that encourages their participants to take risks in trying new skills.

- Outdoor leaders should model themselves as learners in the facilitation of the experience. This allows participants to see the outdoor leader as a growing learner who gained skill competency over time and that the outdoor leader's role is not to intimidate but to share abilities for others to learn from.
- An essential teaching strategy is maintaining instructional core values: Respect the basic human dignity of others, preserve the safety of participants as the prime responsibility, be prepared to lead in the field, and create positive learning moments.
- Finally, effective outdoor leaders do not have to have all the answers; rather, they need curiosity and the ability to explore answers with their participants and model lifelong learning strategies as they share and practice outdoor pursuit skills with the participants.

Personal Readiness and the Right to Opt Out

Each person should be in a state of readiness to participate and aware that anyone may opt out of an activity (which may then be modified to suit the participant's readiness). Outdoor leaders should not exercise pressure to perform to coerce participants to participate; instead, support and encouragement may be helpful in building confidence and readiness. When participants feel safe and capable, they are more apt to commit to the skill or experience that is in front of them. Most often support and encouragement is enough to lead the participant to the skill.

Perceived Fear Versus Anxiety

Fear inhibits performance, whereas anxiety at the right level increases performance. Increasing perceived risk without increasing real risk is one means of increasing anxiety and elevating the experience for participants. Facilitating emotional responses that are representative of personal accomplishments can leave participants with greater confidence, self-esteem, and camaraderie when the experience is shared as part of a team challenge.

Fear should be recognized as a healthy red flag in the decision-making process. Fear should be a catalyst for rational thought, or logical, solution-oriented thinking that facilitates good judgment and ultimately is integral to a positive experience. Fear-induced learning to say no or to take an alternative approach to a challenge should be reinforced as positive.

Social Responsibility

Everyone has a personal responsibility to do the following:

- Follow instructions.
- Perform tasks as expected.
- Look out for others in the group.
- Contribute in an appropriate manner to make the experience better for others.
- Avoid risks that can compromise the safety of others.
- Realize that there are smart risks and harmful risks associated with every outdoor pursuit.
- Respect all participants' skill levels and comfort associated with each activity.
- Be willing to support others and exercise patience as others are trying.
- Be willing to practice and help coach others; we all learn at different rates.

Teachable Moments

Teaching outside is more than just covering a given subject outdoors; outdoor leaders need to facilitate learning in outdoor experiences. Teaching outside is not a simple act, but with sound facilitation, rich learning moments are possible. Direct experiences offer numerous opportunities to connect participants to deep learning moments.

To reach these moments in facilitation, be prepared to do the following:

- Probe participant responses with questions that have them dig deeper; beneath the surface of questions and comments lie deeper dimensions of participant perceptions.
- Take the time to explore what participants experienced when something unique occurs in the learning experience.
- Create moments that are adventurous, exciting, challenging, liberating, fulfilling, and even magical.
- Look for simple things to support the learning experience; they can contribute to profound moments as much as the grand experience.
- Question the value of the moment for participants and yourself—how do these moments shape your understanding and growth?

- Look for personal accomplishments by your participants and subtly draw their attention to this learning connection.
- Recognize when significant moments emerge, connecting participants to the skill, to the environment, or to their understanding—celebrate the "Oh yeah!" moment.

Balancing Risk and Control

Compounding the complexity of all types of learning and how people learn in experiential activities is the fact many could perceive the learning environment as chaotic. The result is fear due to control concerns.

- Outdoor leaders need to discern what is actually controllable, preventable, anticipated, and planned for.
- By the nature of the learning process, learning outdoors can expose participants to degrees of risk.
- Due to the risk, outdoor leaders are required to have competency in the skill being taught.
- Outdoor leaders need to focus on the participants' experience and not on their own ability or inability to perform.
- The issue of risk and control involves being able to garner enough control over the planned activity, gauging participant ability and anticipating how environment, skill levels, and leadership can prevent the activity from taking control of the experience. The outdoor leader must always balance the needs of the group and individual learners with the progression of the planned lesson—people first!
- The outdoor leader does not give up control but practices due diligence by creating an environment with a calculated level of risk that allows for short-term failures and long-term successes as participants gain confidence and learn constructively.
- Outdoor leaders must ensure the mental, physical, and emotional health of all participants. Minimally, the maxim "Do no harm" is a requirement for all outdoor leaders.
- A fundamental challenge for outdoor leaders is balancing risk, challenge, growth, and appropriate learning. If there is no real risk involved, no real challenge, no growth, was there even an experience worth noting?
- Outdoor leaders guide participants to achieve a new level of skill or insight, promoting

self-determination and competence, which requires a time of transition or dissonance.

- The planning goal is to create opportunities that stretch participants without breaking them; thus outdoor leaders must be adept at creating opportunities for optimal dissonance and intentional in establishing opportunities for future growth and motivation to participate in future outdoor activities.
- When assessing the risk of an outdoor activity, outdoor leaders must focus on *how to be in a place* outside with participants.

There is no denying the risk inherent in teaching away from the support, comfort, and controlled environment of institutional structures. A well-led learning endeavor does not just happen; instead, the outdoor leader plans for the appropriate degrees of risk. Meaningful education cannot be easily packaged. Does the risk of the experience reside in the difficulty of the activity or within the relationship between participant and peers and the outdoor leader? Almost certainly, some outdoor leaders rob participants of learning experiences by ending the process with an excuse or by providing the answer because the risk proved too great for the leader. An outdoor experience requires degrees of risk; it requires leading participants to engage in an experience that will allow them to grow in a positive way.

Planting the Seed: The Genesis for More Adventure

A well-facilitated experience plants the seeds for more activity and adventure outside. Everyone has a personal Mount Everest that may change over time. The aim for facilitating outdoor learning is to have participants wanting to do and learn more.

- Direct learning experiences can allow people to actualize their dreams—one does not always have to go to Everest to achieve this experience!
- The confidence that comes from making dreams reality is a catalyst for planning new adventures outside.
- Initial experiences may be with the support of a class or program, and over time they become completely self-directed as the participant gains confidence and competence along with the willingness to continue to explore outdoor pursuits.

- Outdoor education promotes concrete, practical problem solving as participants encounter tangible challenges that connect them to learning.
- Outdoor education allows participants to experience recreation and activity that promote healthy lifestyles and that can be integrated into a lifelong pursuit of outdoor activities.
- Outdoor education is the nexus between a unifying mode of learning that enables participants to gain hands-on skills as well as cognitive and social skills, including problem solving, decision making, communication, critical thinking, and cooperation. In a highly competitive global market, we can no longer afford to cultivate minds untested by concrete, practical problems of the world.
- Testing ideas in action—experiential education—is one of the most powerful means available for promoting new learning by building on a participant's prior knowledge and appreciation for a particular subject or activity.
- Outdoor leaders must understand how participants can learn from outdoor experiences and how they can measure the experience to determine what they learned.
- Not all experiences are genuinely or equally educative. For learning purposes, the experiential process contributes to participant growth in the intellectual domain, physical domain, and even the moral domain of engaging with others.
- The aim of outdoor education is future growth and whether participants will be able to transfer what they learned to future settings.
- If cultivated by the outdoor leader, the direct experience has the potential to create learning conditions that lead to further growth. The experience can strengthen participant motivation and initiative to learn more and do more in a particular activity, to explore similar experiences, and to further engage with others in future experiences.
- The responsibility of the outdoor leader is to create the conditions for experiences that foster self-esteem, learning growth, and personal awareness. This knowledge could help participants learn in other areas in life, giving them the ability to anticipate and respond to particular life situations, bonding their confidence of what they have learned with knowing what they can or cannot do as a result of direct experiences.

Outdoor leaders must have the vision to see the growth potential in every participant.

Designing Outdoor Lessons

Formal attention to structuring outdoor experiences has seen tremendous growth in the last few decades. However, there is room for improvement in practice before many see the full potential of outdoor education. Numerous fields of expertise constitute a particular pursuit that requires certain levels of competency to exceed simple recreation or leisure. Outdoor education offers experiences that hopefully suit participants' interest to learn skills for physical and cognitive purposes.

The outdoor experience must be suited to the ability and interest of a particular group and most importantly to the skill level of the outdoor leader. The purpose of the lesson plan thus should live up to the *designed purpose:* We are going outside today to learn these skills for this reason using this equipment. Outdoor leaders must anticipate and respond to the questions and problems that are naturally associated with each pursuit, requiring them to have more than just knowledge of skill.

Not all outdoor pursuits require the same expectations from the participant and the outdoor leader in terms of ability, knowledge, and risk. Each activity in this text is unique and should be modified to fit the outdoor leader's particular teaching environment. The ability to discern these complexities stems from the ability of the outdoor leader to design a program that is based on best practices, which are derived from the accumulation of working knowledge, which is derived from firsthand experience. The importance of personal experience in delivering the lesson is critical when designing a quality learning experience.

However, best practices simply are not enough. The outdoor leader must have the ability to implement the lesson plan safely. Each participant is expected to engage in each activity—it is not an abstract experience that occurs within the comfort of a building in front of a medium that transmits information. Direct experience requires the outdoor leader to take into account the challenges of the environment, plan for a variety of skill levels, and support participants as they gain confidence in a particular skill. Outdoor leaders cannot just allow experience to be the design of the lesson plan. The lesson plan is much more than a plan; it's the ability to live the plan outdoors with others.

Quality Lesson Plans

Teaching outside tends to be expensive due to equipment requirements and transportation to learning sites. The challenge of the experiential process is allowing participants ample time to practice skills, which can take considerable time in a scheduled unit—more than what was planned for! Quality rests with the outdoor leader taking the time to explore what is necessary to make a quality learning experience. Because experiential education attempts to teach holistically, it can take longer to accomplish the lesson, but it is increasingly effective over time due to the rich learning experiences that can be had outdoors. The outdoor leader must develop organization skills for time management, equipment allocation, and participant well-being. There is no time for fumbling around when teaching a lesson in the outdoors.

The success of outdoor instruction depends upon the quality of the experience. The basic elements contributing to the quality of the experience will be determined by outdoor leaders who have established practices by *walking the talk.* These planning qualities apply to all lesson plans in this text; they are based on actual experiences and are experiential in nature—the participants are doing as part of the learning process. The lesson plans are infused with the following qualities:

- **Purpose:** Each lesson has intentional learning designed as a central feature—there is a specific outcome for the learner to achieve.
- **Authenticity:** There is an actual doing component for each participant, using proper equipment in a safe environment conducive to learning.
- **Planning:** Planning is a deliberate act, and the outdoor leader has an active role in preparing the outdoor lesson to ensure a quality experience.
- **Organization:** Each lesson is planned; lessons are clearly laid out, set up in advance, and professionally delivered by a competent outdoor leader.
- **Orientation for social etiquette:** Certain behavior is expected of each participant, imparting a sense of stewardship among the group when engaging in the activity—a community of learners upholds a set of spoken or in some instances unspoken rules of engagement for each outdoor pursuit.

- **Monitoring:** Each participant is monitored and receives constructive feedback to foster self-esteem and ensure growth and competency in the outdoor pursuit.
- **Assessment:** All participants are expecting and should receive critical and constructive feedback on their performance, allowing them to feel good about their progress while indicating how they can continue to grow.
- **Reflection:** Time is provided to engage in reflection for self-assessment. This time is guided by the outdoor leader to ensure learning and that personal connections are made to the outcome.
- **Lifelong engagement:** Opportunity is given to practice and explore the outdoor pursuit, showing participants how they can incorporate outdoor activities in their lives outside the program.
- **Fun and acknowledgment:** All participants deserve the opportunity to be recognized for what they are able to do—their personal best in any activity—and this opportunity should occur in a fun, supportive environment that encourages participation and camaraderie. Most times it is more than just skills; outdoor education is about discovering oneself with others and forging lifelong relationships based on shared experiences.

In planning any outdoor lesson, the outdoor leader must focus on the learning process as listed here and ask: What specific learning and knowledge do I intend for participants as a result of engaging them in a particular experience? The answers to this question can guide, but do not dictate, the overall plan. To reach an outcome, the outdoor leader needs to consider subsequent choices of instruction by being flexible and not limiting the unique ways people can learn; rather, the outdoor leader embraces learning styles and abilities of participants. To ensure participants reach the intended outcome, outdoor leaders must plan for checkpoints to determine how to best adjust the plan for their individual learners to have the best possible learning experience. Outdoor leaders must ensure that the purpose—the outcome—is the focus of the experience. The means to measure learning should not be separate from the outcome, nor should the outdoor leader lose sight of the lesson purpose despite the experience and the environment.

The planning process opens the experience to empower participants to contribute to the learning process by being active members in decision making, working with others, communicating effectively, and problem solving. By engaging in this open process, outdoor leaders have the opportunity to receive participant feedback so that they can plan and adjust to the needs of their learners. This ensures that the planned activity maintains a course of experiential direction that is realistic and useful due to participant ownership in the planning process. In addition, this level of engagement by the outdoor leader and participants provides for meaningful understanding of why they are focused on particular learning goals in an outdoor pursuit.

A quality learning experience depends on clear expectations that include shared responsibilities between the outdoor leader and the participants. Clarity results in participants who are actively involved, opportunities for them to articulate aspirations for learning and personal development, and opportunities to participate in their assessment and monitor their growth. The key for the outdoor leader is to allow for flexibility in designing outdoor lessons to balance the multitude of interests. However, outdoor leaders should not allow the outcome to expand far beyond the plan—keep the outcome and participants in the forefront of your thinking by asking, "What is best for my participants at this moment in the lesson?" Essentially, the outdoor leader should balance flexibility with the integrity and coherence of the lesson plan by not sacrificing purpose, clarity, and the outcome for each activity.

Much of what outdoor leaders provide is support for participants as a mentor. This support recognizes learning as a lifelong process, and mentoring of participants may prove to be more effective as you monitor their progress and assess their accomplishments. Monitoring and assessment will be a well-defined, invested process, moving the instructional relationship beyond the simplicity of evaluating progress by scoring a test. During the planning process, participants have the opportunity to be involved in the expectations for them, and they better understand the role of the outdoor leader as a coach, not a judge. Furthermore, when participants are involved in actual experiences with the outdoor leader as part of the learning experience, they see their outdoor leader not as separate from their experience but as a person involved in their skill performance and understanding of the outdoor activity.

Essentials for Outdoor Lessons

Outdoor leaders must assess the ability of the people who have entrusted them to provide accurate feedback designed to encourage their learning, not destroy their self-esteem. The challenge is how to best assess participants in an outdoor environment. Positive and corrective feedback for participants is essential. As outdoor leaders, we can ask the following question: How can assessment of someone's progress in an outdoor pursuit contribute to quality, and how can we help our participants assess their own performance? These growth indicators should assess growth as a continuous process that is moving each participant to reach competencies expected in a particular pursuit.

The outdoor leader must incorporate the experience itself in the measure of whether the outcome was met—the environment for the learning cannot be separated from the measure. Outdoor leaders must regularly challenge their participants to question their actions and abilities with the aim of improvement. To do this, the outdoor leader must be able to demonstrate what quality looks like, not just talk about it.

A simple lesson-planning technique that many outdoor leaders use to facilitate learning is a step-by-step approach to ensure that the experiential aspect of the learning experience is not lost to an overabundance of teacher talk and that participants have a sound point of reference to work from—the 4 Ds. We have gravitated to the following checkpoints in planning a quality outdoor lesson:

- **Describe:** Briefly frontload the experience by telling the participants what they will be doing, describing the experience to help them prepare, helping them set their expectations for each activity, and fostering curiosity and motivation by revealing your own experience, thus personalizing the value of the experience.
- **Demonstrate:** Show key aspects of the skill. Help participants to see what they will be doing and the standard that is expected of the skill, providing the opportunity to set realistic personal goals.
- **Do:** Give the participants ample time to practice the skill. Be present and provide feedback, direction, or challenges when needed. Support participants' efforts to gain confidence in the outdoor pursuit.

- **Debrief:** Help process the learning experience for participants: what they learned, how they did, how they can improve, what they did well, what they will do next time, and so on.

The debriefing is an excellent opportunity to provide feedback based on the learning outcome of the lesson. The feedback needs to be communicated in a manner that builds willingness to participate in future activities but does not promote a false sense of ability to perform with competency. The debriefing can lead to a more formal assessment (discussed later) or serve as an informal gauge of how participants are progressing.

Therefore, there is a pressing need for the outdoor leader to engage in continual monitoring and assessment as participants learn and practice each skill. However, avoid the testing mentality when measuring learning. The outdoor leader should promote the belief that in outdoor activities, there is improvement over time that can be measured through reflection. Reflection is a deliberate strategy to debrief the internalization of knowledge. To reflect on an experience is to look back over the experience and extract personal learning.

Reflection is an integral part of the learning process and should begin at the start of the learning experience (the Describe checkpoint) in the form of questioning: Have you done this before? How did you experience this activity in past? What skills do you have that are related to this experience? For reflection to be meaningful, it should be focused on the activity itself and not a discussion of unrelated experiences (although they could be important in another time and place). Effective reflection comes from the ability of the outdoor leader to question the participants' experience and to help them to reconnect to their own learning—a connected knowing.

Reflection is not an ending phase in the learning process; rather, it occurs throughout the learning experience, even in the Demonstrate checkpoint, through questions such as these: Does this look familiar? Did you do this in the past? Have you seen this before?

Reflection is also part of the Doing checkpoint. There must be time to practice the skill, with guided, constructive feedback coaching the participant through the skill.

Reflection is critical to the debriefing, but at no time is it to be separate from the learning process as something to be saved for the end of the lesson. If guided effectively, reflection on the learning process is defined by the outcome set in the outdoor activity. Thus reflection enables learners to examine their actions and learning against the outcome measures they established and to use constructive feedback to strengthen improvement.

Beyond these integrated reflection opportunities, participants should be offered a variety of structured and unstructured activities that support reflection (i.e., one-to-one question-and-answer sessions, simulations, small-group discussions, focused conversation) to ensure that intended and serendipitous learning goals are addressed in lesson-plan closure and extensions for future engagement. Reflection is inseparable from the intended outcomes of the learning experience. In order to be evaluated, outcomes must be measurable.

Planning Lessons

A wise practice for any outdoor leader is to plan the lesson well in advance of the participants' arrival. We have broken the planning stages into the following progression: presession plan, in-session monitoring, and postsession follow-up. Before getting to the details of the lesson plan, outdoor leaders must assess their skill, instructional capacity, and lesson expectations as a benchmark to ensure a safe and positive learning experience. Participants' age, readiness to learn and comfort level with the outdoor pursuit, and physical abilities need to be considered when planning the sessions. As well, the outdoor leader needs to be comfortable and prepared to contribute to the learning experience. At any time during the lesson, the outdoor leader has the final say in gauging the degree of challenge to ensure safety.

The following section outlines plan implementation. An essential trait for implementation is organization; *know the plan and work it*, remaining flexible to build on quality and safety. It is prudent to clarify any organizational policies and procedures and build this awareness directly into the plan. In addition, it is important for the outdoor leader to establish guidelines and community standards (acceptable behaviors linked directly to suggestions for social etiquette) to help set specific learning goals.

In living out your lesson in the field, use the following considerations as a framework:

- The outdoor leader needs to balance the needs of the participants with program expectations.
- The lesson plan should respect the participants and promote experiential engagement in an outdoor community of learners.
- Every lesson will require preparation and practice to accomplish outcomes. The outdoor leader may at times require a coleader to ensure quality and safety; seek others for support.
- The outdoor leader's qualifications must include not only physical skills and fitness and relevant certifications (if appropriate) but also the ability to lead people.
- The outdoor leader must be familiar with the location and environment before allowing the lesson to unfold. This requires the leader to survey the area before developing the lesson plan—site characteristics must be built into the plan.
- Not everything can be known in advance. Current conditions such as unpredictable weather can have a large effect on an outside activity, so a lesson must be flexible. Be aware of the anticipated weather and insist on appropriate clothing to help to ensure a positive, healthy, and safe learning experience.

Presession Planning

The outdoor leader is responsible for not only preparation for the activities but also the many administrative tasks that are associated with a quality lesson. The following is a list of suggestions based on experience:

- Gather required equipment and perform a check to ensure the gear is in working order and safe to be used as intended in an outdoor lesson.
- Consider potential locations to conduct your outdoor lessons.
- Obtain any necessary permissions.
- Send information packages to participants (e.g., schedule, equipment lists, medical forms).
- Set up a training schedule for any support staff and coleaders to make sure all instructors are at the same skill level and are clear on their roles and the lesson expectations. This allows the outdoor leader to build in safety checks and emergency plans. Firsthand knowledge of the activities and assessment structure is essential.

- Update the emergency plan (figure I.1), taking note of any changes in policy for your organization.
- Collect informed consent forms for minors and pertinent waivers or liability releases (signed, of course). It is advisable to use existing, approved program forms.
- Collect medical information from participants. For programs that convene over an extended time, update these forms on a regular basis. Furthermore, take time at the beginning of sessions to discuss each form with participants (or their caregivers in the case of minors). All outdoor leaders and coleaders should be aware of medical concerns, including allergies.
- Update the duty form (figure I.2) to keep planning responsibilities organized. These duties can be shared among the coleaders and the participants, giving them an active role in the planning responsibility. Be fair in delegating the assignments.
- Begin updating the field-at-a-glance form (figure I.3) that will contain important information for the outdoor leader and coleaders as they plan lessons. This form can be used as a quick reference in the field.
- Determine what activities can be taught along the route and who will teach them. This will save time and avoid missed opportunities to make the learning authentic.
- Develop backup instructional plans to prepare for unpredictable weather conditions. Criteria for what weather will postpone a lesson should be made apparent to all participants and coleaders.
- Develop a monitoring plan to keep track of the participants at all times.
- Issue a personal equipment list to every participant.
- Keeping track of the details can make the difference in having a positive and safe learning experience. Therefore, a final check on instructional materials and the working order of equipment is critical.
- For extended lessons requiring overnight stays, it is advisable to leave your instructional route card (see the following section) with the proper authorities and with your program administration.
- Finally, review the emergency plan before the sessions start.

Instructional Route Card   Examine potential outdoor sites and begin forming the instructional

To maintain the highest level of safety during the outdoor pursuit (backpacking), the leadership team and participants will follow the established guidelines and rules. This emergency plan will be left with the proper authorities along with the original route card outlining the trip.

Trip Details

Trip destination: Fox Hollows, Terratory Dr., Antigonish County, Nova Scotia

Group size: 18 persons

Trained in first aid: 4

Outdoor leader: Name

Planned duration: 2 days, 1 night

Departure time: Wednesday, November 8, 2008, 10:00 a.m.

Arrival time: Thursday, November 9, 2008, 11:30 a.m.

Safety Points

1. The emergency signal is three blasts of the whistle. The whistles are only to be used for this purpose.
2. The group will stay on the selected route unless an emergency results in an immediate evacuation.
3. All participants must have their whistle on them.
4. The buddy system will be in place during the entire trip.
5. All participants are responsible for taking a ready-to-eat first meal.
6. All participants are responsible for a personal water supply for hydration.
7. Group members will not deliberately engage in high-risk activity.
8. At least one cellular phone will be taken on the trip.

Injury and Evacuation

1. If an accident occurs, the casualty will be assessed on-site and it will be determined if evacuation is necessary.
2. If the injured person cannot be extracted from the site, a group of no fewer than three people will travel to the trailhead (Fresh Air Shelter) to notify the appropriate emergency personnel. This will be based on routes within the route card that have been decided upon before the trip.
3. The evacuation site will be the Fresh Air Shelter (6FGR 785458 Map 11F).
4. First person on-site will initiate first aid if an accident occurs.
5. All injuries, symptoms, and illnesses will be reported through the buddy system regardless of whether they seem small or insignificant.
6. Outdoor leader has the right to cancel or end the trip due to current or pending weather conditions.
7. Emergency bearing will be north—340°.

Figure I.1 Sample emergency plan.

Outdoor Pursuit

Name	Task	Deadline	Comments	Complete
Participant name	Collecting informed consent forms		Forms were passed out 2 weeks in advance of the trip.	
Coleader name	Collecting medical forms		New forms are needed to keep current. Last trip was over 3 months ago.	
Outdoor leader name	Menu checks		Establish cooking groups and ensure appropriate meals (balanced).	
Coleader name	Group gear check		Two stoves are not working properly; batteries are low for the GPS.	
	Group first aid kit check		Small bandages need replacing; restock moleskin.	
	Participant gear check		One participant did not have all the required gear and is borrowing needed equipment before the next check.	

Figure I.2   Sample duty form.

Outdoor Pursuit

Logistics	Group	Preparation
Outdoor pursuit:	Outdoor leaders:	Pretrip meeting dates:
Departure information	Participants' names and phone numbers:	1.
Date:	1.	2.
Time:	2.	3.
Arrival information	3.	4.
Date:	4.	***Equipment check***
Time:	5.	Date:
Emergency plan updated:	6.	***Menu check***
	7.	Date:
	8.	***First aid kit check***
General comments:	9.	Date:
	10.	Kit carrier:
	11.	Map numbers:
	12.	***Final weather check***
	13.	Date:
	14.	Trip outlook:
	15.	Day 1
	16.	Day 2
	17.	Day 3
	18.	Day 4
	19.	Medical forms checked:
	20.	Route card checked:
	21.	Emergency contact and phone number:
	22.	
	First-aiders:	
	Participants with related skills:	

Figure I.3   Sample field-at-a-glance form.

route card (figure I.4) that will outline the travel location for each lesson plan. The route card is a systematic method of planning and recording your route. It is useful for several reasons:

- It encourages you to examine many important details of your trip such as direction, distance, time, terrain, and hazards. Such a close examination will often disclose points that were overlooked in preliminary planning.
- It is a written record for you to use if lessons require remote areas where a map and compass are necessary. If you are not proceeding at the calculated pace, you will be informed soon enough to make changes.
- It is a written record for you to leave with the appropriate authorities along with the field-at-a-glance form. They will take the appropriate action if you do not return at a prearranged time.

Of course, you must ensure that you follow the prescribed route (or one of the alternative escape routes you have recorded) so that in the event a search must be organized, it is directed to the right area.

Risk Assessment Every teaching location should be assessed in advance to determine suitability for the lesson and to note possible risks. This assessment should be part of the training sessions with coleaders. The first step is to assess the inherent risks of the activity. Outdoor leaders need to take into account many things, including their own skill level, the skill level of the participants, and the potential for risks to occur based on the location, overall environment, past experiences of the leaders (their ability to lead), and activity.

The outdoor leader must always be thinking in terms of equipment concerns, environmental concerns, and participant concerns. Figure I.5 shows a sample risk assessment chart to help you mitigate these concerns and assess the site. The question at this point in managing the risks is this: Are any of these risks preventable? The list is not exhaustive, but the plan to deal with any threat, perceived or real, depends on the outdoor leader's ability to continually assess the situation while on a trip.

Instructional Route Plan

Outdoor leader: _____

Lesson: _____

Date: _____

Start 6FGR	
End 6FGR	
Leg bearing	
Estimated distance (meters)	
Vertical rise/fall	
Estimated time	
Terrain characteristics	
Teaching assignment	

Figure I.4 Sample route card.

Type of risk	Real threat	Perceived threat
Lost		
Weather change		
Capsize (kayak or canoe)		
Loss of gear		
Nutritional concerns		
Participant separation		
Sudden medical emergency		
Accidental injury		
Wildlife (insects and animals)		
Gear failure		
Group behavior		
Hypothermia		

Figure I.5 Sample risk assessment chart.

In-Session Monitoring

As the outdoor leader, you need to be on time, organized, and committed to your program. You need to be inviting and show confidence that you can lead people in the outdoors. The following are considerations that are key to delivery and implementation of the lesson plan.

Before the Lesson Begins Setting a positive tone is essential in leading any learning experience. More can be gained in a positive learning environment that supports learning progress than in an environment where participants feel forced, under duress, or afraid. The outdoor leader should be positive and welcoming, forming a genuinely supportive connection with participants.

- When greeting your group, be inviting, be friendly and smile, be energized and organized, and build a sense of fun and motivation.
- Provide participants with a brief overview of the lesson with outcome indicators. This can be done as an advanced organizer—Today at a Glance: a piece of chart paper or the underbelly of a canoe that lists the lesson activities, goals of the day, and scheduled breaks that are on the instructional docket.
- Take the time to make contact with the participants. This will build trust and respect for your program.
- All coleaders and support staff should be on-site and introduced to the participants. This allows relationships to form and assists in developing an outdoor learning community.
- For every lesson, take attendance; know who will be on-site and in the field.
- Check participants' personal gear to make sure they have everything on the list that was distributed before the lesson. All participants and leaders must have all the required gear on the list before departure.
- Check to ensure all participants are dressed appropriately for the outdoor lesson.
- Practice the check-in plan for continually monitoring participant numbers and review the emergency call word that signals an immediate end to an activity. The participants should have enough practice checking in and know

the importance of keeping track of each other and staying with the group (buddy system).

- Who is teaching what activities? This should be decided in advance of the session. As each activity is underway, the other support leaders can help set up the next activity—this will maintain program flow.
- Have lesson equipment and related materials ready for the field. Extra instructional supplies should travel with the group.
- Check required group gear and make sure the stocked first aid kit is part of the outdoor leader's travel gear.
- Confirm all paperwork is prepared to travel with the outdoor leader, including field-at-a-glance form, medical information forms, emergency plan, instructional route card, assessment sheets, participant skills log, and copies of the lesson plan for all leaders.

As the Lesson Unfolds As the lesson is being lived, it is important for the outdoor leader to maintain awareness not only of the skill progression but also of group and individual needs. Thus the outdoor leader needs to be connected and focused on the learning session, living the plan alongside the participants.

- Monitor group health by scheduling water and washroom breaks, watching for fatigue, and providing snacks breaks during extended lessons (be sensitive to allergies and follow institutional policies for food handling).

- Attend to participant levels of engagement and adjust when necessary to maximize involvement.
- Monitor safety by determining what risk factors are acceptable for participants at any time in the field. Teaching outdoors requires analysis of whether the risk inherent in the outdoor pursuit is appropriate for the participants.
- If you have concerns during the lesson, review the following risk progression chart (figure I.6) and review the pertinent risk management protocols established by your program.

The progression helps outdoor leaders assess the activity being taught. In short, the outdoor leader must decide whether to remain engaged in the lesson, modify it, or immediately end the activity to avoid increasing the risk and placing more participants in danger. In all circumstances, reduce risk through sound planning and anticipation—this is essential in being able to recognize inherent risks by evaluating warning signs of impending problems. The outdoor leader makes the final assessment of whether the risk is acceptable or whether it is too great and should be avoided.

Managing any degree of risk depends on sound preparation. When an incident occurs, never dismiss its severity. You must evaluate and reassess the safety of each participant. In short, every mishap, minor or major, must be

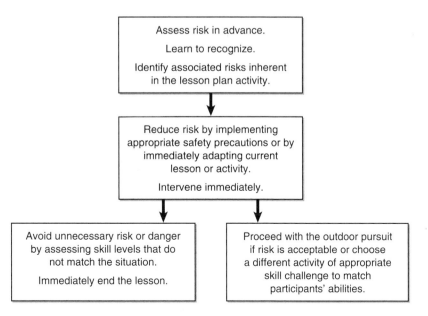

Figure I.6 Risk progression chart.

dealt with according to the risk management plan for the lesson. Risks can be managed, and when it is clear that the situation is beyond your ability, pull out!

The following is a list of key assessment areas that should influence a risk management plan for every outdoor lesson.

- Assessment of the emotional and physical state of the group—beyond morale
- Assessment of self (skills and mental state)
- Assessment of the current conditions—beyond the plan
- Assessment of the coleaders
- Assessment of the equipment—operational
- Assessment of the backup alternatives

After the initial assessment has been conducted, ask this question: Has the situation gone beyond the intention of the pursuit, and if the activity continues could the situation worsen? The outdoor leader must balance the expectations of the planned lesson that were established with the participants and program administration. Is the situation beyond those expectations? In making the decision to pull an activity or lesson based on safety, begin with the previous assessment list and then consider the following:

- What are the program rules and policies that govern off-site excursions?
- Evaluate your initial instinct—should you continue?
- Can further risk be prevented, or is the threat a continued element that goes out of the perceived column into the real?
- After consultation with the coleaders, is there agreement that the situation is not going to improve or that without immediate help participant safety is in jeopardy?
- Is the only way to manage the existing incident to access outside help immediately?

In preparing for an outdoor lesson, all levels of risk must be considered. Learning and teaching outside is a challenge for many. Therefore, the outdoor leader must balance not only the risks that can confront a group but also the risks that confront individual participants, which may differ in severity and are just as real. A sound practice in planning for a lesson is to discuss perceived and real risks with the participants in balance with group and individual expectations for meeting the learning outcomes. Everyone involved in the lesson should be informed of the safety points that govern the lesson.

Safety considerations are based on the outdoor leader's judgment of the situation, the environmental conditions at the time, and most importantly, the maturity of those involved in the lesson. If an incident does occur, a solid plan is the best course of action, and there is considerable comfort in knowing that external authorities informed of your trip are aware of your planned course of action. A prudent practice for any outdoor leader is to keep a record of future considerations as part of the lesson-planning process.

Postsession Follow-Up

An outdoor leader should strive to be a reflective practitioner in order to improve the quality of teaching and the instructional abilities of coleaders. Ask yourself the following instructional questions: What could I do differently next time? What should I do next time? What would I do next time? Teaching requires reflection that is centered on lesson improvement. Therefore, an important phase in the lesson plan is the postplanning phase. This stage allows the outdoor leader to make quality learning connections regarding lesson delivery.

As part of connecting the experience, do the following:

- Plan processing time during and immediately after the lesson.
- Probing questions and guided discussions will help coleaders connect their instructional ability and the quality of the learning experience.
- Determine what materials are needed for the next session.
- Identify what skills need to be practiced and reviewed for the next lesson.
- Organize the assessment sheets.

As part of the gear check, include the following:

- Gear cleanup
- Gear maintenance and repair
- Equipment-return checklists

As part of the considerations for outside instructional space, include the following:

- Method (how to better deliver in the location)
- Location (keeping or changing the location)
- Pace (whether lessons need to be lengthened or shortened for skill development; based on assessment)

Assessment

with Amanda Stanec

Assessment is essential for learning, improvement, and growth resulting from engagement in outside lessons. Effective assessment focuses on three key areas:

- The participant's knowledge of the pursuit (cognitive domain)—knowing
- The ability to perform essential skills (psychomotor domain)—doing
- The value in the experience of participating (affective domain)—valuing

Every outcome in this text has been carefully chosen for its value for participant learning. The outcomes assist outdoor leaders in measuring what participants know, are able to do, and value as a result of their participation in the outdoor lesson. The challenge is to conduct authentic assessments in the field while the participants are interacting with the skill sets and in the natural environment. Outdoor learning can prove difficult to assess. However, this does not mean outdoor leaders should opt out of determining what their participants know, what they are capable of doing, and what they appreciate and value as a result of engagement. In addition, participants have a right to know their levels of competency in the foundational skills of each outdoor lesson.

The outdoor leader must engage in the assessment process as an ongoing feature in the learning. As learning stems from direct experiences, the participants take an active role in gauging their progress with the guidance of the outdoor leader. Skill competency is critical for engagement in a safe, positive activity, but it is also important to focus on the process versus just the end result. The aim for the outdoor leader is to provide positive, challenging learning experiences. In the outdoors, the leader becomes more of a facilitator in guiding the participant to learning connections from a particular experience. Participants are taking part in experiential education beyond mere participation as they actively make connections to the knowledge, skills, and values they will take from that experience.

Value of Assessment

It is challenging to assess a large number of people in a physically active setting, and assessment is further complicated because of the abundance of space and range of involvement in complicated lessons. To further complicate the situation, outdoor leaders often wonder about standards. For example, who sets the standard? Are all participants able to achieve the standard? These are just a couple of questions that need to be addressed before any assessment of physical activity, including in the outdoors.

The outdoor leader must consider types of assessment to ensure the best gauge of how a participant is progressing in a particular lesson. To optimize assessment practices, outdoor leaders should understand key terms and how they are directly related to the assessment process. Assessment can be a valuable tool for the following reasons:

- Gathers data for achievement (e.g., rubrics, checklists, peer and self-assessment forms)
- Measures results from rubric indicators specifically connected to the outcomes of the activity
- Contributes to overall evaluation—testing and examination of skill performance and knowledge indicators of the outdoor lesson
- Contributes to grading, a number value that represents the participant's achievement in the outdoor pursuit
- Minimizes the real risks of participation by ensuring safe progression where personal and group skills sets accurately match individual and group challenges and expectations
- Provides skill-specific, individualized feedback that is helpful for setting future goals
- Helps outdoor leaders modify their teaching strategies to increase participant learning
- Helps programs examine the big picture in terms of what is delivered throughout a program and how it can be altered and improved
- Reveals participant understanding and progress in an outdoor lesson
- Provides indicators to determine the quality of the lesson delivered by the outdoor leader

The outdoor leader should have tangible assessment markers in the following areas of participant growth: knowledge of the pursuit, ability to perform the skills associated with the pursuit (e.g., successful navigation of an outdoor activity challenge), and what was valued from experiencing the pursuit, which can be gathered as part of the debriefing or the closure for each lesson.

Learning Connected to Assessment

The complexities of outdoor education are more than just content that extends the knowledge base delivered outside. The very nature of teaching outside demands that the outdoor leader has an appropriate background, is comfortable in the environmental context of the course material, has the ability to perform the selected skills associated with the pursuit, and has enough familiarity with outside environments to be able to teach effectively. These abilities ensure an environment of instruction that is conducive to learning. Therefore, the outdoor leader needs two primary strengths in order to teach effectively:

- Content-experience knowledge
- The ability to teach outdoors as a dominant aspect of instruction

The outdoor leader must be able to frame experiential lessons in a way that individualizes instruction through a variety of teaching styles yet stays focused on the outcomes of the lesson. It is also critical that outdoor leaders learn how to assess participants using techniques to give specific skill feedback. There is little argument against not providing corrective feedback to participants, but the act of assessment should not remove the outdoor leader from the learning process—avoid keeping your nose behind a clipboard, focused on checkmarks and numbers. You must be focused on the learning process; thus, attention should be on the participants. The assessment tool should be one that is field friendly and can be attended to during pauses that do not interrupt or remove you from the learning process.

A rubric is one example of an effective assessment tool for the field. A rubric describes the elements for gauging participants' performance based on predetermined outcomes or assessment tasks, and it includes scoring competencies for each element. A well-designed rubric is useful in illustrating each learner's progress. As stated earlier, progress can be individual or as a part of a smaller or larger group.

To develop a rubric, outdoor leaders need to consider exactly what they would like their learners to be able to know, do, and appreciate and then list criteria based on the outcomes that itemize tasks within a category as clearly as possible. The fieldbric (a rubric that is used in the field) is a sample self-assessment tool that can be given to participants before or after the lesson. It tells the participants the standards that they are working toward. Moreover, outdoor leaders should revise the rubric once it has been used to determine if any modifications are necessary. Figures I.7 through I.9 are sample fieldbrics to help guide you in developing your own.

The outdoor leader and participants must share the responsibility for gauging learning and areas for improvement. All participants should be reflective when they ask: How am I doing in this outdoor pursuit? Where can I improve? And outdoor leaders should ask how they can best support the next round in learning.

Assessment Tips

Processing a lesson is critical to the learning experience. The ability of the outdoor leader to have participants articulate what they learned in relation to the lesson objective highlights the experiential aspect of the learning process. The key is for outdoor leaders to help participants make learning connections, reflect on the experience, articulate the pivotal areas where the learning was anchored in the intended outcome, and if possible, discuss where they can improve their performance.

Making specific connections to the lesson objective has the participants take ownership of the experience and their gained knowledge and ability. Careful communication between the outdoor leader and the participants offers a quality learning approach—building on what is known and applying it in new settings to develop new competencies and understandings. Furthermore, the learning needs to be measured and assessed to improve the lesson and to determine a benchmark for what the participants learned.

When using assessment forms, consider the following:

- Keep the assessment focused on the lesson outcomes.
- Prevent one person from dominating a discussion-based assessment.
- Avoid doing all the talking; telling participants what they learned is not always helpful.

- Allow the participants to represent to you what they learned. Comments should be specific only to improve future engagements.
- Teach learners how to assess peers objectively.
- Use assessments to offer skill-specific feedback to the learners.
- Integrate various assessment techniques to process the learning connections, just as various teaching styles should be used to cover content.
- Develop questioning techniques to explore what was learned from the lesson, including prompting questions (initiating the discussion), probing questions (digging deeper for understanding), and questions that redirect (focusing on the outcome or further explaining a particular statement).
- Whenever possible, assess learners in an authentic environment (e.g., assessing learners' ability to maneuver a mountain bike around obstacles as they bike through an obstacle course).

Get Outside

A quality learning experience requires preparation—the outdoor leader needs to be mindful of the plan, participant abilities, appropriate environmental setting, and attention to participant growth. There are many aspects to developing a plan for teaching outdoors, and in order to deliver a safe learning experience, preparation cannot be left to the last minute. As outdoor leaders, we are responsible for the learning environment, and our actions and inactions contribute to the development of a supportive community of learners. When participants are invested in their own learning and are supported to take risks or are challenged to develop their skill competencies, the reward is often improved self-esteem, confidence, and the interest to continue developing their outdoor skills, allowing them to stay outside and to explore and grow.

You can find fulfillment and personal satisfaction at the end of a day spent in outdoor pursuits.

Participant: _____

Range: 1 = Beginning   2 = On the way   3 = Almost there   4 = There!

	Criteria	Score	Total	Areas for improvement
Personal	– Set a good example for others. – Contributed to a positive experience for others. – Demonstrated positive environmental stewardship. – Always knew where we were on the map. – Looked out for welfare of others. – Shared positive outlook and good humor.		___ 12	
Leadership	– Took navigational lead. – Maintained group within travel guidelines (e.g., lead, sweep). – Ensured economic walking pace set and maintained by group. – Set and maintained suitable walk and rest schedule. – Monitored pace, place, and physical and mental state of group.		___ 10	
Followership	– Followed leader's instructions. – Supported others in leader role. – Offered positive feedback where appropriate.		___ 12	

Figure I.7   Fieldbric sample 1: Hiking self-assessment.

Location: _____ Date: _____

Scale

	Beginning	On the way	Almost there	There!
	1	2	3	4

Criteria	Rating	Noted area for improvement
1. Site selection		
2. Shelter construction		
3. Packing		
4. Knots		
5. Fire making		
6. Stove operation—cooking		
7. Food line		
8. Organized site and gear		
9. LNT practices		
10. Leadership		

Self-Evaluation

Developed and demonstrated an understanding for a personal wilderness ethic:

_____

_____

_____

_____

_____

Outdoor Leader's Comments

_____

_____

_____

_____

_____

_____

Mark: _____

Figure I.8   Fieldbric sample 2: Core camping.

Participant: _____

Range: 1 = Beginning   2 = On the way   3 = Almost there   4 = There!

	Criteria	Score	Total	Areas for improvement
Safety	– PFD check – Safe canoeing procedures – Launching and docking (or entering and exiting) – Lifts and carries – Positions and trim		_____ 20	
Flatwater skills	– Changing positions – Pivots – Displacement – Forward straight line (J-stroke) – Backward straight line (reverse J-stroke) – Inside-outside turns – Inside-outside circles – Stopping – Power stroke – Paddle recovery – Staying in tandem – Dock landings		_____ 48	
Water works	– Swim with swamped canoe – Paddling swamped canoe – Canoe-over-canoe rescue		_____ 12	

Overall out of 80: _____

Figure I.9   Fieldbric sample 3: Flatwater paddling.

Core Camping Skills

▼ Rolf Kraiker, Debra Kraiker, and Andrew Foran ▼

When one has been accustomed to the comforts of civilized life—the small ones, I mean, for they are the only ones that count—the beginning of a wild, free life near to nature's heart begets a series of impressions quite new, and strange—so strange. It is not that one misses a house of solid walls and a roof, with stairways and steam radiators. These are the larger comforts and are more than made up for by the sheltering temple of trees, the blazing campfire and the stairway leading to the stars.

– Albert Bigelow Paine, *The Tent Dwellers* (1993)

Most people lead lives that are sheltered from the wilderness existence of their ancestors. The thought of being alone in a wilderness environment far away from the normal support systems of modern life can be daunting. But with adequate skill and preparation, the reality is that the most dangerous part of any wilderness excursion is usually the vehicle ride to and from the start and end points. With some basic skill preparation, camping in the wilderness is a safe and enjoyable experience with many rewards. To ensure a positive outdoor experience, outdoor leaders must conduct comprehensive pretrip preparation, and most importantly, outdoor leaders and participants must stay within their skills and abilities.

Certain components of any wilderness trip are essential regardless of the mode of transportation; however, unique opportunities and challenges are present for trips that involve camping and core skills. A winter trip by a dogsled team provides ample room to store gear, but the risk of extreme cold mandates special equipment and considerations. Some destinations might be equally accessible to hikers or canoeists, but paddlers have the option of bringing much more gear comfortably because the capacity of a canoe is greater than what can be carried on foot by backpack.

Equipment

Group Equipment

- Rope of different sizes and types (cotton, nylon); to be used for knots and shelter building
- Magnesium blocks and flint
- An example of each type of stove and fuel for each (pressurized gas, nonpressurized fuel, mixed gas, and wood)
- Matches or lighter
- Tent
- Outer tarp—the fly and groundsheet
- Down sleeping bag and synthetic sleeping bag (mummy and rectangular)
- Closed-cell foam sleeping pad and self-inflating sleeping pad
- Food dehydrator
- Food storage containers such as food barrels
- Expedition-sized pack
- Knife (solid, single-piece knife with at least a 10-centimeter [4-inch] blade)

- Folding saw
- Hatchet

Personal Equipment

- Day pack
- Personal hygiene bag (nylon stuff sack)
- Change of clothes
- Rain gear
- Hat
- Sunscreen
- Sunglasses
- Bug repellent
- Personal first aid kit and prescribed medications
- Utensils, mug, plate or bowl (nonbreakable and suitable for the outdoors)
- Personal water bottle

Equipment Care and Maintenance

- When not in use, store stoves according to manufacturers' specifications.
- All pot sets and utensils should be cleaned thoroughly after field use.
- Restock the toilet paper and hand sanitizer.
- Tarps and ropes should be inspected after use for wear; small holes in tarps can be repaired with red sheathing tape such as Tuck Tape (a construction tape that weathers well on plastic tarps) and fraying ropes replaced.
- Dry tent parts and tarps after use.

Site Selection

A wide variety of sites can be used for teaching core camping skills, from practicing outdoor stove cooking in an urban area to camping in the wilderness. The ideal site includes a range of geographical features and topography that offer choices and learning opportunities for the lessons in this unit. If the ideal site is not available, most wooded outdoor spaces will suffice.

Social Skills and Etiquette

- Participants should gain an appreciation for the environment and practice LNT skills.
- Participants should stay on any groomed trails while walking to the site.
- Avoid making new trails and respect any vegetation in the area.
- Participants should practice LNT at all times when partaking in core camping skills.

• After addressing personal needs and responsibilities, participants should make a conscious effort to make the experience positive for all.

Risk Management

Most risk management considerations are included in specific lessons because part of the learning experience is to identify, assess, and manage risk. However, following is a general list of risk management considerations:

• Keep the group within specific boundaries.
• Participants never travel alone. A buddy system should be created to ensure all are present for necessary check-ins.
• If participants move away from the instructional site, it is only with your permission and on your instructions.
• Establish a whistle or a recognizable call word that all participants know. It could be a word that will bring all participants together for further instructions or emergencies.
• All participants should carry a sounding device (whistle) at all times that is only to be used in case of emergency. There should be an emergency signal such as three loud whistles with a short pause between each.
• Cutting tools are to only be used by those deemed responsible. Depending on age and maturity, constant visual supervision may be required.
• All fires and stoves should be kept well away from tents, rain gear, and any flammables.
• Demonstrations are required on safe lighting and shutting down of open flames and extinguishing fires to avoid mishaps and accidents.

Unit Organization

The core camping unit serves as an overall introduction of core skills needed for any camping in the wilderness. The lessons focus on skills needed to have a safe, productive, and enjoyable camping trip. Some of the lessons will require patience, practice, and maturity as participants engage in activities from tying knots to building shelters and working with open flame around fires and stoves. Thus, you need to ensure all safety precautions are in place, remind participants of the lesson expectations, and monitor all participants.

Lesson Plans

Lesson 1: Campsite Selection. This lesson provides participants with the knowledge and experience to select a campsite. Participants will focus on choosing a campsite that is durable and avoids any safety hazards such as flood zones, dead tree limbs, and animals.

Lesson 2: Knots and Ropes. This lesson forms the basis for other lessons such as shelter building and securing tents. The focus of the lesson is teaching participants when and how to use knots to support core camping practices. Participants will learn about types of rope and how to tie important knots needed for trips in the wilderness.

Lesson 3: Tents, Shelters, and Sleeping Bags and Pads. This lesson will teach participants how to live in degrees of comfort in the outdoors. Participants will learn how to set up tents as well as how to build specialized shelters using only tarps, rope, and nature. Participants will be able to examine some of the sleeping gear that is commonly used in the outdoors.

Lesson 4: Backpacks. When going on any backpacking trip, whether it is overnight or an expedition, it is important to know how to use a backpack. Participants will learn how to pack a backpack as well as how to put on the pack and wear it correctly. Not knowing these essential skills can make the trip uncomfortable, and participants could hurt themselves if the skills are not done correctly.

Lesson 5: Stoves. This lesson will ensure that participants can distinguish among the types of stoves on the market and the fuels that accompany each. Participants will learn the pros and cons of each stove and the ideal conditions in which it should be used. Participants will also be able to safely light and operate each stove.

Lesson 6: Fires. This lesson provides participants with the knowledge and experience to gather materials and build and ignite a fire. Participants will also learn the importance of ensuring that a fire is completely put out. While gathered around the fire, the group will have the opportunity to build a community circle and participate in activities such as campfire treats, games, and singing.

Lesson 7: Food Preparation and Menu Planning. In this important lesson, participants will learn how to plan a meal focusing on group needs on an outdoor trip. Participants will also learn how to pack this food as well as how to safely handle and cook food in the outdoors.

Lesson 8: Knives, Saws, and Hatchets. These tools are extremely important in the outdoors, but when used incorrectly they can be extremely dangerous. In this lesson, participants will learn the situations in which each of these tools would be used most effectively and how to use each safely.

Lesson 9: Checklists and Specialized Kits. This is an essential part of the planning stage of any outdoor trip. Participants will learn how to create checklists, focusing on the important equipment that will be needed on the outdoor trip. By creating a thorough checklist, participants can help ensure that the trip goes more smoothly and that they are prepared for the unexpected.

Terminology

- **alpine butterfly**—A versatile knot used widely throughout outdoor activities such as shelter building and climbing. In regards to shelter building, this knot can be used as a pulley to tighten the guideline.
- **blended fuels**—Prebought fuel tanks made of a mixture of propane and butane. These fuels are best used in the warmer months and are not effective in the cold.
- **bowline**—A versatile knot used to tie a non-slipping loop in the end of a rope that can be easily untied even after being under a heavy load.
- **clove hitch**—Knot used to hold onto things, such as building a button to keep more tension on an outer tarp or to peg down a corner of a shelter to a tent peg, tree, or tree root.
- **debris hut**—Shelter made from dead and down trees that is easy to set up against a fallen log or hill using logs, tree branches, leaves, boughs, and grasses. Can be an effective short-term shelter if built correctly.
- **fly**—Outer protective layer of a tent that guards against moisture and wind.
- **guideline hitch**—A friction knot used to form an adjustable loop that can be quickly slipped to either tighten or loosen a line.

- **igloo**—A traditional Inuit shelter that uses blocks made of snow to build a domelike shelter. This is a durable and structurally sound shelter that can be depended on for the long term if built well.
- **loft**—The thickness of a sleeping bag, which will determine how warm the bag is.
- **magnesium block**—The block is shaved onto a ball of kindling to help start a fire using flint. Magnesium will burn in any condition and burns at about 3,000 degrees Celsius (5,432 degrees Fahrenheit).
- **mummy bag**—A sleeping bag tailored to the human body with a hood built in.
- **naphtha**—White gas or camp fuel.
- **quinzhee**—A shelter built out of a mound of snow that is hollowed out. A door should be built going upward into the shelter so as to keep as little heat as possible from escaping.
- **reef knot**—Knot used to tie two pieces of rope together that are the same diameter.
- **ridgeline**—The main rope of a shelter that acts as the backbone, keeping the tarp up.
- **scat**—Animal feces.
- **sheet bend**—Knot used to tie two pieces of rope together that have different diameters.
- **shucking**—Taking off a backpack.
- **snow trench**—An emergency shelter built by digging a trench in the snow and then placing logs, branches, leaves, boughs, or tarps on top to waterproof it. Recommended only for one overnight use.
- **sparker**—Flint and steel tool used to light a fire or a stove.
- **tinder ball**—Small twigs, pieces of birch bark found on the ground, dry leaves, old man's beard (hanging tree moss), ferns, wood shavings, and any other natural material used as kindling to start a fire.
- **topography**—The relief features or detailed mapping of an area on a map.
- **Tuck Tape**—Red construction tape that weathers well on plastic tarps; used for small repairs to prevent leaking.
- **widower**—Tree that is dead, partially fallen, or under dead or broken limbs.

LESSON 1

Campsite Selection

Overview

An ideal campsite is a blend of both what is desirable and necessary (figure 1.1). Outdoor leaders seem to have a constant debate with their participants: Is there a perfect campsite? The challenge is to find a place to call home in wilderness areas. To find that site, many factors need to be taken into consideration: carrying capacity (factoring in environmental conditions and number of participants), skill levels of participants, wildlife, scenic and historical significance, and for some, the challenge to push into unexplored regions of the world. Fundamental to the entire trip process is planning for the campsite based on previous visits or deciding as you go and weighing the advantages and disadvantages of each location. In addition to ensuring a campsite is enjoyable and comfortable in a variety of weather conditions, it's also important to evaluate the site for potential hazards. The campsite is central to many trip memories and should not be decided on casually.

Figure 1.1   When setting up your home away from home, you have many factors to consider, including carrying capacity and scenic significance.

Learning Objectives

- To select an appropriate campsite that is durable
- To recognize natural hazards
- To select a campsite that will meet the group's needs

Risk Management

- You must have updated medical forms for each participant, a stocked first aid kit suitable for the location and activity, a reliable contact aware of your location and expected times for returning, and proper hiking formation for keeping the participants on the set trail and together.
- At the site, you need to be aware of potential hazards (i.e., cliff edges, water sources, or other environmental threats) and articulate these concerns to the participants.

- All participants should be aware of the designated boundary in which they are expected to stay. This helps ensure that participants select a campsite where you can monitor the group.
- Review with participants the emergency signal (whistle or designated call word) to end an activity and to bring the group together.

Activity 1: Features of Campsite Selection

The reality is that every site selection is an exercise in compromise. Regardless of how much thought and preparation goes into selecting a site, in a wilderness setting circumstances can change quickly and contingency planning is essential. Participants will select a campsite based on safety hazards, environmental factors, and what is suitable for the group.

Skill Cues

- Participants, in groups of four to six, look for an area that is not environmentally fragile and is able to support a group (carrying capacity).
- Participants try to determine if the site is durable and relatively level.
- Participants look at hazards, including weather, animal dens and trails, and widowers. A widower is a tree that is dead, partially fallen, or under dead or broken limbs.
- Participants can try to locate areas that not only are safe but also have scenic views and admit breezes, which aids in the reduction of pesky insects.
- The site should have easy access to other points of camp: cook shelter, sleep shelter, and locations for supporting human waste.

Teaching Cues

- Circumstances often dictate that compromises have to be accepted when it comes time to settle into camp, but having a checklist of desirable and important criteria will help ensure that any site offers as pleasant a stay as possible.
- Have a site tour where each group discusses the pros and cons of its selected campsite.
- When site tours have been completed, have participants pack all equipment away, leaving the campsite as it was when entered.

Activity 2: Desirable Campsite Features

Wilderness travel is frequently more about the journey than the destination. A good campsite will contain all the features that make it suitable, but it also should provide some enjoyment with the potential of being a trip highlight (figure 1.2).

Skill Cues

- Participants identify beautiful characteristics such as vistas at sunrise or sunset and shade trees for relief from the sun.
- Assess the location for easy access to recreational opportunities, such as a sand beach for swimming, areas to explore, and space for the group to gather and build community by engaging in common activities.
- Participants determine location based on safety, including emergency evacuations or ease of rescue personnel being able to reach the group.

Teaching Cues

- Circumstances on a wilderness trip often dictate that compromises have to be made when it comes time to settle into camp.
- Review the pros and cons of the site as a group before beginning the process of setting up camp.

Figure 1.2 . This secluded cove offers a view and space for tents.

Activity 3: Evaluating Campsites for Drainage

Campsites that look great when the sun is shining can become a nightmare if a sudden storm brings significant precipitation. In many parts of the world, this is a constant concern that ranges from discomfort to a safety threat. In groups, participants will assess that their campsite is properly situated away from flood zones.

Skill Cues

- Ideal campsites should be reasonably level to provide a comfortable platform for sleeping.
- There should be a slight slope to the campsite for water to drain away if it should begin to rain.
- Look to make sure the area is not a punch bowl, an area that is lower than the surrounding terrain from numerous angles, serving as a bowl that catches rainwater and allows the water to pool.
- Sandy, gravelly soil tends to shed or absorb water quickly and dry quickly, but mosses will absorb water and stay damp longer after rainfall.

Teaching Cues

- Ensure that all participants are examining their potential site for water hazards.
- Participants should be able to identify locations suitable for sleeping sites that have minimal drainage problems.

- A few buckets of water can be used to test site drainage, illustrating whether or not the site sheds water in practice the way it did in theory.
- Vegetation growing at a site can provide clues to how much water is available. Guide participants through suggestions and inform them of areas such as moss growth and how they may be reservoirs for water retention.
- Take a campsite tour with participants and have them present the advantages and possible water hazards.
- Have participants show and tell: Why did they pick a particular location, and what are the pros and cons of their group decision?

Activity 4: Evaluating Campsites for Additional Hazards

Local knowledge is important when evaluating campsites. Features that might be desirable in one region might present hazards in a different region.

Skill Cues

- Examine the site for any toxic plants that might grow in the region and make sure none grow in traffic areas. Some plants cause skin irritations strong enough to require medical attention even after only slight contact.
- Examine the trees for any signs of wind damage or lightning strikes; most storms follow somewhat similar patterns, and previous evidence of storm damage can provide clues about what might happen in the future.
- Check the site for tripping hazards along the natural pathways. What might not seem to be a significant problem in the daylight might lead to an accident at night.
- Check the site for other hazards that might cause injuries, such as branches at eye level that might injure an inattentive participant.

Teaching Cues

- Conduct a discussion with the group to determine if anyone can think of problems that seem to be small but are actually important hazards to recognize when selecting a campsite.
- Ensure participants are aware of any hazards they may encounter when choosing a campsite.
- Have participants keep a hazards list as they experience the activity, and then have them present the major and minor hazards.

Activity 5: Evaluating Campsites for Animal Risk

An important factor to consider when looking at a potential campsite is personal safety from animals.

Skill Cues

- Take precautions and be aware of animal habitats, looking for any signs of animal life such as trails and territorial markings.
- Look for scat at the site that might suggest carnivores routinely pass through the area. Perhaps trees reveal claw marks from animals.

Teaching Cues

- The first step is to do extensive research into the types of animals that might present problems in locations you will travel through.

- Bring in track and scat samples or pictures to show participants what to look for.
- Have a group discussion about the implications for site selection if a site has obvious signs of animals.
- Do a group tour through the site to discover animal signs and discuss their implications.
- Be aware of any insects that pose a threat to participants. This may require going back to participants' medical forms.

Lesson Closure

- What are some challenges and characteristics of selecting a campsite?
- What are natural hazards that everyone should be aware of when selecting a campsite?
- As a group, why did you select a particular campsite over another site?
- What additional considerations have to be made when selecting a campsite (e.g., are objects such as the canoe secure, will the tent pegs hold through the wind, can the gear be stored in a safe environment)?

LESSON 2

Knots and Ropes

Overview

The goal of this lesson is to develop the participants' ability to tie and apply basic knots when camping. Knots are a must-know skill in order to survive in the wilderness, from building shelters for comfort to hanging food for the safety of the group. Participants will have the opportunity to learn a variety of knots that will provide for a multitude of possible applications while camping in the wilderness.

Learning Objectives

- To learn about the types of rope along with their advantages and disadvantages
- To tie six basic knots useful for core camping skills
- To apply knots in appropriate contexts when camping in the outdoors
- To understand the purpose of each knot
- To know proper terminology of knots and rope

Activity 1: Rope

The forces placed on the rope can be significant; therefore, great care must be taken in selecting the right rope for the task. It is important to practice with various ropes because not all knots work well in all types of rope (figure 1.3). Experience will teach you what to use.

Skill Cues

- Participants identify the various ropes.
- Participants demonstrate how to care, pack, and store rope.

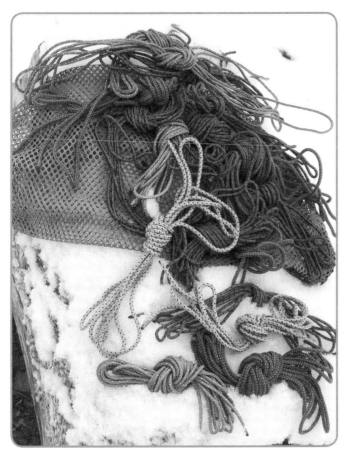

Figure 1.3 Stored rope should be packed (wrapped in halves) to prevent tangling and knotting.

- Participants explain the rope types in terms of pros and cons.
- Participants practice packing a variety of rope bags for transport or storage.

Teaching Cues

- Provide participants with a variety of ropes to touch and work with.
- Give participants information on the types of rope along with the pros and cons. Nylon woven sheath rope is a broadly used rope but is expensive. Nylon braid rope is cheaper and works well in many applications but can be slippery. Cotton rope is easily affordable, but when it gets wet in the outdoors, it will retain water and become heavy, which is not beneficial when packing up or if temperatures drop to freezing, resulting in a difficult experience in breaking camp.
- Pack rope into halves: Fold each length by half a number of times until compact; then tie the compact rope into an overhand knot. This keeps the lengths from tangling and knotting up when stored.
- Store rope after it has dried.

Activity 2: Bowline Knot

The bowline knot is an extremely versatile knot that is easy to untie even after considerable pressure and tension have been placed on the length. Because the bowline is a strong knot that forms a loop that will not slip under force, it serves as an excellent knot to anchor the rope to almost any object.

Skill Cues

- Participants practice tying a bowline knot around a tree or fixed object.
- Form an eye in the rope with the standing part of the rope running underneath. Run the free end of the rope up through the eye, making a loop below the eye.
- Take a turn around the standing part and feed the free end back down through the eye and hold. Pull the standing part to tighten the knot (figure 1.4).

Teaching Cues

- The standing end of the rope is the part of the rope that you do not work with while tying a knot. The standing end could be several centimeters or meters in length.
- A loop is when the rope crosses under or over itself to form a loop.

Figure 1.4 A bowline knot—note the tail.

- The free end of the rope is the working end, the part of the rope you are using to move in and out to create the knot.

Activity 3: Square (Reef) Knot

The square knot is a popular knot, but it must be tied correctly or it will be difficult to undo or it will fail by slipping. The square knot is an excellent knot used to join two ends of a rope together, resulting in a longer length. This knot works best with ropes of equal size.

Skill Cues

- Take the right rope over the left rope and twist down, under, and around the left rope. Then take left over right and twist over, under, and through the loop.
- Pull the two free ends to tighten the knot (figure 1.5).

Teaching Cues

- Make sure that both parts of the rope are exiting the knot together.
- Check to make sure the knot is not slipping by pulling on the two lengths, creating tension on the knot.

Figure 1.5   The square (reef) knot—note that the ropes are a similar size.

Activity 4: Sheet Bend

The sheet bend is an excellent knot for joining two ropes of different diameters to make a longer length (figure 1.6). In its double form, the knot will even hold slippery nylon rope.

Skill Cues

- Create a loop and pinch with fingers. Take the other rope and bring it up through the loop around the rope where you're pinching it. Take the free end of the rope and put it over the loop but underneath itself.
- Pull the free end of the working rope tight.

Teaching Cues

- If participants understand the single sheet bend, demonstrate the double sheet bend.
- When creating the loop down, under, and around, continue under the working rope and around again, and then pull back through and under the working rope to pull tight.
- The working rope is the end of rope you do the work with, usually tying around the other end of the rope.

Figure 1.6   The sheet bend—note the different sizes of the two ropes.

Activity 5: Alpine Butterfly (Preacher Knot)

The alpine butterfly is useful when a secure loop is required at any point along a length of the rope. An easy knot to tie, it also remains reasonably easy to undo even after considerable pressure and tension.

Skill Cues

- Wrap the rope around your hand. At the end of turn 1, position the rope close to your fingertips. Continue round and complete turn 2 back near your thumb.
- Pick up the turn near your fingertips and wrap it around the other two turns.
- Pull the rope through and tighten by pulling on the loop and the ends. This creates the secure loop in the rope (figure 1.7).

Teaching Cues

- Participants can complete the secured loop in the middle of the rope and then follow up by bringing the rope around an object and back through the loop. using a guideline hitch if preferred.
- The knot is commonly tied around the hand, making it easy to ensure that the second crossing of your hand is near the fingertips and away from the two ends.
- When the knot is completed, it is best to pull on the loop and both ends to set the knot.
- The alpine butterfly knot should look the same: two loops along the rope separated by a loop sticking up from the middle.

Figure 1.7   The alpine butterfly can support a larger loop.

Activity 6: Guideline (Taut-Line) Hitch

The guideline hitch is a friction knot used to form an adjustable loop. It's a favorite among campers because the knot can adjust the tension, slipping to tighten or loosen a line, and then holds fast under load. The knot is excellent for tarp and tent construction.

Skill Cues

- Pass the working end of the rope around an object (usually a tree), bring it back alongside the standing part of the rope, cross the standing part, and hold.
- Continue wrapping inside the loop, making a round turn around the standing part of the rope. Repeat, making two or three more loops around the standing part of the rope.
- Bring the free end back across the loops to the outside and complete a half hitch. Cross the rope over the standing end down, under, and back up through the loop just created.
- Finish by snuggling the hitch firmly (figure 1.8). Load slowly and adjust as necessary.

Teaching Cues

- Ensure participants are creating the loops around the standing end of the rope, going back toward the tension (the tree or anchor object).

- When tying the knot off, make sure the participants go in the opposite direction than the wraps around the standing end.

Activity 7: Clove Hitch

A clove hitch is an all-purpose hitch that is easy to tie and untie, holding onto objects firmly. A clove hitch is a great knot for creating buttons (secure holds on flapping tarps) when building shelters.

Skill Cues

- You can complete the hitch around your hand or around a post, but you must be able to take it off the post for use.
- Make one loop in the rope where you would like the knot to be, crossing right over left.
- Create another loop on the right side of first loop, crossing right over left with the rope.
- Cross the loop on the left over the top of the other loop and slip your hand up through the loops. The rope should create a cross where both ends of the rope can be pulled to tighten the knot.

Teaching Cues

- Ensure participants are creating the first two initial loops by crossing right over left.
- When participants complete the knot, the left loop should cross over the loop on the right, creating an *X* with the rope that allows the ropes to tighten when pulled on either end (figure 1.9).

Lesson Closure

- Have participants identify the types of rope available along with the pros and cons of each.
- Do a complete review of all knots, making sure all participants understand the appropriate times to use the knots and how to tie them.
- Have participants take part in a relay race where groups create a line of rope to go from one tree to another using a certain number of knots in the proper places.
- Have groups pack up their own rope bag.

Figure 1.8   The tail of the guideline hitch can be pulled to easily undo the knot.

Figure 1.9   Keep the side loops of the clove hitch snug to the rope as you tighten the knot.

LESSON 3

Tents, Shelters, and Sleeping Bags and Pads

Overview

Tents, shelters, sleeping bags, and sleeping pads are critical equipment on an extended trip. As with other pieces of equipment, each gear choice comes with pros and cons, but the bottom line is the participant's level of comfort with an informed choice and the environment in which the equipment will be used. In some instances because of seasonality and geography there is no choice in equipment selection—safety and practicality override trend and style. Most outdoor leaders follow the rule of functionality over fashion. It is essential that participants are comfortable, warm, and dry when staying in the outdoors.

Participants should have a firm understanding of this equipment, including all the styles and materials that are available. Each outdoor pursuit will call for different equipment. For instance, when hiking, participants are going to want a smaller, more lightweight tent because they will be carrying it around for the duration of the trip. Knowing what you will need for the trip is essential to ensure that you will be comfortable and the trip will be safe and enjoyable.

Learning Objectives

- To set up a variety of tents
- To build three types of shelters with the appropriate knots and know the functionality and importance of each type
- To build a shelter for different weather and locations
- To understand the types of sleeping bags and pads available, including styles and materials

Risk Management

When teaching how to build shelters, make sure participants are aware of the materials and trees they are using to construct their shelters. Everyone should be aware of the dangers of using dead trees and tree limbs—there can be danger when putting a load on, as well as when the weather changes over the stay. A strong wind or snow will place even more stress on the dead trees or tree limbs. Avoid widowers.

Activity 1: Tent Selection

Tents come in a variety of styles, but there are two main factors that influence which type of tent is appropriate: weather and comfort. Tents that are designed to withstand the weather have aerodynamic shapes that shed water and wind easily. Tent construction will vary depending on the temperature range the tent was intended for. Lightweight tents often require staking, whereas freestanding tents can be set up almost anywhere but usually weigh more. In low-risk situations where weather is unlikely to be a problem, it may be acceptable to use tents designed more for comfort than function.

Skill Cues

- Identify the parts required for setup.
- Know how to set guylines under tension even when it's not possible to drive stakes or there's a good chance that stakes won't hold in high winds.
- Match the physical characteristics of a given campsite to the setup requirements for various tents.
- Use colored tape to mark poles of different sizes to make setup faster.
- Prepare a repair kit with key components to ensure a tent can be set up no matter what happens because emergency repairs can be made.
- Select the right style of tent to match anticipated weather conditions for a variety of outings.

Teaching Cues

- Hold a group session to discuss the advantages and disadvantages of various tent styles.
- Demonstrate ways to improve waterproofing by treating flies and groundsheets, sealing seams, and selecting a suitable site.
- Demonstrate how to use the pole-repair sleeve and other repair items that should accompany an outing.
- Conduct competitions that have groups doing timed trials to determine which styles of tents are easiest to set up.

Activity 2: Sleeping Shelters

There is no single perfect way to build a sleeping shelter. The most common example is the traditional A-frame tent style with a ridgeline between two trees and then a tarp hung across and pegged out in the four corners. Once the outer tarp is secured, a smaller groundsheet should be put directly underneath to keep the group dry from any moisture from the ground. A groundsheet that extends beyond the main tarp could capture precipitation that drips off the outer tarp. Although this style is the most common, it may not be the best for all situations. Weather, group size, temperature, and site location all play an important part in determining how the sleeping shelter should be built. Participants can get creative building their shelter as long as they are aware of the needs that their shelter should fulfill.

Skill Cues

- Participants use the correct knots when building their shelter.
  - A bowline should be used to tie the first end of the ridgeline to the tree.
  - When securing and tightening the other end, an alpine butterfly knot should be used first and then a guideline hitch should be used to make the guideline taut.
  - A clove hitch should then be used to peg out each of the corners.
  - If participants need to tie two ropes together, a reef knot or sheet bend should be used depending on the diameter of the ropes.
- Participants experiment with building strategies to construct a unique shelter that fits group members and will keep them dry.
- When building the shelter, choose a site that will minimize the impact on the area.
- Participants inspect their tarps and use Tuck Tape to fix any holes.
- Selecting and constructing an appropriate shelter depends on the weather, including the location of the shelter in relation to wind and any weather conditions such as rain.
- Participants should have a rationale for building their sleeping shelter the way they did.

Teaching Cues

- Build shelters on durable surfaces that will be able to recover quickly after staying in the shelter overnight.
- Ensure that the groundsheet covers slightly less area than the outer tarp to prevent water from pooling overnight in the groundsheet.
- Encourage participants to take height and size of the shelter into consideration. A smaller, lower shelter will maximize heat and keep the group warmer in colder conditions (figure 1.10), whereas a larger, higher-built shelter is better suited for warmer outings.
- Allow participants to select their own site based on the low-impact criteria that you set out for them (see LNT practices in unit 3, Environmental Ethics).
- Walk around to each of the groups while construction of the shelters is underway. Do not comment on the shelters yet, but be there to answer any questions or give any help that may be required.
- Bring everyone together and go from one shelter to another, getting the groups to point out the pros and cons of each shelter. This is also a time for the groups to see each other's creativity. Once the tour is over, participants can go back to their shelter to improve it based on the suggestions from the rest of the group.
- Participants should understand that this skill could be used for making an emergency shelter to provide quick shelter for someone who is hurt, sick, or wet or to secure the environment due to a sudden change in the weather.
- Emergency shelters should be built quickly. Safety is more important than low-impact camping; therefore, an emergency shelter should be built in the first appropriate site that the group finds.

Figure 1.10 Before bunking down for the night, consider the height and size of your sleeping shelter in relation to weather conditions.

Activity 3: Cooking Shelters

A cooking shelter is an easy shelter to build, and it is also one of the most important shelters. In a large storm it is important that your group be able to eat; thus it is important to have a cooking shelter built for such an occasion. The cooking shelter is simple and usually can just be a tarp hung over a ridgeline with a slight angle in the tarp and with all four corners tied off to trees (figure 1.11). The cooking shelter should be higher so that the cooks are able to stand and work under the tarp. The height allows for a well-ventilated space and keeps the tarp away from the heat source. Always remind participants that they are not to walk through the cooking shelter but should go out and around so they do not accidentally kick over the stove or anything on the stove.

Skill Cues

- Build a cooking shelter in a spot that is 70 adult steps away from the sleeping location. A flat, durable area with little vegetation at risk of catching on fire is appropriate.
- Participants should build their cooking shelter to match the size of the group and both current as well as forecasted weather conditions.
- Participants must be able to secure the tarp so that it is taut and angled enough to protect against the elements and tight enough that rain cannot pool and snow cannot pile up on the tarp flaps. However, the tarp also needs to be high enough for safety when operating the stove.
- Participants use appropriate knots when building their shelter.

Figure 1.11 The cooking shelter provides a dry space for preparing meals.

Teaching Cues

- Remind participants of safety concerns, emphasizing that they should walk out and around the cooking shelter when going to get something that they need.
- Emphasize the importance of a shelter for not only cooking but also keeping warm and dry when eating the meal.

Activity 4: Natural Shelters (Debris Huts)

Debris huts offer a simple solution to building a shelter when traveling in a heavily wooded area. If you want to travel as lightly as possible and immerse yourself in nature, a debris hut can be an excellent shelter to build. The only materials required are dead and down sticks, the woods, and your imagination (figure 1.12). Humans have been using debris huts since the time of hunters and gatherers. If built correctly, this shelter can be warm even without the use of a fire, which can easily be added if desired. The trickiest part of constructing this shelter is waterproofing it, but if you can find leaves, grass, and sheets of bark or are camping in an area heavy with down birch trees, this problem can be remedied quite easily.

Skill Cues

- Leaves and small twigs lying on the ground can be used to help waterproof at the end of construction.
- Use larger sticks that are dead and down to make the frame for the debris hut.
- Weave smaller sticks among the larger sticks.
- Stuff leaves and place large pieces of broken bark across the sticks to form the walls and roof.

Figure 1.12 Debris huts are composed of dead and down sticks.

- In a birch forest, large pieces of birch bark can be layered to create a shingle pattern to help provide protection from the rain and intense sun, but the bark should be on the ground because pulling it off the birch tree causes a great deal of damage.

Teaching Cues

- Instruct participants to make the debris hut only large enough to accommodate the members of their group (one or two people) so that they will be warmer.
- The hut should be constructed with a low roof to maintain heat.
- Encourage participants to use natural features that they can place other sticks around, such as a fallen tree or large, low, hanging branches.

Activity 5: Quinzhees

Quinzhee is the Inuit word for snow shelter and is similar in shape to an igloo, but it requires much less time to build and is made of a pile of snow rather than many blocks cut from the snow (figure 1.13). A quinzhee does not require a snowbank; it only requires a large pile of snow that will be able to bond to itself so that when it is dug out, it will eventually become a solid, hollow dome that makes a warm shelter. For the strongest quinzhee, the walls at the base should be much thicker than at the top because the base will have the greatest weight to support.

Skill Cues

Piling the Snow

- Pack the surface snow lightly with a shovel.
- Pile snow in a dome shape that is 2 meters (2 yards) high and 2.5 meters (2.7 yards) wide at the bottom.
- During the process of piling snow, break up chunks of snow and lightly pack to form the dome shape.
- If built on a slope, the door area should be on the down side and extra snow should be piled to form the entrance.
- To ensure consistent wall thickness after digging out, several 30-centimeter (12-inch) dry sticks are inserted into the walls of the dome, although the base of the walls should be thicker and gradually get thinner as you near the top of the shelter.

Digging Out the Quinzhee

- Begin by digging in where the group has decided the door is to go.
- To avoid caving in the door, use test sticks to check progress before digging upward.

Figure 1.13 This person is digging out the sleeping area in the quinzhee.
Courtesy of Sean Dwyer.

- The digger inside the quinzhee continuously pushes snow out through the open door while other participants remove the snow.
- Once in far enough, the digger digs to one side and up, creating a space to the side of the doorway where the digger can kneel slightly.
- In a kneeling position, a shortened shovel can be used to easily scrape off snow chunks and pass them out through the door opening.
- Participants on the outside of the quinzhee use their shovels to remove the snow passed out by the digger.
- The digger needs to dig out the inside walls consistently to avoid caving in one area.
- The digger should dig until all the sticks are encountered, ensuring that the walls are thicker at the base and gradually get thinner as the shelter walls move upward.

Finishing the Inside

- Use the last of the snow removed from the walls and ceiling to create an even floor surface, making a sleeping area that is higher than the top of the doorway.
- A bed area that is higher than the doorway will prevent intrusion of cold air and will allow the participants to heat the interior of the quinzhee.
- Use the handle of the shovel to make two or three ventilation holes about halfway up the walls (the shovel handle can be dismantled to allow for plunging). Ventilation is important, especially if a candle is lit inside to help raise temperature and glaze the inside walls.
- Smooth the interior surfaces of the walls and roof to remove peaks of snow, which can cause water to drip as the interior heats up. A smooth roof and walls will allow water to drip down to the sides.
- Light a candle inside the quinzhee to heat and glaze the interior snow surface.

Teaching Cues

Piling the Snow

- The snow needs to bond because it has been disturbed and piled.
- Due to the bonding ability of snow, nearly any snow conditions are suitable for building a quinzhee.
- Before digging out, the snow pile should be allowed to set for 2 to 3 hours, but this setting time can be skipped for instructional purposes if you need to complete the shelter within 1 hour.
- One lesson should be sufficient to pile snow. The digging-out and finishing process should take two lessons.

Digging Out the Quinzhee

- Removing snow from the walls inside is a time-consuming, tiring process.
- Participants should take turns digging to avoid becoming too tired, wet, and cold, as well as to share the experience.

Finishing the Inside

- The formation of the walls and roof needs to be done consistently so as to allow the water to drip down to the base.
- A higher floor area in relation to the doorway is crucial to warmth in the shelter.

Activity 6: Emergency Winter Shelter (Snow Trench)

Snow shelters such as the quinzhee and the igloo can take a great deal of time to create. If you are in an emergency situation and need to build a natural shelter quickly

Figure 1.14 While others continue to dig the snow trench, this participant sets the logs to support the tarp roof.
Courtesy of Sean Dwyer.

for protection against the elements, then the snow trench will be the best natural shelter to build (figure 1.14). However, this shelter is not built to be comfortable. The snow trench is not as large as other shelters and is recommended only for overnight use.

Skill Cues

Digging the Trench

- A large snow depth of approximately 1 meter (1 yard) is necessary to build a trench; however, snow can be piled up to help with wall height.
- Measure the area needed for the snow trench. Measurement is easy if all participants lie on the ground in sleeping formation and allow a little extra space for gear storage.
- Dig the trench with vertical walls and almost to the ground, leaving a small layer to help with insulation when sleeping.

Covering the Trench

- Obtain dead and down logs and place them across the top of the snow trench approximately 50 centimeters (20 inches) apart.
- One option for covering the trench is to spread a tarp over the top and cover the edges with snow to seal out drafts, snow, and rain.
- Another option is to cover the roof of the trench with several down tree branches and then a layer of snow.
- The floor should be covered with a tarp and sleeping pad for warmth and comfort.
- The door is created by starting a hole 2 meters (2 yards) from the edge of the trench.
- Dig the door straight down and then inward until access to the interior of the trench is complete.
- Cover the entrance with a tarp and gear to help prevent heat loss and entrance by curious animals.

Teaching Cues

Digging the Trench

Knowing the area is important to avoid digging into obstructions such as fallen logs, large rocks, or boggy areas.

Covering the Trench

- The trench is below the surface of the snow, so it is not as warm as the quinzhee because cold air can easily sink into the sleeping area. However, it is faster to dig in emergency situations.
- If the trench is built on the edge of slope, the door can be dug upward and into the hut to create an air trap so that cold air does not enter.

Activity 7: Igloo

For thousands of years, Inuit hunters have constructed igloos as a means to hunt and stay alive on the barren Arctic tundra, and the igloo has become one of the most famous symbols of the Arctic and the Inuit people. The igloo is the warmest of all the winter shelters and is also the most stable. If you are staying longer than one night, an igloo is best to build because of its ability to keep its inhabitants warm, as well as because it is stable and will last for a long time. More effort and tools are required to build an igloo, but the participants will not be disappointed in the finished product—it will be a very memorable activity (figure 1.15).

Skill Cues

Phase 1

- Mark a circle in the snow and pack down the snow to make a solid base.
- Push a small peg into the center of the circle to act as a reference point.
- This center point is crucial because all the blocks will have to be trimmed taking into consideration the center.

Phase 2

- Using a handsaw or a block mold (sold by many outdoor suppliers), cut blocks of snow out of nearby drifts.
- Most of the blocks should be fairly large, approximately 60 by 30 by 30 centimeters (24 by 10 by 10 inches).
- Arrange the blocks around the outside of the circle.
- As each block is put in place, the butt ends of the blocks (or sides that butt with the next block) must be trimmed to align with the center of the circle.

Figure 1.15 These participants are closing in the dome of their igloo with formed snow blocks.

Phase 3

- Now that a complete circle of blocks has been made, two more important cuts must be made in the base level.
- A good base will ensure that the igloo comes together to form a dome shape.
- For the first base cut, pick a starting block in the circle and use the handsaw to trim the top plane of the entire circle into a gradual incline.
- Designate some participants to work from the inside of the igloo. As the building continues, the inside workers will seal themselves in.
- The door can be cut once the igloo is three or four layers of blocks high.
- All parts of the igloo are trying to fall inward toward the middle. The wedge shape of the blocks and the fact that the net force on any given wall is zero means the structure will support itself.

Phase 4

- Put the second row of blocks in place.
- Trim the blocks in the same way as the first row.
- The butt ends of each block must be trimmed to line up with the center of the floor.
- Once the entire row is in position, the top plane of the tier will also be slanted to point toward the center of the floor.

Phase 5

- Continue with this process as you construct the third row and so on to the top.
- As the roof closes in, the last block will have to be shaped to plug the final opening.

Teaching Cues

- This activity is best done as a group project because many blocks are required to complete an igloo.
- The fact that the first row of blocks is sloped in toward the central point helps to bring the walls of the igloo inward; without this slope, the igloo will become a cylinder.
- Bring participants together and place a block on the top of the first row to show how the second tier of blocks should slope inward once they are seated on the first tier.

Activity 8: Sleeping Bags

A good night's sleep is essential to ensure the safety and enjoyment of wilderness travel. Selecting comfortable sleeping equipment involves a combination of expected weather conditions and personal preferences. A sleeping bag should provide enough insulation to maintain a sleeping person's core temperature comfortably within the range of temperatures anticipated on an outing. In addition, the bag should allow body perspiration to evaporate slowly in order to prevent heat loss through conduction (see lesson 1 in unit 19 on the CD-ROM for information about heat loss).

Skill Cues

- Participants practice fluffing their sleeping bags to restore loft after the bags come out of a compressed stuff sack.
- Participants practice entering their sleeping bag (rectangular and mummy bags using a liner).
- Participants repack their sleeping bags using the provided stuff sacks.
- Participants recognize the difference between a three-season or summer sleeping bag and a four-season or winter sleeping bag.

Teaching Cues

- Hold a group discussion of the merits of various sleeping bags. Have samples available.
- Know the advantages and disadvantages of different cuts:
  - Rectangular—These sleeping bags are ideal for shorter trips closer to home. They are roomy, allowing more body heat to escape, but they are also bulkier, making them harder to pack. The main advantage of rectangular bags is that they are much cheaper to purchase.
  - Mummy—These sleeping bags are tailored to the human body, being narrow at the feet, wider at the hips and shoulders, and then narrow again at the neck and head, including a hood. Because these bags are shaped similarly to the human body, less body heat escapes. The mummy sleeping bag packs lighter and smaller and is better suited for longer trips. The biggest downside is that some people find them to be constricting.
  - Barrel shaped—These bags are a combination of the previous two. A barrel sleeping bag is slightly tapered but does not offer a hood. It is roomier than the mummy sleeping bag and warmer than the rectangular sleeping bag, but it is still bulky to pack and not as warm as the mummy sleeping bag.
- Each sleeping bag has a tag that tells the lowest temperature recommended for using that bag by itself. Additional accessories, such as a liner, will contribute to the maximum temperature that the sleeping bag is recommended for.
- Know the advantages and disadvantages of covering materials:
  - Nylon—Durable and dries quickly, but uncomfortable against skin and easily slides off the sleeping pad at night.

- Cotton—Comfortable, but harder to keep clean, may be damaged by insects, and dries slowly, which could lead to hypothermia concerns when sleeping in a wet bag.
    - Liners—May make a bag more comfortable, warmer, and longer lasting.
- Know the advantages and disadvantages of insulating materials:
    - Down—More compressible, lighter, and warmer, but loses almost all insulation when wet. Down bags are more expensive than synthetic sleeping bags, but in the long run they will last longer than the synthetic sleeping bag.
    - Synthetics—Similar to down, but their strength lies in retaining insulating value when wet. These sleeping bags are also good for people with allergies.
- Show examples of loft or thickness in determining how warm the sleeping bag will be.

Activity 9: Sleeping Pads

Regardless of how good a sleeping bag is, it won't provide a comfortable night's sleep if there is no insulating barrier between it and the ground. Most people expect the sleeping pad to act as the mattress of a bed, but realistically the sleeping pad insulates you from the ground and is designed to keep you comfortably warm. In addition to providing insulation, a sleeping pad will also prevent moisture transfer from the ground, and it will provide extra comfort by padding out any unevenness (figure 1.16).

Skill Cues

- Identify the differences among and advantages of the sleeping pads.
- Reroll the sleeping pad for packing purposes.
- Operate a self-inflating sleeping pad and deflate the pad for packing purposes.
- Develop familiarity with the most common types of pads.

Teaching Cues

Hold a group discussion about what sleeping pads are better suited for different trips. Have samples available.

- Closed-cell foam—More durable and resilient to moisture than a self-inflating pad; however, it's bulkier than the self-inflating pad.

Figure 1.16 An assortment of typical sleeping bags and pads used for backcountry camping.

- Self-inflating—These open-cell pads allow excellent insulation from the ground. Self-inflating pads are lighter and easier to pack, but they are more susceptible to moisture and are much easier to damage and harder to fix.

Lesson Closure

- Review the advantages and disadvantages of sleeping systems.
- Review objective analysis of basic gear needs compared with high-end specialized equipment, emphasizing cost-effective essentials as opposed to trendy bells and whistles.

LESSON 4

Backpacks

Overview

Backpacking can be a rewarding and memorable activity, but participants need to be comfortable to gain the benefits of this outdoor pursuit. The challenge is to adjust the pack so that a participant is carrying weight safely. This requires the right fit and distribution of packed items. Not all packs are created equal; thus participants need to be familiar with the features, styles, and sizes that are suitable for the type of trip.

Packing the backpack is a challenge and can take time and practice, but when you actually go on the trip, the time spent finding the best way to pack your pack will be well worth it. It is also important to learn how to properly don (put on) and shuck (take off) a pack, preventing back injuries. Once the pack is on, participants need to know how to make adjustments for comfort, allowing them to focus on the beautiful surroundings and not pain caused by the pack.

Learning Objectives

- To know how weight distribution and common equipment should be packed
- To learn how to put on a backpack alone and with help from a partner
- To practice adjusting the pack once it has been donned

Activity 1: Packing a Backpack

There is no single correct way to pack a backpack, but certain suggestions for streamlining and weight distribution can aid in a more enjoyable backpacking experience. The key to this activity is to share ideas with the participants and stress creativity and problem solving as they strategize ways to make room.

Skill Cues

- Participants inspect their packs for broken straps or buckles. The strap system will help maintain comfort.
- Participants sort equipment into piles based on weight and high-need accessibility.
- Begin packing according to the following criteria:
  - At the bottom, pack light items such as the sleeping bag and other items that are not required until in camp at the end of the day.
  - In the middle of the pack and closest to your back, pack the heaviest items. This way the pack is balanced from top to bottom so you don't feel too top or bottom heavy. Such items may include clothes, pot sets, stoves, food, and tent components.
  - At the top of the pack, consider lighter items that may be essential throughout the day, including rain gear, a tarp, an extra change of clothes, and a jacket in case the weather changes quickly.
  - In the top compartment (the hood), include small items that will require easy access throughout the day, such as a journal, camera, binoculars, snacks, first aid kit, GPS, or survival kit.
- Streamline the packing: Try to pack as much inside the backpack as possible, keeping the items balanced from side to side and up and down, so as to avoid having a multitude of items dangling from the pack.

Teaching Cues

- Streamlined packs will cut down on damage to equipment, prevent the loss of equipment, and eliminate the risk of getting snagged when going through thick trees and bushes.
- A balanced pack assists in hiking because the participant will not feel off kilter during the hike.
- If you have to pack something on the outside of the pack, make sure that it is secured and fitted tight to the pack.
- Important items such as clothes or the sleeping bag may be packed in a dry bag or other waterproofing bag. It is easier to keep items dry than to dry them in the field.
- Fuel should be packed below food and in external pockets if possible in case fuel bottles leak.
- Use compression straps to center the items and stabilize the load—a more compact pack is the goal.

Activity 2: Putting on a Pack

Putting on a pack, especially one packed for a longer trip, can quickly lead to an injury if done incorrectly. This activity will introduce three ways to put on a pack that reduce the chance of injury.

Skill Cues

Donning the Pack

- Participants loosen all body straps before donning the pack.
- Participants exercise care by following the skill progression:
  - Lift the pack to the knees by holding onto one of the shoulder straps and the grab loop at the top of the pack (figure 1.17).
  - From the knees, continue to hold the grab loop while putting one arm through one of the shoulder straps.
  - As the arm slides through the shoulder straps, lean forward, and keeping the back straight and legs slightly spread for balance, shift the pack onto the back.
  - Once the pack is on the back and one shoulder strap is on, maintain a slight lean forward while sliding the arm through the other shoulder strap.
  - The donned pack is ready for adjusting.

Donning the Pack With a Partner

- The partner donning the pack starts with the back toward the other person and the pack in between them.
- With legs slightly spread and knees slightly bent, the lifting partner lifts the pack by the shoulder straps to the knees.
- The lifting partner holds the pack in place while the donning partner slides arms through the shoulder straps, again leaning forward for better balance.
- The donned pack is ready for adjusting.

Figure 1.17 Donning the backpack by using the knee lift.

Lift and Flip

The third method to don a pack should only be done by more experienced participants who have the required upper-body strength and a healthy back.

- Place the pack at the feet with the shoulder straps facing front.
- The feet need to be shoulder width apart and the knees slightly bent.
- Reach down and slide arms through the shoulder straps, grabbing onto the sides of the backpack securely (figure 1.18*a*).
- When ready, stand up quickly, hold on tight, flip the bag over the head, and place—not throw—the pack onto the back (figure 1.18, *b-d*). Participants should have a partner spot them.
- Remain leaning forward or else the momentum of the pack will pull you backward.
- If done correctly, the shoulder straps should be positioned on the body and the donned pack is ready for adjusting.

a

b

c

d

Figure 1.18 Donning the backpack by using the lift and flip.

Teaching Cues

- Make sure all participants lift with their legs, emphasizing starting with bent knees—you may need to demonstrate this to avoid lower back injuries due to lifting heavy packs improperly.
- All participants should finish leaning forward with feet spread shoulder width apart, providing a more balanced position.
- Make sure all participants go at their own pace and only try the methods that they feel comfortable with.
- Supervise each lift to make sure all steps are followed, and coach participants through each step.
- Encourage participants to use each other instead of you for the partner carry so everyone has hands-on experience with the methods.
- Encourage participants to spot each other when they are donning their packs so they are not pulled over if they lose their balance.
- Closely monitor participants during the lift and flip. They will tend to lift and throw the pack too hard until they get a feel for how much strength is required.

Activity 3: Fitting a Pack

This activity will teach participants how to adjust the pack so that they can remain comfortable for the day. As participants hike, they should be able to enjoy the outdoors and not be distracted by discomfort or even pain from the backpack. A properly fitted pack will not eliminate all physical stress on the body, but it will allow comfort in degrees. Refer to figure 1.19.

Skill Cues

- Bend forward slightly with feet shoulder width apart. Check that the hip belt is directly over or just above the hipbones, fasten the buckle, and tighten the strap only until it is comfortably tight.
- Straighten posture with only a slight forward lean, and one shoulder strap or both can be tightened until snug. The fit should barely allow a hand to slide in between the shoulder blade and top of the shoulder strap.
- Adjust the top loader straps until the top compartment of the backpack is just touching or within reach of the back of the head (still leaning slightly forward). Once standing straighter, the pack should no longer be touching the back of the head and the participant can cinch the final straps on each side of the hip belt.
- Adjust the sternum strap and fasten the buckle together. You do not need to have it done up all day, but if you want to take some stress off the shoulders for a short time, fastening the sternum strap will give some relief.

Teaching Cues

- You need to match participants with a properly fitting backpack. Make required adjustments to the back harness before beginning the hike.
- Remind participants that they do not need to have every strap cinched up as tightly as possible; it can be cinched only until they feel comfortable with securing the load to their body.

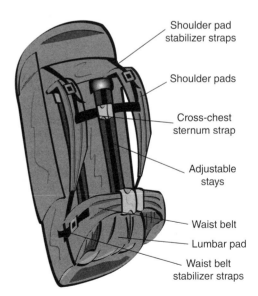

Figure 1.19 Properly adjusting the straps on your backpack can help minimize physical stress on the body.

Adapted, by permission, from WEA, 2009, *Hiking and backpacking* (Champaign, IL: Human Kinetics), 63.

- Take as much time as possible with this step, making sure everyone has a pack that will fit correctly and that is adjusted appropriately.
- Women may not be as comfortable with the sternum strap, so ensure that the pack fits them in the shoulders correctly and use packs that are designed specifically for female participants.

Activity 4: Shucking a Pack

If the pack went on the back, sooner or later it will have to come off. Shucking a pack is not as easy as it sounds when done properly to prevent back injuries. An unacceptable practice is for participants to unbuckle and drop their packs.

Skill Cues

- Leaning slightly forward, loosen the shoulder straps and unbuckle the hip belt.
- Take one arm, slide it out from the shoulder strap, reach across your body, and grab onto the opposite shoulder strap (or the grab loop at the top of the pack). The hand of the arm still in the shoulder strap should hook the thumb or grab onto the strap to secure the pack (prevent it from flopping off your back).
- In one smooth motion, slide the pack off your back and onto your leg with a bent knee. Slide the backpack slowly off your leg onto the ground.

Teaching Cues

- Monitor participants as they shuck their packs one at a time.
- Coach each step in the skill progression.
- Stress the importance of not dropping packs from the back; this can damage the pack and packed gear.
- With the pack on the ground, loosen all the straps so the backpack is ready to be donned. Having a loaded pack with a participant struggling to slip an arm into a tight shoulder strap or tight top loaders will make adjustments difficult.
- Have participants work in pairs to prevent injuries, if necessary.

Lesson Closure

Have participants practice donning backpacks again and follow you for a short hike that has varied terrain. The actual walking experience with a loaded pack will inform participants of comfort, fit, and needed adjustments. Going up and down small inclines will provide valuable information on posture during a hike, helping participants maintain a healthy body position along with comfort.

LESSON 5

Stoves

Overview

Backcountry cooking is an art form and a necessity. There is no debate that healthy meals will contribute to the overall experience for participants. A warm and filling meal results in a happy camper. Technology has evolved, and compact, lightweight stoves have allowed wilderness cooking to become a sophisticated skill. However, learning to cook on any stove is a skill that needs to be developed, and learning how to light and operate a camp stove is not a simple skill to master in one attempt. Learning to operate a stove takes time and repeated attempts to get the meal just right.

Learning Objectives

- To be able to distinguish among the types of stoves and match up each stove with the appropriate fuel
- To safely light and operate a variety of stoves
- To boil a liter (1 quart) of water
- To properly shut down a stove
- To know the pros and cons of various stoves and fuels

Risk Management

- Follow the lighting specifications of each manufacturer.
- Use only approved fuels and store fuel in approved canisters.
- Before participants practice lighting the stoves, inspect and light all stoves to ensure safety.
- If participants are having trouble starting a stove, they should turn off the stove and wait a few moments before attempting to light the stove again.
- An empty pot should be on hand to cover a stove that is flaring or burning out of control.
- Make sure fuel supplies are stored well away from the instructional area.
- Demonstrate shutdown procedures to all participants.
- Remind participants that they should not step over a burning stove or pick up a lighted stove.
- Participants also are not to lean over the stove when lighting it; they must keep well away from the burner.
- Allow for ample cool-down time before stoves are packed.
- Participants should be closely supervised at all times, and you should ensure that each participant is comfortable lighting and operating each type of stove.
- Allow only one stove to be lit at a time under your supervision.

Activity 1: Identifying Types of Stoves and Fuel

Stoves come in a variety of styles, each with advantages and limitations (figure 1.20). There are four types of stoves: those that use pressurized liquid fuels, those that use pressurized gas containers, those that use mixed fuel, and wood-burning stoves. Personal preference will play a large role in stove selection, as will group needs and skills, fuel accessibility, and environmental concerns.

Skill Cues

- Participants examine a variety of stoves (pressurized gas, blended fuels, liquid gas, and wood) and complete a comparison chart that rates the following information: fuel consumption, fuel accessibility, burning efficiency, ease of operation, field-friendly repairs, and advantages and limitations.
- In groups, participants prepare an overview of their stove of choice.

Teaching Cues

- Provide data sheets on the performance of each stove in the field.
- Consider sustainability: Liquid-fuel stoves allow you to refill and reuse the fuel canisters (if inspected and safe for continued use), whereas pressurized canisters do not have the refill option. Liquid fuels include white gas (also known as *naphtha*

Figure 1.20 An assortment of typical backcountry stoves, including pressurized gas, pressurized liquid, and wood-burning stoves.

or *camp fuel*), kerosene, or methyl alcohol. These stoves are more complicated to light due to the need to preheat the generator in the stove.

• Simplicity may be the most valued characteristic. For example, the main strength of pressurized gas such as propane is the ease with which it can be used. Propane stoves are already pressurized, requiring no pumping, and they have few moving parts, allowing for low to no maintenance. For outdoor trips, you can get small .5-kilogram (1-pound) tanks that last an extended time and burn efficiently even in extremely cold temperatures. The largest drawback of the propane stove is that the tanks are not refillable and may not be recycled everywhere once the trip is over, requiring you to pack the tank out over the rest of the trip.

• An example of blended fuel is butane mixed with propane. Stoves that use blended fuels are similar to propane stoves in that they are relatively easy and safe to use with low maintenance. However, also similar to propane stoves, they require pressurized tanks that are not refillable and must be disposed of properly. Cold weather can also affect these stoves, lowering their effectiveness.

• Wood-burning stoves rely on a ready supply of twigs at camping sites. It is difficult to regulate heat with these stoves because it takes time to build or reduce flame height. One of the major advantages of wood-burning stoves is that they are the only type of stove that isn't restricted on commercial airlines (many fuels cannot be transported on airplanes). These stoves also have a constant fuel source depending on where you are practicing your outdoor pursuit.

• Discuss the disadvantages and advantages of the stoves, taking into account participant feedback and knowledge of seasonality—how temperatures, dampness, geography, altitude, and access to fuel types can affect the performance of each stove.

Activity 2: Lighting the Stove

Stoves are an essential part of low-impact camping. All participants should be able to safely assemble, start, and operate the various stoves. Participants should be in the correct position to light the stove so that they can stay safe in case of flare-ups. This activity will show participants where and how to set up, light, and shut down a variety of stoves.

Skill Cues

- Participants practice with matches, lighter, and sparker (steel and flint tool).
- Participants check their stove for leaks or loose attachments, and in some instances they assemble their stove using the proper fuel.
- Participants must demonstrate proper body position while lighting and then shutting down the stoves following the step-by-step procedures.

Teaching Cues

- Each group should rate the stoves on compactibility and ease of lighting, shutting down, and operation.
- Use a variety of ignition sources: lighter, match, and sparker.
- Any stove should be set up in an area that is sheltered from wind yet far enough away from combustible materials (including duff and litter) that a sudden flare-up won't cause problems. Use approved windshields according to the manufacturer's specifications.
- Explain that dead and down sticks should be the only fuel used in wood-burning stoves and that they should be gathered over a wide area to prevent depletion.
- Demonstrate the assembly and lighting of all stoves, including body position when lighting the stoves. Emphasize having the face away from the burner and being in a position where the body is safely away from the flame source.
- Set up the stove on a durable natural surface to limit impact.
- Demonstrate care and maintenance procedures for the stoves.

Lesson Closure

- Review the types of stoves and their advantages and disadvantages.
- Give participants one of the stoves and require them to safely light the stove and boil 1 liter (1 quart) of water.

LESSON 6

Fires

Overview

Many participants feel that the campfire is the best part of the outdoor experience. Building a warm fire is a skill that cannot be overlooked; beyond aesthetic and social benefits, in some instances a fire means survival. Building a fire takes practice and patience, and the skill cannot be left to chance in the backcountry. All participants should have the ability to build and maintain a fire and follow LNT practices while doing so (see unit 3 for more on LNT practices).

Learning Objectives

- To learn how to build and ignite a fire
- To understand the safety precautions around the fire area
- To experience a recreational campfire
- To learn how to put out a fire

Risk Management

- Teach in a wooded area close to a water supply. If the area is not near water, filled containers should be within reach of the fire at all times.
- Another important consideration is selecting an area that has an ample supply of fuel and can accommodate a group building various fires.
- Participants must understand the correct way to gather and break large sticks for the fire.
- When shaving magnesium with a knife, participants need to be cautious.
- Another consideration for this lesson would be to advise the local authorities (i.e., department of natural resources) of your plan and lesson location, abiding by fire regulations for the area. This may require you to obtain permits or contact landowners for permission.

Activity 1: Building a Fire

Fires should be located in an area that provides shelter from the wind and also presents no risk that the fire will expand beyond the designated area. Ideal locations include durable surfaces (bare rock or mineral soil) free of plant debris. Working in small groups, participants will build a fire using natural materials and will develop their skills by experimenting with ignition sources.

Figure 1.21 The beginnings of a twiggy fire using a natural fire starter (a piece of birch bark found on the ground).

Skill Cues

- Participants use an existing location or select an appropriate fire location based on LNT practices.
- Once the site is prepped, participants assemble essential components before igniting the fire: tinder, kindling, and fuel (figure 1.21). The components should be prepared by breaking them into small pieces and then organizing them from smallest to largest. Preparation is the key to a reliable start.
- Participants make a tinder ball of small twigs; pieces of birch bark found on the ground; dry leaves; old man's beard (hanging tree moss) if not raining, foggy, or drizzly; ferns; wood shavings; and any other natural material that will give them an advantage in lighting their fire.
- Participants practice using the following techniques:
  - Use both flint and steel to light the tinder ball alone.
  - Use magnesium shaving pieces, making sparks with flint to ignite the shavings that will in turn ignite the tinder ball.
  - Use matches or a lighter to ignite the tinder ball.
  - Use homemade or commercial fire starters.
- Participants practice making tepee fires:
  - Make a tinder core in the center of a fire pit.
  - Place kindling above the tinder ball by setting the kindling vertically around tinder and leaning the tops together to construct a tentlike structure above the tinder.
  - Be ready to place more kindling until coals begin to form.
  - A hubcap or fire pan is recommended.
- Participants practice making log-cabin fires:
  - Begin with a tinder core in the center.
  - Place two branches on left and right side, then two more branches atop those. Repeat until the logs are higher than the tinder.
  - Place a layer of thinner branches across the top layer of branches to cover tinder.
  - A hubcap or fire pan is recommended.

Teaching Cues

- Adhere to the LNT principles and use an existing ring fire, construct a mound fire or a platform fire, or use a fire pan if necessary.
- Provide samples of the raw materials necessary for fire building. Assign people to gather materials and then review the merits of the gathered materials as a group.
- Placing a long branch between two stumps, creating a pressure point, and bending it until it breaks is an easy way to create smaller pieces of wood. Participants should not be gathering sticks any larger than their wrists; small pieces are more beneficial to building a fire.
- The first component in starting fires is tinder. Tinder consists of highly flammable materials that react quickly to an open flame and burn robustly but are usually quickly consumed. The role of tinder is to create enough heat to ignite the kindling. Typical sources of tinder might be dry grasses, little pieces of twigs, or crumpled bark from down trees. Often there are sources of tinder that might not be evident and require research to discover. For example, resins from some evergreen trees often contain chemicals that ignite easily and burn with intense heat.
- In regions that support birch trees, the thin bark that can often be gathered from the forest floor contributes to an excellent tinder ball due to the flammable natural oil in birch.
- Because the flames from tinder don't last long, tinder should be placed under kindling, and additional kindling must be added as soon as the tinder ignites.
- Kindling can be either gathered at a location or made on-site by cutting thicker pieces into thinner pieces or using small, dry twigs.
- Kindling is simply thin pieces of dry wood that ignite fairly easily, developing a small bed of coals and flame that can be used to ignite larger pieces of fuel.
- When the weather is inclement, dry kindling can often be found by looking for dead twigs on the lower branches or base of trees because the branches above keep the lower branches dry.
- Prepare enough kindling to have an ample supply for starting the fire, and make sure there's enough left over that it would be a simple matter to restart the fire by laying fresh kindling on a coal bed.
- Larger burnable items such as sticks constitute the fuel for a fire. Small-diameter sticks will burn fairly readily, but larger sticks should be split to ensure that they burn efficiently.
- One of the best sources for fuel logs is windfalls—dead and down trees that were caught so that they do not rest on the damp forest floor. The wood is naturally air dried and isn't subject to the rot that happens once trees fall to the ground. Longer, larger pieces of fuel can often be reduced to suitable length for fires by breaking them using the crotch of a large tree, but a collapsible saw is faster.
- Making saw cuts halfway through logs can aid the process of splitting fuel logs.
- It is important that the rocks do not contain splits and cracks. When the rocks heat, trapped water in fissures and cracks can heat to a vapor, forcing expansion of the rock and resulting in an explosion, sending shards of rock into the group.

Activity 2: Recreational Campfire

with Tiffany Hayne and Leanne McPhee

Most campfires are lit for social purposes. There is something fascinating about glowing coals and flames, and campfires are a great way to pass an evening. A campfire is a special ceremony. It will come to play a bigger part in campers' memories than anything else. The happy hours spent around the dancing flames will live forever in the campers' hearts as shared memories. The outdoor leader must plan a campfire and not leave this experience to chance. This activity provides some suggestions.

Skill Cues

- Participants are given the material to cook a range of campfire treats, such as s'mores and hot dogs (first night only due to spoilage).
- Participants lead activities and games, which can take place while they are sitting around the fire enjoying the community spirit.
- Participants can sing songs, tell stories (personal or scary), share what they are thankful for, talk about dreams, or play games.

Teaching Cues

- You must plan the campfire and have the necessary materials on-site.
- No fire will ever work out just as it was planned, but it is good to have some sort of intention as well as backup activities.
- Some activities require you to begin modeling them, such as songs, rules for games, and of course cooking snacks to enjoy around the campfire.
- S'mores (graham crackers, chocolate pieces, and roasted marshmallows made into a sandwich) are snacks that most people enjoy but do not eat very often. Another bonus to having s'mores is that participants are allowed to be more intimate with the fire. Participants are often attracted to fire, but use some safety precautions as described previously.
- Spider dogs are a fun way to cook and eat hot dogs. Slit the end of a hot dog with an *X*. Place the hot dog on a roasting stick or fork and cook over the fire. The ends will curl to look like a spider. Have a contest for the most realistic spider.
- Have a list of campfire songs that many participants will have heard and with encouragement will sing as a group. Allow participants to lead songs; you will be amazed at the variety of songs people know. Bring along copies of song sheets.
- Have a few games on hand to keep the group's interest.
  - Continue the Story is great for any age; simply change the storyline to cater to the age of the participants. You can start the story off, with each participant taking turns adding a line or two. You can go around the campfire a couple of times. If the story gets out of hand, just start another story and reverse the direction of the previous storyline.
  - In Twenty Questions, one person thinks of a person, place, or thing and the rest of the group determines what it is by asking up to 20 questions that can be answered with only *yes* or *no.* You can limit each person to one question.

Risk Management

- Running, horseplay, and even walking in the campfire area are not allowed, even when no fire is lit. Clearly define the boundaries of the campfire area.
- No loose clothing is allowed. Nylon pants are also discouraged because they are highly flammable.
- Long hair must be tied back.
- When the fire is burning, it must always be attended. Designate this responsibility to participants if appropriate.
- Depending on the age of the participants, it may be appropriate to have one or two designated people to poke or add wood to the fire when necessary or even to start or douse the fire.
- Campfire snacking rules should be considered, such as maximum number of roasting sticks used at a time to minimize the number of sharp objects and people trying to roast a snack at one time.
- Only participants who have roasting sticks or are tending to the snack should be allowed to stand in close proximity to the fire.

Activity 3: Dousing the Fire

An essential skill in conducting the campfire is putting it out before leaving the area or heading off to the tents or shelters. Old roots in the soil can ignite and burn underground for quite some time after campers leave the area, often surviving a dousing of water that would extinguish most fires. This is one reason why fires are built on mounds or platforms. Therefore, it is important that participants learn how to put out a fire.

Skill Cues

- Participants need to anticipate the time it takes for the fire to die out, leaving only embers and ash.
- The group discontinues putting fuel on the fire and stirs the hot coals, exposing coals buried under the ashes.
- Participants slowly douse the fire with water. After allowing the fire to smoke and steam until few or no hot coals are evident, participants douse the fire with water again, continuing to stir the ashes and cold coals to ensure the fire has completely gone out.
- A third or fourth application of water may be required. Keep stirring to ensure all coals are cold.
- In the morning, the final camp chore to break camp is scattering the cold ashy remains, following LNT practices for dispersing the ashes over a wide area outside the campsite.

Teaching Cues

- Monitor the time frame for allowing the fire die out.
- Make sure there is an established water site and filled containers are beside each fire in case of emergency and for dousing.
- Each participant needs to be involved in dousing the fire and checking to make sure the coals are cold.
- You should be the last one to leave the fire, ensuring gear is stowed, the fire is out, and participants are settling in with no concerns for the night.

Lesson Closure

- Review how to start a fire, types of fires, and LNT practices.
- A good way to perfect fire-building skills is to have fire-making competitions. Set up a fire pan for each group of three or four people. Suspend a string above each site. Have participants gather the raw materials and let them organize the materials beside their fire pit. On your signal, the participants must lay out the raw materials and light a fire that grows tall enough to burn through the suspended string. The first fire to burn through the string wins the competition.
- Have participants share something they learned about each other from the fireside activities.
- Have participants share what their favorite part of the campfire circle was and why.
- Have participants share games and other ideas that are fun and educational.
- Review how to put a fire out.

LESSON 7

Food Preparation and Menu Planning

Overview

An otherwise good trip might leave sour memories if the food was of poor quality, whereas an otherwise miserable trip can leave fond memories if the meals make up for the difficult conditions. Food on wilderness trips needs to be easy to carry, well balanced, easy to prepare, pleasing to taste, and filling! Meals can make or break a wilderness trip.

Learning Objectives

- To know how to plan meals for a wilderness trip, taking into consideration group needs, nutrition, caloric intake, and other factors
- To know how to efficiently pack each meal so that all food is organized by meal, easy to find, and simple to cook in the field
- To know how to safely prepare for cooking a meal
- To know how to safely handle and cook food in an outdoor setting

Risk Management

- Consider allergies when planning the menu.
- The menu plan should consider food spoilage based on the duration of the trip.
- Regular in-camp practice should ensure proper sanitation that extends to food preparation and cleanup that is consistent for each cooking group.
- All garbage is to be disposed of and stored correctly while in the outdoors—everything that you pack in must be packed out.

Activity 1: Menu Planning

Menu planning needs to be carefully done well in advance of the trip. There must be enough food so that all participants' dietary needs are met, but this must be balanced with what is reasonable to take on a trip—food should be healthy and nutritious, but in manageable quantities that can be carried. Planning a menu needs to take into account not only caloric requirements to suit the season and activity but also allergies, religious sensitivities, and the amount of food that will be suitable for the group. Other considerations should be group requirements such as likes and dislikes. All participants should enjoy the menu as much as possible, although realistically not everyone is going to be completely happy with the finished menu plan.

For extended outdoor pursuits, the group may want to consider dehydrated meals, and in some instances such meals will be a necessity, not a choice. Dehydrated meals cut down on the weight of the food as well as the space required for packing. An essential feature when planning is to balance nutrition with the ability of the group to pack, load, and carry the meals. As the outdoor leader, you must consider the cooking requirements of each meal and the skill level needed to create the meal.

You have to balance all these requirements with the question of whether the food will keep until the time comes for it to be prepared.

Skill Cues

- Develop lists of food from each of the following food groups: protein, vegetables and fruits, milk and dairy products, and grains. Classify the choices by refrigeration requirements, what can be dried before the trip, or what substitutes can be included (i.e., substitute milk and egg powder for milk and eggs, dried onions for chopped onions, and so on).
- Plan a 2-, 4-, 6-, and 8-day menu chart with three meals per day and morning, afternoon, and evening snacks. Include the following information for each chart: equipment needed to prepare the meal (number of stoves, reflector ovens, nesting pots, fry pans), how to modify recipes or ingredients to accommodate the trip plan (route, weight, spoilage), health concerns associated with the meal selection (diabetes, lactose intolerance, allergies), and how the menu will be modified to prevent potential health concerns.
- Use a dietary calculator to determine caloric intake of a full day's meals. (Dietary calculators are easily found on the Internet. Some examples include the Dallas Dietetic Association's Calorie Calculator at www.dallasdietitian.com/resources/calcalc.asp and the Health Calculator at www.ivillage.com/diet/healthcalc, which includes daily caloric requirement as one of the fields you can calculate.) Identify the caloric intake of active and moderately active men and women of various ages to determine the average daily caloric intake needed. Determine whether the menu matches the needs of the group based on the outdoor pursuit.

Teaching Cues

- Provide sample menus and analyze suitability for the trip based on ease of preparation, transportation, nutrition, ability to pack without refrigeration, dietary restrictions of participants, and quality based on your own experience.
- In many countries, government agencies publish nutritional dietary guidelines. These can form the basis of menu planning for a wilderness excursion.
- Some food items are more suitable to wilderness travel than others because refrigeration isn't an option. Often there are suitable substitutes available, and menu planning requires knowledge of viable options.
- It may seem onerous to plan menus for extended trips, but it's quite acceptable to devise a 5- to 7-day menu and then simply repeat it for the rest of the outing.
- Menus should take into consideration restrictions that cooking options might impose, such as fuel consumption, time and seasonality, and the need to boil water as part of the hydration and cooking requirement. There are restrictions to the amount of fuel that can accompany a group.
- Cooking fires are discouraged because they consume large quantities of wood. All meals should be planned based on the use of single-burner (or some instances dual-burner) backcountry stoves.
- Travel in the wilderness can be unpredictable. Menus need to be planned with flexibility in mind, such as quick breakfasts and lunches for time management, alternative meals such as soup on cold days, and quick meals to maintain a travel schedule.
- In addition to planning each meal for the duration of an outing, good menu planning will also include a buffer of meals to cover unexpected delays. This may include emergency meals for additional unplanned days spent in the outdoors or cold days where the group may need a bowl of soup to warm up.
- Some foods present a severe health risk to people with allergies. Participants with allergies need to be identified and the menu needs to accommodate any

health concerns posed by the allergies. These ingredients should not be part of the menu plan.

• Good menu planning attempts to match the calories of the meals to the activity planned during the day, the weather, and the weight and age of each participant.

Activity 2: Food Packing

There is no one perfect way to pack food for wilderness outings; instead there are many ways, each with advantages and limitations. Wilderness travelers must make informed decisions and choose the most appropriate methods based on the demands of the trip.

Skill Cues

• There are three methods for packing food:
  – Option 1: Organize food as a daily package (breakfast, snack, lunch, snack, dinner, snack). This method ensures an appropriate amount of food for each day; however, the method may have to be altered for flexibility and to accommodate bulky items.
  – Option 2: Another way to pack food is to organize materials into categories (e.g., pasta packed separately from the dried tomato sauce, allowing pasta to be used with a different topping if desired). Pack breakfasts, lunches, suppers, condiments, drinks, soups, and snacks separately. This method makes it easier to change meals based on circumstances and usually results in more compact packaging.
  – Option 3: Participants can pack individual meals in their own bags with all the ingredients already measured and ready to go. Designate three meal containers or storage containers as breakfasts, lunches, and dinners. Then pack each bag in the appropriate container in chronological order with the first meal that will be cooked on top for easy recovery.
• Regardless of packing method, label each bag for what meal it belongs to, including any recipe information with the meal. (You will not remember once you're in the field, and guesswork can backfire!)
• Keeping food dry is important. Participants should pack the food in waterproofed barrels, in sturdy sealed bags, or vacuum-packed bags. (Note: Some supermarkets will vacuum-pack food for consumers.)
• Garbage is another important consideration: Cut down on packaging as much as possible so you do not have to carry much garbage around during your time in the outdoors and to prevent microtrash, which tends to get left behind.
• Understand food safety and how to pack and transport foods to ensure foods are not exposed to conditions for bacterial growth or moisture.
• Fresh meats must be kept frozen until ready to prepare. Wrap frozen foods in several layers of newspaper and then package them in plastic bags so that any dripping does not contaminate other foods.
• Drink crystals, hot chocolate, coffee, and teas should be packed at the top of the food container to allow for quick access.

Teaching Cues

• Divide participants into three groups. Provide menus and have groups package foods. Team 1 has a vacuum bagger, team 2 has a variety of plastic food bags, and team 3 has larger plastic bags. Once food is packaged, discuss volume and waterproofing. An alternative method is to break the participants into four groups: breakfast, lunch, dinners, and condiments, snacks, and desserts. Each group is responsible for packing and labeling all food in that category and then packing those meals into the designated areas depending on the preferred method.

- Do the waterproofing test: Submerge empty food packs or food barrels in water for 10 minutes. Examine insides for moisture before packing the food.
- Provide the barrels or bags that all the meals will be packed in. Have participants pack meals. Discuss ease of packing, ease of retrieving foods, volume, and waterproofing.
- Before the trip, leave packages for 2 weeks in a cool, dry place to prevent moisture or mold. Keep all perishable food in the fridge or freezer and do not pack until immediately before going into the outdoors.

Activity 3: Cooking Styles

The cooking equipment available will determine what can be cooked and prepared in the field. Weight restrictions of the trip are another factor to consider. Baking allows menus to expand to endless possibilities. Cooking depends on the skill of participants, size of stove, menu options, amount of fuel, and season. The desired cooking style will ultimately come down to the outdoor pursuit (figure 1.22).

Skill Cues

- In groups of three or four, participants determine what cooking equipment they need and prepare the recipe.
- Determine what cooking method is needed for the meal—boiling, frying, sautéing, saucing, or baking—and how this could be prepared in the outdoors.
- Participants identify baking methods used in the wilderness and discuss the pros and cons of each method. They also identify five recipes that can be baked using each of the methods.

Teaching Cues

- Provide cookbooks and varied sets of baking equipment to groups of three or four people.
- Have teams plan a 4-day menu that can be cooked with the equipment provided.
  - Baking methods: dutch-oven cooking, reflector oven used on a wood-burning stove, outback oven, billy-pot baking
  - Cooking methods: grill, griddle, cooking food in foil, cooking on a spit
  - Styles of cooking: one-pot meals, bases with toppers (e.g., spaghetti noodles with sauce on top), roasting directly over wood-burning stove
- Any added water needs to be filtered or boiled before rinsing or rehydrating foods.
- Cooking pots can be kept shiny by smearing a thin film of dish soap over the outside of the pot before cooking over fire.

Figure 1.22   The preparations for a backcountry supper.

Activity 4: Campsite Hygiene

Food can be a magnet, attracting unwanted animal visitors into the campsite. Methods for protecting the food vary depending on the type of food and the type of animals. Though it is important to keep the food safe, the reality is that lingering odors from scraps left over from food preparation are what draws animals in the first place.

Skill Cues

- Carefully manage odors and remnants of meals prepared at the campsite by keeping cooking equipment, eating utensils, plates, bowls, and mugs clean. Do a group boil and dispose of gray water according to LNT practices.
- Prepare and eat meals atop a groundsheet that will catch any scraps. When the meal is over, carry the groundsheet well away from camp and shake it into a compost bag. With a cloth, wash off spills and stubborn stains. Air out lingering odors. The cook tarp and all food equipment go up the food line at the end of the day.
- Keep a hand towel easily available near the kitchen area. Participants should not wipe hands on their clothing, which could leave lingering food odors that go into the tent at night.
- Any food items that aren't needed should be kept in sealed containers or suspended by a food line (see unit 3 on environmental ethics).

Teaching Cues

- Before retiring to bed, make sure no food is stashed in clothing pockets. All food should be kept in the same safe location.
- Everything in personal hygiene kits should be stored in the food container. For example, a bar of soap is not normally thought of as food, but most soap is made from animal products and can be considered a tasty treat by many animals.
- Any scented products could attract unwanted animal visitors; therefore, in some places the clothes that participants wore while cooking may have to go up the food line.

Activity 5: Food Safety

When planning menus for wilderness adventures, the luxury of freezers and refrigerators is not available. In remote settings food poisoning can be life threatening at worst and a debilitating illness that can alter the wilderness experience at best. Knowing how to preserve foods from bacterial growth, packing prepared foods in a way that keeps them safe from bacterial growth, and knowing how to handle food during cooking are essential. When you are in a remote location without indoor plumbing, you need to take extra precaution to ensure that you are handling food as safely as possible.

Skill Cues

- Participants must be able to recognize the signs and symptoms, common sources, and conditions for growth of common food poisoning and water contaminations such as *E. coli,* salmonella, staphylococcus, *Clostridium perfringens,* botulism, and giardia.
- Participants reduce moisture content. For example, hard cheeses can be prepped by leaving them unwrapped in small pieces on a cutting board. Vacuum-packing the cheese after reducing the moisture content makes the cheese less likely to mold.
- Participants preserve some menu choices by wrapping them in cheesecloth that has been soaked in vinegar and then covered in a layer of wax.
- Participants blanche vegetables before dehydration to ensure aging enzymes are destroyed.

Teaching Cues

- Bacteria need moisture, time, food, and sometimes anaerobic conditions for growth. For wilderness excursions, the factor that can be controlled is moisture. Without moisture, bacteria cannot multiply and divide.
- Food can be made less attractive to bacteria by adding sugar, salt, or acids (i.e., vinegar or lemon juice)—you need to know the food choices!
- Discuss the typical signs and symptoms of food poisoning. Have cue cards with symptoms of various types of food poisoning, names of common food poisoning, and time of onset after ingesting foods. Have groups research and match food poisoning type with symptoms and time of onset.
- Discuss the impact that food poisoning could have on wilderness excursions and examine first aid and contingency plans in the event that one or more participants experiences food poisoning.
- Allow participants to dry a variety of foods and vacuum-pack them for future trip use.
- Explain the difference between dehydrated foods and freeze-dried foods.
- Provide a variety of meals. Have groups determine possible sources of food contamination, and discuss how meals can be prepared and packaged to avoid food contamination.
- Identify methods to safely prepare water for human consumption on wilderness trips.
- Examine methods used by pioneers to preserve foods and discuss how the methods worked.
- Know how to safely handle food when packing as well as when cooking.

Risk Management

- Once you are reasonably confident that the site does not have a high probability of an animal encounter, organize the components of the site in a triangular configuration.
- Gear and equipment will be kept in one segment of the triangle, food storage and kitchen preparation will be kept in another portion of the triangle, and sleeping quarters will form the last segment of the triangle. A sound practice is a minimum of 70 adult steps away from each of the camp locations listed above.

Lesson Closure

- Good food and enough of it is essential to having happy campers. Ask participants to share their favorite backcountry meal.
- Review major concepts of the lesson and strategies for finding the balance between individual and group needs and preferences in menu planning.
- Review the importance of food safety and the hazards of attracting wildlife. Participants should understand how to take precautions in food preparation and storage while in the wilderness.
- Have participants review types of food that are commonly brought on a camping trip, along with the variety of ways in which the food can be prepared.

LESSON 8

Knives, Saws, and Hatchets

Overview

Most wilderness trips benefit from ready access to cutting tools, but inherent risk is involved in using these tools. Cutting tools commonly found on wilderness trips fall into three broad categories: saws, knives, and hatchets. Each has advantages and disadvantages.

Learning Objectives

- To safely and appropriately use saws, knives, and hatchets
- To learn how to sharpen a knife and a hatchet
- To know the appropriate time to use all three cutting tools in relation to low-impact camping

Risk Management

- Use of cutting tools is at your discretion as the outdoor leader. Depending on the age and maturity of the users, constant visual supervision may be required.
- Practice makes perfect and is essential when outdoor excursions take groups into regions far beyond medical care.
- Placing safety first is paramount when cutting tools come out. It only takes a second for an injury to occur and alter the entire experience. Participants need to know the safety instructions for each cutting tool before they are given the chance to practice.
- All cutting tools must be sharp—a dull tool is just as dangerous as an inexperienced user.

Activity 1: Knives

Knives are probably the most practical cutting tool on the equipment list and are one of the most important pieces of equipment. If participants are competent and exhibit awareness of the safety concerns involved, they should each carry a pocketknife at all times on a wilderness trip. Knives can be used not only to shave magnesium for lighting a fire and kindling but also to split larger pieces of wood.

Skill Cues

- Participants must cut or shave away from their body and be in the proper position, kneeling and being as tall as possible while leaning over the piece of wood.
- Participants shave small pieces of kindling that could be used for kindling in a fire bundle.
- A more advanced skill is to split a larger piece of wood using a one-piece knife with a blade no shorter than 10 centimeters (4 inches). Place the wood standing up on a solid, stable, flat cutting block. Put the edge of the blade directly on the wood with the top of the handle close to the wood so as to use as much of the

blade as possible. Then use a smaller piece of wood as a hammer and hit the back of the blade until the blade is in the piece of wood. Use the smaller piece of wood as a hammer again, hitting the tip of the blade that is still sticking out of the log (figure 1.23).

Figure 1.23 Splitting kindling into smaller pieces—note the knife position.

Teaching Cues

- Safety is vital when dealing with cutting tools.
- Make sure participants are aware that cutting tools are off-limits unless their use is supervised or has been approved.
- Cutting or sharpening activities should always be done in a direction that moves body parts away from the cutting edge. No one should be in front of the cutter.
- Ensure that participants are using the sheath for the knife if the knife has one. Whenever a knife is not in use, it should be in its sheath at all times.
- Sheath knives are useful in tackling larger cutting tasks, but they are more dangerous to handle and bulkier to carry.
- Dull knives are more dangerous than sharp ones. Demonstrate sharpening technique for both a touch-up sharpening to hone a dull edge and a more vigorous sharpening to reshape a cutting edge damaged through inappropriate use.

Activity 2: Saws

A saw is the safest cutting tool for wood with a larger diameter. Folding saws that protect the blade when folded are the most practical choice for wilderness travel. Nonfolding saws can be made safer by cutting a slit in a piece of bicycle inner tube and stretching the tube over the cutting surface, thus fashioning a sheath to protect the blade.

Skill Cues

- Participants should always demonstrate controlled cuts when using the saw so as not break the blade by bending it with jerky movements and to avoid hurting themselves in case they hit a knot in the wood when sawing.
- Participants should never saw above their heads in case they drop the saw or the piece of wood they are sawing falls loose.
- Participants should not saw any piece of wood that is larger than their wrist. These pieces can be split using the knife method described in activity 1.

Teaching Cues

- Safety is vital when dealing with cutting tools.
- Make the group aware that cutting tools are off-limits unless their use is supervised or has been approved.
- Cutting or sharpening activities should always be done in a direction that moves body parts away from the cutting edge.
- Bring along several types of saws and conduct a group discussion to highlight the advantages and disadvantages of each.

Activity 3: Hatchets

Hatchets are the most dangerous of the three cutting tools. They are best suited to cut large pieces of wood to use in building a fire that may be required for an emergency to dry participants or warm them in extreme weather conditions. In a survival situation, you must take into consideration the safety and well-being of your participants—a large fire may be a necessity.

Skill Cues

- The safest and most effective way to use a hatchet is to first stand the piece of wood upright. Then place the edge of the hatchet on the top of the wood while it is standing on the cutting block, looking for natural cuts in the wood called *checkmarks.* Using another piece of wood as a hammer, tap the hatchet until it is securely embedded into the log. Then strike the back of the hatchet into the block so that it is acting as a wedge.
- Once the larger block has been split into smaller pieces of wood, kneel with knees shoulder width apart, raise the hatchet just past the waist, hold the cutting edge of the hatchet against the piece of wood, and strike down onto another log, a cutting block, allowing the force of the blow to split the wood into smaller pieces.

Teaching Cues

- Safety is vital when dealing with cutting tools.
- Make the group aware that cutting tools are off-limits unless their use is supervised or has been approved.
- Cutting or sharpening activities should always be done in a direction that moves body parts away from the cutting edge.
- Hatchets are the most dangerous cutting tool on wilderness trips. Ensure that participants are not swinging the hatchet to split smaller pieces of wood so that the hatchet does not slip and hit their body. Most often a swinging hatchet will miss the intended target and embed the cutting edge into a leg.
- Participants should not be allowed to use a hatchet until they have demonstrated that they understand all safety procedures.
- Hatchets need to be kept sharp. Demonstrate sharpening techniques, using a file to get rid of nicks and a stone to hone the edge. Use a piece of lumber to support the axe head.
- Work sharpening tools away from the cutting edge.

Lesson Closure

- Review the advantages and disadvantages of the cutting tools and when to use each type of tool.
- Ensure participants understand all safety precautions when working with knives, saws, and hatchets.

Checklists and Specialized Kits

Overview

There's nothing more frustrating on a camping trip than realizing that something important was forgotten at home. The easiest way to prevent that problem is to develop checklists for every aspect of a camping trip. At a minimum, there should be at least four checklists for every camping trip: a group equipment list (see figure 1.24), personal equipment list (see figure 1.25), duty roster (see figure 1.26), and menu list (see figure 1.27).

- Topographic maps and compasses
- Whistles
- Pocketknife
- Toilet paper, trowel, and hand sanitizer
- Plastic bags
- Sleeping bag (2-3 season)
- Sleeping pad
- Rope (various lengths for shelters and food lines)
- First aid kits
- Duct tape
- Tarps
  - Shelter (sleeping and cooking)
  - Groundsheets (sleeping and cooking)
- Pots and pans
- Stove
- Burning fuel (funnel)
- Repair kit (specific to the pursuit)
- Water-purifying equipment
- Large water jugs
- Tents
- Small bucksaw
- Matches (strike anywhere; stored in waterproof containers), lighter, candle, and fire starters (in waterproof case)
- Backpack
- Cell phone, satellite phone, radio, or personal locator beacon (PLB)

Figure 1.24   Sample group equipment list.

Learning Objectives

- To brainstorm items that should be on each checklist and in each kit
- To determine what items are placed on the checklist and what items go into each kit
- To value the importance of checklists in planning before going into the outdoors

Activity 1: Checklist—Equipment Kits

The need for organization is apparent when leading others for extended lengths of time. The checklist is essential not only for organizing yourself but for modeling organization for participants. Your challenge is not to try to remember everything but to be accountable to the safety of participants through systematic, thorough checks.

Standard Equipment

- Personal hygiene (toothbrush, toothpaste, soap, towel, hand sanitizer, tampons)
- Sunscreen and lip protection
- Sunglasses
- Journal and pencil
- Personal first aid kit (containing personal medications)
- Watch
- Eating utensils and a mess kit (pot, bowl, mug)
- Personal water bottle
- Rain gear (top and bottom)
- Flashlight with extra set of batteries and spare bulbs
- Bug repellent

Optional Equipment

- Camera and spare batteries (in a waterproof container if water is a threat)
- Binoculars
- Day pack to carry a change of clothes and assorted items

Dress

Include wool or synthetic materials as much as possible, and think in terms of layering (try to avoid cotton clothing).

- 3-4 pairs of wool socks
- Clothes for the day: T-shirt, long-sleeve shirt, pants, sweater, windbreaker, heavy outer jacket
- Backup clothes: T-shirt, long-sleeve shirt, pants, sweater, long underwear, underwear, fleece, shorts
- Sturdy footwear
- Ball cap and wool hat

Figure 1.25 Sample personal equipment list.

Skill Cues

- Participants generate a general list of group equipment and supplies required for a particular outdoor pursuit.
- Participants generate a list of personal equipment needs and justify the merits of each item.
- Participants identify the specialized equipment needed for a specific outdoor pursuit (see figure 1.28). For example, a hiking trip will have different equipment requirements than a paddling trip.
- Each of these three broad categories can be further subdivided into more detailed itemization of the necessary items. For example, the overall list might have a subcategory that breaks down the first aid kit.
- Repair kits are usually activity specific and hopefully are rarely needed. If the repair kit is well prepared in the first place, a visual inspection to ensure that nothing is missing should be just as effective as going through a checklist.

Name	Task	Deadline	Comments	Complete
Krista	Collecting permission forms	May 21	Forms were passed out 2 weeks before the trip.	✓
Steve	Collecting medical forms	May 18	New forms are needed to keep current. Last trip was over 3 months ago.	✓
Beth	Menu checks	May 23	Establish cooking groups and ensure balanced meals.	
Shamus	Group gear check	May 11	Two stoves are not working properly; batteries are low for the GPS.	✓
Danielle	Group first aid kit check	May 20	Small bandages need replacing; restock moleskin.	✓
Kris	Participant gear check	May 24	Three participants did not have all the required gear. They are borrowing needed equipment before the next check.	

Figure 1.26 Sample duty roster.

Teaching Cues

- Once the checklists are developed, packing the items should follow a fixed pattern to make it easy to notice if any items are missing. Sometimes the packing system is more important than the checklist. For example, organizing kitchen hardware and eating utensils into one pack where everything has a place means it may not be necessary to go over a checklist; a quick glance at the kitchen pack should easily determine if anything is missing.
- Equipment kits change depending on the activity, and they also change over time as needs change or equipment evolves.
- Spread out equipment based on one of the generated lists and lead a group discussion to evaluate the components. Ideally, every component in a kit should serve multiple functions.
- Conduct an equipment inspection to make sure functionality and maintenance needs are met. This is an excellent way to model trip preparation.

Activity 2: Survival Kit

People do not intentionally set out to get lost; usually it happens during a moment of inattention when they are distracted and they lose their bearings. It is important to bring a survival kit with additional equipment on all trips.

Skill Cues

- Participants identify the survival tools needed in case they get separated from their party or the bulk of their equipment: a pocketknife, matches or a lighter, a whistle, a paraffin-wax candle, a collapsible aluminum bread pan (to warm water by fire), an emergency snack, an ouch pouch (small supply of first aid items), flagging tape, and a compass.

Item	Ingredients (per group of 10)	Checked by
BREAKFAST		
Oatmeal	55 grams (2/3 cup) per person	
Cream of wheat	120 grams (2/3 cup) per person	
Pancakes	520 grams (4 cups) of pancake mix	
Bannock	400 grams (4 cups) of flour, 155 grams (1 1/3 cups) of powdered milk, 4 teaspoons of baking powder, 4 tablespoons of margarine	
Red River cereal	60 grams (3/4 cup) per person	
Hash browns	800 grams (4 cups) of diced, dehydrated potatoes	
LUNCH		
Tripper lunch	Wheat crackers and cheese Pitas with bean dip (spicy and nonspicy) Mini pitas with peanut butter, honey, or jam Beef or turkey jerky Baby carrots	
Soup	Select from a variety of dehydrated options	
Macaroni and cheese	520 grams (5 cups) of any noodle you wish, 180 grams (1 cup) of cheese mix (may add in ground beef or turkey and vegetables)	
SUPPER		
Tacos	910 grams (2 pounds) of ground beef, 2 tablespoons of vegetable chili mix, 40 soft taco shells, 240 grams (2 cups) of grated cheese, 55 grams (1/4 cup) of dried tomatoes, taco seasoning	
Pepperoni pilaf	2 sticks of dry pepperoni (spicy and nonspicy; may substitute with lentils or beans), 400 grams (2 cups) of dried potatoes, 95 grams (1/2 cup) of dried vegetables, 840 grams (4 cups) of rice	
Lentil and bean casserole	12 grams (1 cup) of onion soup mix, 50 grams (1/4 cup) of dried vegetables, 300 grams (1 1/2 cups) of kidney beans, 100 grams (1/2 cup) of lentils, 225 grams (1 cup) of dried tomatoes, 840 grams (4 cups) of rice	
DESSERT		
S'mores	1 box of graham wafers, 4 milk chocolate bars, 1 large bag of marshmallows	
Apple cobbler	200 grams (2 cups) of flour, 1 tablespoon of baking powder, 80 grams (2/3 cup) of powdered milk, 180-270 grams (2-3 cups) of dried apples	
SNACKS		
Granola bars	Select a variety of flavors	
Dried fruit	Select a variety of fruits	
DRINKS		
Tea		
Coffee		
Juice mixes		

	Breakfast	Lunch	Supper	Desserts	Snacks
Total number of meals					

- Include instructions with each meal.
- Confirm that there are NO food allergies to the ingredients in each meal.

Figure 1.27 Sample menu list.

Canoeing Equipment

- Canoe shoes (old sneakers)
- Kneeling pads
- Glasses strap
- Extra rope (securing packs and gear)
- Bailers
- Painters
- Canoes
- PFD with whistle attached for every participant
- Paddle for each participant (extra for each canoe)

Hiking Equipment

- Hiking boots
- Hiking pack, 60-80 liters (16-21 gallons)
- Bear repellent (at least one per small group—bear spray, bear banger)

Cross-Country Skiing Equipment

- Hat and mittens or gloves
- Outdoor winter clothing
- Snow boots
- Backpack (size depending on the length of trip)
- Ski boots
- Poles
- Skis

Figure 1.28   Sample specialized equipment for three outdoor pursuits.

- Shelter from the elements is an important survival tool that can be handled by carrying a small waist bag that contains rain pants and top, or twine and a plastic sheet that is 2.5 meters by 2.5 meters (8 feet by 8 feet) to construct an emergency shelter, as well as enough mesh to cover the face and hands in locations where biting insects are a problem.
- Participants practice a mock survival situation by using their survival kits and practicing a simulated survival for a few hours to determine how they could improve the kit.
- All of these items can be carried in a small daypack or waist bag.
- This practice needs to become a safety habit, much like buckling the seat belt in a car.

Teaching Cues

- Group discussions that begin with a case study or scenario provide the opportunity for dialogue among participants.
- Survival kit contents may vary depending on the hazards present in any given destination.

- Participants should be able to visualize any potential problems that they might encounter in a survival situation and make suggestions for kit contents that could improve the chances of survival.

Lesson Closure

Review key components of checklists and specialized kits and how their usage may enhance a trip.

References and Resources

Curtis, R. 2005. *The backpacker's field manual.* New York: Three Rivers.

Drury, J.K., B.F. Bonney, D. Berman, and M. Wagstaff. 2005. *The backcountry classroom: Lessons, tools, and activities for teaching outdoor leaders.* 2nd ed. Guilford, CT: Falcon.

Harvey, M. 1999. *The National Outdoor Leadership School's wilderness guide.* New York: Fireside.

Navigation

▼ Sean Dwyer ▼

No matter where you go, there you are.
— Confucius

Navigation is a core skill that should be an integral component of most outdoor activities. Getting lost is unlikely if you are properly versed in the skills of route planning, map and compass use, and GPS use with a map. Navigational competency thus reduces risk significantly when exploring the outdoors.

Familiarity with an area significantly diminishes the likelihood of disorientation. However, a variety of natural (e.g., seasonal, snow, no snow), environmental (e.g., weather, fog) and human (e.g., forest harvesting activity) factors can make what was once familiar landscape appear foreign, leading to errors in directional travel.

Knowing how to use navigation equipment and materials is crucial for safe travel in the outdoors. A trip into the wilderness can become uncomfortable and disheartening when you're left with the sinking feeling of being lost. Knowledge is power, and nowhere is this truer than in the wilderness. Trees all look the same, streams appear that are not marked on a map, hills are unexpectedly followed by more hills, there are no signs to guide the traveler, and you may realize that after walking for hours, you are back where you started. Having the ability to navigate will provide the confidence to safely lead others during an outing.

Many types of maps can be used for navigation, ranging from hand-drawn maps, park pamphlets, and site maps to more complex topographic maps produced through aerial photography. Topographic maps contain many features that allow for more complex navigation using land features and a compass. These maps give a vivid representation of the overall landscape, including waterways, municipalities, landmarks, elevations, distances, and vegetation. Topographic maps can be purchased from local suppliers, natural resources departments, or local sporting goods stores. Digital topographic maps are also available and are flexible so that you can print just the section you need.

GPS works in conjunction with mapping instruments and uses satellite technology to locate positions on the earth's surface (land and water). This technology can be used to link GPS and a home computer to load digital maps on the GPS unit for use in the field. Routes and landmarks can be shared between both sources and even between users of the technology. GPS and mapping routes for popular tourist attractions may be sold on CD-ROM or downloaded from the Internet. Maps for outdoor explorations such as hiking, mountain biking, snowmobiling, and even rafting trips in the Grand Canyon are available to buy and load into a personal GPS unit.

Equipment

Group Equipment

For the Outdoor Leader
- 1 demonstration compass
- 1 roll of surveying tape
- Permanent markers
- Spare batteries for GPS units
- Checklist for signing out maps, compasses, and GPS units (see figure 2.1)

For Participants
- 1 compass
- 1 topographic map
- 1 GPS (or 1 GPS for every two participants)
- 1 pencil, eraser, and ruler

Personal Equipment

Clothing and footwear suitable for outdoor conditions

Equipment Care and Maintenance
- Take care not to drop compasses or GPS units.
- If GPS units are not weather resistant, do not use them in inclement weather.
- Laminated maps will last during repeated use and wet weather but will be disfigured by pencil markings. Map bags and cases allow maps to be removed and marked on.

Site Selection
- Sessions can be conducted indoors and outdoors in an open field or in a forested setting.
- An area that has plenty of topographical features will be conducive to learning about map features and navigation.
- According to group maturity and skill level, sites should be chosen on natural collectors, or defined boundaries that contain participants within a specific area, preventing them from getting lost as they learn and practice their navigation skills.

GPS/compass #	Student names
1.	
2.	
3.	
4.	
5.	
6.	
7.	
8.	
9.	
10.	
11.	
12.	
13.	
14.	
15.	
16.	
17.	
18.	
19.	
20.	

Figure 2.1   Using a sign-out checklist ensures that all GPS units and compasses are returned at the end of the lesson.

From K. Redmond, A. Foran, and S. Dwyer, 2010, *Quality lesson plans for outdoor education* (Champaign, IL: Human Kinetics).

Social Skills and Etiquette

- Participants need to listen well during sessions to better understand the many components of each lesson.
- Navigation can be challenging for some and quite effortless for others who have a natural sense of direction and a knack for learning new concepts.

Risk Management

When navigating outdoors with a group, it is important to organize and plan activities such that all participants know where they are and can easily and safely return to a common meeting location. If the lesson is taking place in an expansive outdoor location, the risk of getting lost is high if you haven't taken the necessary precautions:

- Have all participants carry a whistle.
- Develop and communicate with a whistle code.
- Walking while looking down at a compass, map, or GPS unit can cause a participant to run into an obstacle or fall down a hillside.
- Instruct participants to stop, look at their device to make navigation judgments, look up, and proceed toward their destination.

Unit Organization

The many tools of navigation work together naturally because they are based on the cardinal directions of north, south, east, and west. This unit proceeds with basic operation of a compass, which is perhaps the most commonly recognized navigational tool. The sequence of lessons is designed to allow participants to build on knowledge and skill. As participants learn to use the compass, they will integrate the ability to read maps and then incorporate technology by using GPS in the field.

Lesson Plans

Lesson 1: Compass Parts and Use. Using a compass requires instruction and adequate practice. The group will learn the parts of the compass and how to dial and follow a bearing. Once participants are comfortable with the compass, activities at the end of the lesson allow them to practice their skills.

Lesson 2: Components of a Topographic Map. In this lesson, participants will be introduced to the components of topographic maps and how they are used in navigation. Many participants may be used to city maps and other simple maps. Topographic maps contain much more information and require practice. Components of this lesson include map features, elevations and contours, and grid lines.

Lesson 3: Using Map and Compass Together. This lesson combines the skills of the compass and map. Participants will gain experience finding a bearing from start to finish, aiming off with a compass, and adjusting for declination. The map and compass individually are great, but together they are much greater.

Lesson 4: GPS (Part 1). A GPS unit is a powerful piece of navigation technology. Most people are savvy with technology and will experience success with this lesson. Participants must realize, however, that any electronic equipment has limitations. Components of this lesson include understanding the satellite system, using GPS controls and screens, marking a location (waypoint or landmark), and navigating a waypoint or landmark.

Lesson 5: GPS (Part 2). This lesson is an extension of the previous GPS lesson. Participants will explore further features of GPS that are more specific to route planning and finding.

Experience using Track Log, Speed and Distance of Travel, and Backtrack functions will greatly increase understanding of the navigational functions of a GPS unit.

Lesson 6: Using GPS and Map Together. Participants have already had experience using a map and compass together for navigation. This lesson builds on earlier lessons by showing how GPS can be used in conjunction with a map. Using the Mark function on the GPS unit and the grid lines on a map, participants can accurately pinpoint their location. A route is simply a collection of locations (waypoints or landmarks) that can be easily taken from a map and entered into a GPS. Participants will experience how easy it is to plan a route using a map and then follow it precisely in the real world using a GPS unit.

Lesson 7: Route Planning. Navigation involves planning how to get from one location to another. Route planning is similar except that it involves several small legs to make one large route. Route planning involves such considerations as energy conservation, vistas and points of interest, and all aspects of safety.

Lesson 8: Route Selection and Finding. Planning and following a route with a group demands common sense and safety. Planning a route requires time and detail to attention. Despite this, sometimes unforeseen events and obstacles may require a change to the route plan. This lesson contains several tips that should be considered when planning a route.

Lesson 9: Geocaching. The final lesson in this unit involves a navigation activity with a GPS called *geocaching*. Using GPS, participants will search for caches set by the outdoor leader and by the general public. Participants will gain respect for the activity by visiting a cache and following the etiquette involved with items in the cache. Geocaching is a lifelong pursuit that uses skills taught in this unit.

Terminology

- **aiming off**—Following a bearing to the left or right of tricky locations such as stream and trail junctions. Aiming off to the left means going to the right when the stream or trail is encountered to find the junction.
- **Backtrack function**—GPS function that allows the user to reverse the direction of travel on a route.

- **bearing**—A horizontal direction from north measured in degrees.
- **cache**—A sealed container that is hidden for the purpose of geocaching.
- **cardinal directions**—The most common directions used for navigation: north, east, south, and west.
- **contour lines**—Lines on a map that show elevation above or below sea level. Each line connects areas of the same elevation.
- **declination**—The difference in angle between magnetic north and grid north.
- **east declination**—The magnetic-north line falls to the right or east of the true-north and grid-north lines.
- **easting**—The eastward distance measured on a topographic map.
- **geocaching**—An outdoor activity that uses a GPS unit to find caches hidden by others.
- **Global Positioning System (GPS) unit**—A navigational system using satellite signals and electronic handheld devices to find locations on earth.
- **grid north**—Used as north on a map and represented with blue grid lines; grid north varies from true north because it is a flat representation of the earth's surface on a map.
- **landmark**—A specific location either on a map or marked with a GPS unit.
- **leapfrogging**—Repeatedly identifying an object in the near distance or positioning a person in the near distance to maintain the proper bearing while navigating over a longer distance.
- **legend**—A chart on a map that identifies the meaning of symbols.

- **magnetic north**—An area in the earth's magnetic field that varies over time; its direction is indicated by the red compass needle.
- **map scale**—Ratio of a distance on a map to a distance in the real world; topographic maps are commonly 1:50,000, which means that 1 centimeter (.4 inch) on a map equals 50,000 centimeters (19,685 inches) in the real world.
- **Mark function**—A function on a GPS unit that allows the user to name and record the coordinates of a location (landmark or waypoint).
- **northing**—The northward distance measured on a topographic map.
- **safety bearing**—A bearing that can be followed at any time during an expedition that will lead to a certain destination such as a power line or highway.
- **topographic map**—A type of map that shows detailed features of a large area, including elevation.
- **Track Log**—A digital representation on a GPS screen that records the movements of the user as a line (bread-crumb trail).
- **true north**—If a line were drawn on the actual earth from the north pole to the south pole, it would indicate north; it is a curved line because it wraps around the earth's surface.
- **Universal Transverse Mercator (UTM)**—A grid system developed to indicate locations on the earth using east and north values.
- **waypoint**—A specific location either on a map or as marked with a GPS unit.
- **west declination**—The magnetic-north line falls to the left or west of the true-north and grid-north lines.

LESSON 1

Compass Parts and Use

Overview

Many people acknowledge the compass as one of the most important pieces of outdoors equipment but simply pack it along without the proper training and know-how. Integrating the use of a map strongly increases the effectiveness of the compass. Knowing how to use the two in concert enables users to navigate wherever they need to go and return safely. This lesson is designed to allow participants to use the compass as a navigation tool.

Learning Objectives

- To properly hold and orient a compass
- To identify the parts of a compass
- To recognize the cardinal directions and degrees on a compass dial
- To dial and follow a bearing
- To understand how pacing is integrated with the use of a compass
- To use the skill of leapfrogging to follow a bearing over a long distance

Equipment

- 1 compass for each participant or pair of participants
- Appropriate outdoor dress

Risk Management

- Conduct outdoor sessions in a location free from obstacles and traffic.
- Participants will be looking down as they use the compass and will require an area that is risk free.

Activity 1: Parts of a Compass

Knowing the terminology is essential for using the compass as a navigational tool. Providing the background knowledge of compass basics allows outdoor leaders to coach their participants through the skills, calling out specific steps that hinge on participants using the compass correctly. Knowing the parts is the starting point.

Skill Cues

Identify the parts of the compass as outlined in figure 2.2.

Teaching Cues

- Review the cardinal directions (north, south, west, east).
- Using the compass, have participants turn and face various directions as you call them out.

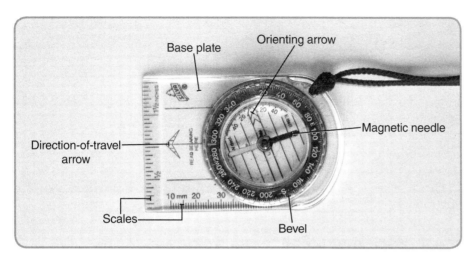

Figure 2.2   Knowing the parts of a compass is important for learning how to use one.

Activity 2: Using a Compass

Improving the use of any skill starts with small steps. This activity demonstrates the simple technique of how to hold a compass when in use.

Skill Cues

- Hold the compass by placing it flat in the left or right hand.
- The lanyard should be positioned back toward the user with the beveled (ruled) edge facing forward; the direction-of-travel arrow will be facing forward also.
- Use the free hand to rotate the compass housing dial marked with degrees of rotation.
- The compass should be kept level for best results.

Teaching Cues

- This activity is an extension of learning the parts of the compass.
- Emphasize how each part contributes to the use of the compass as a navigational tool.

Activity 3: Dialing and Following a Bearing

On the base plate of most compasses where the direction-of-travel arrow meets the compass dial, there is a small black or white line and the words "Read bearing here."

Skill Cues

- Twist the compass dial until the desired bearing is placed over the "Read bearing here" line.
- By shuffling the feet, turn in a circle until the red arrow (north arrow) is positioned within the thick orienteering arrow at the base of the compass dial—red is now in the bed (see figure 2.3).

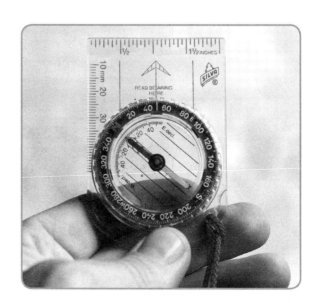

Figure 2.3   "Red is in the bed." The user is ready to follow a bearing of 50 degrees.

- Walk forward while maintaining the position of the red arrow in the bed.
- Keep the compass level for best results.

Teaching Cues

- Maintain the position of the compass by keeping the lanyard and rear of the compass toward the body.
- Do not rotate the compass itself while finding a bearing.
- Name a bearing and have participants dial the bearing and turn to put red in the bed.
- Then check to see if all participants are pointing in the same direction and move throughout the group, checking bearings and answering questions.

Activity 4: Pacing and Following a Bearing

Find a pebble or other small object and place it on the ground at the feet. This activity practices consistent pacing and following a bearing.

Skill Cues

- Dial the compass to north (0 degrees) and walk forward 10 even paces.
- Dial the compass to 120 degrees and walk 10 paces following the compass and keeping red in the bed.
- Add 120 degrees by dialing the compass to set it at 240 degrees and walk 10 paces forward; the pebble or object should be at the feet.

Teaching Cues

- Participants should spread out in a large area to avoid overlapping while completing the steps.
- The pebble or object should be at the feet if pacing was correct and consistent.
- Participants get immediate feedback based on the proximity of their object.

Activity 5: Following a Bearing

If traveling a long distance on a bearing, it is easy go astray; this is called *navigational drift*. The skill of leapfrogging will help reduce or eliminate straying off track when following a bearing over long distances. Leapfrogging can be accomplished using landmarks or a partner.

Skill Cues

- After following a bearing to the first landmark, place red in the bed again and look up to identify a second landmark.
- Walk toward this landmark and repeat the process until the final destination is reached.
- To leapfrog with a partner, one person goes in the desired direction to a distance of 20 to 30 meters (22-33 yards).
- Hold the compass and align red in the bed.
- Instruct the partner to move until aligned with the direction-of-travel arrow.
- Move to stand immediately behind the partner.
- Repeat this process as many times as necessary until the desired destination is reached.

Teaching Cues

- Once the bearing has been dialed, look in the distance and identify a landmark.
- Walk toward the landmark without constantly looking at the compass.
- To proceed in a new direction, follow the procedures in the skill cues by dialing a new bearing and placing red in the bed.
- Leapfrogging using a partner is much more accurate than using landmarks because directions can be given to move left or right and align with the desired path.
- Practice in a large open space and drop a cone with each leapfrog; once complete, participants look back and see if the cones are perfectly aligned.
- Partners should take turns leapfrogging so they both practice this skill.

Lesson Closure

- Participants should understand the importance of using the compass correctly during navigation to minimize errors.
- Review steps for the following:
  - Finding the bearing when given a direction or landmark
  - Finding the direction of travel when given a bearing
- Review the activities and use them to lead up to the components of a map.
- Liken pacing to the scale on a map whereby navigation over distances requires awareness of the distance traveled and yet to be traveled.
- Increasing distances traveled increases difficulty and magnifies errors of compass navigation.

LESSON 2

Components of a Topographic Map

Overview

Reading a map is similar to any literacy: Practice is needed and context is essential. Unfortunately, the ability to read a map is not as widespread as it was in years past. There have been great improvements in cartography that have standardized the map-making industry, resulting in greater accuracy and detail. However, better maps do not supplant the need to be able to translate what is on the map—the abstraction—to the concrete world. The ability to read a map is another basic skill that by itself cannot tell you where you are going, but only where you are.

Learning Objectives

- To explore the features of a map (legend)
- To understand grid lines and scale on a map
- To understand elevations with contour lines
- To use the UTM system for pinpointing locations on a map
- To use a practical example to understand eastings and northings (in conjunction with UTM coordinates)

Equipment

- 1 map for every two participants
- Appropriate outdoor dress

Activity 1: Introduction to Map Features

The ability to read a map starts with the components of a map. Each part of the map contains essential information on how to best use the map in the field.

Skill Cues

- Individually or in pairs, participants look over a topographic map and discuss what they can see.
- Participants look at the legend of map features or conventional signs and search for them on the map.
- Map scale is the ratio of a distance on a map to a distance in the real world (e.g., 1:50,000 where each blue grid line square equals 1 square kilometer [.5 square mile]).
- The map number and index of adjoining maps tell which map to buy to continue navigating off the currently held map.
- Blue areas on the map are water; green areas are forested or vegetation, which could make hiking difficult; and white areas are open barren or grassy areas, which make navigation and walking much easier.

Teaching Cues

- Lead participants in their discovery by prompting, "What does the map tell you?"
- Try to use local maps and encourage participants to recognize features that are familiar to them. Ask, "Do they look the same on the map?"
- Consider having participants compare an aerial photograph (1:12,500 scale) to a local topographic map (1:50,000 scale).
- Discuss map scale. Point out the meaning of the numbers representing the map scale. For example, if the scale is 1:50,000, it means that a distance of one unit on the map represents 50,000 of these units in the real world. As a visual, simply lay a pencil on the map and explain that the distance covered by the pencil in the real world is 50,000 pencil lengths.

Activity 2: Elevations and Contour Lines

Though maps are two-dimensional, they are representations of a three-dimensional world. An essential map-reading skill is translating contour lines into hills, slopes, mountains, and valleys—critical geographic features for translating where you are in the real world.

Skill Cues

- On a topographic map, elevations are denoted by brown lines called *contour lines.*
- Contour lines spaced closely together mean a steep slope, whereas contour lines farther apart mean lessening steepness.
- Contour elevation is denoted in the margin on the map and tells how much elevation is gained between contour lines (e.g., 15 meters [50 feet]).
- If the contour interval is 15 meters (50 feet), describe the height and steepness of the contour lines in figure 2.4.

Teaching Cues

- Contour lines provide crucial information for travel by foot. Many slopes may be impassible due to danger from steep descents or the fatigue that would result from climbing a steep hill when an alternative route could be planned to skirt around the hill on more level land.
- Pick landmarks and have participants identify the elevation.
- Pick known hills in the surrounding area as examples of how contour lines function.
- The direction of flow of brooks and streams can be determined by looking at contour lines.
- Tightly arranged contour lines denote steep cliffs.

Activity 3: UTM Grid

Understanding UTM allows participants to easily use the compass in conjunction with the map as a means of traveling from a fixed point A to a destination point B. UTM allows the user to plot these points on a map easily and accurately. In simple terms, UTM allows participants to go from big picture to small picture—where they are in the world, country, and district—in a coordinated system. Understanding the series permits participants to better grasp navigation using six-figure grid references, which are similar to zip codes that help pinpoint where they are on a map. Only six numbers are used for UTM in this activity as an introduction for quicker and easier reference. Typically, easting and northing numbers have more digits, which will be seen in activity 4.

Figure 2.4 The top diagram shows an overhead view of terrain that gradually elevates until dropping off steeply to the right. The bottom diagram shows what this terrain would look like in a side view.

Skill Cues

- To find a map location, use the numbers or UTM located on the border of the map.
- *Easting* is the number that tells position east and west.
- *Northing* is the number that tells position north and south.
- Each block represents 1 square kilometer (.5 square mile), with each line segment equaling 1,000 meters (1 kilometer) on a 1:50,000 topographic map.

Teaching Cues

- Figure 2.5 is an example of using UTM.
- UTMs are six-figure numbers, such as 856452, with 856 representing easting and 452 representing northing. Note that easting numbers are listed first (think of going in the house and then up the stairs).
- The third digit refers to the number of tenths from the line immediately to the left (easting) or below (northing) the landmark or position of interest.
- A position on the line would be denoted by a zero for the third digit (e.g., 760850).

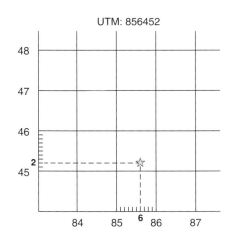

Figure 2.5 Determining a location on a topographic map using easting and northing on a UTM grid.

Activity 4: Determining UTM Coordinates

Determine the coordinates for the point X marked on the map (figure 2.6).
- To determine UTM coordinates, think of going in a house (easting), then up the stairs (northing).
- On a topographic map, use the numbers written in blue on the bottom axis and side axis of the map.

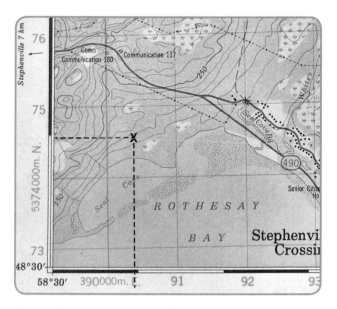

Figure 2.6 Sample map for activity 4. On a color topographic map, the numbers along the bottom and side axes would be blue.

- The UTM coordinate system uses the numbered grid lines on the map. To understand how to give the coordinates of a point, look at figure 2.6.

Skill Cues

Determining the Easting

- The easting will be expressed as a six-digit number followed by the letters *m E* (see example on grid line 90 for this map).
- The *X* sits between grid lines 90 and 91.
- Select the smallest number (in this case, 90).
- To determine the last three digits, estimate how many meters away from the 90 line your point is located. In the example, point X is 300 meters (328 yards) east of the 90th grid line.
- The easting for point X will be written down as 390300m E.

Determining the Northing

- The northing will be expressed as a seven-digit number followed by the letters *m N* (see example on grid line 74 for this map).
- The first two numbers for the northing for this map will always start with 53. This is simply an index number for this particular map.
- The next step is to determine which two grid lines the point is located between. In the example on the map, the *X* lies between lines 74 and 75. Always pick the smallest number as your next two digits (in this case, 74).
- Now for the last three digits: Each block in this grid for a 1:50,000 scale equals 1 square kilometer (.5 square mile). This means that the distance between line 74 and line 75 is 1,000 meters (1,094 yards). To determine the last three digits, estimate how many meters above the 74 line point X is located. In the example, point X is 750 meters (820 yards) above the 74th grid line.
- The northing for point X will be written down as 5374750m N.

The UTM coordinates for point X on the map are 390300m E 5374750m N. Using only a six-figure grid reference, as in activity 3, the UTM coordinates would be 903747.

Teaching Cues

- Participants may be confused about all the extra numbers.
- Make sure participants understand that we only use some numbers because we are in our local area. The other numbers refer to our place on the entire earth.
- Confusion about which numbers to use can easily be resolved by referring to the numbers used for the grid lines on the map.
- When showing students this process, use a map that will have different numbers for easting and northing to avoid confusion as in the example above.

Lesson Closure

- Review how the information on the map represents the real world and that practice is needed to be able to view a map in this way.
- Use maps in an outdoor setting to tour the area and compare features on the map with landmarks and geographical features.

Using Map and Compass Together

Overview

When following a bearing with a compass, it is important to stay on track at all times. Straying from the direct path and resuming with a compass will cause the user to travel on a parallel but incorrect path, and missing the destination completely is likely. Shorter legs or parts of a journey are easier to follow, more rewarding, and more accurate. Mistakes are also easier to correct.

Learning Objectives

- To find a bearing from a map with a compass
- To learn how to aim off to find a bearing for tricky locations such as stream and trail junctions
- To understand how to compensate for declination when taking and following a bearing

Equipment

1 map, 1 compass, and 1 pencil for every two participants

Activity 1: Finding a Bearing From Start to Finish

The activities in this lesson are best conducted using a full map. This allows the participants to see firsthand the range a map can offer in distance, geographic features, and supporting components needed to plot points of origin and destination.

Skill Cues

- Identify start and finish locations on the map and draw a pencil line to connect them.
- Lay the compass flat on the map and position the side of the base plate along the line.
- The back end of the compass must be positioned at the start with the front of the compass positioned toward the destination (figure 2.7a).
- Turn the compass dial so that the orienteering arrow within the dial is parallel with the grid lines and is pointing north or toward the top of the map (figure 2.7b).
- Check the "Read bearing here" line for the bearing.

a

b

Figure 2.7   Finding a bearing: (a) Line up the edge of the compass with the start and finish points, and ensure that the arrow is pointed in direction of intended travel; (b) line up the orienting lines with the grid lines, ensuring that the orienting arrow points north to the top of the map.

Teaching Cues

- If participants are at the start location (outdoors), the bearing can be followed.
- To follow this bearing, turn the body until red is in the bed and proceed toward the destination.
- The compass must be placed on the map correctly to determine the proper bearing.

Activity 2: Aiming Off With a Compass

When trying to find a specific location such as a trail junction, you might be uncertain whether you are to the right or left of the junction after coming out of the woods onto the trail. Aiming off is a technique whereby you purposely change the compass bearing to situate yourself to the right or left of the intended target location. Then, when encountering the trail, you will know which way to travel to find the trail junction.

Skill Cues

- Aiming off is purposefully veering to the right or left of the intended destination.
- Use the compass to find the bearing and add 5 degrees to travel slightly to the right of the intended destination; subtract 5 degrees to travel to the left of the intended destination.
- After adjusting 5 degrees, simply put red in the bed again and proceed toward the destination.
- Aiming off must be predetermined (e.g., road, lake, hill) so that upon arrival, it is known whether to go left or right to reach the intended destination.

Teaching Cues

- This technique is useful because it is difficult to arrive exactly at the intended target, and once close it is often a gamble to travel to the left or to the right to reach the destination.
- Aiming off to the right lets users know that once they are in line with the destination, they are to travel to the left.
- This technique is especially useful when finding a location along a lake, a fork in a stream, or a trail junction.

Activity 3: Declination

Declination refers to the difference in angle between magnetic north and grid north. Understanding declination is critical in order to navigate correctly. Topographic maps throughout the world have declination unique to that location. The declination is located in the margin of a map.

There is a distinction among true north, grid north, and magnetic north that should be clearly understood. True north is represented by the north pole and a true-north line that connects the north and south poles. Grid north is different from true north in that grid-north lines are represented on a map with a flat surface. The earth's surface is not flat and the true-north lines are curved. Therefore, these lines cannot be the same. Grid north is used for declination; it is represented on a map by blue grid lines that are used in navigation. Magnetic north is an area of the earth's magnetic field in which the direction is indicated by the red needle on a compass. The difference in location of magnetic north and grid north is accounted for by adjusting declination. This is different in all areas of the world. Since the earth's magnetic field (magnetic north) varies over time, it is necessary to make adjustments for this on maps as time passes.

Skill Cues

- When magnetic and grid north are in line, adjustment for declination is not necessary.
- West declination means that the magnetic-north line falls to the left or west of true north and grid north.
- East declination means that the magnetic-north line falls to the right or east of true north and grid north.
- West declination means that declination degrees are added to the compass bearing.
- East declination means that declination degrees are subtracted from the compass bearing.

Teaching Cues

- The rhymes "West is best" and "East is least" help with setting the correct declination, with "best" meaning to add and "least" meaning to subtract.
- For west declination, add declination (e.g., 22 degrees) when going from the map to the land; when taking a field or land bearing and verifying it on the map, subtract declination (e.g., 22 degrees). The reverse applies to east declination.
- Declination is necessary when traveling outdoors to avoid following an incorrect route and missing the intended destination.
- The blue grid lines on a topographic map represent grid north.
- In a large, open area, use the map to find the magnetic-north bearing and follow it to illustrate following a bearing without adjusting for declination.
- Practice setting declination and following the new bearing to arrive at the intended destination.
- Set declination incorrectly and follow this compass bearing to demonstrate the error involved.
- Take a bearing off the map, follow it without adjusting declination, and see what happens.
- Illustrate how following an incorrect bearing leads you more off track as the distance traveled increases; the angle opens considerably within a short distance.

Lesson Closure

- Review the procedures for using the map and compass together to follow a bearing.
- Emphasize the procedures for setting the correct declination to avoid becoming disoriented or even lost.

LESSON 4

GPS (Part 1)

Overview

GPS technology has increased the attractiveness of navigation and has made getting around easier and more convenient. Battery life and satellite reception are drawbacks that make GPS navigation risky if relied upon too heavily. Most often, though, conditions are favorable for GPS use and provide intricate abilities to seek out locations.

Learning Objectives

- To gain insight into the system that allows GPS to function
- To explore screens and functions of the GPS unit
- To mark a location (waypoint or landmark)
- To navigate to a remote location

Equipment

1 GPS unit for every two participants

Risk Management

When using GPS units in the outdoors, participants should be aware of obstacles while walking and using the device.

Activity 1: Satellite System

It is hard to imagine, but in the outer limits of the sky is a network of satellites designed to send signals to earth for our use in determining our position in the world. GPS was first developed for the United States military for defense purposes, but in recent years GPS technology has evolved for personal use, including geocaching and recreational uses in numerous outdoor programs. Outdoor leaders cannot simply ignore the versatility of the GPS and not incorporate the technology into their leading capabilities, nor can they completely rely on the technology as a means in which to lead participants in outdoor activities.

Skill Cues

- Turn GPS unit on and watch as the unit receives signals from satellites within the horizon and sky (figure 2.8).
    - Identify that there is an antenna that is either internal or external that receives satellite signals; some GPS units need to be held upright whereas some may be held flat.
    - The screen is a representation of the sky, showing the position of the satellites and giving a reading of the signal intensity.

Teaching Cues

- GPS units communicate with satellites to help identify the user's position on earth.
- A greater number of satellite signals received by the GPS unit means more accurate determination of actual location on earth.
- Continue to monitor satellite reception until the GPS unit advises that it is ready to navigate.
- Once satellite signals are received, a value in meters or feet is given that will inform the user of the accuracy of the unit.
- Accuracy will vary; satellite reception is influenced by the horizon, hills, clouds, and density of vegetation.

Activity 2: GPS Screens and Controls

The GPS user manual that accompanies the unit upon purchase will be most helpful for this lesson. You should become familiar with the

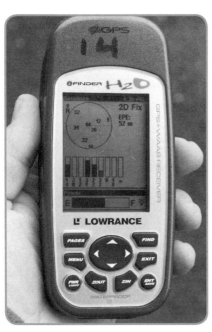

Figure 2.8 A GPS unit that is receiving signals from the sky to acquire position, waiting for a 3D fix.

operation of the GPS and practice using it in the outdoors before instructing participants.

Skill Cues

- Explain the most commonly used features of the GPS unit.
- Scroll through the screens to help with this orientation to the capabilities of the GPS.

Teaching Cues

- This lesson should help participants gain an understanding of the functions of the GPS. Gauge the pace of the lesson by the participants' level of comprehension and avoid moving to the next step until all participants understand.
- Pairing participants helps with understanding because one participant tends to listen and provide instructions while the other uses the functions and operates the GPS.

Activity 3: Marking a Location (Waypoint or Landmark)

The power of location—knowing where you are and remembering how to get back to that exact location—is fundamental to using a GPS unit. The usefulness of the GPS extends beyond just telling users where they are. Users can save locations along their travels that will assist them in their outdoor journey.

Skill Cues

- Scroll through the pages to the main menu and select Mark (functions will vary from one GPS unit to another).
- Some units have a quick step to the Mark function by pressing and holding the enter button or cursor button.
- Follow procedures to name the waypoint and assign a symbol that will be meaningful when displayed on the map page.

Teaching Cues

- Upon selecting Mark, direct participants' attention to the UTM or degree coordinates on the screen.
- These coordinates should be familiar to participants if they have completed the activities on using a map and compass.
- Impress upon participants that no matter where they travel, this location is saved and can be called upon at any time for the GPS unit to lead them back to that location.

Activity 4: Navigating a Waypoint or Landmark

The ability to develop any skill depends on ample opportunity to experiment and grow with trial and error. This activity, though simple in structure, permits the experiential process for participants to gain confidence using GPS technology in the field.

Skill Cues

- After marking a location, walk 30 to 50 meters (33-55 yards) away.
- Use controls to select Find and find a list of waypoints or landmarks.
- Select the waypoint by scrolling to select and highlight it; then press the enter button.

- Select the Go To option.
- The screen will change, displaying a compass-type dial with a navigating arrow that exists only during the activation of the Go To function.
- Follow the navigating arrow to locate the proper position.
- Monitor the decreasing distance display as progress is made toward the waypoint.

Teaching Cues

- Some GPS units require that the user start walking before the navigating arrow functions properly, and others act as a compass full time and will show accurate direction when the user is standing still.
- Encourage participants to keep moving to maintain the effectiveness of the GPS unit and walk until the distance reads as close as possible to zero.
- Participants should note how close they returned to the marked location and offer explanations for why they may not have returned to the exact spot.
- Changes in satellite reception affect accuracy and should be expected when using GPS.

Lesson Closure

- Review the steps of marking and navigating waypoints or landmarks.
- Inform participants that the skills learned in this lesson are among the most common functions of a GPS unit.

LESSON 5

GPS (Part 2)

Overview

As participants grow in their proficiency to navigate with GPS, you can advance your group with more challenging GPS techniques. The following activities progressively advance a participant's skill and allow for more sophisticated application of GPS technology.

Learning Objectives

- To gain further insight into the functions of the GPS unit
- To use Track Log (bread-crumb trail) to keep track of personal movements
- To use speed and distance functions to better understand movement while using GPS
- To mark a route of several locations (waypoints or landmarks) using GPS
- To use the Backtrack function to assist with following the reverse direction on a route

Equipment

1 GPS unit for every two participants

Risk Management

Participants should be aware of obstacles while using GPS in the outdoors.

Activity 1: Track Log (Bread-Crumb Trail)

Experiencing how the GPS can track travels reveals the usefulness of the GPS as a tool that can assist groups in exploring their natural surroundings.

Skill Cues

- Scroll to the Map screen to get a visual representation of the user walking on the map.
- Participants walk and notice that as progress is made along the map, the path of the user is marked by the Track Log or bread-crumb trail.

Teaching Cues

- The slightest variations in the user's path can be seen on the GPS screen.
- After participants have seen this function, erase the log and have participants walk in a large area to spell their name.
- Participants' names should be spelled out on the screen as satellites track their path.
- The scale of the screen may have to be adjusted to see the full name on the screen.

Activity 2: Speed and Distance of Travel

GPS technology offers many useful features such as monitoring traveling speed. This tool can prove critical when managing the estimated times of arrival for extended trips.

Skill Cues

- A GPS unit can record the total distance covered on an outing, check the distance of a running or cycling race, and even check driving speed if the speedometer in an automobile is broken.
- Scroll to the page containing information on speed, average speed, maximum speed, odometer, and trip odometer.
- Select the Reset function to clear all information to read zero.
- While walking, notice the current speed.

Teaching Cues

- Lead participants on a walk and occasionally jog and sprint.
- Reassemble the group and have participants check their average speed, maximum speed, and trip odometer.
- Poll the group to see who had the highest average speed and determine the fastest runner by checking maximum speeds.

Activity 3: Marking a Route

A route consists of a series of waypoints or landmarks that are followed toward a final destination.

Skill Cues

- Walk around the local area and mark several locations with the Mark function.
- Set up a route by saving the waypoints, to which the user must assign a file name.

Teaching Cues

Conduct this activity in an area where you can monitor all participants for safety and assistance.

Activity 4: Backtrack Function

Upon completing a route, the user can return by selecting the Backtrack function, which will allow the user to follow the route in the reverse direction.

Skill Cues

- When following a route with GPS, select the Backtrack function to return to the start at any time.
- Follow the navigation arrow the same way as when following the route.
- The GPS automatically reverses the direction of travel when the Backtrack function is selected.

Teaching Cues

- Selecting the Backtrack function takes the guesswork out of reversing the direction.
- A second option for following the route back to the start is to retrace the steps by aligning the current track (bread crumbs) with the previously laid Track Log. Following the Track Log may be safer because previously encountered obstacles will be easily negotiated and the area and terrain will be more familiar.

Lesson Closure

- Review all the skills that participants have acquired with the GPS.
- Encourage participants to practice these skills on their own if they have access to a GPS unit.

LESSON 6

Using GPS and Map Together

Overview

Skills often require flexibility and creativity; it is seldom that a skill does not cross over into another area. Map and compass use is obvious, but taken for granted is map and GPS use. These skills should not be seen in isolation but rather as skill sets that can improve the quality of the outdoor experience and enhance the safety of the experience.

Learning Objectives

- To understand how GPS and maps can be used together for navigation
- To use the Mark function on a GPS to pinpoint current location on a map
- To enter a predetermined map route into a GPS unit and save it as a route

Equipment

- 1 GPS unit for every two participants
- 1 topographic map for every two participants

Risk Management

If conducting this lesson in the outdoors, take care to ensure that the group does not become separated.

Activity 1: Where Am I?

At any time, a person's location can be established by use of a GPS unit and a map (figures 2.9 and 2.10).

Skill Cues

- Find a known location in a familiar area and mark the location (Mark function) with the GPS.
- Check the UTM coordinates on the GPS screen.
- Use the UTM coordinates (easting and northing) to check the location on the map.

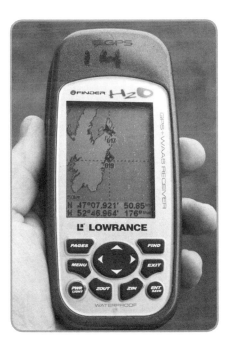

Figure 2.9   A GPS with position acquired and shown on a map screen.

Teaching Cues

- The accuracy of the GPS will determine the success of this activity.
- Participants should recognize that this is a skill that can be used if lost in the wilderness.

Activity 2: Entering a Map Route in a GPS

Designing and entering a wilderness route into a GPS unit can be done at home or in class.

Skill Cues

- Plan a route by selecting multiple UTM coordinates from a map.
- Enter the complete UTM coordinates into the GPS as separate waypoints.
- Select the Mark function and enter the UTM coordinates by editing each waypoint.
- Elevations can also be edited by checking contour lines from the map.

Figure 2.10   Finding the waypoint on the map.

Teaching Cues

- Participants plan a fictional route or one that can be followed on an outing.
- Once the route has been created, the total distance is displayed.
- The total distance is measured by straight lines, which may not be realistic when actually walking the route in the outdoors.
- Shorter legs of the trip will provide a more accurate route distance.

Lesson Closure

- The GPS unit can be a powerful tool for navigation, but it has limitations of which participants should be aware.
- Participants should take extra batteries on excursions and recognize that inconsistencies in satellite signals should prompt them to stay aware of their location and surrounding topographic features.

LESSON 7

Route Planning

Overview

The ability to plan an outing in the outdoors is an essential skill. A critical component of the excursion is the route plan. A well-planned trip takes into account a detailed plan that balances the ability of the group, the complexity of the terrain, and the purpose of the activity. To state the obvious, route planning is essential for risk management.

Learning Objectives

- To understand the many options and variables to be taken into account when planning a route
- To recognize safety as a top priority when planning a route
- To learn how to determine a safety bearing and understand its significance

Equipment

- 1 map for each pair of participants
- 1 compass for each pair of participants
- 1 pencil for each pair of participants
- 1 ruler for each pair of participants

Activity 1: Start to Finish—What Route?

Developing the skill to plan a route requires the ability not only to read a map and plot destination points but also to interpret the terrain and judge the ability of the group to embark on the journey. A fundamental for route planning is being able to visualize the natural area and decide on the most appropriate direction of travel.

Skill Cues

- Identify a start and a finish location on the map.
- Use a light pencil to decide on a route to follow from start to finish (see figure 2.11).
- Consider contour lines, waterways, trails, and vegetation densities.

Teaching Cues

- Select start and finish locations that allow for alternative routes.
- Communicate start and finish locations in UTM coordinates to review and reinforce this skill.
- Participants take turns presenting their route to the group (an overhead projector would be useful).
- If participants chose different routes, discuss why one route was chosen over another.

Activity 2: Determining a Safety Bearing

Every good plan needs a backup. This is true for all outdoor pursuits. Most often an outdoor leader will have determined a safety bearing for every leg of the route and will have built this into the plan.

Skill Cues

- Before following a route, it is important to determine a safety bearing in case the group becomes disoriented or lost.
- Study the area and look for features that run long distances (such as roads, lakes, and power lines) and are in range.
- Determine the bearing by placing the compass on the map, pointing the direction-of-travel arrow toward the feature, and lining up the orienteering arrow with the grid lines on the map.
- Read the bearing on the compass dial at the "Read bearing here" line and record it on the map margin or in the route plan.

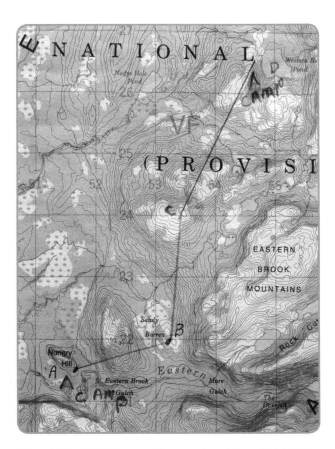

Figure 2.11 Mark the map with several small legs of a trip (A to B, B to C, and C to D).

Teaching Cues

- Participants should recognize this step as a safety precaution and that good planning means planning for unforeseen circumstances.
- Following a safety bearing may mean traveling through tough terrain but will lead to safety and security when lost.
- Draw a side profile of the elevations of the route.
- Seeing the elevation changes from this perspective might lead to changes in the route, especially if many contour lines are crossed.

Lesson Closure

- Review key points to consider when planning routes.
- Reinforce the safety aspect of planning a route to avoid becoming lost or wasting time once in the outdoors.

LESSON 8

Route Selection and Finding

Overview

Most often the ability of outdoor leaders to lead participants safely and ensure a positive experience depends on their experience. Deciding on a route is a skill that requires firsthand knowledge of what to expect. A map can only tell us so much; our experiences have to help fill in the gaps for participants. The ability of outdoor leaders to guide their participants comes from sharing tips, techniques, and field wisdom. Not everything that was planned for becomes the lived experience for the group, and outdoor leaders have to develop the most essential skill of all for outdoor pursuits—flexibility.

Learning Objectives

- To recognize the need to sometimes modify the planned route for a better route that will enable the group to avoid problem areas and get back on route as soon as possible
- To realize that trying to stay on the intended route is better accomplished with plans for shorter routes
- To understand how aiming off can save valuable time when trying to find specific locations such as a stream or trail junction
- To learn how to navigate around large obstacles (pond, canyon) without going astray from the desired bearing

Equipment

- 1 map for each pair of participants
- 1 compass for each pair of participants
- 1 pencil for each pair of participants
- 1 ruler for each pair of participants

Risk Management

- Take care that the group does not get separated.
- A particular area may be conducive to allowing participants some freedom, especially if surrounded by natural features such as streams and roads that can act as natural boundaries.

Activity 1: Short Legs Are Better Than Long Legs

A challenge in using navigation skills is accuracy. This is further complicated when natural obstacles confront traveling groups. A simple way to balance these barriers is to practice shorter legs of travel.

Skill Cues

- Shorter legs of travel are better for keeping on track (figure 2.12).

- Identifying several small legs within a long route allows for repeated success and security that the correct route is being followed.
- Traveling long distances between waypoints can lead to uncertainty because the attention span can become challenged after being on the trail for a long time.

Teaching Cues

Mark progress along a route with a pencil to keep track of progress and current location.

Activity 2: Aiming Off With a Compass

Navigation is like trying to hit a tiny target over a huge geographical area while working solely from plotted

Figure 2.12   Shorter legs of travel can increase navigational accuracy, ensuring a safe return to camp.

point to point. Good practice requires reading the map with the intention to look for a more definable geographic location. It's much easier to hit a lake compared with a dot in the middle of the green space. A sound practice in navigation is to aim off with the purpose of hitting a specific or elusive target.

Skill Cues

- Aiming off means purposefully veering to the right or left of the intended destination.
- Use the compass to find the bearing and add 5 degrees to travel slightly to the right of the intended destination; subtract 5 degrees to travel to the left of the intended destination.
- After adjusting 5 degrees, simply put red in the bed again and proceed toward the destination.

Teaching Cues

- This technique is useful because it is often difficult to arrive exactly at the intended target, and once close it is often a gamble to travel to the left or right to reach the destination.
- Aiming off to the right lets users know that once they are in line with the destination, they are to travel to the left.
- This technique is especially useful when finding a location along a lake, a fork in a stream, or trail junction.

Activity 3: Navigating Around Large Obstacles

Not all natural barriers will show up on a map. In wilderness travel, participants will often encounter barriers that cannot be walked over. Thus, it is necessary to be able to navigate around a swamp or lake; otherwise it may be impossible to continue the journey without a raft or canoe.

Skill Cues

- With the bearing dialed on the compass, look across the obstacle and look for a clearly distinguishable feature such as a unique treetop, a large boulder, or a cove or inlet in a lake.
- Maintain the compass bearing and place the compass in a secure location.
- Proceed around the obstacle, finding the safest if not the most direct route.
- Upon arrival at the landmark or feature, resume navigating with the compass.

Teaching Cues

- Pick a feature that it is easy to recognize from the new perspective on the other side of the obstacle.
- The compass should not be followed when walking around the obstacle because it will lead the user on an incorrect path that is parallel to the intended path.

Lesson Closure

- Safe travel and expending as little energy as possible are the goals for route selection and finding.
- Inform participants that if confusion sets in, it is a good practice to return to the last known location and rethink strategy.
- Panic and confusion lead to mistakes in navigation, so a clear mind is necessary to make good judgments.

LESSON 9

Geocaching

Overview

Geocaching is a fun and energetic activity that allows participants to challenge their navigational abilities, and for some groups the potential exists to build in healthy competition. Geocaching is an outdoor pursuit that is growing in popularity as handheld GPS devices become more affordable. Degrees of success are not just limited to the technology, however; in many instances a map and compass will help participants find the hidden canister (cache) with the aid of the GPS.

Learning Objectives

- To be introduced to geocaching as an exhilarating outdoor pursuit using navigational skills
- To understand the worldwide system of caches that has been set out for finding by the public
- To set up a personal account for geocaching to hide and find caches
- To find caches in the community and wilderness
- To learn how to use a cache and how to preserve its integrity for other users

Equipment

- 1 GPS unit for each pair of participants

- 1 roll of surveyor's tape
- Cache (UTM) coordinates

Risk Management

- The risk of getting lost is slight because caches are set close to the location of the outdoor program.
- Establish a boundary to let participants know how far the caches are set in order to prevent participants from going astray.
- Maintain close contact with participants during this activity to avoid becoming separated if geocaching is to be away from the regular instructional area.

Activity 1: Outdoor Leader Preparation—Getting Connected

Geocaching is about experiencing the outdoors firsthand, finding something that is hidden, signing in on a log sheet when the find is made, and exchanging treasure. The fun is in the hunt, and the hunt depends not only on the accuracy of the GPS but also on the ability of the participants to read their maps and follow clues that are sometimes provided. Setting up an exciting geocaching event requires some advance work to find interesting areas to hide the cache.

Skill Cues

- Set out the course before the lesson begins.
- At least two or three caches should be set out for each participant or pair of participants.
- Assign one close and one far cache for participants to locate.
- Upon finding a cache, participants sign the log sheet provided.
- This figure represents a lead-up activity to geocaching. The figure is meant to be photocopied by the outdoor leader. Each row in the figure is designed to be cut into strips. Students are provided with a strip of paper containing coordinate information and a clue to find the cache. The teacher sets up this activity by hiding several pieces of flagging tape and writing a number on each piece. The number is recorded in the left column followed by the coordinates and finally a clue to help students zero in on the flagging tape (cache).

Teaching Cues

- Caches should be set close to the ground so that they are not identifiable until participants are led within close proximity by the GPS.
- Provide students with a strip of paper containing coordinate information and a clue to find the cache (see figure 2.13).
- Set up this activity by hiding several pieces of flagging tape and writing a number on each piece. The number is recorded in the left column, followed by the coordinates and a clue to help participants zero in on the flagging tape (cache).

Activity 2: Finding Public Caches

Geocaching is about the find. This activity builds a sense of team and reinforces many navigational techniques. One option is to use the existing geocaching framework. Visit www.geocaching.com to register as a user to hide and seek caches. Caches are small containers, usually plastic, that are hidden in the outdoors by a registered person on the Web site. They contain trinkets and items that can be traded among several caches at other locations. Locations of caches are provided by UTM and map

001	0431588 5421127	Great shortcut to play a game
002	0431128 5421039	Small tree
003	0431422 5421207	We've got the power
004	0431177 5420969	No sign
005	0431005 5421382	Two culverts
006	0431110 5420832	Edge of trees
007	0431364 5421319	On shortcut trail
008	0431195 5420851	Reserved—sorry!
009	0431304 5421339	Birches—at least 10
010	0431077 5420889	Fire!
011	0431035 5421361	Course starting when?
012	0431065 5420865	Grass clump
013	0431364 5421294	Is this a brook or a trail?
014	0431362 5421090	Bench area
015	0431219 5421331	This tree didn't make it!
016	0431135 5420824	You can't put it in park here!
017	0431072 5421412	Black hole
018	0431403 5421116	No grass

Figure 2.13 The outdoor leader will create geocaching clues and coordinates specific to the geographic location.

locations that can be found using a GPS or identifying landmarks on a map. Caches are located throughout the world.

Skill Cues

- Participants are given UTM coordinates of caches.
- Participants mark waypoints and edit them by entering UTM coordinates.
- Select a waypoint and select the Go To function to begin navigating.
- Once on location, enter UTM coordinates in the GPS and proceed by following the Go To function.
- Upon finding the cache, open it and see what is inside.
- Most caches contain a notebook for finders to sign their name and record the date to document the event.

Teaching Cues

- Ensure that participants respect the cache and do not remove any items without placing an item.
- When finished, participants should hide the cache as they found it.
- Impress upon participants the importance of not sabotaging the cache; other users expect the cache to be present and in good condition.
- Encourage participants to set their own cache or set a cache as a group and monitor it throughout the year for visits and exchanges.
- Inform participants that if they are planning a trip anywhere in the world, they can check the Web site and geocache while exploring their vacation destination.

Lesson Closure

- Review the ethics of geocaching.
- Review the GPS skills needed to geocache.
- Highlight the thrill of seeking caches and the enjoyment that can be gained from this outdoor activity.
- Discuss the experience of geocaching and inform participants of caches that are set all over the world.
- Answer any questions or address problems that participants had while trying to locate caches.

References and Resources

Burns, B., and M. Burns. 2004. *Wilderness navigation: Finding your way using map, compass, altimeter and GPS.* 2nd ed. Seattle: Mountaineers Books.

Kjellström, B. 1994. *Be expert with map and compass: The complete orienteering handbook.* 2nd ed. New York: John Wiley and Sons.

Environmental Ethics: Caring for Resources

▼ Andrew Foran ▼

The one thing about canoe tripping that I love is getting to places where no one has been, or so I let my group think. I know we have been to this location many times, but good practices create the feel for the uncharted—the unexplored—the undiscovered, and this gives the group that sense of wilderness.

– Steve Cook, Nova Scotia Outdoor Leadership Development Program, 2001, McGowan Lake, Nova Scotia

As environmental concerns continue to mount globally, it is becoming increasingly difficult to feign ignorance when it comes to our personal practices and interactions with the natural world. An emerging social awareness is becoming formalized in a standard of practice ranging from home practices with recycling to Leave No Trace (LNT) principles that govern outdoor educational programs—in other words, outdoor ethics.

The word *ethics* conjures a judicial notion of good and bad practices. However, this interpretation may be problematic because what was acceptable as an outdoor practice years ago may be disputed as unacceptable in current recreational uses of natural settings. This evolution of ethics and our relationship to the natural world is changing from a consumptive perspective to one of preservation. For the purposes of this book, ethics will balance outdoor practices that preserve the natural world for other groups to enjoy. The suggestions in this chapter are based on actual practices, keeping in mind the readiness and maturity of the groups that outdoor leaders will encounter.

In its simplest application for outdoor educational practices, ethics is what a person will do when no one is looking. Ethics govern our personal and group decisions on how we behave in our interactions with the outside environment.

As natural settings continue to disappear at alarming rates and signs of misuse and abuse are evident due to ignorant recreational practices, there is mounting pressure to do more to protect what is left of the outdoors. This chapter introduces practices that stem from attitudes that protect the outdoors but at the same time allow participants to enjoy what the natural world has to offer us. Thus this chapter is about ethical practices based on LNT and beliefs that preserve a range of environments from woodlands to seashores, arid lands, and wild grasslands.

Equipment

Group Equipment

- Pencils and notebooks for participants
- Trowel (1 per group)
- Modeling clay
- Regular and large resealable bags
- Scoop of kitty litter in small paper lunch bag
- 5- to 8-centimeter (2- to 3-inch) food strainers (1 per cooking group)
- Rolls of cheesecloth (1 per cooking group)
- Pot sets (1 per cooking group)
- Stoves (1 per cooking group)
- Toilet paper, single ply (1 roll per group)
- Hand sanitizer (1 dispenser per group)
- Expedition-sized tent (1 for demonstration)
- Tarps and ropes for shelter building (1 set per shelter group)
- Tents (1 per group)
- Nylon bag for soil collection
- Hubcaps (1 per fire group)
- Food lines and carabiner (1 set per cooking group)
- Food bag, garbage bags, plastic grocery bags, and compost bags for each group

Personal Equipment

- Day pack
- Personal hygiene bag (nylon stuff sack)
- Change of clothes
- Rain gear
- Hat
- Sunscreen
- Sunglasses
- Bug repellent
- Personal first aid kit and prescribed medications
- Utensils, mug, and plate or bowl (nonbreakable and suitable for the outdoors)
- Personal water bottle

Equipment Care and Maintenance

- When not in use, store stoves according to manufacturer's specifications.
- All pot sets and utensils should be cleaned thoroughly after field use.
- Restock the toilet paper and hand sanitizer.
- Tarps and ropes should be inspected after use for wear; small holes in tarps can be repaired with red sheathing tape such as Tuck Tape (a red construction tape that weathers well on plastic tarps), and fraying ropes should be replaced.
- Tents, tarps, and ropes should be dried and stored according to program equipment standards.

Site Selection

For this session to be effective, a variety of sites may be required; however, a wooded site edged with a field and brook would be adequate. Mixed forests offer an environment that contains a variety of flora and fauna and many potential teaching moments to raise awareness.

An important consideration for this topic is land durability, how often the unit will be taught at the location, and participant numbers. These considerations may determine whether continued use is possible; a less-than-pristine area may be more realistic to teach the skills, allowing participants to master LNT practices before engaging in outdoor pursuits. As an outdoor leader, you may very well be leading your participants into a variety of unique environments, and seasonality can also alter LNT practices. Therefore, you should practice the LNT skills in the location best suited for your program needs.

Social Skills and Etiquette

Be sure to obtain permission to use all land areas for teaching and traveling. As the outdoor leader, it is your responsibility to request permits and permissions in advance. On-site, the expectation is for the group to follow the seven Leave No Trace (LNT) principles:

- Plan ahead and prepare.
- Travel and camp on durable surfaces.
- Dispose of waste properly.
- Leave what you find.
- Minimize campfire impacts.
- Respect wildlife.
- Be considerate of other visitors.

Reprinted, by permission, from Leave No Trace.

For more information on LNT and practices that are specific to sensitive environments, visit www.lnt.org and obtain more information to ensure the seven principles are being observed and practiced to the fullest in your program.

Risk Management

Before entering the designated area to learn and practice LNT skills, it is important to remind participants about working within designated boundaries. Make sure each person is clear on the area to be used (use flagging tape if needed and remove the tape when finished), employ a buddy system, and check to make sure each person is carrying a whistle (remind each person of the emergency signal—three short whistle blasts, a short pause, and three more short whistle blasts).

Another helpful tip is to have a recognizable call word that alerts participants that you need to bring them together for further instructions or discussion. This word should be recognizable and distinct. Furthermore, this word can be used to end the activity for safety reasons as a preventative measure in managing risk.

To increase the standard of safety, check to make sure each person has a daypack and personal medications, that you have the group first aid kit, and that you have an updated medical form for all participants.

Another concern for this unit is the use of stoves. You may need to demonstrate safe lighting and shutting-down procedures. Furthermore, kitchen operations need to be reinforced to avoid mishaps around the stove. As well, open fires cause concern; fireside behavior will be a needed discussion before groups are engaged with the lesson.

The following is a brief list to consider:

- You should have a checked and stocked first aid kit suitable for the location and activity.
- A reliable contact should be aware of your location and expected times for returning.
- Establish proper hiking formation, keeping the participants to the set trail and together.
- At the site, be aware of potential hazards (cliff edges, water sources, or other environmental threats) and articulate these concerns to participants.
- Remind all participants to be aware of the designated boundary in which they are expected to stay during the activities.
- Strongly warn participants not to eat anything found or to add found food to prepared meals.

Unit Organization

The environmental ethics unit serves as a core unit for all outdoor pursuits. The lessons presented here focus on ethical practices in the outdoors and the need for personal and group awareness. Some of the topics will require group maturity and open-mindedness as participants engage in lessons that range from human waste management to personal comfort sacrificed for wilderness preservation. A key consideration in this unit is the need for participants to connect to the natural world; thus, you must be open to lessons that allow for natural sensitivity to the outdoors.

Lesson Plans

Lesson 1: Connecting to the Natural World. The activities for this lesson are commonly referred to as *earth education*. The value of this lesson is to create awareness for participants, allowing them to understand the fragility and beauty of the natural world. The purpose is reconnecting to nature and establishing a commitment to preserve and protect the environment.

Lesson 2: Trail Impact. This lesson introduces participants to soil and the impact that people can have in fragile places. Participants will connect soil layers to the causes of trail erosion and creation of social trails.

Lesson 3: Campsite Selection. The focus of this lesson is selecting a site as part of the core camping skill set. Participants will balance the group size and the carrying capacity of a specific environment. Furthermore, participants will identify differences between pristine locations and sensitive environments versus established sites.

Lesson 4: Human Waste Management. Human waste management is a challenging lesson. This topic requires group maturity and open-mindedness. Participants will learn how to select and dig proper catholes and latrines or recognize kybos (trail toilets). Another focus for this lesson is activities that deal with personal hygiene.

Lesson 5: Cleaning Dishes in the Backcountry. This lesson is an extension of hygiene as it applies to kitchen practices, specifically cleaning dishes, pots, and leftovers. Participants will engage in activities that allow them to deal with gray water, discerning between sump holes and scattering, broadcasting water, and handling food scraps.

Lesson 6: Campfires. The campfire is the best part of outdoor excursions for many people. However, if not practiced properly, campfires can have a devastating impact in some environments. Participants will learn how to practice fire-building techniques that are sensitive to the conditions of specific locations. The activities for this lesson will focus on mound fires, hub fires, or using existing fire rings. A commonly overlooked skill is how to best gather fuel to avoid depletion.

Lesson 7: Environmental In-Camp Practices. The final lesson engages participants in the best backcountry washing practices, including brushing teeth. This lesson will also include activities that allow participants to practice prepping for a trip that takes packaging into consideration. As well, participants will set their own food line and know the ethical value of this essential skill.

Terminology

- **broadcasting**—Using a spoon or ladle to flick small amounts of gray water over a large area well away from camp.
- **campsite selection**—Choice of area that is durable enough to support camping activities for the number in a group.
- **carrying capacity**—The ability of an area to serve as a campsite for a group of people; the maximum number that an ecosystem can support.
- **cathole**—A small hole dug into the organic layer allowing for human feces.
- **cheesecloth**—A coarse filter used for straining liquid.
- **compost bag**—A biodegradable plastic bag used to hold food scraps; can be composted when participants return home.
- **ecological attitudes**—Personal view and values regarding the environment.
- **ecosystem**—The abiotic and biotic components of the environment in a given area.
- **ecotone**—A transitional area between two or more diverse communities, such as a forest and grassland. The ecotonal community commonly contains many organisms of the overlapping communities, as well as organisms that are characteristic of and often restricted to the ecotone.
- **erosion**—The process of wearing away and dispersing rock and soil particles over time.
- **fire pan**—A durable, reusable container that can hold and withstand a small fire, such as a hubcap.
- **fire rings**—Scorched and blackened ring or rocks in a circle marking a fire pit.
- **food line**—Rope system used to haul food off the ground, preventing animal attraction.

- **gray water**—Water used to clean dishes.
- **kybos**—Small wooden boxes that have a toilet seat; found along portages and heavily used trails to serve as a toilets.
- **latrine**—A group location for human waste.
- **microtrash**—Small pieces of waste packaging that fall to the ground and become overlooked during cleanup.
- **ponding**—Areas along a trail that are widened from improper hiking or erosion where water pools after heavy rains, forming temporary ponds.
- **soil compaction**—When the litter layer is trampled so that it is no longer loosely packed but is compressed and hard.
- **soil profiles**—Soil consists of layers. Duff (litter) is organic material natural to the area, such as leaves, plants, twigs, and sticks, that decomposes into the organic layer; A horizon is finely reduced organic material; B horizon is mineral soil thoroughly mixed with organic material; and C horizon is unmodified parent material.
- **sump**—A cathole for strained gray water.
- **switchbacks**—A trail designed to loop or zigzag up steep sections of a hill versus a straight trail up or down a hill.
- **trail system**—Existing or established trails used for hiking.
- **trail widening**—Areas along a trail where hikers repeatedly stepped off the main trail, widening it.
- **trampling**—Evidence of vegetation affected by human interaction; a trail beaten through a grassy area.
- **vegetation**—Natural plant growth of an area.
- **waste management**—Practices to deal with the generation of human waste in outdoor settings.

LESSON 1

Connecting to the Natural World

Overview

The challenge many people face when entering an outdoor environment for educational purposes is being comfortable. The desire to connect to the natural world is essential for anyone to develop an ethical practice while engaged in outdoor pursuits. If people have no connection or understanding of the environment or the importance of developing a particular attitude, they will miss the importance of preservation practices. Connecting activities allow people to become aware of the natural world, reconnect to the outdoors, and form personal understandings of the natural world, and with that knowledge they will be better informed on how to best act in natural settings. The following are nonthreatening but representational activities to help outdoor leaders awaken participants to their place in the world.

Learning Objectives

- To develop senses in natural settings: listening, smelling, feeling, and seeing
- To form a personal ecological connection to the natural world

Activity 1: Silent Hike

During the hike, stress the importance of silence and listening to inner thoughts along with the sounds of the natural world. The goal of this activity is to begin using other senses, which is better realized when not engaged in distracting conversations.

Skill Cues

- Maintain absolute silence during the hike.
- Make observations during the hike:
  - Look for something that sparks your curiosity.
  - Try to smell new or familiar smells.
  - Look for signs of humanity.
  - Listen for something natural.
  - Touch something gently as you pass.
  - Look for something you know well.
  - Look for an amazing color.
  - Try to feel differences in air movement, temperature, scent, and so on.

Teaching Cues

- Select an established trail system and plan a hike duration that will be long enough to accomplish the observation list.
- Respectfully position the importance of absolute silence during the hike.
- You may need to strategically place yourself in the hiking formation to act as a reminder for silence.
- The pace needs to be slow enough to give participants time to allow their senses to become attuned to the natural world. A responsible participant may need to lead the group at this pace.

- When you arrive at the designated area, allow the group to settle before breaking the silence. You may need to gesture the sign of silence.
- Process the experience by eliciting participant responses about what they observed during the hike.
- Be prepared to probe participant responses for fuller explanations.

Activity 2: Solo Watch

The solo watch gives participants personal time in the natural world. Most outdoor engagements are social affairs; solo time in the outdoors is often an uncommon experience. This activity allows participants to reconnect to nature on a personal level and to help develop their understanding of a particular place.

Skill Cues

- Within the designated area, participants find a place to sit for an extended time within sight of a designated meeting area.
- During their solo watch, they focus on one particular sense that resonates with their sitting place. Try to extend and connect this observation from the silent hike.
- Participants draw or write their observations in a field notebook to try to capture their experience.

Teaching Cues

- Remind participants of safety concerns and the need to stay within the designated boundary.
- Remind participants of any environmental hazards.
- Give participants whistles.
- Remind participants of the emergency signal.
- Demonstrate the signal, not using the whistle that will be used when requesting the participants to return to the designated meeting area.
- You may need to provide an example of what you expect of their writings or drawings.
- Learning to sit and reflect is a practiced behavior. You may have to judge the appropriate length of time based on the participants' maturity.
- When the participants return to the designated meeting area, have them share their observations via a nature gallery.
- Be prepared to further the discussion by linking ecological attitudes and thoughts to support participant observations.

Activity 3: Painter's Palette—Color Your World

Exploring is a natural response to being in the outdoors, but this aspect of our curiosity may not be as prevalent as it was during childhood. Each participant explores the designated area and looks for natural colors of brilliance.

Skill Cues

- Participants explore the designated area, seeking colors that resonate with them.
- When the participants return to the designated meeting area (when hearing the call signal), they begin naming the newfound color for an up-and-coming paint company.
- Participants present their new color to the group.

Teaching Cues

- Encourage creativity and names that reflect the place and the new color.
- To help the participants, have a variety of paint samples on-site and read a few of the names as examples.
- Remind the participants of the return signal.
- Remind participants of the boundary in which they are permitted to explore.
- Remind participants of the need to be respectful of nature and to only bring back color samples that will not cause harm to any living organism.

Lesson Closure

- To bring closure to the lesson, read a passage or poem or share a story that brings human connection to the environment to the forefront.
- Take time at the end of the lesson to have each participant offer a key discovery of how the environment connects to the personal as a way to review the activities.

LESSON 2

Trail Impact

Overview

The intention of this lesson is to increase awareness of the need to exercise good judgment and ethical trail practices. The importance of trail impact is revealed when participants are brought to areas that have been damaged by the simple pursuit of hiking. Critical to this lesson is your ability to motivate participants to consider how they affect outdoor spaces and to practice sound trail techniques. For this lesson, take the opportunity to introduce soil and its characteristics as part of the natural environment. Understanding soil will be necessary in future lessons.

Learning Objectives

- To learn proper hiking techniques based on LNT practices
- To learn how to recognize impact
- To learn basic soil layers and characteristics

Activity 1: Trail Erosion

Many trails are experiencing degrees of erosion. In a location that offers various trails, design a short hike for participants to identify signs of erosion and human impact. This is an opportunity for participants to practice sound hiking practices. Key features would be washouts, mud holes, rocky stretches, and exposed tree roots (figure 3.1*a*).

Skill Cues

- Identify worn places along the trails.
- Identify material piles—places where soil is piled due to runoff.

a   *b*

Figure 3.1   Trail erosion: *(a)* A typical worn trail—it's been washed out, leaving large stones. *(b)* A switchback skirting a hill—stay on the trail and avoid shortcuts straight up or down the hill.

- Identify examples of ponding.
- Identify areas along the trail that have become widened.
- Identify path cuts caused by hikers taking shortcuts. This is a common form of impact along switchbacks.

Teaching Cues

This activity is an opportunity to demonstrate and practice proper hiking techniques—single-file lines and staying to the designated trail. As the participants identify each feature, provide the reasoning for the impact based on human interaction with the local environment and suggest prevention methods.

- Worn places may be due to groups congregating in a particular area for extended rest or water breaks, dropping packs at the side of the trail, sitting in vegetated areas, and trampling and breaking the undergrowth. Encourage participants to stay on the trail or take breaks in durable areas.
- Trail areas along steep grades may have material piles caused by water from spring runoff or heavy rains. If the ground is unable to absorb the water due to soil compaction from previous use, the result is a temporary ground stream that washes loose soil material and deposits it at a low point.
- Ponding is the result of water runoff collecting in a low point on a trail. Don't skirt to the side to avoid the mud—the result will be a widening trail. Encourage your group to use gaiters and lightweight hikers. If possible, have sandals for these sections of the trail. This requires you to know the area and trail conditions during the varying seasons.

- Hikers traveling side by side cause trail widening. Encourage single-file travel and passage around obstructions that can cause groups to become bottlenecked, resulting in a large number of people trampling a small area as they wait their turn to go around windfall or rocks.
- Discourage shortcuts, especially on switchback trails (looping or zigzagging trails) (figure 3.1*b*). Switchbacks tend to be in steep areas, and shortcuts intersect the gradual trail along the steepest section of the landscape. When these areas become compacted, the soil will easily erode away. Without intervention, it will be challenging for nature to recover from this level of impact.

Risk Management

- Be aware of the trail quality and instruct the group to keep together during the lesson.
- All participants should be aware of the trail conditions and should not stray into identified hazard areas.

Activity 2: Understanding Soil Layers

During the short hike, bring the group to an area where the soil layers are exposed. This will allow participants to easily identify how the ground beneath their feet is layered (see figure 3.2). Such knowledge will help participants better understand how trail impact occurs, reinforcing the need to practice proper trail techniques. All areas have a unique soil signature. It is your responsibility as outdoor leader to understand the soil characteristics of the area and how this area is able to rebound through natural regenerative processes.

Skill Cues

With a blank copy of the soil-profile diagram (figure 3.3), participants examine the exposed soil layers and write the characteristics that they are able to observe. This activity will allow participants to identify the layers of soil that compose a profile and how each layer is important to the natural environment.

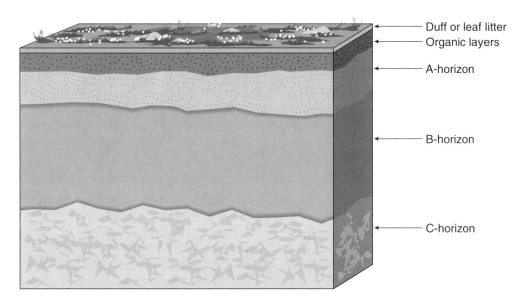

Figure 3.2   Soil layers in profile.

Teaching Cues

- The duff layer is organic material natural to the area. This is the material that decomposes. As it breaks down, it becomes a sticky brown material, humus, that weakly cements soil particles together and can resist rain and compaction within limits.
- The A horizon is a more finely reduced organic material.
- The organic layers and A horizon are normally able to absorb quantities of water from runoff, preventing drastic effects of erosion.
- The B horizon is mineral soil thoroughly mixed with organic material.
- The C horizon is unmodified parent material and perhaps the original material of the place or was deposited there by gravity, water runoff, or glaciers.
- The final layer is bedrock.
- On average it can take up to 200 years to form 1 centimeter (.4 inch) of soil. This is an exceedingly slow rate of renewal, which indicates the challenge of trying to restore damaged areas naturally.

Activity 3: Avoiding Social Trails

A typical human behavior is to follow the path of least resistance from one place to another and to consistently follow a determined route. As this path becomes established in a camp area, other participants follow it. This is referred to as a *social path,* a route that others use repeatedly to move from one area to another. This route can quickly become an established path. This activity should be taught in a durable setting such as a field.

Skill Cues

- Participants walk a single-file line across a field a few times.
- In another section of the field, the group crosses the field, but participants take their own route and do not follow anyone else.

Teaching Cues

- Ask the participants to comment on the observed impact on the field.
- List the pros and the cons from each method of crossing the field.
  - Single file concentrates the impact in a single-use area. The impact is immediate and apparent, affirming the need to hike durable areas.
  - When scattered and random, the impact is not immediate. A scattered hike has the advantage when crossing open spaces through grasslands.
- You may need to lead the participants through questioning and discussing the connection from the field walk to traveling along trails.
  - Hiking in a single-file line is a way to contain and control trail damage.
  - In a camp setting, following random routes prevents the formation of social trails. Camp areas are not subject to frequent use; therefore the random routes will have time to rebound.
  - In camp, use lightweight, smooth-soled camp shoes to minimize impact.

Lesson Closure

- Take time at the end of the lesson to review travel techniques for hiking.

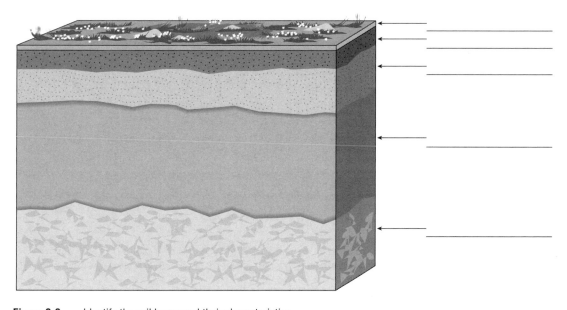

Figure 3.3 Identify the soil layers and their characteristics.

From K. Redmond, A. Foran, and S. Dwyer, 2010, *Quality lesson plans for outdoor education* (Champaign, IL: Human Kinetics).

- Remind participants of the importance of staying to established trails and using the trail system for the purpose it was intended.
- Have participants perform a skit that demonstrates the unique relationship of soil to an area and how human use in the area creates impact. Participants can act out sound practices and undesirable hiking behaviors.

LESSON 3

Campsite Selection

Overview

Living in the outdoors requires preparation for nighttime. The overnight camp experience may be the highlight of many outings. However, preparing to spend a night or a few nights in wilderness requires you to prepare participants to put ethical considerations into practice. This lesson will allow participants to determine suitable camp locations that will balance their numbers within a particular natural setting, aiming to preserve the area.

Learning Objectives

- To recognize suitable campsite locations
- To practice LNT skills in establishing a campsite
- To discern the positives of the camp location and the inevitable impact that may occur

Activity: Setting Up Shelter

In groups of four to six, participants scout out a suitable location within the designated boundary to set up tarp shelters (for sleeping and cooking) or tents. Remind the participants to think in terms of preserving their natural surroundings; thus durability may be required over comfort—a complex consideration when selecting a campsite.

Skill Cues

- Participants should find sites that are not in sensitive areas.
- Each group should try to determine the durability of the site.
- Safety considerations need to be considered during site selection, including dead tree limbs, flood zones, and animal routes.
- Saplings should be avoided while setting guidelines (securing ropes).
- The site should be a minimum distance of 60 meters (200 feet or 70 adult steps) away from water sources. Participants need to pace this distance, gaining the visual perspective needed in establishing a site.
- Participants provide a tour of their site while explaining the ethical benefits of the site.

Teaching Cues

- Confirm each site selection for durability. Have groups present the reasons for their selected sites and have the participants evaluate the site according to LNT principles.
- Compare pristine versus established sites.
    - Durable pristine sites are acceptable to use considering frequency of use.
    - Established sites are the first choice as means to preserve pristine areas unless they show signs of moderate wear and do not seem to be rebounding well.
- In balancing the carrying capacity of the campsite, shelter and tent sites should be limited to four to six people and these groups need to be spread out.
- Avoid sensitive areas, including ecotones, vegetation that is susceptible to trampling and has a limited ability to rebound (e.g., meadows), and animal trails or nesting sites (to prevent habitat destruction). Prevent social impact by avoiding other camping groups (gives groups a sense of solitude in wild settings).
- In established sites, keep shelters to designated areas, use existing social trails, and use existing fire pits.
- After the lesson is complete and equipment is packed away, have participants sweep the area by fluffing vegetation, returning any litter and duff to the shelter location, and removing any indicators of human activity.

Lesson Closure

- Which type of shelter was easiest on the environment: tents or shelters?
- What are the environmental benefits of using an established campsite over a pristine location?
- Did any groups debate their choice based on LNT practices as they searched out a suitable location? What key points were raised?

LESSON 4

Human Waste Management

Lesson cowritten by Sarah Skotty

Overview

Spending time in the outdoors will require participants to answer the natural call to relieve themselves. This lesson presents a range of possibilities for managing human waste in a sanitary and ethical manner, preserving natural resources. The challenge of this lesson is to create an environment where participants feel comfortable discussing the topic of human waste in a mature and respectful way.

In addition, certain practices are required for specialized environments. Environmental and geographic conditions could alter the method of waste disposal depending on the area. How you teach participants about waste disposal in one environment may differ greatly compared with another area (e.g., river canyons, desert environments, northern locations, higher altitudes, coastlines). Each environment requires a specific technique; consult LNT to ensure that the correct practices are in use.

Learning Objectives

- To dig a cathole, minimizing the chance that someone else will find human waste and maximizing the rate of decomposition
- To discern management practices in sensitive environments and understand practices for high-use areas
- To practice and value the need for sanitary practices, minimizing the possibility of spreading disease associated with human waste and contaminating water sources
- To understand and practice the need to pack out what was packed in, preserving the area for natural wildlife and for future visitors

Activity 1: Catholes

Each group of four to six participants will have a trowel, single-ply toilet paper, and hand sanitizer in a stuff sack. The groups scout out suitable locations within the designated boundary to dig a cathole (figure 3.4) for the purposes of depositing human excrement. Remind participants about the soil layers and the need to have a whistle on their person, even during body breaks.

Skill Cues

- Participants determine a cathole location away from camp and trails (try not to select sites where future travelers may wish to camp) that allows privacy and is 60 meters (200 feet or 70 adult steps) away from water sources.
- Participants practice digging a hole in the soil layers. Decomposition is to be promoted; thus the soil layers need to contain organic material versus sandy mineral layers.

– Remove the duff and litter and keep it in a pile.
– Dig at least 15 centimeters (6 inches) deep into the organic layer and 10 to 15 centimeters (4-6 inches) in diameter.
– Simulate a bowel movement sitting on a fallen log or using a tree for support.
– Replace some of the organic material, stirring it into the feces (use premade mud balls).
– Use small amounts of toilet paper and place it in personal plastic baggies.
– The baggie goes into the participant's personal stuff sack (hygiene bag).
• Participants replace the duff and litter and flag the area with natural materials that clearly indicate a previous user.
• Participants clean their hands with soap and water or sanitizer.
• For urine, participants locate appropriate areas (thick humus covering or rocky areas away from water sources).

Figure 3.4 A typical cathole is dug down 15 centimeters (6 inches) into the organic layer.

Teaching Cues

• Catholes are to be dug 60 meters (200 feet or 70 adult steps) away from water for bowel moments.
• If camping in the area for more than one night or if camping with a large group, cathole sites should be widely dispersed. Considering the impact and the environment, the latrine option may serve better (see activity 3).
• Model and encourage the use of natural toilet paper that can be left behind; leaves or smooth rocks can prove to be good substitutes.
• Encourage participants to pack out all toilet paper in plastic baggies kept in their personal stuff sacks (hygiene bags).
• For safety purposes, toilet paper is not to be burned in catholes, and for sanitary reasons, it is not to be burned in the campfire.
• Have participants dilute their urine with clean water, preventing the odor and salts from attracting unwanted animals, and avoid urinating on vegetated areas.
• It is best to bury feces below the timberline (the upper limit of tree growth) because digging catholes above the timberline damages tundra plants. Waste management above the timberline will require different strategies.

Activity 2: Packing Out Human Waste

Certain times of the year (specifically winter), high-use areas, and environments in river canyons or other sensitive areas close to water sources will require participants to pack out human waste. Another consideration is that feminine hygiene products will need to be packed out in addition to other generated waste products such as toilet paper.

Skill Cues

- Participants retrieve their personal hygiene bag.
- Participants construct their own pack-out kit using a scoop of kitty litter in a regular-sized resealable bag, a paper bag, toilet paper, modeling clay, and a heavy-duty resealable bag.
- Participants practice collecting simulated feces (modeling clay) because a cathole could not be dug.
  - Place one hand inside the paper bag, grab onto the feces pile, scoop up the waste, and pull inside the paper bag, turning it inside out.
  - Take the baggie with kitty litter and sprinkle the litter into the paper bag (this will help absorb the liquid and odors when the feces begins to break down). The toilet paper follows.
  - Double up: Place the paper bag in the regular-sized baggie and seal it. Then place the package in the heavy-duty resealable bag.
  - This hygiene bag then should go into the participant's personal stuff sack.
- Female participants practice placing a tampon or maxi pad in their hygiene bag.

Teaching Cues

- Pack-out material has to be organized before the lesson.
- Encourage the use of natural forms of toilet paper.
- In winter, catholes are not always possible because of frozen ground, thus requiring people to pack out all their waste.
- Have female participants crush an aspirin to put in their baggie to help control odors.

Figure 3.5 Personal poop tube using ABS material.

- Burning toilet paper or tampons is not recommended due to the high temperatures required for complete burning and amounts of fuel required to accomplish the task.
- Show participants other options such as container systems that can be purchased to manage human waste.
- You may wish to invest in more permanent waste management systems or build your own for each participant.
- Remind participants that when they return home, they must dispose of their waste materials in a proper manner.
- You may demonstrate packing-out techniques beyond the personal baggie option used for winter, such as durable poop tubes constructed from ABS tubes (figure 3.5).

Activity 3: Latrine

Considering the vastness of many landscapes, various methods may be needed to manage human waste. Additionally, a group may be required to spend more than a couple of nights in a particular area. This activity demonstrates an alternative method for managing human waste if catholes are not an option: the latrine.

Skill Cues

- Participants scout out a suitable area for digging a latrine (ample duff layer and soil base).

- Dig the latrine 60 meters (200 feet or 70 adult steps) away from water sources.
- Dig a hole in the organic layer that is 30 centimeters (12 inches) deep and 45 centimeters wide (18 inches).
- After each use, participants shovel in soil to cover and stir in the feces.
- Practice closing up the latrine: Replace all soil and organic material, scatter any extra material, and replace the duff.

Teaching Cues

- Stress the importance of keeping the removed soil accessible and loose for easier return and covering.
- Keep the duff separate for restoring the latrine site to its original state.
- This option is to be used if catholes are not suited for the environment.
- Remind participants that privacy is a critical consideration for many people.
- Participants must pack out their toilet paper or use natural alternatives.
- Explain the necessity of using established outhouses and kybos (only for human waste, not trash or organic waste) when traveling (figure 3.6).

Figure 3.6   A standard outhouse.

Activity 4: Surface Disposal

Surface disposal may be required when catholes are not appropriate and packing out is not the best option for the environment (i.e., desert conditions, high altitudes, coasts, arctic locations). This method must be practiced before taking trips into these environments.

Skill Cues

- Participants locate a flat rock away from the camp and trail in a spot that is as shielded from public viewing as possible. Minimum distances still apply—60 meters (200 feet or 70 adult steps) away from water for bowel moments and urination.
- Each participant makes mud balls for simulated feces.
- Using a sturdy stick, each participant smears the mud into a thin layer covering the rock surface.
- In practice locations along coastlines, participants throw their rock as far as possible into the intertidal zone, where the human waste will be broken down naturally.
- Toilet paper is to be packed out in the participant's personal hygiene bag.

Teaching Cues

- Do not use modeling clay; it is not natural to the outside environment and may result in materials that will not break down without impact.
- The thin layer will decompose faster as a result of direct sunlight in arctic or desert environments.
- In coastal areas, make sure the deposit site is well away from swimming activities.

- Because there may be no organic soil in deserts, there will be a lack of micro-organisms that are essential to the natural breakdown of human waste. Additionally, the moisture and organisms that break down human waste in catholes are not likely to be present. In these situations, if a suitable location away from other visitors and potential water locations is not possible, it is best to pack out human waste.
- If a cathole is used because there was no choice, decomposition requires the heat of the sun to help break down the waste. Therefore, the catholes should be shallow, on south-facing slopes, and far away from trails, camps, and water sources to maximize decomposition and minimize harmful environmental impact.
- Stress surface disposal for deserts.
- Surface disposal in the arctic is an acceptable practice during the popular travel season due to the low number of visitors and long hours of sun exposure. When there is limited sunlight, the breakdown of feces is slow and therefore packing out is often the best option.
- If traveling in an area where contact by others is evident, use a cathole, preferably in an area of unfrozen ground where organic soil is present and where damage to vegetation is minimal.
- If catholes are not possible because of deep snow, ice, or frozen ground, packing out may be the only option.
- Catholes in snow only hide waste until the snow melts; then it lies on the snow and ground. Instead, let your waste freeze and then pack it and your toilet paper out.
- If urinating, imagine the drainage system of the area, because snow will melt in the spring and participants need to avoid contaminating water sources. Always cover urine stains (yellow snow) with clean snow.
- Toilet paper should be packed out.

Lesson Closure

- Which of the waste techniques are problematic or most challenging?
- Of the methods experienced during the lesson, which seems most reasonable when on an outdoor pursuit? Why?

LESSON 5

Cleaning Dishes in the Backcountry

Overview

In the backcountry, cleaning dishes is a chore that must be attended to after every meal. This lesson presents techniques for dishwashing, enabling the group to uphold the current standard in hygiene, camp cleanliness, and wilderness preservation.

Learning Objectives

- To learn cleaning techniques for hygienic purposes
- To learn how to dispose of gray water
- To learn how to prevent illnesses due to improper sanitary practices

Activity 1: Cleaning With Hot Water

Oftentimes utensils, mugs, bowls, and plates can be simply and effectively cleaned with hot water. After cooking a light lunch, participants will clean their personal kitchenware and cooking groups will take responsibility for their cook set.

Skill Cues

- Participants cook a light lunch; backcountry pizzas, spaghetti, or vegetable soups are easy possibilities.
- Using a large pot, swish hot, boiled water on used personal kitchenware until it is clean.
- Plates and cutlery may be soaked and swished in a large pot of hot water.

Teaching Cues

- Scrub lightly using fingers or a designated washcloth to avoid splashing hot water.
- For more stubborn cleanup, soak the dish before swishing.
- Cooking and cleaning groups should be limited to three or four people.
- This method requires no soap.

Risk Management

- Lighting a stove is required to heat a light lunch.
- Take precautions to prevent scalding from the hot water boiled for dishwashing or burns due to stove flare-ups.
- Follow safe practices for stove lighting and group cooking in an established backcountry cook site and exercise proper sanitation practices; incomplete or improper cleaning and food-handling practices may lead to food poisoning.

Activity 2: Recycling Gray Water

Participants will dispose of their gray water as a tea.

Skill Cues

- Strain dishwater and dispose of food particles in the compost bag of the cook group.
- Bring gray water to a rolling boil and drop in the tea bag of choice.
- Let tea steep to the desired strength.
- Sit back, relax, and enjoy the fruit of responsible environmental practices.

Teaching Cues

- Emphasize this process as a convenient and fast method of backcountry cleanup.
- Have leaders model this practice to help break down participant reticence.
- Discuss the environmental benefits of water conservation and taking responsibility for personal waste.
- Help participants discover that the tea masks the tainted water, enabling them to adjust to the concept of gray tea.
- Consider extending this activity to hot chocolate or other drinks.
- In the initial introduction of this activity, strain the water to be used for tea.
- This is a soapless activity.

Activity 3: Sump Method

A sump is a filtration system (primarily for food-particle removal) for gray water before the gray water is disposed of in a cathole. A cathole offers a natural filtration system for gray water. The three sump methods are a litterbag, cheesecloth, or kitchen strainer.

Skill Cues

Preparation

- Dig a cathole (15 centimeters [6 inches] deep into the organic layer) in a location just outside the kitchen area and not toward the trail, sleeping shelters, or water (60 meters, 200 feet, or 70 adult steps).
- Save the covering duff layer and soil to restore the cathole to its original condition when leaving the site.
- Wash kitchenware with minimal soap or no soap, using natural scrubbers or a dishcloth.
- When the dishes are cleaned, dispose of gray water using one of the following methods.

Litterbag

- A litterbag is a plastic shopping bag one-quarter full of duff (figure 3.7). Drainage holes are located in the center bottom of the bag.
- The bag is suspended over the cathole.
- The gray water is then poured into the bag. The duff catches food particles, allowing the wastewater to drain into the cathole.
- The litterbag is stored inside another plastic shopping bag to contain seepage and is kept with the garbage.
- Pour clean water into the sump to dilute the odors from the gray water.

Figure 3.7 The litterbag is one-quarter full of duff and placed in a cathole.

Cheesecloth

- A piece of cheesecloth is cut from the roll and pegged over the cathole (figure 3.8).
- The gray water is carefully poured onto the cheesecloth. The cloth strains out the food particles and allows the wastewater to go into the sump hole.
- Pour clean water into the sump to dilute the odors from the gray water.
- When the cleanup is complete, the cheesecloth is then stored with the garbage.

Figure 3.8 Pegged cheesecloth.

Strainer

- A kitchen strainer (metal mesh) can be used in place of the cheesecloth (figure 3.9).
- After the gray water is poured, the strainer will have to be emptied of food particles and cleaned.
- Pour clean water into the sump to dilute the odors from the gray water.

Teaching Cues

- Designate the location of the cathole and dig it before cleaning.

- Practice the three sump methods and then dispose of gray water in one of the three sump disposal areas.
- Explain each sump method as an ethical backcountry practice in bear country (to avoid attracting bears).
- Sump methods may be used to ethically dispose of personal gray water and the wastewater from group pots.
- Consider assigning one of the three disposal methods to each cook group. When the participants dispose of their gray water, have them discuss the pros and cons of their assigned method.
- Monitor sumps to ensure they are flushed with clean water to minimize the chance of attracting unwanted wildlife.

Figure 3.9   Working together to strain dishwater for broadcasting.

Activity 4: Broadcasting

Another method of disposing of gray water is using a kitchen strainer to strain the dishwater and then scattering the gray water in minute amounts over a large area well removed from the campsite.

Skill Cues

- Cooking groups strain their dishwater into an empty pot.
- One participant cleans the strainer into the compost bag.
- Another participant takes the pot of gray water and a spoon well outside the camp area (at least 60 meters, 200 feet, or 70 adult steps) and walks and flicks water out of the pot, scattering the gray water over a large designated area.

Teaching Cues

- Encourage minimal to no soap use. Even biodegradable soaps can alter pH levels in soil.
- This technique would not be advisable in bear country.
- On extended trips, consider using a kitchenware boil to sterilize personal and group equipment.

Lesson Closure

- When the cleanup is complete, ask each group to list the pros and cons of each cleanup method.
- Debrief participants as to their preferred method and why it is an ethical field practice.
- Why is it not acceptable to wash dishes at the lake edge or in a stream?
- Why is it acceptable to scatter the gray water beyond the camp area?

LESSON 6

Campfires

Overview

Many outdoor enthusiasts believe that a campfire is one of the highlights of an extended trip. Fire is a powerful force that can warm tired bodies, dry wet clothing, and allow a group to bond through song and story. However, fire can also scar and destroy the beauty of the natural settings that many of us enjoy on our outings. Thus there is a great deal of responsibility to not only keep participants safe around a campfire but also build fires that are ethical. To teach this lesson effectively, a wooded area with an ample supply of downed branches is required.

Learning Objectives

- To build a variety of low-impact fires
- To gather fuel sources, leaving minimal impact
- To practice techniques that promote LNT principles when dismantling the fire

Risk Management

- Provide each fire group with a hubcap or fire pan. This helps keep fires small and manageable.
- Teach in a wooded area close to a water supply.
- Remind participants to abide by safe practices as they work around the fire zone and to not cross over or walk through a designated fire zone for any reason.
- Advise the local department of natural resources of your plan, abide by all fire regulations for your area, and obtain permits if necessary.

Figure 3.10 If using a hubcap as a fire pan for the mound fire, make sure the hubcap is made of durable metal.

Activity 1: Mound Fire

A mound fire is a simple way to construct an ethical fire with little effort, provided that the needed materials are at hand. A mound fire is a pile of mineral soil that separates the heat from a fire pan from the ground, preventing unsightly scarring (figure 3.10).

Skill Cues

- Have the participants lay out a groundsheet larger than the intended fire-pan area to catch embers.
- The group is responsible for gathering sandy, rocky material and mineral soil in a large stuff sack. The collected material can be mounded on top of the groundsheet.
- The mineral soil needs to be at least 10 centimeters (4 inches) thick.

- Participants gather fuel for the fire.
- Place the hubcap on the mound and make a twiggy fire.

Teaching Cues

The following points apply to all fire types and will not be repeated:

- A suggestion to efficiently model and practice this lesson is to break the participants into groups, each with the responsibility for one of the fire types.
- Groups can then present their fire type and ethical considerations.
- Gathering fuel should take ethics into consideration. To avoid depleting the fuel source (branches, twigs, and downed sticks) around the fire zone, have participants walk out from the fire site and gather fuel that is small enough to break by hand. A simple guide would be wood sized from pinky to thumb, appropriate for building a twiggy fire.
- Smaller pieces will burn more efficiently.
- Do not gather wood from standing trees.
- Collect only what is required for maintaining a small fire for the night.
- Keep fires contained within the hubcap.
- At the end of the fire session, make sure the fire is completely out. Use water and scatter the ash and cold coals over a large area far from the fire zone.
- Have the group dismantle the mound of mineral soil, returning the material to its original location.
- Fluff the area around the fire zone, restoring a more natural look versus a trampled area.
- Remind participants of the importance of putting out all fires regardless of type and location.

Activity 2: Fire Ring

A fire ring is an example of an established campsite (figure 3.11).

Skill Cues

- Clean out any signs of garbage that may not have combusted during a previous fire.
- Keep the fire inside the existing ring.
- At the end of the lesson, participants put out the fire using water and stirring the coals until all are cold to the touch.

Teaching Cues

- Refer to the teaching cues for activity 1.
- If your camping location has an existing fire ring, use it instead of creating another fire zone. However, always carry a fire pan or hubcap just in case!
- If your campsite has more than one fire ring, dismantle the others, hiding the evidence and restoring the area to a more natural look. Choose the existing ring based on the durability of the area.
- Remind participants of the importance of putting out all fires regardless of type and location.

Figure 3.11   Using a fire ring does not mean you can build a bonfire. Keep all fires small to conserve wood and to promote safety.

Activity 3: Pan Fire

In highly durable areas where there are exposed rocks or site conditions that can support a group, a fire may be easily made in a fire pan. A fire pan is a compact metal base that holds coals and ash and prevents black scarring of the surrounding rock (figure 3.12). The rock easily absorbs the heat without scorching the ground and vegetation in the area.

Figure 3.12   A pan fire on a slab of rock.

Skill Cues

- Select a rockscape that will accommodate a group and contains an abundance of rocks.
- Participants gather various rocks with little to no disturbance of the natural landscape and construct a flat, stable platform to hold the fire pan.
- Participants gather twig-sized fuel and break the twigs into even smaller lengths to ensure burning and to keep the burning embers contained within the pan.
- At the end of the fire, participants carry the cold pan and scatter the remains.

Teaching Cues

- Refer to the teaching cues for activity 1 (page 129).
- The pan is small and light enough to carry at the top of a backpack.
- The pan allows for easy scattering of ash and charcoal bits that may still remain. Return all rocks to their original location.
- Remind participants of the importance of putting out all fires regardless of type and location.

Lesson Closure

- Have the participants list as many uses as possible for a campfire.
- Discuss the value of a fire for the group experience.
- As a reminder, list the safety considerations to follow during the fire.

LESSON 7

Environmental In-Camp Practices

Overview

The intention of this lesson is to answer the various "What do I do about . . . ?" questions that participants eventually ask. A positive experience in the outdoors requires that all participants are knowledgeable of simple practices such as maintaining a clean body, brushing teeth, and managing food and snacks. These topics are essential for preserving personal health and for maintaining the natural camp.

Learning Objectives

- To practice personal hygiene by taking a backcountry shower
- To learn the proper technique for brushing teeth
- To manage food and set food lines

Activity 1: Washing in the Backcountry

Personal hygiene is essential to a healthy and enjoyable experience. Extended trips require time for washing. Not only does this time allow participants to feel good about themselves, but it also preserves the safety of the group by minimizing health concerns. Essential to this skill are privacy and simplicity without compromising the environment.

Skill Cues

- Participants select a shower site and hand-washing location that is 60 meters (200 feet or 70 adult steps) away from water sources and the campsite yet is close enough to source an adequate water supply.
- Using a tarp, ropes, and carabiners, hang an enclosed shower area, constructing an improvised shower curtain.
- Using a large pot or water container, practice bringing a large quantity of water to the bathing location—lugging water is not an easy chore.
- Water luggers will supply the bather with the water source.
- Participants simulate the washing procedure in a dry run.
  - Rinse body.
  - Lather.
  - Rinse body.
  - Dry off.
- Participants practice washing their hands for actual experience. Repeat to ensure clean hands.

Teaching Cues

- This activity requires an adequate water supply.
- Remind participants that this is teamwork—every group member must take an active role in helping each other. Have participants work in groups of four to six.
- Hand sanitizers do not remove dirt; they are just a quick fix.
- The shower site needs to be able to handle copious amounts of water. Drainage is essential to ensure the group does not result in a mud pit and ponding.
- Use biodegradable soaps in small amounts.
- Demonstrate minimal soap usage—a thumbnail-sized dollop may create enough lather.
- Avoid rinsing in a stream or lake; participants potentially could introduce containments (sunscreen, insect repellent, soap residue) into a sensitive freshwater source and alter the environment.
- Remind the water luggers that their value in this team exercise is to supply enough clean water for thorough cleaning.
- Do not rush the final rinse; each participant needs to ensure that no soap residue is left behind that could cause skin irritation later.
- Remind all groups to restore the washing site, removing evidence of usage.

Activity 2: Brushing Teeth

Oral hygiene is another critical area related to personal health. Brushing teeth and flossing are essential daily maintenance procedures that should not take a second or third level of priority on extended trips. Most often, participants will see this daily ritual as an inconvenient duty and avoid it.

Skill Cues

- Participants find a location 60 meters (200 feet or 70 adult steps) away from water sources and the camp.
- Participants bring a cup of drinkable water (filtered or treated) and their personal hygiene bag.
- Participants remove duff (litter), scuff a small hole, and dispose of their used toothpaste and rinsing spit.

Teaching Cues

- Inform participants that swallowing toothpaste is not recommended.
- Try to use environmentally friendly forms of toothpaste that contain baking soda.
- Remind participants to restore their brushing site.

Activity 3: Repackaging

The adage many outdoor leaders follow when planning for extended trips is that whatever a group brings in for an outdoor pursuit should be less on the way out. Trip planning should remove excess weight and trash, eliminating littering potential before the trip. A great rainy-day activity is to have the group plan, repackage, and prepare a light meal that can be consumed in the field in the near future (hopefully for the lesson on cleaning dishes in the backcountry). The objective of this activity is to reduce the amount of packaging that accompanies food purchases. It is a preventative exercise that helps manage generated waste in the field.

Skill Cues

- Provide each cooking group with the ingredients for a light meal. Participants repackage their meal, reducing the amount of garbage that accompanies the group.
- Participants practice organizing their meal into separate reusable bags, removing cardboard (cut out the instructions and include them with the meal).
- Participants should assess potential sources of litter (microtrash) that inadvertently ends up on the ground and under leaves: bread-bag clips, twist ties, plastic caps, and so on.
- Participants pack their meal with their travel gear.

Teaching Cues

- Model repacking techniques using plastic baggies that are labeled for the meal of the day.
- Remind participants that plastic baggies can be reused for future trips if cleaned properly.
- Include cooking instructions within the food contents—memory does not always suffice on extended trips.
- Label the plastic baggie with the meal's name and date to be consumed. This provides a means to monitor the menu and manage food to avoid spoilage.
- Assess the group meal again for potential microtrash.

Activity 4: Food Scraps

In a perfect world, we would never generate waste and all our meals would adequately fill us with no leftovers. However, that is not always the case; not all cooked food is consumed. Ideally, the food brought in should not be packed out, considering the inability to maintain the freshness of food due to lack of proper storage. Schedule this activity close to an eating time (preferably after the activities on cleaning dishes in the backcountry and repackaging; this may be an opportune time to have food waste), and provide each group with a cook set, food bag, compost bag, and predetermined menu.

Skill Cues

- Groups have their own food bag containing their meal of the day and a compost bag.
- Each cook group prepares a light meal.
- Each participant reserves a small portion of food.
- Participants clean their personal eatery equipment using the strainer.
- Participants place unconsumed food in the compost bag to be packed out.

Teaching Cues

- Participants are often uncomfortable with the thought of carrying garbage, let alone compost materials.
- Do not encourage the burning of food waste.
- Remind participants of the hazards of trying to bury food waste (i.e., attracting animals).
- Food waste will be carried out by the participants, and during an extended trip, a food line will be used for storage.

Activity 5: Food Lines

An essential skill for extended trips is the food line. All food and scented products should be hung up and away from animals. One of the principles of LNT is to prevent human contact with animals—camps have a tendency of attracting unwanted visitors. To protect participants and wildlife from unwanted encounters, a food line is necessary. Have each cook group practice hanging a food line, and remind the participants of safety when hoisting the food line with a heavy object that could potentially swing and hit a bystander.

Skill Cues

- Participants strain food particles from the gray water and dispose of food particles in the compost bag.
- Cook groups clean the cook site of any incidental droppings and include those in the compost bag.
- Cook groups put unused food in the compost bag, waste in the group garbage bag, and unused food back in the food bag.
- Participants gather their personal hygiene bags and include these with the food bag, along with all cookware and eating utensils.
- Groups find a location 60 meters (200 feet or 70 adult steps) away from camp.
- Groups use two ropes and a carabiner to set a food line without damaging the tree limb.
- Groups hang the food line. Using a small but strong rope, tie one end onto a stick to heave over a sturdy tree limb. Set the food line according to figure 3.13.

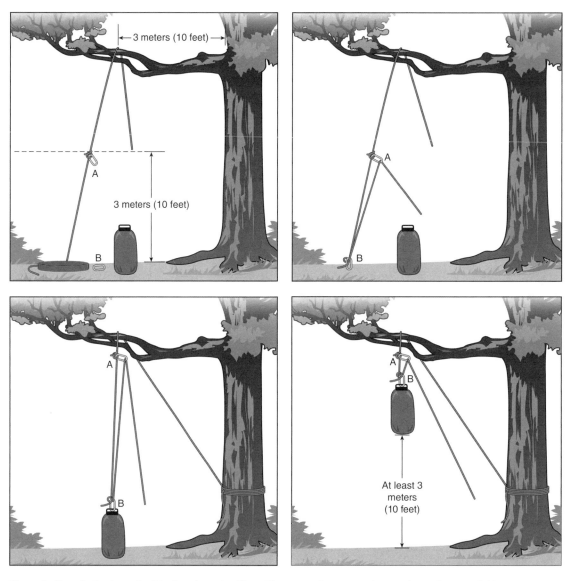

Figure 3.13 A simple method for hanging a food bag. There are other ways—be creative and use available resources.

Based on R. Curtis, 2005, *The backpacker's field manual* (Princeton, NJ: Princeton University). Available: http://www.princeton.edu/~oa/training/bearbag.shtml.

Teaching Cues

- Avoid setting a food line in the dark; it will prove to be a frustrating experience.
- Do not hoist the food and equipment alone; this should be a group effort.
- Do not allow the food line to cut into the branch because this may damage the limb and possibly kill it. Use carabiners to take pressure off the single rope.
- For large and heavy amounts of food and equipment, more than one line may be required; reasonable weight (able to be lifted without undue stress) should be expected per line.
- Large-limbed trees would be an asset in practicing these skills.

Lesson Closure

- What other steps could you take to deal with the little things involved in avoiding environmental impact?

- Of all the LNT skills learned, which practice could you maintain as a part of your everyday life? What we do in the wilderness should support what we do at home, and home practice must in turn preserve the natural world.

References and Resources

Curtis, R. 2005. *The backpacker's field manual.* New York: Three Rivers.

Drury, J.K., B.F. Bonney, D. Berman, and M. Wagstaff. 2005. *The backcountry classroom: Lessons, tools, and activities for teaching outdoor leaders.* 2nd ed. Guilford, CT: Falcon.

Hampton, B., and D. Cole. 2003. *Soft paths: National Outdoor Leadership School.* Mechanicsburg, PA: Stackpole Books.

Harvey, M. 1999. *The National Outdoor Leadership School's wilderness guide.* New York: Fireside.

van Matre, S. 1990. *Earth education: A new beginning.* Greenville, WV: The Institute of Earth Education.

Hiking and Backpacking

▼ Sean Dwyer ▼

How frequently the reward of beauty is associated with the dignity of toil, as if nature consciously reserves her noblest effects for those who take some care to earn them.

– Sir Arthur Lund

Hiking and backpacking provide avenues for personal adventure. The outdoor enthusiast is in for a treat every time, whether trekking along marked trails or venturing into the backcountry. There are many common practices that make hiking and backpacking adventures safe and enjoyable.

Hiking and backpacking differ slightly. Generally, hiking is a day trip where departure and return occur within the same day. Hiking appears easy. However, whether hiking for only an hour or for a full day, there is the potential for personal injury, getting lost, encountering wild animals, or having trouble maintaining proper body temperature.

Backpacking involves spending one or more nights in the outdoors, covering much greater distances. Although it seems obvious that a backpacker would carry a backpack filled with specialized equipment, the hiker should carry a pack, too. Many people have found themselves in trouble even while on small hikes. Weather and dehydration are two common threats to hikers who are unprepared for the conditions. Hikers should carry a basic first aid kit, food, water, and adequate layers of clothing in case conditions turn inclement. Backpackers need to be fully prepared to cook meals and set up shelter in preparation to spend the night.

Equipment

Group Equipment

Refer to each lesson plan for a list of equipment.

Personal Equipment

- Participants require suitable outdoor clothing for the weather conditions.
- Long pants should be worn when traveling through wooded areas, especially when gathering firewood.
- Gloves may be needed for cleanup efforts in streams and local parks.

Equipment Care and Maintenance

- All equipment should be in excellent working order.
- Old or damaged equipment should be replaced to limit discomfort when on the trail.
- An equipment maintenance kit consisting of items such as needle and thread, wire, pliers,

extra plastic clips or hasps, extra webbing or straps, and patches should be taken on any long adventure.

Site Selection

- Study the objectives of each lesson to choose the best site for the lesson.
- Bearing in mind ethical practices in the outdoors, select sites that are effective for instruction but do not compromise the integrity of the outdoor environment.

Social Skills and Etiquette

- Participants should gain an appreciation of and respect for the environment.
- Participants need to follow instructions and cautions provided by the outdoor leader.
- Participants should respect all equipment, especially hiking and backpacking items belonging to the outdoor leader, in show-and-tell sessions.

Risk Management

- Be aware of the potential hazards that exist in an outdoor setting, including unstable footing, steep and slippery trail sections, sharp branches, participants separating from the group, and fire safety.
- Encourage participants to bring to your attention any equipment that is not in proper working condition.

Unit Organization

The lessons in this unit provide a general introduction to hiking and backpacking. Lessons include information regarding equipment, group organization, outdoor ethics, fire building, and expeditions.

Lesson Plans

Lesson 1: Hiking and Backpacking Equipment. Group gear and personal equipment are crucial to successful hiking and backpacking. In this lesson, participants will learn about some of the hiking and backpacking gear that exists and why each item is necessary. Participants need to understand that certain items must be packed to avoid jeopardizing safety and comfort.

Lesson 2: Ethical Practices in the Wilderness. Enjoying the natural environment is intimately linked with preserving it. Outdoor enthusiasts must accept responsibility for their actions when pursuing activities in natural surroundings. This lesson presents the principles of Leave No Trace (LNT) and proper waste disposal. Limiting the impact of human activities in the environment is the common thread throughout this lesson.

Lesson 3: Day Hike. A short hike of only an hour can demonstrate many principles that must be considered when taking a group on a hike. A full day hike will allow for more in-depth experiences where the group can become more involved in the activity. This lesson emphasizes the importance of staying together in a group and making a suitable trip plan with a clear itinerary. It also discusses walking pace and rest stops to ensure consideration and respect for all participants.

Lesson 4: Fire-Building and Lighting Techniques. Having a fire in the wilderness can be a calming and enjoyable experience. This lesson presents fire-building and lighting techniques to get the flames going. More importantly, it highlights precautions to ensure the safety of the environment and all participants. Site selection and dousing the fire need to be considered long before the gathering of wood or the strike of the first match.

Lesson 5: Footwear and Foot Care. The happier the feet, the happier the hiker. The duration of the hike and the terrain to be negotiated will determine the type of footwear needed. This lesson focuses on footwear for hiking and backpacking and foot care while on the trail. Maintaining happy feet will result in happy faces while on the move, at camp, and at the end of the trail.

Lesson 6: Backpacks. In this lesson, participants gain an appreciation of the many uses for backpacks, from the smallest daypacks to largest expedition packs. Personal needs and how much gear is to be carried will determine the pack required. Participants will gain experience in properly packing a backpack and will learn about sizing and the many adjustment features for maximizing comfort.

Lesson 7: Maintaining Comfort and Safety in Camp and on the Trail. This lesson highlights several tips for staying comfortable and smiling during the entire outing. Managing loads along the trail and commonsense practices around camp are addressed. Group cohesion and shared responsibility are key to the safe enjoyment of the outing.

Lesson 8: Backpacking Expedition. The culmination of this unit is an expedition with the group. Participants are involved in the planning and get a chance to put into practice their new knowledge and experience. Equipment, safety, route planning, and trip itinerary are all key factors that participants will have to incorporate into the trip plan. Opportunities to share highlights and reminisce with peers are an important part of the planning process as well.

Terminology

- **bar tacking**—Series of stitching perpendicular to the strap on a backpack that is very strong and used to attach straps on backpacks.
- **bivy bag**—Waterproof emergency sack similar to a sleeping bag commonly used by mountaineers as an alternative to a tent.
- **economic walking pace (EWP)**—Walking pace that uses the least amount of energy and can be maintained for extended lengths of time.
- **gaiters**—Knee-high, and often waterproof, leggings that keep debris and water out of the tops of hiking boots.
- **hip belt**—Wide belt on the bottom of a backpack that buckles around the hips to bear a lot of the load and keep the backpack from swaying.
- **layering**—Wearing multiple layers of clothing that can easily be put on or taken off according to temperature and activity.
- **Leave No Trace (LNT)**—Techniques for responsible use of outdoor spaces where users leave no indications through garbage, broken branches, or fire residue that they were ever in the area.
- **moleskin**—A blister care product that is soft on one side and adhesive on the other. It can be used to prevent blisters or make walking manageable when a blister has formed.
- **spindrift collar**—Closeable collar under the lid of a backpack that keeps debris out and can be used to extend the capacity of the pack.
- **sternum straps**—Small straps that attach from each of the main backpack straps and go across the chest. The objective is to keep the backpack straps toward the center to reduce strain on the chest and shoulders while carrying heavy loads.

- **suspension system**—The attachment of the main backpack straps to the top and bottom of the backpack; can be either adjustable or fixed.
- **switchbacks**—*S*-shaped trails that skirt back and forth on a slope as an alternative to walking straight up or down.

- **trip itinerary**—Detailed plan of an expedition that includes the time of departure and arrival, a full description of every person on the trip, and the exact route and campsites. It is given to a responsible person who is instructed to notify emergency personnel if the expedition party is late returning or communicates an emergency.

LESSON 1

Hiking and Backpacking Equipment

Overview

Selecting personal gear can be reduced to a simple word—preference. However, certain group gear is a necessity. All equipment choices should be based on safety concerns, necessity (functionality and real purpose), and reliability in the field. With experience comes the inside knowledge that informs the outdoor leader whether the equipment selected is just a frill or whether it serves a purpose outside creature comfort.

Learning Objectives

- To learn about hiking and backpacking equipment and gain insight into the level of preparedness that is necessary
- To discuss the importance of safety and the equipment necessary for safe and comfortable trips
- To ask questions about the equipment to gain further understanding
- To handle and use the equipment to gain experience that will be useful later in the field

Equipment

1-2 backpacks filled with hiking and backpacking gear for show and tell:

- Hiking boots
- Gaiters
- Specialized clothing
- Hat and mitts (for any season)
- Stove and fuel bottles
- Cook set, utensil set
- Toilet paper and alcohol-based hand cleaner
- Biodegradable camp soap
- Waterproof match container
- Assorted fire starters
- Candle lantern
- Knife, multitool, compact saw, and axe

- Flashlight or headlamp
- Map, map case, compass, Global Positioning System (GPS)
- Mosquito net
- First aid kit
- Watch
- Mirror
- Sleeping bag
- Reusable camp towel
- Water filter system
- Rescue and safety rope
- Bivouac bag and emergency blanket

Risk Management

- Ensure that participants travel together when hiking to the show-and-tell location.
- Point out obstacles and risks along the trail.

Activity: Show and Tell in the Outdoors

This activity demonstrates the range and use of the many gear options that are available. If participants understand the relevance of selected items, they will be more inclined to grasp the complexity of an outdoor trip and the challenge of being away from urban supports.

Skill Cues

- This session is a hike and a show-and-tell of hiking and backpacking gear.
- Show participants several examples of equipment.
- Explain the use of each item to participants. This may interest them because many people are unfamiliar with the gadgets that are available for hiking and backpacking.
- Spread a small tarp on the ground and empty the contents of each backpack.
- Discuss the relevance of each item.

Teaching Cues

- Welcome questions from participants at any time throughout the presentation.
- Aim to be entertaining and keep the atmosphere light and interesting.
- Let participants handle the equipment and practice using it (if applicable).
- Present equipment to participants and have them suggest alternative uses for each item; this might be critical in an emergency situation, and bringing items that have more than one use will lighten the load.
- During the show and tell, have pieces of string (or duct tape) everywhere, such as in the pot set, tent roll, and so on. At regular intervals, take a piece of string out and demonstrate a practical use for it to reinforce the value of having such items on the trip.

Lesson Closure

Close the session by answering questions and reinforcing that it is crucial for participants to know how to properly use each item and that the equipment should be in good working order.

LESSON 2

Ethical Practices in the Wilderness

Overview

Preserving the natural world requires outdoor leaders to take their participants to actual settings. If participants can see the beauty of the outdoors coupled with its fragility, and if they understand simple techniques that allow outdoor groups to preserve the resource, they will be more accepting of LNT principles.

Learning Objectives

- To learn simple approaches to help preserve the natural environment
- To learn how to use LNT techniques in the natural environment
- To learn proper waste disposal techniques in the outdoors to prevent long-term negative consequences for the environment

Equipment

Garbage bags

Risk Management

When doing the cleanup activity, wear appropriate protective gloves, clothing, and glasses.

Activity 1: Leave No Trace

A starting point for instilling a sense of values regarding outdoor environments is to have participants begin taking care of the natural resources around them.

Skill Cues

- The purpose of LNT is to leave an area as it was found with no trace that anyone was there, except for footprints that do not cause damage or destruction to the environment.
- It includes no garbage, no tenting on fragile ecosystems, no breaking off living trees or twigs, and no walking across protected bog or marsh areas.

Teaching Cues

- LNT should be adopted by participants to protect the environment from human activity.
- Adherence to this principle should be lifelong and should be passed on to others to help minimize the negative results of human activity.
- Sandy or hard-packed gravel areas are the best areas for pitching tents, building fires, or having group gatherings because there is little or no potential for damaging the environment.
- Teach LNT with a purist attitude to model ethical practices in using and caring for the environment. Students can learn from your actions and gain an appreciation that caring for the environment is a commitment, not an option.

Activity 2: Waste Disposal

Taking responsibility for our actions extends to our interactions with the environment. This lesson brings forward the premise that we all have to manage our waste and determine best practices that will allow us to keep natural settings as pristine as possible.

Skill Cues

- The principle of "Pack it in, pack it out" should be employed on all outings.
- Any food or packaging that is carried into nature should be carried out with nothing left behind.

Teaching Cues

- Participants should come to appreciate the environment and realize that everything they throw into the environment is damaging and unsightly.
- Reinforce the concept that any foreign material disposed of in nature can upset the balance of the local ecosystem.
- Participants should understand that disposing of waste in the environment can be destructive and unsightly.
- Recycling and waste management activities in some areas are effective in managing human garbage and should be used (e.g., trails and high-traffic areas that are commonly used by the general public should be equipped with garbage cans to reduce impact).

Lesson Closure

- Review all aspects of the lesson and reemphasize the importance of caring for the environment for the enjoyment of oneself and others both now and in the future.
- Participants could reflect on ways to improve their treatment of the environment.
- Participants could share stories of local areas that are not cared for by users and comment on the results of such activities.

LESSON 3
Day Hike

Overview

Getting a group outside on a pursuit takes a great deal of planning and preparation; it is never as simple as just going outside and hitting the trail. With practice and time on the trail, many participants will be able to anticipate just what they need to allow for a safe and enjoyable experience. Advance preparation will provide more time to enjoy the company of the group and the benefits of being in the outdoors.

Learning Objectives

- To understand the concepts of safe travel in a group, even on a day hike
- To learn the importance of a lead person and sweep person to keep the group together

- To appreciate the feelings and rights of all group members
- To learn about trip itineraries
- To find an appropriate pace to accommodate all members of the group
- To understand the concept of economic walking pace (EWP)
- To use a topographic map and group demographics to discuss the variables of route planning
- To discuss the importance of rest stops and activities for maintaining cohesion in the group
- To discuss the preventative measures for and productive responses to being lost

Equipment

Trip itinerary forms (see figure 4.1)

Risk Management

- It is vital that the group remains together throughout the entire hike.
- Identify a lead person whom everyone stays behind and a sweep person to bring up the rear.
- The main first aid kit should be toward the rear.
- Primary navigational aids should be toward the front.
- Put slower hikers toward the front of the group to act as pacesetters.
- With larger groups, divide groups into pods of four to six per group.

Activity 1: Keeping Everyone Together

How fast is too fast? How slow is too slow? Finding the balance with a group takes a bit of flexing, but tweaking the pace ensures that all participants are comfortable and able to enjoy the outing versus feeling rushed or held up (figure 4.2). However, keep in mind that a group can only go as fast as the slowest member!

Skill Cues

- Review established rules of conduct for the hike—all participants follow the same path, no one goes in front of the leader, and no one falls behind the sweep.
- The group progresses only as fast as its slowest member.

Teaching Cues

Maintaining contact with all group members is mandatory in a school setting but may be a matter of survival on an outing in the wilderness.

Activity 2: Trip Itinerary

The importance of a trip itinerary grows with the duration of the trip. Small day hikes on well-marked trails may not require such measures; however, always letting someone know where you are going and when you will return is never excessive. A trip itinerary is a detailed plan that tells a responsible person the exact details of a trip, including the route, time of departure and return, number of people, clothing and tent descriptions, mode of travel, medical information, and so on. If the group does not return when stated, the person with the trip itinerary contacts emergency personnel to begin a search.

Group name: _____

Type of event: _____

Participant list with contact and medical information:

_____

_____

_____

_____

_____

_____

_____

_____

_____

_____

_____

Date of application: _____

Date and location of departure: _____

Destination: _____

Route (attach proposed route and safety exits or evacuation route[s])

Date and location of return: _____

Emergency contact person: _____ Phone: _____

Alternate emergency contact: _____ Phone: _____

Type of transportation (indicate number of each): _____

Total number of members traveling: _____

Leader traveling with the group, including contact and medical information:

_____

_____

_____

_____

Listing of emergency contact equipment carried by group (e.g., satellite phone, cell phone and number, and so on):

_____

_____

_____

_____

Figure 4.1   The trip itinerary form contains information that can save lives if a group encounters an emergency or becomes lost.

From K. Redmond, A. Foran, and S. Dwyer, 2010, *Quality lesson plans for outdoor education* (Champaign, IL: Human Kinetics).

Figure 4.2   Hikers savor the view while waiting for the remainder of the group.

Skill Cues

- During a break, provide each participant with a copy of a trip itinerary.
- A trip itinerary is important to let family and friends know where the group is going, a description of group members, the planned route, and the approximate return time.

Teaching Cues

- The trip itinerary gives hope to those who are stranded and assists search-and-rescue personnel in locating people as quickly as possible.
- The trip itinerary should be left with a responsible person who will contact police and search-and-rescue personnel if the return time has passed beyond a reasonable delay.
- Present each feature of the itinerary in sufficient detail.

Links to Trip Itinerary and Trip Plan Forms

- http://mazamas.org/pdf/forms/outdoor-trip-itinerary.pdf
- www.adventuresmart.ca/downloads/TripPlan.pdf
- http://bcmc.ca/forms/BCMC_TRIP_PLAN.pdf

Activity 3: Economic Walking Pace

Many health benefits can be realized simply from walking. By developing proper technique, participants can exact the health benefits while maintaining their personal comfort during the outing.

Skill Cues

- Walking should appear relatively effortless.
- Walking should maintain a rhythm that flows.
- Stride length should be shorter rather than longer and will change with terrain.
- Determine a personal EWP that uses the least amount of energy and can be maintained for hours; this often means slowing down!
- Recognize that everyone has a different EWP, and this should be respected.
- When hiking in a group, pair up with people who maintain a similar EWP.
- When navigating grades, use shorter steps and switchbacks.

Teaching Cues

- Discuss EWP at the beginning of a trek, but it is best determined over an extended distance.
- At the end of a hike, discuss whether the EWP appeared to change from the beginning to the end (i.e., if the pace was slower at the finish, the perceived EWP at the start was too fast).
- Hikers with slower EWPs should be in the front of the pack and frequently monitored.

- Some hikers just want to go, go, go; assign them responsibilities, such as monitoring others, going to the back of the pack to check on things, navigating, and doing observation probes (identifying what is around), in order to use their energy in a positive way and increase their stake in group success and enjoyment.
- Consider providing every participant with a map and list of things to see on the hike (see figure 4.3). Participants then use this list to stop, look around, and become observant.
- Have participants wear pedometers and compare distances. (Note: Pedometers are most accurate when pace is consistent.)

Item	Description	UTM/location
Brook		
Fishing hole		
Steep hill or cliff		
Wildlife		
Berries		
Spruce forest		
Birch grove		
Best lookout		
Place to return another time		

Figure 4.3   Sample list of what to see on a hike.

Activity 4: Route Selection

Determining a route depends on many variables, including fitness levels of the participants, skill levels of the participants and the outdoor leader, and purpose of the activity, including goals of the outing, technical aspects, environmental concerns, and growth potential from the activity. Routes should not be chosen lightly. Once the weighing out of the variables supports the route choice, try to ensure a positive experience for participants.

Skill Cues

- Identify obstacles, hazards, associated risks, alternate route options, and advantages and disadvantages of routes.
- Steep grades require up to 10 times the energy and cover up to three times the distance (shown on a topographical map).
- Soft ground cover such as sand or bog requires more energy than hard-packed trail.
- Plan rest stops that take into consideration challenging trail sections, protection from elements (wind, rain), areas that offer broad vistas, recognized landmarks, navigational features, cultural history, and natural history.

Teaching Cues

- Discuss challenges and choices before each trail section, such as challenge of a hard hike up and over a mountain versus the choice of a longer but easier hike around the mountain. For each trail section, identify the challenges it is likely to present and the options the group has for dealing with the challenges. Analysis of challenges and choices should serve as the basis for route selection.
- After each section of trail, compare expectations with reality.
- Recognize that experience internalizes concepts essential for effective decision making in the future.

Activity 5: Rest Stops

Preventing an accident is the best form of risk management. Key components in prevention versus reaction are proper nutrition, hydration, and rest.

Skill Cues

Rest stops are important and should be used for the following:

- Goals: breaking the hike into sections
- Hydration: water in, water out
- Temperature control: adjustment of layers
- Foot care: blister prevention and treatment
- Pack adjustment
- Navigation: reviewing position, landmarks, and upcoming route
- Communication and monitoring
- Rest and rejuvenation

Teaching Cues

- Use rest stops as needed for all skill cues and available teachable moments.
- Continually reinforce good EWP to avoid the rush and rest syndrome, which leads to excessive perspiration, exhaustion, and decreased motivation. When a very intense pace is set that cannot be maintained, the person gasping for breath is forced to stop and rest.
- The last group to arrive may decide when to move on.
- Avoid resting more than 10 minutes unless absolutely necessary.
- Rest stops should consider weather and trail conditions. For example, if participants are sweating, the rest area should be protected and the stop should be short to avoid severe cooling.

Activity 6: Camouflage Game

Camouflage is an ideal game to play along the trail. Its low energy requirement offers a less-than-obvious rest filled with adventure and excitement.

Skill Cues

- The ideal location for this game is a small clearing surrounded by a wooded area.
- The seeker stands in one spot in the center of the clearing.
- As with hide-and-seek, the seeker counts to 20 and all other participants hide.
- The seeker cannot move from this spot to seek out the other participants once the game commences.

- The hiders must stay as close to the seeker as possible.
- The seeker can turn on the spot and try to identify participants hiding in the woods.
- If caught, participants return to the clearing but are not allowed to help the seeker find other participants.
- Once the seeker cannot find any others, the seeker raises one hand and holds up a certain number of fingers, turning a full circle while announcing that a number is being held up.
- Participants can be caught while they peek to see the number.
- Upon lowering the hand, the seeker invites all participants to come out and whisper to the seeker the number that they saw.
- The first person caught could be it for the next round, or you could select a participant among those who did not identify the number of fingers correctly.

Teaching Cues

- This game is great for a new group when you would like to reinforce name learning for participants.
- Explain the game and be the first person to seek in order to demonstrate the game.
- Participants who hide too far from the seeker will not be able to see the number and will lose the point of the game.
- Hiding as close to the seeker as possible adds to the excitement of the game and encourages participants to be creative in their endeavors to stay as close as possible without being seen.

Risk Management

- Participants must obey instructions not to hide too far from the person who is seeking.
- Participants should use caution when walking and ducking through tree branches to find a hiding spot.

Activity 7: We're Lost—Now What?

Many of us have experienced a temporary sense of being lost, and a few of us have experienced what it means to be geographically displaced. When this occurs away from what is considered recognizable—that is, urban supports—the lost sensation can be magnified. Outdoor leaders should help participants become better prepared to deal with being lost, learn key coping strategies, and learn tips that allow for a positive resolution.

Skill Cues

Lead a discussion of what happens when you become disoriented or lost in the wilderness. The following list offers several practical suggestions, some of which require planning before embarking on the outing.

- Never go into the wilderness alone; always leave a trip itinerary.
- Do not allow the group to separate to try to find the way back.
- Once it is discovered that the group is lost, the group should not proceed any further without making a plan.
- If sure and only if sure, retrace steps to the last known location.
- Consult GPS (if currently in use) and check the track log.

- Mark the location on GPS and check Universal Transverse Mercator (UTM) coordinates on the map to determine current location.
- Move to high ground and survey the area by consulting the map and comparing topographic features.
- Follow safety bearing to a prominent landmark and place the group back on course.
- If in possession of a cell phone or communication radio, call for assistance and help searchers by lighting a signaling fire.

Teaching Cues

- Have participants discuss what they would do if lost.
- Discuss each of the options in the skill cues and determine which courses of action are first and which are reserved as a last resort.
- Lead participants on a hike into the wilderness.
  - Ask participants to identify as many characteristics of the trail and surroundings as they can.
  - After each contribution, have participants indicate whether they noticed a particular feature.
  - The key to this discussion is to highlight how important it is to be aware of surroundings.
  - Point out that it is a good idea to turn around occasionally and view the trail from the reverse perspective.
  - Take participants to an area where they can triangulate their position with a map and compass.

Lesson Closure

- Emphasize that getting lost can be a dangerous situation that results from and can lead to poor judgment and decision making.
- Lead participants back to the starting point and reemphasize points discussed along the way by having participants accept the responsibility of being the lead and sweep of the group.

LESSON 4

Fire-Building and Lighting Techniques

Overview

In environmentally sensitive areas, fires may not be recommended, and in hot climates, fires may not be necessary. Yet for people who hike and backpack in temperate environs, fire-lighting skills can mean the difference between life and death in many situations. Hence, those who travel in the wilderness should practice fire-lighting skills. If the area is sensitive, a practical, environmentally friendly alternative is to provide the tinder, kindling, and wood to practice fire-building strategies and simply discuss fire-lighting strategies. This activity may be done close to the base of operation or on the trail.

Learning Objectives

- To select a suitable site for fire building
- To address the risks of lighting fires in the wilderness
- To understand the components of fire building and the requirements for a fire to burn effectively
- To practice fire-building techniques
- To understand the responsibility of properly extinguishing a fire

Equipment

- Matches for each group of three participants
- Container for water to douse fire
- Small shovel

Risk Management

- Getting burned is the most apparent risk with fire building. Participants must be careful when handling sticks on the fire because burns can occur when repositioning sticks.
- Smoke inhalation is another concern, and participants should use caution, especially in the early stages of lighting the fire (when it is most smoky).
- Participants must be careful exposing clothing and hair to the fire.
- No green wood should be added to the fire because it causes the greatest amount of smoke.
- Wind direction should be noted to find the best position around the fire to avoid exposure to smoke and damage to personal (clothing) or group (tents) equipment.
- Materials made from synthetic fibers such as nylon tents, polypropylene, fleeces, and waterproof and breathable rain gear are extremely vulnerable to sparks and flames; on contact with embers or flame, the material melts instantly and is capable of causing severe burns.
- Burning sticks should not be waved in the air or transported in order to avoid accidental ignition of other sources of wood or clothing.

Activity 1: Fire Site

Where to build a fire depends as much on balancing environmental need as it does safety. Outdoor leaders should consider the many factors needed to facilitate the fire-building process.

Skill Cues

- Sandy areas are the best locations for fire lighting because the underlying ground will not be damaged by fire as would a grassy or mossy surface.
- The overhead area should be noted because a fire could cause overhanging trees to ignite, leading to a forest fire.
- Fires should not be located too near water in order to avoid contamination.

Teaching Cues

- Determining an appropriate site for a fire involves many considerations.
- Participants should be asked what considerations are involved in building the fire at one site versus another.

- Participants should display sensitivity for the environment and suggest a site that has the least impact on the environment.

Activity 2: Fire Starting

A good fire requires three things: fuel, heat, and oxygen. The trick is getting these things in balance to provide the end result—fire!

Skill Cues

- An effective fire starter must be able to burn by itself for as long as possible.
- A fire starter that can burn by itself will stay lit long enough to burn off surface moisture and ignite the larger sticks.
- Progress by adding larger sticks once the fire is hungry and can withstand the extra sticks.
- Care should be taken not to add too many sticks too fast because the fire can be overwhelmed by a reduced oxygen supply.
- Blowing sideways at the base of fire can help fan the flames and cause the fire to roar through the small sticks or tinder.
- Birch bark is an excellent fire starter but should not be stripped from the trunk of the tree; loose pieces can be used to avoid harming the tree.
- Small, dry sticks should be gathered and placed on birch bark prior to lighting.
- The dryness of sticks can be generally determined by how they crack; they should snap easily without requiring repeated bending.
- Larger sticks can be broken by placing them between two trees and prying to the side to break the sticks. An easier method is to lay long sticks on the fire and move them inward once they have burned sufficiently.

Teaching Cues

- There are many commercially available fire starters. Relying on these can leave a participant without the skills to start a fire if faced with an unexpected emergency, but they should be included in a personal survival kit.
- Using available materials in the environment is the best method of securing effective fire-starting skills.

Activity 3: Fire-Building Techniques

Building the fire allows participants to practice the big three: using the right amount of fuel, generating the needed heat, and supplying the required amounts of oxygen. Maintaining a clean fire is never as simple as lighting a match.

Skill Cues

- Crisscrossing sticks or building a miniature log cabin allows the sticks to maintain a flow of air into the base of the fire and ensures that the fire will continue burning; sticks can be continually added in this manner to gradually build the fire (figure 4.4).
- One of the most common approaches to building a fire is to build a tepee structure with larger sticks and stuff the middle with small sticks and tinder.
- The downside to this approach is that as the smaller sticks in the middle burn away, the tepee can collapse.

Teaching Cues

- Air flow is critical to building and maintaining a fire.
- Stacking sticks in the same direction restricts air flow and decreases surface area of the wood presented to the fire.
- Discuss alternative fire-building methods: crisscross (good air flow), log cabin with tepee in middle, star (long sticks that are fed into the fire as they burn).
- Consider appropriate fire size: Cooking fires should be small, whereas fires in an emergency or for warmth should be larger.
- Have a cookout using outdoor cooking techniques over an open fire.
- Have a hot dog and marshmallow roast.
- Have each participant make a hot dog spider by placing a hot dog sideways on a roasting stick and slicing the ends of the hot dog into quarters with two slices on each end. During the roasting process, the sliced portions of the hot dog curl and resemble a spider with eight legs.
- Organize a fire-building competition where participants compete to be the first to boil a kettle of water. Adding some dish liquid to the water before the start of the competition causes the water to boil over the top of the pot and clearly indicates when the water is boiling.

Figure 4.4 To provide good air flow, build a miniature log cabin out of tinder and crisscross the top before lighting.

Activity 4: Putting Fires Out

Dousing a fire involves more than just dumping on some water. Putting out a fire is a deliberate, careful act that requires practiced vigilance. If participants become careless, they may very well find their natural surroundings engulfed in flames because of their inattention to a powerful force in nature—fire.

Skill Cues

- Allowing a fire to burn well down before dousing will reduce the mess and debris of incompletely burned sticks.
- Douse the fire using a container of water; pour water all around the base of the fire to prevent it from spreading.
- Use a stick to stir the embers, exposing ignited areas not doused by the water.
- If the fire pit is in turf or peat, take extra care to ensure the fire is out and there is no fire in the ground.
- A fire is much easier to douse if it has burned down to embers.

Teaching Cues

- Fires need to be fully extinguished before you leave the area (figure 4.5).
- A fire should never be left unattended, even if only a small bed of embers remains; winds could arise and spread small embers to nearby areas of grass and dry sticks, causing an unplanned fire.
- Such a fire could destroy a large land area and upset the balance of an ecosystem.

Figure 4.5 Burn the fire to ash and clean the area so no trace remains.

- Participants should understand that fire is a natural phenomenon in nature, but a major fire caused by humans is unacceptable.
- Some cone-bearing trees (e.g., black spruce) must have their cones exposed to fire in order to be properly prepared for germination.

Lesson Closure

- Remind participants of the safety considerations when having a fire.
- Fire starting and building are skills that need to be practiced in case of emergency.
- Green or living trees and branches are ineffective in fire starting; participants should be able to tell the difference between good tinder and green wood.
- Discuss fire size and environmental impact.

LESSON 5

Footwear and Foot Care

Overview

Taking care of equipment is important, but an equally important maintenance topic is body care. One part of the body that tends to take high levels of abuse is the foot. Caring for the feet requires participants to understand the footwear that is required for hiking and backpacking. A most important skill for participants to practice is how to care for their feet, thus preserving the experience—sore feet can ruin a participant's experience.

Learning Objectives

- To select suitable footwear that matches the demands of the hike duration and terrain
- To ensure proper foot care while on the trail for safety and personal comfort
- To learn tips for keeping feet healthy and happy while hiking

Equipment

- First aid kit (moleskin, scissors)
- Multiple layers of duct tape (for preventing blisters in blister-prone areas)

Risk Management

Participants should wear comfortable and properly fitting hiking boots to aid in foot comfort and to prevent blisters.

Activity 1: Footwear

Not all boots are equal. This activity helps participants see how a boot is structured and the benefits this structure will provide their feet during a hiking or backpacking experience.

Skill Cues

- Light hiking sneakers or trekking shoes are suitable for day hikes on easy and even terrain.
- More challenging terrain on uneven ground requires rugged footwear such as hiking boots with stiff soles and high-cut uppers to provide much-needed ankle support.
- When backpacking, it is especially important to have rugged hiking boots with exceptional ankle support to handle the increased load of a full backpack.

Teaching Cues

- Along the trail, discuss the main elements of footwear (ankle support, sole stiffness, laces, water resistance, sole tread pattern).
- You should be wearing footwear that is suitable for the conditions and purpose of the trip.
- Participants should evaluate their footwear and determine how suitable it is for the current outing.
- Waterproof boots should be used to keep water out, but if they get wet inside, they are slow to dry out and tend to stay wet.
- Over the course of a long hike, waterproof hiking boots can trap water inside, which can leave unpleasant odors (even when dried out at home).

Activity 2: Foot Care on the Trail

Little inconveniences can become big problems if left unchecked. A little blister has the potential to grow and become a constant irritant, taking away from the more enjoyable aspects of the outdoor experience. If left untreated, the blister can become debilitating, making it next to impossible for the participant to hike out.

Skill Cues

- Keeping the feet dry and comfortable on the trail determines comfort while hiking and backpacking.
- Foot comfort and care is aided by dry socks and moleskin (for hot spots or blisters).

Teaching Cues

- Participants should appreciate how foot comfort is critical to enjoyment on the trail.
- Use rest stops to take care of the feet by changing into dry socks or clearing debris from socks.
- Blisters should be avoided by treating hot spots with moleskin to prevent the full development of blisters.
- Demonstrate how gaiters can help keep the feet dry when walking through water and mud and how gaiters are effective in keeping trail debris out of hiking boots.
- Debris and water in the boots can lead to discomfort and contribute to cuts and blisters as debris rubs between the foot and the boot.

- Campfires at night can provide a great comfort to hikers and backpackers and could present a good opportunity to dry out hiking boots (care should be taken not to damage boots with extreme heat).

Lesson Closure

Highlight the importance of safety and foot care—a heavily blistered foot will slow a hiker or make walking impossible without excruciating pain.

LESSON 6

Backpacks

Overview

Internal frame, external frame, day pack, overnight pack, weekender, expedition—selecting the right pack depends on the type of trip, and not all packs are equal in carrying capacity, comfort, or even functionality. Packing a backpack effectively and efficiently, donning a pack correctly, and shucking a pack are important skills to learn. Backpacks require good technique, and if essentials can be mastered, participants will be much more comfortable while carrying their load on the trail.

Learning Objectives

- To recognize the types of packs that are available for various load-carrying capabilities and outings
- To learn how to properly pack a backpack for easy accessibility of important items and for even weight distribution for personal comfort
- To introduce the many features of backpacks that provide comfort when carrying larger loads

Equipment

- Several backpacks filled with hiking and backpacking gear
- Participants' own backpacks and gear (if possible)

Risk Management

- Ensure that participants travel together when hiking to the show-and-tell location.
- Point out obstacles and risks along the trail.

Activity 1: Packing a Backpack

Packing in the proper order is a starting point for an easier carry. Organization is key to packing well so that you can easily access your gear and put it all back together again.

Skill Cues

- Pack light and seldom-used items such as the sleeping bag and some clothing at the bottom of the bag.

- Pack heavier items such as food and water close to the back and in the middle of the pack.
- Pack sharp or protruding objects such as cook sets and stoves in the middle of the pack but not against the back.
- Pack fuel and stoves below food to avoid contamination if a leak should occur.
- Pack frequently used items toward the top of the pack, such as a rain coat, clothing layers, and hat.
- Top and side compartments should contain an emergency first aid kit, water, snacks, map, knife, matches in a waterproof container, camera, flashlight, and radio or cell phone.

Teaching Cues

- Involve participants in this process by having them take turns packing backpacks.
- Ask which items should be packed at the bottom, middle, and top of the pack.
- Ask which items should be stored in the top or side compartments.

Activity 2: Features for Comfort and Adjustability

Most packs have various methods that allow for making minute adjustments to provide maximum comfort (figure 4.6). Understanding weight distribution is important, but fitting a pack properly is critical if a participant is expecting to carry a backpack for any length of time.

Skill Cues

- The suspension system of a backpack is either fixed or adjustable.
- Fixed systems need to be matched to the size of the wearer's back; adjustable systems can be fitted to several sizes.
- The hip or waist belt is one of the most important features on a backpack because when the backpack is secured snugly, the hips receive the majority of the weight (figure 4.7).
- Shoulder straps should be padded and adjustable to help manage loads and keep the pack from swaying too much when walking and negotiating obstacles.
- The sternum strap keeps the shoulder straps together, which helps relieve stress on the shoulders and chest.
- The sternum strap should not be fastened so tightly that it restricts breathing; it should have elastic built in to allow for chest expansion during inhalation.
- A spindrift collar keeps dirt and rain out of the main compartment of the pack.
- Some backpacks have a floating lid that allows for larger loads.
- A map pocket under the top lid keeps the map dry and in good condition.
- Stitching on the backpack should be doubled or bar tacked, which is strong and durable.

Figure 4.6   A typical backpack with a variety of adjustable features.

© Human Kinetics

Figure 4.7   A properly fitted and worn backpack.

- The material of the backpack should have a waterproof coating to help protect contents.

Teaching Cues

- Point out that there are many types of packs, including waist packs, day packs, rock-climbing packs, cycling packs, ski packs (narrow to permit free arm movement), overnight packs, and multiday and expedition packs.
- Explain that backpacks may have different features.
- Fit a backpack on a participant while explaining the features; ensure that the backpack is full in order to clearly demonstrate each feature.
- More features on a backpack generally mean more weight.
- Arrange a hiking trip to have participants experience what it is like to wear a weighted pack for an extended time.
- Participants will practice unpacking and packing a backpack during rest stops and meals.

Lesson Closure

Hike back to the starting point, giving all participants an opportunity to wear a backpack and fit it to their body by adjusting the straps.

LESSON 7

Maintaining Comfort and Safety in Camp and on the Trail

Overview

Camp living is a skill that requires practice and teamwork. Successful camp life depends on the ability of group members to collaborate, share, cooperate, and communicate effectively. A fun camp experience rests on the positive attitude of the participants, and the outdoor leader plays a key role in fostering this camaraderie. Group attitudes can shift during the pursuit; thus it is imperative that the outdoor leader remains in tune with the group every step of the way.

Learning Objectives

- To learn about the importance of comfort and safety while on the trail and while in camp
- To ensure that backpacks are properly adjusted and packed for comfort
- To share duties at camp to ensure comfort and environmental responsibility
- To recognize the importance of communicating personal discomforts and problems to the group for the safety of all
- To recognize dangers associated with setting up a camp for a large group, such as location of fire, location of the cooking area, and firewood gathering

Equipment

Typical equipment of a fully packed backpack

Risk Management

- When in camp, keep all equipment organized and in its place to prevent accidents (e.g., axes, saws, stoves).
- Have procedures in place to ensure that the group stays intact while on the trail to prevent participants from becoming separated.

Activity 1: On the Trail

Individual attitudes are easily strained when physical discomfort dominates the experience. Take the time to prevent much of the trail pain in advance by assisting participants in donning and fitting their packs properly.

Skill Cues

- Ensure that all straps are properly adjusted.
- Participants should not have overloaded backpacks; practice load sharing of common items such as saws, stoves, and cook sets.
- When crossing waterways above the knee, release the hip belt and sternum strap and hold the backpack with only one shoulder strap in the event of a fall.
- When crossing even terrain, give shoulders a break by tightening the hip belt and loosening the shoulder straps slightly.

Teaching Cues

- The backpack should be packed and fitted properly to ensure that the weight is high and toward the center of the body.
- Rain covers for backpacks are useful in keeping contents dry as well as keeping debris out and helping to prevent straps from snagging on trees and bushes.
- When walking through wooded areas, ensure that participants walk far enough apart to avoid being flicked with branches, or else ensure that branches are held for the next person.
- Frequently perform attendance checks or roll calls to ensure that the group is intact and does not spread out on the trail.

Activity 2: Around Camp

This is living! Camp life has the potential to generate numerous positive memories, and it is a shared effort by all participants. Maintaining a positive camp experience requires effort and clear social expectations. A clean, orderly camp is half the battle.

Skill Cues

- Participants set up camp in small pods to keep equipment organized and less likely to be scattered and walked on by fellow campers.
- The campfire should be located away from tents and the cooking area, where stoves and flammable fuels are located.
- Firewood storage, cutting, and splitting should be done on the outskirts of camp to avoid injuries from an axe or saw and from flying wood.

Teaching Cues

- Set up camp and have participants do an inventory of potential dangers.
- Inform participants of their individual responsibilities for keeping the camp orderly and picking up equipment that might be lying around and posing a danger.
- Involve participants in choosing the safest site for tents, cooking, and the fire.
- Encourage participants to communicate any discomforts experienced during time in camp, such as being cold, having blisters or cuts, or any other problems.
- Present safety scenarios that could happen on the trail or in camp and ask for suggestions for dealing with such concerns.

Lesson Closure

- An enjoyable hiking and backpacking trip is declared primarily when all participants have returned free from personal injury.
- Emphasize the importance of all participants accepting a role in ensuring the safety of others.

LESSON 8

Backpacking Expedition

Overview

There is no better way to test the skills associated with backpacking than to lead a trip where participants live out their learning in an actual setting. Experience has a way of teaching us what we are capable of and what we need to practice. Most importantly, the trip can become a landmark experience that changes lives. A backpacking expedition has the potential to allow people, environment, and learning to converge within the pursuit.

Learning Objectives

- To experience the process of planning an expedition with a large group
- To complete a route plan and trip itinerary
- To discuss topics to consider when planning an expedition
- To determine individual responsibilities for participants and small groups
- To plan fun activities during the expedition that involve all group members (e.g., digital-photo scavenger hunt)
- To record and report highlights of the trip to the group while on the expedition and to others when at home afterward

Equipment

- Topographic maps
- Navigation devices (compass, GPS)
- Communication device (two-way radio, cell phone)
- Typical equipment of a fully packed backpack so that participants are fully prepared for a multiday backpacking expedition

Risk Management

- Due to the nature and duration of this trip, it is critical to employ adequate safety practices in planning and practice.
- You must have a quick system of checking attendance regularly during the trip to ensure that the group remains together, such as a checklist of names or numbering system whereby participants call out their own number in order.

Activity 1: Planning the Trip

A good trip starts with a sound plan. Trip planning requires the outdoor leader to attend to the many details that will contribute to a positive, safe experience. However, no trip should be planned in isolation; all participants should actively contribute to planning the trip.

Skill Cues

- Determine the best location for an extended backpacking trip. This can be done with the group as a learning experience.
- Route planning allows participants to apply the skills of navigation and route planning (if learned previously).
- Plan a route that has several vistas that provide excitement and are great opportunities for rest and rejuvenation after long routes.
- Complete a trip itinerary form for the group and include all details that will assist search-and-rescue personnel or assistance personnel.
- Use discussion topics for trip planning:
  - Goals and objectives for the outdoor pursuit
  - Special training and certification
  - Equipment needs, such as tents and canoes
  - Transportation
  - Personal equipment
  - Group gear
  - Gear rentals
  - Park permits
  - Maps
  - Route card
  - Weather concerns
  - Emergency plans
  - Updated medical forms (updated forms and health concerns must be discussed every 3 months)
  - Permission forms
  - Buddy system
  - First aid kits
  - Water purification
  - Trip purpose
  - Areas of concern
  - 24-hour day (one-third traveling, one-third maintenance, one-third relaxation)

Teaching Cues

- Check local regulations regarding wilderness backpacking and camping and determine whether to plan an original route or follow an established, authorized route.
- Involving participants in the planning of a backpacking route can be an educational experience.

Historic Tookalook Trail Hike Day 1

- Our Tookalook Trail adventure begins in _____.
- It is a small town located _____.
- We will arrange accommodations, an orientation session, and a gear check.
- There will be time to explore this unique area.
- Features to see in the area include _____.

Historic Tookalook Trail Hike Day 2

- We will get a shuttle ride to the trailhead.
- Today, we will hike 11 kilometers (7 miles) through the forested trail to _____.
- Natural features in view of this beautiful campsite include _____.
- This is a great warm-up hike that helps folks get used to their packs and hiking hills and uneven terrain.

Historic Tookalook Trail Hike Day 3

- We leave _____.
- The trail passes _____.
- After lunch, the trail climbs at a steady rate.
- By 4 p.m. we arrive at Cramalotin Campsite.
- Total distance for the day is 26 kilometers (16 miles).
- Those interested in an additional 1.5-hour return hike to the summit of Mount Tookalook, departure time is 6:45 p.m.
- The scenic trailside is covered with waterfalls and wildflowers.

Historic Tookalook Trail Hike Day 4

- Lunch is at _____.
- Arrive at trail's end at _____.
- This is where the journey ends, but the memories will last forever.
- Total distance for the day is 16 kilometers (10 miles).

Figure 4.8   Sample activity list for Tookalook Hike.

- Route planning must take into account the number of participants, their physical capability, and their level of experience.
- Completing an activity list form with the participants reinforces lessons taught earlier in this unit on planning and being proactive where safety is concerned.
- Use the sample activity list in figure 4.8 to show students the categories required and the level of detail needed.

Activity 2: Participant Responsibilities

A positive trip requires participants to take responsibility for the outing; all group members need to take ownership of a trip component. Every group needs a trip roster to help prompt participants and keep them accountable for their assigned responsibilities. Every camp should know who is responsible for what chore, and these responsibilities should be shared.

Skill Cues

- Participants should be involved in planning the trip and should also be given responsibilities during the trip.
- Participant responsibilities include firewood collection, fire maintenance, latrine preparation and maintenance, camp setup and takedown, campsite checks, navigation assistance, cooking and cleaning duties, first aid assistance, and picture taking.

Teaching Cues

If participants are involved in all aspects of the trip, they will be more likely to take ownership and experience greater enjoyment and satisfaction in the trip.

Activity 3: Digital-Photo Scavenger Hunt

The ease of using certain technological devices in backcountry experiences has provided many unique learning opportunities—the only necessary ingredient is the creativity of the outdoor leader. Doing fun activities with learning outcomes can lead to rich opportunities for participants to continue discovering new things while in the field.

Skill Cues

- Each group must carry a whistle.
- Group members must stay together within a 5-meter (15-foot) radius.
- All items must be photographed from the trail or trailside.

Teaching Cues

- This activity may be presented as a one-off activity during a rest or lunch stop, or it may extend from the start to finish of the expedition.
- Clearly define boundaries and expectations; all items must be photographed from the trail or trailside.
- Change the list in figure 4.9 to reflect the local topography and ecosystem.

Item	Point value	Item	Point value
Fir tree 1.5 m (5 ft) tall	5	Mushroom red	10
Birch tree 6 m (20 ft) tall	5	Indian pipe plant	25
Squirrel	20	Blueberry bush	5
Picture of another group violating safety or environmental stewardship guidelines	50	Picture of competing groups	5 per person
Gull	15	Moose track	10
Ideal campsite	25	Bear scat	25
Gray jay	15	Good kindling	10
Grouse	30	Fern	10
Worm	5	Picture of people demonstrating environmental stewardship	50

Figure 4.9 Sample scavenger list and point value.

- Consider some skill-related items, such as an east (90 degrees) view from a certain landmark.
- Photographs from the scavenger hunt may be a part of a slideshow and reminiscence after the expedition.

Activity 4: Recording and Reminiscence

Technology has reached new heights, following people into even the remotest areas. The digital camera has allowed many outdoor leaders to facilitate debriefing sessions with participants. The digital image becomes a snapshot in time, allowing participants to actively reflect on the experience—a critical element for experiential learning. The only limit is the outdoor leader's creativity in opening up the reflective worlds of the participants.

Skill Cues

- Record highlights and memorable moments with a daily journal; the more specific and detailed, the better. In the absence of time, use bullets as cues for later detailing.
- Document route and activities with poems, stories, photographs, and video.
- When documenting a trip with images, take a variety of images, some that are close up and show detail and others that show the big picture and vistas.
- Write a magazine article on the expedition.
- After the expedition is over, create a display board of the trip for your organization.
- After the expedition is over, meet to share the memories.

Teaching Cues

- Allocate time in the trip itinerary for reflection, sharing, and recording.
- Consider a daily sharing (maybe at the end of the day) of highlights and memorable moments.
- Schedule a time after the trip for reminiscence such as a potluck or slideshow.
- Add participant reflections, photos, and video clips to the organization Web site.
- Have participants plan other aspects of the expedition such as games and fun activities to be used at rest stops and while at camp.

Lesson Closure

- Participants should understand the extent of backpacking expeditions through their experience in planning and partaking in the event.
- The details of any backpacking expedition depend on the nature and location of the trip.
- Participants should feel a sense of autonomy and personal satisfaction with their involvement in the development and completion of the trip.

References and Resources

AdventureSmart. n.d. Trip plan. www.adventuresmart.ca/downloads/TripPlan.pdf.

British Columbia Mountaineering Club. n.d. BCMC trip plan for outdoor survival. http://bcmc.ca/forms/BCMC_TRIP_PLAN.pdf.

Curtis, R. 2005. *The backpacker's field manual.* New York. Three Rivers.

Goldenberg, M., and B. Martin. 2008. *Hiking and backpacking.* Champaign, IL: Human Kinetics.

Mazamas. 2008. Outdoor trip itinerary. http://mazamas.org/pdf/forms/outdoor-trip-itinerary.pdf.

Rock Climbing

▼ Darlene Thomasina Pidgeon ▼

A few hours mountain climbing turns a rascal and a saint into two pretty similar creatures. Fatigue is the shortest way to equality and fraternity and in the end liberty will surrender to sleep.

– Friedrich Nietzsche

Courtesy of Kevin Redmond.

Climbing comes in many styles, including indoor climbing, traditional climbing, bouldering, competition climbing, mountaineering, big wall climbing, and ice climbing. Although many regard climbing as a dangerous sport, it is dangerous only if you don't know the ropes.

Rock climbing involves climbing up various levels of terrain such as a mountain, cliff, boulder, or artificial wall. Climbs come in various levels of difficulty, which is determined by the steepness of the rock, the size of the hand- and footholds, the direction and position of those holds, and sometimes even altitude.

Climbing demands strength, endurance, balance, flexibility, strong mental will, and the ability to remain calm in uncertain situations. Problem-solving skills develop when the climber tries to figure out the moves of a climb or tries to calm a racing mind so as to get the courage to move a little farther. The best moments in climbing, however, happen when the mind shuts down and you find yourself literally floating on the rock. Everything comes together move after move, leaving you with a sense of appreciation and wanting more.

Rock climbing has drastically increased in popularity in the past decade, which could be due in part to the increase in the number of artificial walls. Indoor climbing provides a relatively safe environment for experiencing the movement of climbing. It provides a good place for beginners to feel more comfortable and learn the ropes, but the drawback is that it is indoors. It is outside where climbers find the spirit of the sport that so many people are addicted to. There is rarely a dull moment, and the sense of adventure and freedom will provide memories and a deep appreciation for the environment. The beauty of climbing is that after all the hard work to get on top of the rock, you can find yourself appreciating a beautiful sunset with the burning feeling of life rushing through your veins. Rock climbing can test your mind, body, and spirit. It can teach you to appreciate life, and it can bring you to places you never thought you'd go.

Improvements in climbing equipment as well as greater focus on physical training to improve skills have pushed climbing dramatically in recent decades. Climbing gyms have opened the sport to more and more people, resulting in the outdoors being enjoyed by more people. This increase in climbers has resulted in some climbing areas showing more wear and tear on trails and foliage and sometimes even waiting lines for certain climbs. Hopefully the increasing numbers of climbers will result in more people appreciating and respecting the great outdoors, thus taking better care of it.

Equipment

Group Equipment

- 1 harness for each participant
- 1 pair of rock shoes for each participant
- 1 helmet for each participant (not necessary for bouldering)
- 1 chalk bag for each participant
- 1 belay device
- 1 carabiner
- Climbing tape or white hockey tape for sore skin on hands
- Bouldering needs: climbing shoes, chalk bag, and bouldering pad (can be shared among a small group)
- Climbing toothbrush (optional; used to clean handholds, not wire)
- First aid kit

Personal Equipment

- Suitable outdoor clothing for the weather conditions, such as elastic-waist pants, T-shirt, and warm pullover
- Layers of clothing for easy temperature regulation
- Gloves for belaying (optional)
- Sunglasses (optional)
- Sunscreen (optional)
- Lip balm (optional)
- Hair elastic to tie back hair

Equipment Care and Maintenance

- Rope
  - Ropes should be kept as clean as possible. They should not be stepped on or put down on sandy or dirty ground because the dirt will become embedded in the rope, thus shortening its life span.
  - Store the rope in a rope bag and avoid direct sunlight and moist environments.
  - Regularly check the rope for signs of wear and tear such as damaged sheath, fraying, and abrasion.
  - If using a nondry rope, be careful to not get any water on it. Beware of puddles.

– Never run a rope over a sharp edge.
– Only dynamic ropes should be used. A dynamic rope is a specially constructed rope that is stretchable (the stretch is what makes it dynamic).
• Carabiners and belay device
– Do not drop carabiners or belay devices. If they drop only a couple of feet, they should be OK; use with discretion. However, if they are dropped from the middle or top of a climb, discard them—they may have suffered internal cracks that have weakened them.
– Keep the carabiners clean and away from dirt. This will lengthen their life and keep the gate opening easily.
• Harness
– Harnesses should be kept as clean as possible.
– Check the harness regularly for signs of wear and tear.
– Store away from direct sunlight.
• Chalk bags
– Chalk helps absorb hand sweat, thus enabling a better grip on the rock. Although some people oppose the use of chalk for aesthetic reasons (it can temporarily discolor the rock), it is the norm and usually is socially acceptable. In some countries, you can buy colored chalk so that chalk marks are not left on the rock.
– Chalk bags are secured around the waist and positioned on the back so that they hang near the lumbar region. This enables easy access for the left or right hand when climbing.

Site Selection

• Considerations for outdoor sites:
– Climbing is most rewarding and adventurous in an outdoor setting.
– Climb only in areas previously climbed and deemed safe for rock climbing.
– Beware of loose rock.
– Boulder fields should have a variety of problems so everyone can find something to climb. If a boulder field is not in the area, climbing gyms usually have areas designated for bouldering.
– If climbing on private land, be sure to check the land owner's privileges and follow regulations.
• Considerations for indoor sites:
– Climbing gyms are ideal for practicing belaying and basic technique; however, for insurance reasons lessons will likely have to take place elsewhere, unless the instructor works for the gym.

– Gyms are good for getting used to heights and for training.

Social Skills and Etiquette

• Participants should gain an appreciation for the environment and practice LNT ethics—take out what is brought in.
• Stay on any groomed trails while walking to the rocks.
• Avoid making new trails and respect any vegetation in the area.
• Do not chip, glue, or break rocks for any reason.
• Use an appropriate climbing toothbrush to erase any tick marks made with climbing chalk for pointing out a hold.
• Do not use wire brushes on the rock; use a soft bristle brush.
• Be considerate of climbers, land owners, and other users.
• With bouldering, do not move any rocks to make falls safer; cover the rock with a crash pad and spot well.

Risk Management

• Climbing can be a dangerous sport resulting in bodily damage or death. Attention should be given to every small detail and equipment should be continually double-checked for security. "Check or deck" is a common motto in climbing.
• The quality of the rock is essential for the climber's safety. Loose rock should not be climbed in case it breaks and falls on the belayer or results in the climber falling with the rock.
• Climb only in designated climbing areas.
• Avoid playing near or at the edge of a cliff.
• Never go to the edge of a cliff to set up a top rope while insecure (not tied in). Always tie into a backup such as a large tree or bolt in case of slippage.
• Never use rusty or spinning bolts for anchors. They should be rust-free, tight, 1-centimeter (3/8-inch) stainless-steel bolts.
• Always wear a helmet in case of falling or loose rock.
• The belayer must pay full attention to the climber while belaying. Do not distract belayers by talking to them.
• Never let go of the brake hand while belaying.

- When lowering a climber, do it slowly and steadily so that control of the rope is maintained.
- Before setting up, ensure that the rope length is appropriate so that the climber and belayer do not run out of rope.
- Buckles and any knots should be double-checked by a partner to ensure that they are doubled back and tied properly.
- Never run a rope or sling over a sharp edge.
- When setting up a top rope, make sure the rope is touching the ground with both ends.
- Always tie a stopper knot in both ends of the rope when rappelling.
- Maintain ropes well so that the rope doesn't get tangled while someone is climbing.
- Never take a climber off belay if you're unsure of what the climber is trying to communicate.
- When setting up a top rope, ensure that the rope runs smoothly and is not over any edges.
- Double-check the top-rope setup to make sure all carabiners are locked, the twist in the sling is done once, and the carabiners are through the correct parts of the sling.
- Pay full attention to the boulderer while spotting and move the crash pad into the appropriate landing zone.
- Do not touch the climber while spotting.
- Beware of any poisonous insects and plants in the climbing area.
- Use climbing tape to prevent tears or cuts in the skin if the rock is sharp.
- Warm up the fingers and hands before climbing.
- Wash hands thoroughly after using sunscreen because it makes the hands oily, increasing the risk of slipping.

Unit Organization

Because climbing is a progressive skill, the lessons are organized to allow the participants to gain confidence and provide ample opportunity for the outdoor leader to assess the skill level of each participant. Confidence and ability are two key requirements that need to be considered when determining the technical aspect and difficulty of each climb—both must be appropriate for the group.

This unit introduces participants to three styles of climbing—rock climbing, bouldering, and indoor rock climbing—with emphases on the value of climbing, the challenges it presents

to the mind and body, the importance of safety awareness when climbing, and developing an appreciation for the environment and the unique places and situations that climbing can bring to your life.

Lesson Plans

Lesson 1: Introduction and Preparation. This lesson will introduce participants to the concepts of climbing, familiarize them with equipment and safety, and introduce them to belaying.

Lesson 2: Top Rope and Belaying. This lesson reviews the previous lesson and covers setting up equipment, setting up a top rope outdoors, and hands-on belaying and climbing.

Lesson 3: Belaying Review and Climbing Technique. Lesson 3 reviews belaying so as to refresh the participants on each step and reinforce safety practices. Basic climbing technique is also covered, enabling participants to progress quickly and move more efficiently, thus tiring less, recovering faster, and climbing more.

Lesson 4: Bouldering and Games. The climbing style called *bouldering* is covered in this lesson, including the safety aspects that are unique to this style. Various climbing games are also described to give the climbers a challenge.

Terminology

- **anchor**—That which attaches the belayer to the rock or otherwise prevents the belayer from being pulled off the belay stance if the leader falls. An ideal anchor relies on at least three bombproof attachment points. (See also *belay.*)
- **approach**—The journey to the base of a crag or route.
- **ascend**—To go up. Climbers ascend a route to get to the top.
- **ascent**—A completed climb; the upward movement or progress of a climber.
- **backstep**—Placing a foot behind the body with the foot on its outside edge, allowing the hip to roll inward closer to the rock.
- **barndooring**—When one's body swings out of balance and often results in falling off due to loss of balance, unless one is strong enough to stay on.
- **belay**—The process of paying out rope to the lead climber, taking in rope for a follower, and protecting the climber in the event of a

fall. Belaying allows a climber to fall and live to try again. Also refers to the place where a climber belays (belay station) and a session of belaying.

- **belay device**—A device that attaches to the climber's harness through which the rope is threaded for belaying. Its primary purpose is to create friction quickly in the event of a fall so the belayer can stop the rope, which stops the leader's fall, simply by pulling against the device.
- **belayer**—Person who is belaying a climber.
- **belay station**—A secure stance consisting of an anchor, a rope, and a belayer with a belay device; the place where a belayer sits, stands, or hangs while belaying.
- **bight**—A bend, loop, or curved section of rope.
- **biner**—Slang for carabiner.
- **bivouac (bivy) bag**—A weatherproof sack that fits over a sleeping bag and serves as an alternative to a tent.
- **bolt**—A permanent anchor in the rock installed individually as a protection device or with other bolts or protection devices as an anchor. The bolt is a metal shaft driven into a hole drilled by the climber and equipped with a hanger to attach a carabiner.
- **boulder**—Big rock typically climbed without a rope. May be from head height to over 6 meters (20 feet). Each boulder may have many distinct routes.
- **boulder field**—An area with many boulders of various sizes that are appropriate for bouldering on.
- **bouldering**—A style of climbing that doesn't use ropes or harnesses. Climbs (also called *boulders*) are short in length; if one falls, one lands on a mat, and rocks are usually no higher than 6 meters (20 feet). This style of climbing is physically technical and can be very powerful.
- **bouldering pad**—A mat 8 to 10 centimeters (3-4 inches) thick and roughly 1 meter (1 yard) square placed on the ground under a boulderer to cushion a fall. Usually made of foam layers of various densities, covered with durable nylon, and equipped with straps so that it can be folded in half and carried from place to place on the climber's back. Also known as a *crash pad*.
- **brake hand**—The hand that holds the rope on the side of the belay device opposite to the climber.

- **butterfly coil**—A method of coiling a rope.
- **carabiner**—A metal ring with a spring-loaded gate used to attach the rope to protection as well as many other things.
- **chalk**—White drying agent used to keep a climber's hands dry.
- **chalk bag**—A small bag used to hold chalk; has a stiff rim worn clipped to the harness or around the waist on a belt, allowing the climber to access chalk while climbing.
- **chalk up**—Putting chalk on the hands before or while on a climb.
- **climbing gym**—An inside facility with artificial walls plastered in plastic holds that are meant for climbing.
- **climbing toothbrush**—A small soft-bristled brush used to brush the climbing chalk off the holds.
- **clipping**—The act of putting a carabiner onto a bolt, the rope, or a piece of protection. "Clipping!" is a common call to indicate to the belayer that you are about to pull up rope to make a clip.
- **clove hitch**—Knot often used to tie a rope to a carabiner.
- **competition climbing**—A style of climbing that involves climbing routes or boulders for competition, usually on indoor walls.
- **crack**—An inward split or break in a rock face.
- **crux**—The most crucial, difficult part of the climb.
- **descender**—Any device used to rappel (e.g., figure eight, rappel rack, stitch plate).
- **doubled back**—Bringing harness webbing loop back through the buckle when putting it on. This is an important part of ensuring that the harness is set up correctly.
- **drop knee**—Rotating the knee inside and down, allowing the foot to push sideways on a high hold.
- **edge**—Straight horizontal or slightly angled hold.
- **figure eight**—Common rappel and belay device shaped in an eight.
- **figure-eight knot**—The most common knot used to attach the climber's harness to the rope; varieties include the double figure eight or figure-eight follow-through.
- **flag**—Counterbalancing the body with an extended leg, which prevents the center of gravity from barndooring.
- **fraying and abrasion**—Visible wear and tear on rope from use.

- **free climb**—Making upward progress using only hands, feet, and other body parts for purchase on the rock, as opposed to direct aid where the climber's weight is supported by a sling attached to a device attached to the rock.
- **free solo**—Free climbing without a rope or protection. A fall is likely to result in serious injury or death. Usually distinguished from climbing high boulders in that free soloing implies a climb of a pitch or more.
- **Gaston**—Hold positioned so that the participant must push or lever against the side of it.
- **gate**—The hinged part of a carabiner that opens to allow the clipping of a rope or piece of gear.
- **gear loops**—The loops attached to the waist belt on a harness that are used to hold gear.
- **gym**—An indoor climbing facility consisting of human-made walls.
- **hand–foot match**—Placing a foot and hand on the same hold.
- **harness**—Device that attaches the climber to the rope so that in the event of a fall, the climber is held by the rope. Modern harnesses include leg loops and a waistband secured by a buckle system.
- **heel hook**—Climbing technique involving the use of a heel to pull down.
- **helmet**—Protection for the head from falling gear or rocks.
- **high step**—Lifting the leg up to reach a high foothold.
- **hold**—Any feature of the rock that affords the climber a place to grip with hands or feet. For indoor use, refers to small, plastic, molded climbing grips.
- **ice climbing**—Climbing ice formations, such as frozen waterfalls or rock faces covered with ice.
- **indoor climbing**—Climbing on an artificial wall indoors.
- **jug**—A big handhold. Also refers to the act of ascending a fixed rope with jumar ascenders.
- **keeper knot**—The knot tied after tying the figure eight to prevent rope slippage.
- **lead**—To climb starting with the rope on the ground, clipping into protection points on the way up.
- **leader**—The climber who ascends a route first, putting up the rope and protection.
- **locking carabiner**—A carabiner with either a twist lock or screw-gate locking mechanism.
- **lower off**—To come down from a route after reaching the top or being unable to climb anymore.

- **lumbar region**—The largest segments of the movable part of the vertebral column.
- **mixed climbing**—Refers to a route with both rock and ice sections. May also refer to a route with both sport and traditional sections.
- **mountaineering**—Climbing at alpine levels; consists of hiking, backpacking, and rock climbing, and may also involve climbing on ice and snow.
- **move**—Refers to the motion between holds.
- **multipitch climb**—A climb with more than one pitch, or rope length.
- **off belay**—Common climbing call from a climber to a belayer letting the belayer know that the climber is safe and no longer requires belaying.
- **outdoor climbing**—Climbing on real rock, ice, or snow.
- **pinch**—Hold that is squeezed between the fingers and thumb.
- **pitch**—Generally a rope's length between belay stations on a multipitch climb.
- **pocket**—Hold where only one, two, or three fingers can fit.
- **protection**—Gear placed on a climb to protect the climber in the event of a fall (e.g., nuts, pitons, cams, bolts, quickdraws).
- **rappel**—The act of self-belaying down the length of a rope to descend.
- **rock on**—Shifting the body weight from one foot to the other.
- **rock shoes**—Shoes designed for climbing that have sticky rubber soles and are usually made of leather and fit snugly.
- **rope**—Usually 60 to 70 meters (66-76 yards) in length and composed of nylon; strong enough to hold falls and normal wear and tear for up to 5 years, depending on frequency of use.
- **sewn sling**—A loop of webbing that has been sewn closed so that no knots are necessary.
- **side pull**—Hold positioned vertically that feels best if grabbed on the side.
- **sling**—A loop of webbing or rope.
- **sloper**—Hold that has no real grip or features and is slanted and balloonlike.
- **smear**—Stepping on the sole of the shoe as opposed to an edge where there are no holds, thus using the friction between the rock and the shoe to step up.
- **spinning bolt**—A bolt that spins, indicating that it may be loose and need tightening or replacement.
- **sport climbing**—School of climbing that generally emphasizes shorter routes, physically

difficult movement, and bolted protection. This includes gym climbing with a spotter and competition.

- **spotter**—A person who carefully watches the person bouldering and is prepared to help soften a fall.
- **switch feet**—Switching the feet while staying on the same foothold.
- **topo**—Map of routes and their names.
- **top rope**—A climb that has the rope anchors preset at the top of the climb.

- **traditional climbing**—Climbing that emphasizes longer routes and removable protection.
- **undercling**—The best part of the handhold is underneath and feels best when holding it from above.
- **V ratings**—An open-ended scale used to rate the difficulty of boulder problems.
- **Yosemite Decimal System (YDS)**—The most common system used in the United States to rate difficulty. Most technical rock climbing is rated on a scale of 5.0 to 5.14 with higher numbers representing harder climbs.

Adapted from Rock Climbing.com. Available: www.rockclimbing.com/Articles/Introduction_to_Climbing/Climbing_Directory_528.html.

LESSON 1

Introduction and Preparation

Overview

An introduction to climbing is necessary to give participants an idea of the types of climbing available. It is essential that the participants learn about the risks involved with climbing and the importance of safety. All equipment and rope work must be well understood before actually climbing. This lesson introduces the sport, risks, safety measures, equipment fitting, rope maintenance, knots, and belaying.

Learning Objectives

- To participate in a proper warm-up and warm-down.
- To learn about various types of climbing (competition climbing, ice climbing, indoor climbing, mountaineering)
- To practice risk management strategies for safety and safe climbing techniques
- To be individually fitted for climbing harnesses and understand the importance of a snug-fitting harness
- To be fitted for climbing shoes and understand how properly fitted shoes make stepping on small footholds easier and help climbers find a better sense of balance on the rock
- To understand and apply principles of rope maintenance to ensure a smooth flow of rope for the climber and make the job of belaying a lot easier
- To learn to tie into a harness with a figure-eight knot and a keeper knot
- To understand and apply basic climbing commands essential to climbing success and accident prevention
- To learn to belay for another climber and apply full focus to belaying with the knowledge that the belayer is responsible for the climber's life

Risk Management

- Climbing can be a dangerous sport resulting in bodily damage or death. Attention should be given to every small detail and equipment constantly double-checked for security. "Check or deck" is a common motto in climbing.

- The quality of the rock is essential for the safety of the climber. Loose rock should not be climbed in case it breaks and falls on the belayer or results in the climber falling with the rock.
- Climb only in designated climbing areas.
- Avoid playing near or at the edge of a cliff.
- Never go to the edge of a cliff to set up a top rope while insecure (not tied in).
- Always be tied in to a backup such as a large tree or bolt in case of slippage.
- Never use rusty or spinning bolts for anchors; they should be rust-free, tight, 1-centimeter (3/8-inch) stainless-steel bolts.
- Always wear a helmet in case of falling or loose rock.
- The belayer must pay full attention to the climber while belaying.
- Do not distract belayers by talking to them.
- Never let go of the brake hand while belaying.
- When lowering a climber, do it slowly and steadily so that control of the rope is maintained.
- Before setting up, ensure that the rope length is appropriate so that the climber and belayer do not run out of rope.
- Buckles and any knots should be double-checked by a partner to ensure that they are doubled back and tied properly.
- Never run a rope or sling over a sharp edge.
- When setting up a top rope, make sure the rope is touching the ground with both ends.
- Always tie a stopper knot in both ends of the rope when rappelling.
- Maintain ropes well so that the rope doesn't get tangled while someone is climbing.
- Never take a climber off belay if you're unsure of what the climber is trying to communicate.
- When setting up a top rope, ensure that the rope runs smoothly and is not over any edges.
- Beware of any poisonous insects and plants in the climbing area.
- Use climbing tape to prevent tears or cuts in the skin if the rock is sharp.
- Warm up the fingers and hands before climbing.

Activity 1: Warm-Up and Warm-Down

Climbing requires strength in the fingers and upper body as well as flexibility in the legs. Do a light cardiorespiratory workout such as walking to the crag before doing the stretches.

Skill Cues

- Arm circles: With straight arms, make slow and large circles to progressively faster and smaller circles. Flick the fingers in and out simultaneously.
- Chest stretch: Stand against a door frame, wall, or corner with both arms lifted to 90 degrees and press the forearms into the wall, keeping the arms at 90 degrees. Maintain good posture. This stretch should be felt in the pectorals.
- Finger stretch: Hold the left arm out with the palm down, and with the right hand, grab the fingers of the left hand and pull the fingers back and up, keeping the arm straight and palm down. Pull again, letting the whole hand lift back and up. Repeat for the right arm.
- Leg stretch: Sitting with the legs stretched apart, bring both hands over to touch the left toes. With the hands, pretend to make a crust on a pie as far and wide as you can go, ending on the right toes.

Teaching Cues

- Begin with a light cardio workout to increase blood flow and body temperature.
- Lead warm-ups in the beginning. Over time, warm-ups can be self-directed by participants.

Activity 2: Types of Climbing

The aim of this activity is to help participants learn about types of climbing. Climbing is a complex and diverse activity that requires various levels of expertise and proactive learning.

Skill Cues

- Climbing can be a solitary or social event.
- Sport climbing: Climbing on rock walls that have fixed bolts in the rock that are used to clip while going up.
- Bouldering: Climbing without a harness or rope. Boulders can range in height but are usually safe enough to fall from without a rope. A crash pad and spotters are used to help break the fall. Bouldering is social and although you can go alone, it is most common to go with a group.
- Traditional climbing: Placing protection into cracks or breaks in the rock while climbing. All gear is removable.
- Big-wall or aid climbing: Climbing that can take from 1 day to many. Climbers often sleep on the wall in bivy bags and can use a mix of fixed bolts and removable gear for protection. Often there are few features to climb, so climbers are left to pull on the gear they place and move piece by piece.
- Competition climbing: Climbing on mostly human-made walls for competition. Competitions can range from a small hometown event to the rock climbing World Cup.
- Ice climbing: Climbing on frozen waterfalls using ice axes and ice screws.
- Indoor climbing: Climbing on plastic holds on human-made walls.
- Mountaineering: Climbing at higher elevations, sometimes with a mix of ice and rock climbing. It is very weather dependent and it is not uncommon to go to a far-off country and end up stranded in a tent or bivy on the side of a wall or mountain for weeks, waiting for bad weather to pass.

Teaching Cues

This is simply a sit-and-listen activity.

Activity 3: Risk Management—A Constant in Climbing

Climbing can prove to be a safe pursuit as long as all participants are informed of and skilled in the best practices that focus on safety and safe climbing techniques.

Skill Cues

Review the risk management tips on pages 171 to 172. See figures 5.1 through 5.4 for some common pieces of rock climbing equipment that should be inspected often.

Figure 5.1   Harness.

Figure 5.2   Shoes.

Figure 5.3   Carabiner.

Figure 5.4   Sling.

Teaching Cues

- Although some of the skill cues will not make sense until later, it is essential to introduce participants to the risks involved with climbing, as well as safety measures. Participants must understand the deadly consequences of being careless.
- It might be helpful to make a printed copy of the points for future classes.
- This lesson could be done in greater detail as a slide presentation during inclement weather.

Activity 4: Fitting Equipment

Participants need to be individually fitted for climbing harnesses to ensure a snug fit for safety reasons. Properly fitted shoes will make stepping on small footholds easier and help the participants find a better sense of balance on the rock.

Skill Cues

Harness

- The participant should step into the leg loops and bring the harness up over the hips to fit like a belt (figure 5.5).
- All buckles on the harness should then be doubled back with an 8-centimeter (3-inch) tail to prevent the webbing from slipping and the harness from coming undone.

- A harness should fit the waist so that two fingers can slide easily between the stomach and the harness belt. It is important that the harness cannot be pulled down over the hips.
- Leg loops should fit so that two fingers can slide easily between the thigh and harness.
- Buckles and any knots should be double-checked by a partner to ensure that they are doubled back and tied properly.

Shoes

- Climbing shoes should fit like ballet slippers and should be snug enough so that stepping on a small edge will feel secure without any rolling of the shoe, thus enabling precise footwork.
- The shoe should be fully tied to provide a better feel of footholds.

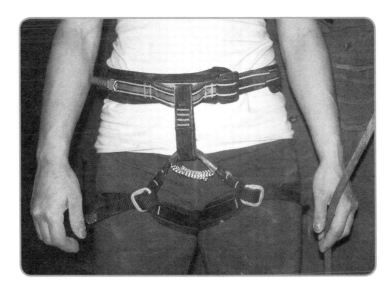

Figure 5.5   A properly fitted harness.

Teaching Cues

To avoid tangles with the harness, arrange the harness on the floor so participants can first step through the leg loops of the harness and then slide the waist belt up over the hips.

Activity 5: Rope Maintenance

Good rope maintenance will ensure a smooth flow of rope for the climber and make the job of belaying a lot easier. Tangles in the rope not only interfere with the person climbing but can be a nightmare for the belayer to untangle with only one hand and only one rope end.

Skill Cues

Method 1—Making a Butterfly Coil

- Grasp one end of the rope in one hand, span the arms, and slide one hand a full arm's length up the rope. This establishes the length of the coil (figure 5.6a).
- Reach down, grab the rope, and take out another full arm's length of rope and set it behind the neck. Continue these motions over and over again until about 3 meters (10 feet) of rope are left uncoiled (figures 5.6, *b-d*).
- Wrap the uncoiled rope around the folded wings from the bottom up. The number and location of wraps is a matter of preference (figure 5.6e).
- Make a bend, or bight, in the free end of the rope and pass this halfway through the top loop formed by wrapping the wings (figure 5.6f).
- Pass the tip of the rope over the top loop and then through the bight (figures 5.6, *g-h*). Pull firmly and then tie and tighten an overhand knot over the bight to finish the coil.

Method 2—Bagging the Rope

- Using a rope tarp or bag, flake your rope into the tarp, remembering to leave the end of the rope tied to a loop on the rope bag to avoid losing it in the flaked rope (figure 5.7).

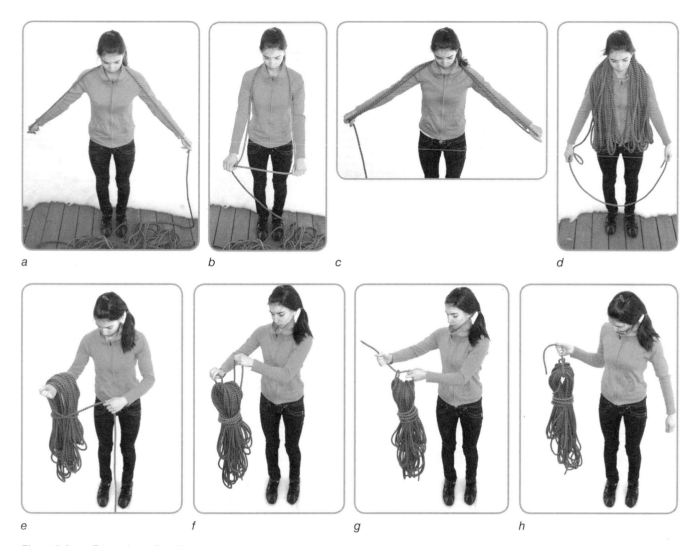

a   b   c   d

e   f   g   h

Figure 5.6   Tying a butterfly coil.
Photos courtesy of Kevin Redmond.

Figure 5.7   Bagging the rope.

- To flake a rope, simply find one end, lay it on the ground, pull the rest of the rope to a point above it, and then let it fall one armful at a time, letting it lie as it lands.
- This ensures that the rope does not get tangled while the climber climbs.

Teaching Cues

- When teaching how to coil a rope, have your back facing the participants, thus avoiding left- and right-hand confusion.
- Although method 2 is easier, a rope bag is not always available and it is helpful to know how to coil a rope.

Activity 6: Tying a Figure-Eight Knot

A figure eight is the most common stopper knot used for tying into the harness. It is strong and it is easy to see if a mistake has been made.

Skill Cues

Single Figure-Eight

- Taking an arm's length and a half of the rope end, fold the rope back on itself to form a bight, leaving the long end on the left-hand side (figure 5.8*a*).
- Keeping the long end in your left hand, twist the bight to the left (figure 5.8*b*). Do this twice.
- Keeping the two twists in place and holding them in the left hand, take the short end of the rope and pull it back to front through the loop that has formed, thus forming a figure eight (figure 5.8*c*).

Double Figure-Eight

After completing a single figure-eight knot, go through the steps again (figure 5.8, *d-g*).

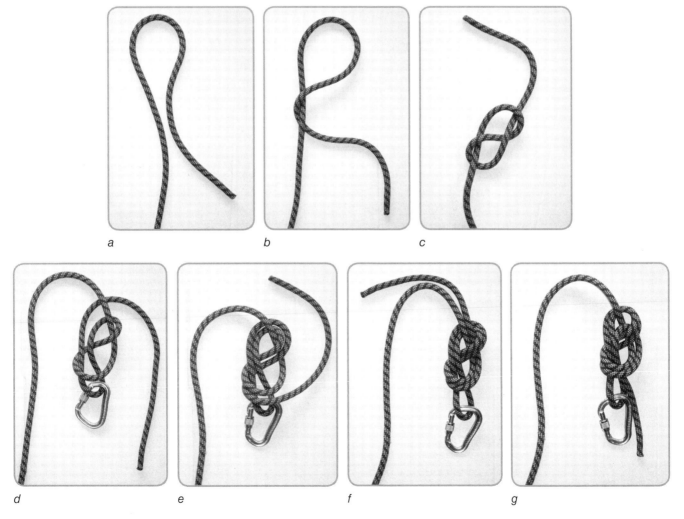

a   b   c

d   e   f   g

Figure 5.8   Tying a figure eight.

Photos courtesy of Kevin Redmond.

Teaching Cues

- It can be easier to refer to the rope as a snake and the end of the rope as the head of the snake that goes through the two twists that the snake makes with its body.
- Another helpful analogy is a snowman:
  - Make a snowman's head (figure 5.8*a*).
  - Choke him (wrap the rope around; figure 5.8*b*).
  - Poke him in the eye (figure 5.8*c*). A common mistake is to poke him in the back of the head.
  - Retrace the first figure-eight knot to tie a double figure-eight (figure 5.8, *d-g*).
- Tie the knot so participants are facing the same direction as you in order to avoid left- and right-hand confusion.

Activity 7: Tying Into the Harness With a Figure-Eight Knot and a Keeper Knot

With basic knowledge of knots, participants can now attach themselves into the harness with a keeper knot.

Skill Cues

- It is essential that participants pay close attention to what they are doing in this activity; any mistake could result in a serious fall.
- Tie the figure eight, making sure that at least .5 meters (2 feet) of rope are between the figure eight and the end of the rope (figure 5.9*a*).
- Thread the rope through the proper tie-in loops that are on the harness, starting from the bottom to the top.
- Pull the knot snug to the top harness loop (figure 5.9*b*).
- Take the end of the rope and follow the exact path of the figure eight, starting at the side closest to the harness and finishing with the strand that comes on the side away from your body (figure 5.9*c*).
- Pull the knot snug and neaten it up. The figure eight follow-through should have two strands of rope that run parallel through the bends of the knot (figure 5.9, *d-f*).
- If it is not a clear eight, then the rope went along the wrong path.
- Next, tie the keeper knot with the tail of the rope. This prevents the figure eight from coming undone.
- Take the loose end and wrap it around the rope twice (figure 5.9*g*).
- Pull the end of the rope through the two wraps, going from the bottom to the top. Pull tight (figure 5.9, *h-i*).
- Attention should be given to every detail and double-checked for safety and security. Accidents can happen if these knots are not tied properly.

Teaching Cues

- Be sure to double-check the knots every time they are tied.
- Ensure that the participants tie into the proper tie-in points on the harness.
- The finished knot should be neat and clearly look like a figure eight.
- Ensure that the participants tie the finishing keeper knot, thus preventing the figure eight from coming undone.

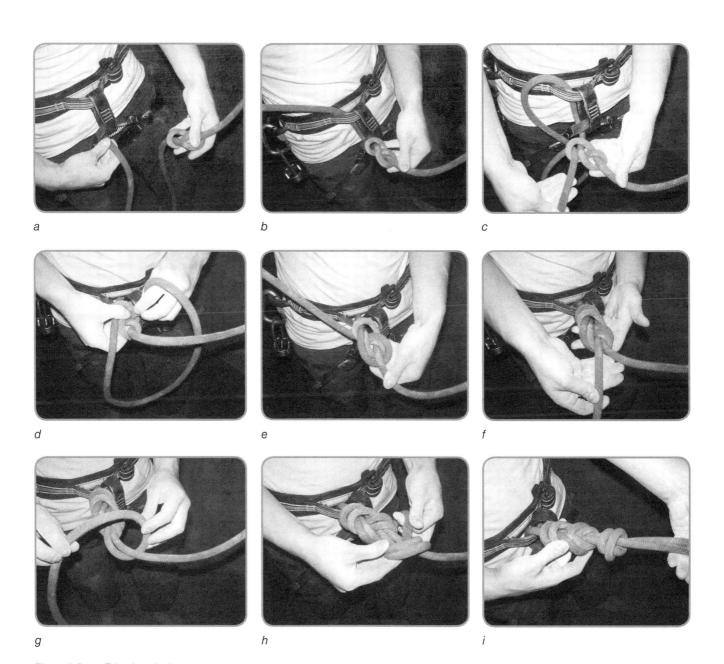

a

b

c

d

e

f

g

h

i

Figure 5.9   Tying into the harness.

Activity 8: Climbing Commands

Clear communication between the climber and belayer is key so that it is well understood what is needed at any given time, helping to prevent accidents. Certain words are chosen for the commands so as to avoid confusion with a like-sounding word.

Skill Cues

- "Climbing" or "Belay on" means that the climber is going to climb and the belayer must start belaying.
- "Climb on" or "Belay on" means that the belayer is ready to belay and the climber is safe to start climbing.
- "Up rope" means to take in any excess slack in the rope.

- "Falling" or "Take" means that the climber will fall and take in any slack and put on the brake hand.
- "Slack" means to loosen the tension rope by letting out a little rope.
- "Watch me" means to watch climbers carefully because they feel like they may fall. This is often said to help the climber feel safe.
- "Secure" means the climber is anchored to another system in addition to the belay that will prevent the climber from falling to the ground.
- "Lower" means that the belayer must lower the climber.
- "Off belay" means that the belayer is finished climbing and either is secure on the ground or is safe at the anchors at the top of the climb and wants off belay.
- "Rock" means that a rock is falling and to move close to the wall to avoid being hit. Most times when a rock falls, it will project away from the wall as opposed to straight down. If the climber is holding the rock, the climber is expected to throw the rock in the direction away from people.
- Sometimes the wind or distance can make it difficult to hear the commands, in which case you should shout extra loud or arrange another method of communication using the rope.

Teaching Cues

Never take climbers off belay if you are unsure of what they are trying to communicate. Unfortunately, this has resulted in accidents.

Activity 9: Belaying

Belaying is holding the ropes for another climber. Belaying is important because the belayer holds the climber's life in her hands. If the climber slips or falls while climbing, the rope will only catch him if someone else is holding the ropes. No climbing is to be done in this activity unless in a gym setting where the ropes are already set up.

Skill Cues

- Participants put their harnesses and shoes on and the climber ties in.
- Participants should understand the appropriate climbing commands and their purpose.
- The belayer must take the rope end that is closest to the tied-in climber, form a bight in the rope, and put this bight through the hole in the belay device (figure 5.10, a-b).
- Pull the bight through the belay device so that the bight is flush with the handle of the belay device.
- Attach a locking carabiner through the rope and the handle of the belay device.
- Attach the carabiner to the belay loop on the harness and then lock the carabiner (figure 5.10c).
- The climber should double-check that the belay device is set up properly and that the gate of the carabiner is locked. The harness should be double-checked to ensure that all buckles are doubled back.
- The belayer should double-check that the climber is properly tied in and that the knot is passed correctly through the tie-in loops and all buckles are doubled back.
- Once safety checks are finished, the belayer tells the climber, "On belay." The climber says, "Climbing."

- If there is a big weight discrepancy between the climber and belayer, anchor the belayer to the ground using something strong such as a tree to prevent the climber from falling farther than necessary.
- Now that both climbers are set up and double-checked, belaying can begin.
- The belayer starts by pulling the slack through the belay device as the partner climbs.
- The belayer uses both hands, one of which is the guide hand, or the hand on the same side of the rope as the climber and the belay device. The other hand is the brake hand and is on the opposite side of the belay device. The brake hand holds the rope from slipping in case of a fall and lowers the climber at a steady, controlled speed when the climb is finished (figure 5.10d).
- Never let go of the rope with the brake hand; the climber's life depends on it.
- Have a third person hold the brake-hand rope farther down as a backup until the belayer feels confident in the skill.
- As the climber goes up, pull the slack through by sliding the glide hand up the rope about 46 centimeters (1.5 feet) (figure 5.10e).
- Bring the brake hand and guide hand up to the same area, keeping the brake hand lower than the guide hand.
- With the guide hand, pinch the rope that the brake hand is holding, remembering to keep the brake hand lower than the guide hand, thus preventing any chance of letting go of the rope with the brake hand (figure 5.10f).
- Slide the brake hand down the rope to the belay device (figure 5.10g).
- It is important to do all of this without the brake hand letting go.
- Keep the brake hand in a locked position below the belay device and behind the hip and thigh when not taking in slack (figure 5.10h).
- Repeat these steps until the climber reaches the top.
- If the climber falls, immediately pull the brake hand to the locked position, as described previously. The belay device takes most of the weight of the climber via friction, but the rope must still be held in the brake position until the climber gives instructions such as "Lower" or "Climbing."
- If the brake hand lets go of the rope in the event of a fall, the rope will quickly slide through the belay device and the climber will plummet to the ground. It is difficult to stop the rope at this point.
- When lowering a climber, do it slowly and steadily so control of the rope is maintained.
- When being lowered, climbers should keep their legs straight and high against the rock to avoid slamming into the rock.
- When the climber has completed the climb and is on the ground, the belay device and carabiner are taken off the belayer's harness, the climber unties, and they switch roles until everyone has had a turn.
- The tension in the rope when belaying should not be so tight that the climber is being pulled up the rock nor so loose that the climber falls more than is necessary. Often if the belay is too loose, the rope will start to fall loose by the climber's knees or feet and the climber will say "Up rope."
- The belayer must pay full attention to the climber while belaying.
- Do not distract belayers by talking to them.

Teaching Cues

- Show an example of belaying before teaching participants how to belay.

- Belaying should be taught step by step, as described in the skill cues.
- Participants must practice belaying before actually climbing.
- It is strongly recommended that participants work in groups of three, with a climber, a belayer, and a spotter holding onto the brake-hand rope for extra security.
- A common mistake when taking in the slack is to use the guide hand to grab the rope below the brake hand. The brake hand cannot slide down the rope without letting go because the guide hand is in the way. The brake hand must not let go. Ensure that the brake hand is held lower than the guide hand when the hands are brought together so the guide hand can pinch the rope.

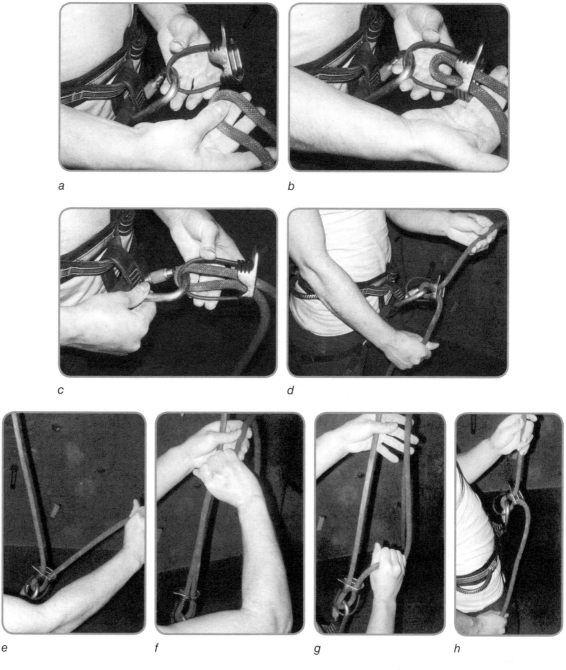

Figure 5.10   Belaying.

- It is vital that participants understand that when they belay, they hold someone else's life in their hands.
- It is necessary to supervise this activity closely for safety.

Lesson Closure

- Constantly reinforce and repeat the importance of safety throughout the lesson.
- It would be helpful to review the material by questioning the participants about the steps for setting up and belaying and why certain steps are important.

LESSON 2
Top Rope and Belaying

Overview

It is common practice to review belaying so as to refresh the participants on each step and to reinforce safety practices. For safe climbing, every participant needs to know how to do the following: Put on a harness, tie a figure-eight knot, tie into the harness using figure-eight and keeper knots, know the climbing commands and their purpose, check a partner for safety, know how to belay, perform rope maintenance, and prevent accidents. These skill sets are not negotiable. This lesson includes setting up a top rope safely outdoors and hands-on belaying and climbing.

Note: If climbing is taking place only inside, learning how to set up a top rope is not necessary.

Learning Objectives

- To learn how to set up a top rope by attaching the rope to an anchor at the top of a climb
- To learn how to set up a belay rope
- To practice belaying technique

Equipment

All previously used equipment plus the following:

- 4 locking carabiners
- 1 sewn sling around 117 centimeters (46 inches)

Risk Management

- Ensure all group members stay together and on the trail to the climbing area.
- Review the importance of double-checking all equipment.
- Avoid playing near or at the edge of a cliff.
- Never go to the edge of a cliff to set up a top rope while insecure (not tied in). Always be tied in to a backup such as a strong, large tree or bolt in case of slippage.

- Never use rusty or spinning bolts for anchors; they should be rust-free, tight, 1-centimeter (3/8-inch) stainless-steel bolts.
- The belayer must pay full attention to the climber while belaying.
- Do not distract belayers by talking to them.
- Never take a climber off belay if you're unsure of what the climber is trying to communicate.
- Never let go of the brake hand while belaying.
- Before setting up, ensure that the rope length is appropriate for the climb so that the climber and belayer do not run out of rope.
- Double-check the top-rope setup to make sure all carabiners are locked, the twist in the sling is done once, and the carabiners are through the correct parts of the sling.
- Always tie a stopper knot in both ends of the rope when rappelling.
- When setting up a top rope, make sure the rope is touching the ground with both ends.

Activity 1: Setting Up a Top Rope

A top rope is when the rope is set up to an anchor at the top of a climb before climbing. Top ropes are relatively safe because if climbers fall, they will fall only a short distance.

The climbing rope runs from the climber to the anchor at the top of the climb and back to the belayer. For simplicity and safety, only areas with top access and already placed permanent bolts are suitable for what is covered in this unit. Top access means that climbers can easily gain access to the anchor of the climb by hiking on easy, safe terrain to the top of the climb. Do not drill bolts for top-rope setup! That goes well beyond the scope of this unit.

Skill Cues

- Ensure that the rope length is appropriate for the climb so that the climber and belayer do not run out of rope.
- Be redundant in any anchor system. Never trust anyone's life to a single anchor.
- Anchors must have at least two good bolts to be suitable for a top-rope setup.
- The bolts should be rust-free, tight, 1-centimeter (3/8-inch) stainless-steel bolts.
- If the bolts are so close to the edge that it is unsafe to reach them, anchor to a tree and bolt before reaching for them.
- Put one locking carabiner through each bolt with the locks facing away from each other.
- Put the sling through each carabiner (figure 5.11a).
- Take the sling that is now attached to both carabiners and separate the sling by grabbing the top, inner part of the sling and twist it once (figure 5.11b).
- Put two locking carabiners through the twisted part of the sling and the untwisted part (figure 5.11c). If this step is not done properly and a bolt fails, the rope and anyone attached will plummet.
- The slings should naturally equalize so there is equal weight on each bolt.
- The angle of the triangle that forms between the sling and two bolts should be no bigger than 90 degrees; 45 degrees is ideal.
- Find the middle point of the rope.
- Put the middle point of the rope through the two lower carabiners.
- Lock all four carabiners.

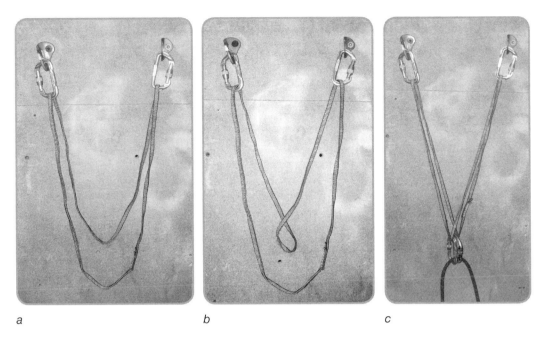

a   b   c

Figure 5.11 Setting up a top rope.

- Tie keeper knots in both ends of the rope.
- Shout "Rope!" to warn anyone at the base of the cliff that the rope is coming down.
- Throw the mostly coiled rope over the cliff. The rope must be thrown outward to prevent it from getting caught in any cracks or snagged on any trees on the cliff.
- Coiling the rope will help it go farther.
- If the rope gets stuck, haul it up and try again. This issue could be resolved when rappelling, but rappelling is not covered in this unit.
- If the rope is running over a sharp edge, the setup will have to be removed and extended by using a longer sling that will go over the sharp edges.
- The extended sling will not be sliding or moving like the rope will be, so it is OK to have the sling over the edge.
- The person who set up the top rope should return to the base of the climb the same way she got up there. Do not rappel; it is not covered in this unit.

Teaching Cues

- It is important that participants remember to lock the carabiners when finishing the setup.
- The twist in the sling is crucial to serve as a backup. If one bolt fails, the other will be loaded, thus saving the climber's life.
- It is necessary to check whether the twist is done properly and to show what happens when it is improperly done. Participants should remove one carabiner from one of the bolts and pull on the two lower carabiners. The carabiners should not fall off but catch in the twist that was put in the sling, thus serving as an essential backup.
- If this step is not done properly because the twist was done wrong or the carabiner was put through the wrong spot and a bolt does fail, the rope and anyone attached would plummet.
- For more details on climbing anchors, check out *Climbing Anchors* by John Long and Bob Gaines (2006).

Activity 2: Setting Up and Practicing Belaying

As with any pursuit, practice leads to better performance and confidence. This activity is sequenced to allow for ample practice time, giving participants more experience in developing their belaying techniques.

Skill Cues

- Follow the instructions in activity 7 of lesson 1 and review by showing a step-by-step example of belaying and going over all safety precautions.
- Participants should work in groups of three, with a climber, a belayer, and a spotter holding onto the brake-hand rope for extra security.
- Participants should put their harnesses on and the climber should tie in and the belayer set up.
- Beware of any large weight discrepancies between the climber and belayer.
- The climber should double-check that the belay device is set up properly and that the gate of the carabiner through which the rope is passed is locked. The harness should be double-checked to ensure that all buckles are doubled back.
- The belayer should double-check that the climber is properly tied in, the knot is passed correctly through the harness, and all buckles are doubled back.
- Climbing commands should be used at all times to ensure clear communication.
- Never let go of the rope with the brake hand—the climber's life depends on it.
- Watch for the common mistake of grabbing the rope with the guide hand below the brake hand, which results in the brake hand letting go.
- The belayer must pay full attention to the climber while belaying.
- Do not distract belayers from their job by talking to them.
- When lowering a climber, do so smoothly and slowly. It will make the trip more comfortable for the climber.
- When the climber has completed the climb and is safe on the ground, the belay device and carabiner are taken off the belayer's harness, the climber unties, and they switch roles until everyone has had a turn.

Teaching Cues

- Participants must understand that when they belay, they hold someone else's life in their hands.
- It is important to supervise this activity closely for safety.
- Pick easy climbs when starting out. The climber will make it farther and will enjoy it more, and the belayer will get more practice at belaying.

Lesson Closure

- Review the steps of setting up a top rope and all safety aspects involved.
- Ask the participants how they feel about their belaying skills.
- Discuss the highlights and fears experienced by the participants.

Belaying Review and Climbing Technique

Overview

It is common practice to review belaying so as to refresh the participants on each step and to reinforce safety practices. Learning basic climbing technique can enable a climber to progress quickly through various levels of climbs. It will help the climber move more efficiently, thus tiring less, recovering faster, and climbing more.

Learning Objectives

- To review belay setup and the practice of belaying
- To understand that for safe climbing, it is critical to establish a sound routine that is grounded in consistent setup and execution of skill
- To understand and apply basic climbing technique such that the participant learns where to put energy for the most efficient use of a maneuver
- To learn to apply focus and precision to footwork and its importance to executing a successful, efficient climb
- To understand that sloppy footwork may result in a foot slipping off and other dangers
- To use good handholds in supporting balance and stability; a well-positioned handhold will make all the difference in whether the climber will be able to hang on

Risk Management

- Review all risk management points from lessons 1 and 2.
- Often accidents occur when climbers start to feel more comfortable with what they are doing, so it is important to continually monitor safety checks.

Activity 1: Setup and Practice of Belaying

For safe climbing, it is critical to establish a sound routine that is grounded in consistent setup and execution of skill.

Skill Cues

- Review all risk management points.
- Following the instructions in activity 7 of lesson 1, review belaying step by step and talk through all safety precautions.
- Participants should work in groups of three, with a climber, a belayer, and a spotter holding onto the brake-hand rope for extra security.
- Top ropes should be set up on as many climbs as possible to shorten waiting lines.
- Safety checks are mandatory on all top-rope setups.
- Climbers should set up for climbing and belaying and do their safety checks before each climb.

Teaching Cues

- When climbers show 100 percent competence in belaying, the group can break into pairs so more climbing can be done.
- Participants should be on full watch for each other's safety and under your supervision.

Activity 2: Basic Climbing Technique

Ability will improve with improved technique. The key to climbing is knowing where to put energy for the most efficient use of a maneuver. Mastery of even basic technique requires practice.

Skill Cues

- Keeping the arms straight while climbing will be less tiring and enable climbers to move around easier because their body won't be so tight to the wall.
- Avoid lock-offs or pulling up with the arms.
- Bring one leg up at a time and move one hand at a time.
- Try to maintain three points of contact with the rock, such as two feet and one hand moving to one foot and two hands.
- Keep most weight on the feet because the legs are much stronger than the arms.
- If your weight is on the legs, you can move the hands from one hold to the next slowly and calmly without needing to grab for the hold.
- Try to stay in balance while climbing.
- Climb mostly with the inside edge of the shoe as opposed to the toe.
- Avoid overgripping the handholds. Concentrating on the feet will help prevent this. A secure foot means a secure mind and thus less overgripping.
- When in a secure position, rest with straight arms, shake out, and lean back a little.
- Before climbing and when resting, look at where the climb goes. Look at the handholds and footholds. Plan the next move. This will help the climb go more smoothly because you know where you're going and will save energy.
- Remember to look for rest positions while climbing and take advantage of them.
- Try to put hands and feet in the positions that they should be in for the next move. This will reduce the amount of foot and hand switching, thus improving skill and speed.
- Relax and remember to breathe deeply while climbing.
- Chalk up often. Climbing chalk absorbs hand sweat and can make a handhold feel less greasy.
- If the forearms get pumped, shake them out between rests while climbing and massage them when finished with the climb.

Teaching Cues

- Have participants do a climb as if they were zombies. Some bending is OK, but the point is to climb with straight arms, thus increasing use of the legs.
- Get the participants to practice three points of contact while maintaining balance. While climbing back and forth on a small section of rock, encourage them to feel the difference in balance when they completely shift the weight from foot to foot.

Activity 3: Footwork

Even something as small as having precise footwork by paying attention to foot placement makes all the difference in executing a successful, efficient climb. Footwork is how you place the foot on the hold. If it is done sloppily instead of efficiently, the foot may slip off.

Skill Cues

- Good footwork is a trademark of the best climbers; it can override strength and help climbers be more efficient, thus having more endurance.
- When placing a foot on a hold, look for the best and biggest spot to step on.
- Do not make the next move until the foot placement is accurate and trustworthy.
- A secure foot placement means less overgripping with the hands.
- Trust the foot placement and the shoes.
- The more shoe is on the rock, the more traction there will be.
- Try to push the body's weight into the foothold.
- Go through and practice footwork drills:
  - Backstep: Place a foot behind the body with the foot on its outside edge, allowing the hip to roll inward closer to the rock.
  - Drop knee: Rotate the knee inside and down, allowing the foot to push sideways on a high hold.
  - Hand–foot match: Place a foot and hand on the same hold.
  - Flag: An extended leg counterbalances the body and prevents the center of gravity from barndooring. Barndooring is when one's body swings out of balance and often results in falling off due to loss of balance, unless one is strong enough to stay on.
  - Rock on: Shift the body weight from one foot to the other.
  - High step: The leg lifts up to reach a high foothold.
  - Backstep: Place a foot behind the leading foot and then move off that foot.
  - Heel hook: Use the heel on a hold to take weight and to move higher. Pull with the hamstrings.
  - Switch feet: Switch the feet while staying on the same foothold.
  - Smear: Where there are no holds, step on the sole of the shoe as opposed to an edge, thus using the friction between the rock and the shoe to step up.

Teaching Cues

- Practice the Quiet Feet game. This exercise will get participants to concentrate on secure, precise foot placements and a controlled climbing style. Participants should climb quietly so as to make as little noise as possible when placing feet on holds. This helps build better footwork because great effort is made to place feet precisely.
- Have participants find small footholds and move between them. Practice putting full weight on the holds, switching feet, matching feet, and crossing through.
- Have participants practice the previous footwork drills while climbing.

Activity 4: Handholds

Support for the climber's balance and stability is not limited to the feet. A well-positioned handhold makes all the difference in whether the climber will be able to hang on.

Skill Cues

- Handholds come in many shapes, sizes, and positions. Big handholds that are close together and positioned with the best part for grabbing on top are ideal, whereas small handholds that are far apart and in an awkward position can make a climb a lot more challenging.
- Try not to grab the handhold tighter than necessary.

- Look at the position of the handhold. Does your hand go on top, on the side, or underneath?
- Look for the best spot on the handhold to grab. Where is it biggest?
- Find the best spot to grab and create an opposing force that will make the hold feel better.
- Change position and balance by turning the hips or chest so you find a position that lets the shoulders do the pulling and maximizes the angle of the handhold.
- Go over types of handholds:
  - Edge: Straight horizontal or slightly angled hold. Can be crimped or openhanded. Crimped means using the fingers in a crimped position with the thumb wrapped over the fingers; it is stressful on the joints but usually stronger. Openhanded is simply hanging with the fingers straight.
  - Jug: Large hold that feels like a bucket.
  - Side pulls: Hold positioned vertically that feels best if grabbed on the side.
  - Gaston: Hold positioned so that the participant must push or lever against the side of it.
  - Pinch: Hold that is squeezed between the fingers and thumb.
  - Pocket: Hold where only one, two, or three fingers can fit.
  - Sloper: Hold that has no real grip or features and is slanted and balloonlike. Hanging with straight arms and under the sloper maximizes the amount of skin in contact with the hold. As you move past slopers, they become harder to hold.
  - Undercling: The best part of the handhold is underneath and feels best when holding it from above.

Teaching Cues

- Have the participants find the various handholds on the rock and practice ways to hold them.
- If climbers are having difficulty in reaching a handhold, suggest moving the body in different positions, finding higher feet, or turning the foot to the outside edge and reaching. Climbing is many times an unsolved puzzle, but beware: Many people prefer to solve the puzzle themselves!

Lesson Closure

- Ask the participants how they feel about the belaying and how confident they feel with their safety checks.
- Ask participants if the technique drills helped improve their climbing.
- Review how technique is just as important as strength in making a difficult climb.

LESSON 4

Bouldering and Games

Overview

Bouldering is a type of climbing where the climber goes no higher than 4.5 to 6 meters (15-20 feet) off the ground. It is one of the simplest styles of climbing because all it requires is shoes and a chalk bag. Most climbers will also bring a crash pad to land on in case they fall. Bouldering can be a solo event, but often climbers are found in small groups. This is a good thing because climbers frequently need a spotter to make a boulder problem safer for them in case they should fall. Boulder climbs are referred to as *problems* as opposed to *routes.* They are shorter and usually have many cruxes or difficult moves that require solving. Bouldering is a powerful style of climbing that requires explosive, dynamic movement as opposed to a static style of climbing.

Spotting is an important part of bouldering safety, and it is important to learn how to spot properly. If there is no outside bouldering area, climbing gyms usually have designated bouldering areas. All risk management still applies to inside climbing.

Learning Objectives

- To experience bouldering where the climber goes no higher than 4.5 to 6 meters (15-20 feet) off the ground
- To apply the safety of crash pads to bouldering
- To understand and apply explosive and dynamic movement as essential components of successful bouldering strategies
- To recognize and apply spotting as an essential skill
- To keep constant attention on the person engaged in activity when spotting
- To participate in a variety of climbing games designed to give climbers a challenge

Equipment

- Crash pads to share among groups of three or four
- Climbing shoes
- Chalk bags

Risk Management

- Always have a spotter and crash pad when bouldering.
- Spot properly to minimize risk for the climber and spotter.
- Move the crash pad to the appropriate landing zone for the climber.
- Be aware that how crash pads are organized can increase or decrease the risks of spraining ankles; watch for overlapping or gaps.
- Warm up well on easier boulder problems; bouldering is often found to be more physically demanding.
- Do not encourage the participants to go higher than they feel safe climbing.
- Have more than one spotter if necessary.
- When climbing down a boulder, use the easiest path and a spotter and crash pad if necessary.
- Take spotting seriously—it is a major method of injury prevention.

Activity 1: Spotting

Spotting is an essential skill. It means keeping constant attention on the person engaged in activity.

Skill Cues

- A spotter is considered the safety net when climbing without a rope.
- The objectives of a spotter are as follows:
  - Soften the fall of the climber.
  - Protect the head and neck.

Figure 5.12 Learning to spot is a crucial skill for safety in bouldering.

– Position the crash pad under the vicinity of the landing zone in case the climber should fall.
– Direct the climber to fall on the crash pad if the climber begins to fall.
– Organize the crash pads so that they cover rocks and there are no gaps or overlaying bulges that could cause an ankle to roll if the climber lands in that area.
• The spotter should keep the arms extended and below the climber's back following the climber as she climbs (figure 5.12).
• If the climber falls, the spotter should ideally catch him under the lats.
• Pay close attention to the position of the climber's body and the direction that she is going to climb so as to have an idea where she may fall.
• If the climber is using a heel hook, spot his back closely because if he falls and the heel stays on the rock, he will fall headfirst.
• Keep the thumbs close to the hand.
• Use more than one spotter for higher boulder problems.
• Use more than one crash pad if necessary.
• Do not touch the climber while she's climbing.
• If the spotter starts to feel uncomfortable with the height of the climber, he can get more crash pads and more spotters and inform the climber that he no longer feels safe spotting her and that she climbs further at her own risk.
• When moving the crash pad, always keep the climber in sight to avoid getting landed on in case the climber should fall.

Teaching Cues

• Try to keep in mind the weight and size differences between spotter and climber.
• Be sure that climbers always have a spotter and crash pad.
• Remind participants that as spotters, they must move the crash pad under the climber.

Activity 2: Bouldering

Bouldering is a great way to practice many climbing techniques and to keep fitness levels up for the sport of climbing.

Skill Cues

• Before starting a boulder problem, have a spotter and crash pad ready.
• Before starting a boulder problem, make sure the participants know where the safest and easiest climb down is and have a crash pad and spotter ready if necessary.
• To prevent injuries, warm up well.
• Bouldering is a relatively simple style of climbing and involves a lot of figuring moves out.
• Look at the hand- and footholds to get an idea of where the problem goes before trying it.

- If the rock is steep, concentrate on engaging the abdominal muscles and pulling down with the toes.
- If you're going to fall, look at where the pad is so you know where to jump, and be sure to bend the legs when landing.
- Do not go higher than you feel comfortable going.

Teaching Cues

- Many boulder problems require patience in order to solve the sequence of movement required to finish the problem.
- The sequence for one participant may not work for another, so it is important that climbers work the sequence out to suit their own climbing style and capabilities.
- It is not uncommon to find the climb down just as hard as going up. For this reason, ensure that a spotter and crash pad are always available.

Activity 3: Games

Games and competitions designed to challenge your personal best are a fun and engaging way to enhance the climbing skills learned in this unit.

Skill Cues

Game 1: Add-On

- Add-On is a game where one climber creates a problem by choosing two handholds to start and moves with the use of two additional handholds.
- The next climber must follow the first climber's sequence and then add on two new moves. The next climber does the previous four moves and adds on two more, and so the game continues.
- A turn is considered compete when the climber sticks the last hold of the sequence and adds two new moves.
- Usually any foothold can be used.
- People are eventually removed from the game if they cannot do the moves already made up or cannot add on.
- The last climber able to do all moves and still add on when no one else is able wins!

Game 2: Blind Climbing

- The participants blindfold themselves and work with a partner to get up the rock.
- Climbing blindfolded is not only fun but can help participants learn how to grab onto a hold because they are forced to feel for the best spot.
- It is not recommended to play this game outside because the landings may not be level and climbers should be able to see where they are going to land should they fall.

Teaching Cues

Game 1: Add-On

- Encourage participants to make easy moves in the beginning so everyone gets a turn.
- The game should traverse the rock and not go high.
- This game requires the participants to pay attention to what the other climbers do.
- It also requires some memory so that climbers can succeed on their turn without asking questions about the next move.
- If many participants get out of the game early on, they could start another game on another part of the rock so there is more climbing and less standing around.

Game 2: Blind Climbing
- The climber's partner should help the climber by telling the climber where the hold is.
- Footwork is just as important as handholds in this exercise.

Lesson Closure

- Ask the participants which kind of climbing they preferred and why. Many reasons are sure to come up, which helps explain why climbers prefer a certain style of climbing.
- Ask the participants to highlight any particular event that helped them appreciate the sport and the environment that they were climbing in.
- Remind participants to always double-check equipment and err on the safe side when climbing.

References and Resources

Long, J., and B. Gaines. 2006. *Climbing anchors*. 2nd ed. Guilford, CT: Falcon Press.

Animated Knots by Grog. www.animatedknots.com.

Climbing Australia. www.climbing.com.au.

Rockclimbing.com. www.rockclimbing.com.

Tradgirl. www.tradgirl.com.

Mountain Biking

▼ Amanda Stanec ▼

When man invented the bicycle he reached the peak of his attainments. Here was a machine of precision and balance for the convenience of man. And (unlike subsequent inventions for man's convenience) the more he used it, the fitter his body became. Here, for once, was a product of man's brain that was entirely beneficial to those who used it, and of no harm or irritation to others. Progress should have stopped when man invented the bicycle.

– Elizabeth West, *Hovel in the Hills* (2000)

Mountain biking is a lifetime activity enjoyed by people of all ages. Though mountain biking competitions do exist, the majority of people who mountain bike do not do so to compete in races. Rather, many people mountain bike for fitness training, for the pure enjoyment of exercising in nature, and for social reasons.

Ideally, adequate resources would allow outdoor leaders to incorporate mountain biking in a way that individualizes instruction for all participants, regardless of experience. Mountain biking is a perfect activity to introduce to young people because it is a lifetime activity that welcomes all ages and experience levels. By implementing this unit in a safe and upbeat environment, outdoor leaders will open the eyes of many young people to how the outdoors can serve their recreational needs throughout life.

Participants can benefit from a solid mountain biking unit in many ways, both immediately and years down the road. Once basic skills are acquired, participants might be more inclined to join or form a community mountain bike club. This allows participants to extend their active involvement beyond the program. In addition, through mountain biking, participants will improve their cardiorespiratory fitness, leg strength, balance, and eye–hand coordination. Mountain biking is the perfect activity to maximize time spent outdoors and to just enjoy nature.

Where is mountain biking best taught? Anywhere! Glorious trails are not required to teach basic to advanced skills and tricks. Consider purchasing bike sets that rotate among community partners, allowing other people the opportunity to learn mountain biking techniques. The final evaluation should be led by the outdoor leader and could be a group bike ride on a beginner trail.

"It's just like riding a bike!" Some participants will not have ridden a bike in many years, and this is a great quote to get them comfortable with biking. By carefully planning lessons, offering challenges on each skill, and setting a mastery motivational climate (rather than competition among the group), participants will learn new skills and experience great success.

Equipment

Group Equipment

- 1 helmet per participant
- 1 mountain bike with a water-bottle cage mounted to the bike frame for each participant

- Several bikes with cages on the pedals for intermediate participants so they can gain strength on the upstroke of their pedal rotation
- Several bikes with clipless pedals for more advanced participants
- Several pairs of bike shoes in a variety of sizes so participants who are more advanced can begin practicing clipping into the pedal
- First aid kit properly stocked for the activity
- An instructional route card (optional; but due to the potential distances that can be covered, it's encouraged)

Personal Equipment

- Shorts or pants that will not get caught on spokes or obstacles
- Layered clothing for easy temperature regulation
- Padded shorts and other advanced clothing for long rides (optional)
- Sunglasses (to keep unwanted dust away from eyes)
- Sunscreen and lip balm as needed
- Backpack hydration system or water bottle for each participant with participant's name clearly marked
- Bike gloves to aid with gripping and for protection from falls
- Identification so that participants get used to riding with an ID that includes name, address, phone numbers, allergies, and emergency contact person

Equipment Care and Maintenance

- Participants will learn about bike maintenance and should be required to clean and dry their bike at the end of each lesson. Necessary items for cleaning and maintenance include
  - cleaning fluid for washing the bike,
  - degreaser,
  - hand cleaner,
  - chain lubricant, and
  - grease.
- At least one complete set of bike tools is required:
  - Allen wrenches, including a long-handled (20-centimeter) Allen wrench
  - Screwdrivers (flathead and #2 Phillips)
  - Bike-specific wire cutters
  - Chain tool
  - Chain-wear measuring tool
  - Pair of pliers
  - Rubber mallet

- Puncture kit (for standard tires)
- Track pump (to help participants repair a tube on the ride without losing valuable class time)
- Tire levers
- Several floor bike pumps
- Include a spare-parts box that contains the following:
  - Extra tire tubes that will fit the bikes (correct valve size)
  - Tube patches and repair kit
  - Zip ties (electrical ties)
  - Brake pads
  - Chain-joining pins
- Storage for the bikes (e.g., baby barn and approved bike trailer if equipment is to rotate through various community programs)

Site Selection

Participants should first bike around the grounds of the program site so that they can become familiar with their bike and their skill level before moving to the actual location of the program. Trails in this unit should be at a beginner level. Beginner trails are wide, not too steep, and free of major obstacles. In other words, avoid taking participants on advanced rides that are rooted out or have a narrow, single track. Advanced trails are not necessary for incorporating mountain biking into a program. Setting up obstacle courses on the program site is often enough for participants to practice necessary skills that they can transfer to trails:

- Very small logs or blocks of wood provide developmentally appropriate obstacles for practicing stump-hopping techniques.
- Trees or any large pieces of equipment allow for sharp turns, simulating the skills required to steer properly and to gain confidence in steering, balance, and coordination.

Access to mountain bike trails, gravel roads, and so on provide the best conditions for mountain biking. Additionally, hills afford the opportunity to learn proper pedaling and balance technique while ascending and descending.

Social Skills and Etiquette

Participants need to become familiar with hand signals. Mountain bikers often are required to bike through towns in order to reach trails from their homes. Thus, proper knowledge of bike etiquette both in traffic and on trails is necessary for participants to be adequately prepared for a safe and enjoyable mountain biking experience.

- Communication and courtesy: Cyclists must ride on the same side of the road as traffic and adhere to all traffic signals. While riding in a group on roads shared with vehicles, those riding at the front of the pack should shout "Car up" and those riding at the back should shout "Car back" to alert fellow riders of surrounding vehicles. While riding on trails, be aware that the following people have the right of way in the following order: (1) the rider heading uphill, (2) a group of children, and (3) the largest group.
- Environment: Following LNT principles, participants should not leave anything (i.e., food, bike parts) on the trails.
- Trail maintenance: Avoid taking participants on wet trails because this will cause further damage to the trails.
- Tailgating: Never tailgate! Participants should stay far enough behind that if a rider in front crashes or slows down suddenly, they have time to stop. A good rule of thumb is to stay back three bike lengths from the biker ahead.
- Pass with care: Announce yourself well in advance and let the rider ahead of you know that you are coming. Specially, use commands such as "On your left" or "On your right" so that hikers, joggers, and fellow bikers are not startled.
- If open fields are required for skills, outdoor leaders must ensure they have the proper permission to use the space for training.

Risk Management

Several risk management topics must be covered before participants ever sit on a bicycle. The level of risk will vary depending on how outdoor leaders provide practice for participants. For example, learning to steer a mountain bike on an advanced trail would pose great risk for beginner mountain bikers. However, learning how to control a mountain bike on a field or patch of grass at school or community center would not. In addition, it is important that outdoor leaders keep in mind the following:

- Participants cannot mount bikes unless they are wearing properly fitted helmets.
- Helmets that have been involved in an accident should never be used again.

- Participants must know and adhere to proper start and stop signals given by the outdoor leader.
- Participants must know how a bike should fit them and learn how to adjust the bike so that they are able to ride it safely.
- Extra care should be taken to guard bikers from descending rapidly down any rocky or rooted surface.

Unit Organization

Lessons in this unit begin with sizing your bike and move on to actual mountain biking activities on and off the program site. In this unit, participants will learn about mountain bikes and maintenance, steering mountain bikes through obstacles, hopping logs, and proper etiquette on trails. Each lesson provides modifications so that participants of beginner, intermediate, and advanced levels all have the opportunity to learn new skills and improve on previous skills. Outdoor leaders should plan for individualized instruction for participants of all skill levels—beginner, intermediate, and advanced.

Lesson Plans

Lesson 1: Bike Safety and Sizing Your Bike. Certain safety issues should be covered before participants ride the bikes, and this lesson covers these concerns. Participants will learn how to properly fit their helmets and bikes to ensure both safety and comfort.

Lesson 2: Identifying Bike Parts and Bike Maintenance. Because bike shops may not be easy accessible and paying others to maintain bikes becomes costly, it is important that participants learn how to clean and lubricate bikes. In this lesson, participants learn the names of bike parts along with their functions and how to clean and maintain bikes.

Lesson 3: ABC Quick Check, Gear Changing, and Pedaling Technique. In mountain biking, terrain often varies greatly, and riders need the skills to adjust from a rapid descent to a steep climb. In this lesson, participants will learn how to optimize both gear-changing and pedaling technique so they will have confidence when approaching varying terrain.

Lesson 4: Ascending and Descending Hills Without Obstacles. This lesson builds on the previous one whereby the focus is on technique in order to prepare for trails. Key skills taught in this lesson include balancing during ascending and descending, braking, and pedaling on hills.

Lesson 5: Environmental Awareness and Maneuvering Around Obstacles. Teaching riders to respect the trails and environment as well as preparing them to ride on the trails and safely avoid obstacles (e.g., trees, other riders, hikers) are the primary focus of this session.

Lesson 6: Ascending and Descending Hills With Obstacles. In this session, participants first learn safety concerns and technique for riding up and down hills with obstacles. The majority of the session will afford participants time to practice these skills in an authentic environment. It does not matter whether these obstacles are natural (e.g., trees, shrubs) or unnatural (e.g., large cones, any other equipment available to serve as obstacles).

Lesson 7: Hopping Logs and Other Obstacles. Participants learn proper hopping technique and are given time to practice this technique through an obstacle course.

Lesson 8: Small-Group Ride and Etiquette. The larger group will be placed into smaller groups of five to six riders. It is recommended that group members have similar bike control and speed so that all members of the group are comfortable and at ease. Once skill cues and routes are given to riders, they ride the trail while following all proper etiquette.

Terminology

- **cassette**—Consists of different-sized sprockets that are bolted together. Smaller cassette sprockets give the rider a higher and more difficult gear, resulting in maximum speed. The opposite is true for larger cassettes.
- **chain**—The chain allows the back wheel to rotate when the rider is pedaling by attaching the chainset to the cassette.
- **chain ring**—Three of these rings combine to form the chainset. Larger chain rings give the rider a higher and more resistant gear but allow the rider to move faster than the lower chain ring.
- **derailleur (front and rear)**—This component allows the chain to shift from gear to gear.
- **fork**—Connects the front wheel to the bike and controls the front wheel suspension. The more rigid the fork, the less suspension the rider will have.
- **frame**—This is the main part of the bike. The seat, handlebars, wheels, and all other components are added to the frame.

- **gears**—Gears allow the rider to pedal at varying rates of difficulty in order to achieve varying rates of power and speed. The higher the gear, the more difficult it is to pedal. Conversely, the lower the gear, the easier it is to pedal, but less power exists to propel the rider forward.
- **pedal (platform, cage, and clipless)**—Pedals allow the rider to push the cranks around and in turn move the bike chain. Typically, beginner riders use platform pedals (foot sits on top of pedal), intermediate riders use cages (foot sits on top of pedal but toes are in a cage), and advanced riders opt for clipless pedals (cleats clip into a mechanism on top of the pedal). Cages and clipless pedals allow riders to gain power on the upstroke as well as the downstroke.
- **tubes**—Tubes are located in the tire of the bike and are pumped up to varying pressure levels depending on the terrain. Mountain bike tubes are pumped up much less than road bike tubes, although exact ranges depend on the tire. Kilopascals (kPa) or pounds per square inch (psi) ranges are often printed on the tube itself.

LESSON 1

Bike Safety and Sizing Your Bike

Overview

Do not allow participants access to the bikes until they understand all components of bike safety. The intention of this lesson is to build awareness so that participants will have a positive and safe experience. Knowledge is a key aspect in acquiring any skill.

Learning Objectives

- To learn safety cues and guidelines to be followed throughout this unit
- To learn how to properly fit a bike helmet
- To learn how to properly size a bike

Activity 1: Bike Safety—Warm-Up and Introduction

Is it necessary to teach traffic signals and riding safely in traffic during a mountain bike unit? Absolutely! Participants will almost always come across motor vehicles or traffic signs at some point during a mountain bike ride.

Skill Cues

- Always ride on the same side of the road as vehicular traffic (i.e., right side of the road in North America) and use bike paths whenever available.
- Obey all traffic signs and lights just as drivers of vehicles must do.
- Wear a bicycle mirror on your helmet or handlebars when riding on any roads or streets (i.e., anytime you are not on trails).
- Regardless of the location, always look over your shoulder before making a turn and use proper hand signals.
- When riding with others, make your own decision in terms of following or waiting while crossing a street and so on.

Teaching Cues

- Inform participants of the skill cues for this activity and check their understanding by asking questions.

• Remind participants that they will receive an exit slip at the end of the class to measure their understanding of these rules and safety procedures and that they will not be able to ride until they have demonstrated mastery of these topics.

Activity 2: Helmet Sizing

When cyclists wear helmets that fit, they are more likely to avoid serious injury during a crash. Head injuries are the leading reason for serious injuries to children using wheeled equipment. Since the human skull is just 1 centimeter (.4 inch) thick, it can be shattered if a properly fitted helmet is not used.

Skill Cues

• Size: Be sure the helmet sits on the head (should not move around when shaking the head) and that all straps are snug yet comfortable.
• Fit the width of two fingers between the eyebrows and front of the helmet (wearing helmets high on the head is a common mistake).
• Adjust buckles or slides on the side strap so they are right under the ear.
• Tighten the chinstrap until you can fit just one finger between the strap and the chin.
• Have a buddy double-check the fit (figure 6.1).
• Participants present the helmet fit to the outdoor leader.

Teaching Cues

• Style: A single-impact crash helmet is designed to protect the head against a single hard fall. Never use a helmet that has been involved in a previous accident.
• Standards: Make sure that the helmet has a label stating that it meets safety standards of an organization such as CSA (Canadian Standards Association), CPSC (Consumer Product Safety Commission), or Snell.

Figure 6.1   Properly fitted bike helmets.

Activity 3: Bike Sizing

When cyclists ride bikes that fit them well, they are more likely to ride with greater ease and more power (figure 6.2). Thus, it is important that all participants understand how to properly fit a mountain bike so that they can do so after they leave class.

Skill Cues

• Straddle the top tube.
• Both feet should be flat on the ground while wearing shoes.
• When riding a hard tail, about 8 to 10 centimeters (3-4 inches) should be between the tire and the ground when lifting the bike by the handlebars. When riding a full suspension, this distance should be less (2.5-5 centimeters [1-2 inches]).

- Seat height: With the ball of the foot on the pedal, participants should demonstrate a slight bend at the knee when the pedal is at the bottom of the stroke.
- Seat angle: The nose of the saddle should be level with the rear of the saddle.

Teaching Cues

- Have two participants mount bikes (one bike will fit while the other will be slightly big). Ask the rest of the participants to choose which bike fits and explain why this is the case.
- Ask participants to state the steps of properly fitting a bike.
- Remind participants without disabilities to offer peer assistance in bike sizing to those participants who need help. Choose the peer helpers strategically and ensure that peers take turns partnering up with participants with disabilities.

Figure 6.2   A properly fitted bike—note the slight bend of the knee.

Risk Management

- Participants are not allowed on the bike unless they are wearing a properly fitted helmet.
- Participants are not to ride unless they are instructed to do so.
- Do not use helmets used in a previous crash.
- Check each bike before issuing to a participant—make sure the bike is functioning properly.

Lesson Closure

Spread bike safety exit slips (see figure 6.3) on the ground. Ask participants to move to an exit slip and to complete the slip. Once exit slips are collected, verbally quiz participants on the following so that you can revisit items that need reinforcement before the next session:

- What are the steps of helmet fitting?
- How many fingers should fit between the eyebrows and the top of the helmet?
- What side of the road should a cyclist travel on?

Name: _____ Date: _____

1. What side of the road do cyclists always ride on?

_____

2. True or false: Traffic signs do not always apply to cyclists.

_____

3. True or false: Cyclists should always look over the shoulder before turning any direction.

_____

4. True or false: Leaders are responsible for all cyclists behind them.

_____

5. True or false: It is OK to ride without a helmet if you are just going down the road for a few minutes.

_____

6. True or false: Helmet and handlebar mirrors keep cyclists from being startled by traffic or other riders.

_____

7. True or false: Cues such as "Car back" or "Animal up" are helpful for alerting peers of surroundings.

_____

On my honor as a participant at _____, I promise to always follow bike safety rules throughout this unit so I do not put myself or my peers in any unnecessary danger.

_____

(Participant signature)

Figure 6.3　Bike safety exit slip.

From K. Redmond, A. Foran, and S. Dwyer, 2010, *Quality lesson plans for outdoor education* (Champaign, IL: Human Kinetics).

Identifying Bike Parts and Bike Maintenance

Overview

Participants must be able to identify bike parts; wash, adjust, lubricate, and repair bikes; and check for problems before riding. This lesson makes a great rainy-day activity. The bike maintenance part of this lesson should be taught indoors so that small parts do not get lost.

Learning Objectives

- To identify parts of a bicycle
- To be able to wash, adjust, and lubricate a bicycle

Activity 1: Identifying Bike Parts

In order to ride safely, participants should inspect the bike before riding. To do this well, they must be able to identify bike parts. After familiarizing themselves with the diagram provided, participants can demonstrate their understanding of bike parts through an active game.

Skill Cues

- Participants receive a labeled diagram of a mountain bike (figure 6.4) and follow along as the purpose of each part is explained.
- Parts covered include handlebars, gearshifts, suspension forks, tires, pedals, front and rear derailleurs, chains, chain rings, cassettes, brakes, saddles, and frames.

Teaching Cues

- Put participants into groups of two or three on one side of the area with bikes on the other side.
- Call out "Rear derailleur," and the first rider (1) writes down the part on a sticky note, (2) sprints up to the bike (slowing down at a clearly marked boundary before approaching the bike), (3) places the sticky note on the appropriate part on the bike, and (4) returns to the group. Once finished, call out another bike part and the next person will go, and so on (see figure 6.4 for a list of bike parts for this activity).
- When the activity ends, give the groups time to self-evaluate their performance.
- Take a few minutes to discuss each part by having participants explain the purpose of the part.

Risk Management

- Participants should be well spaced so they do not run into one another during this activity.
- Having extra shoes with appropriate soles will help ensure that all participants are equipped with proper footwear for this activity.

Figure 6.4 Mountain bike parts. Shocks will be present only if bikes have full suspensions.

From K. Redmond, A. Foran, and S. Dwyer, 2010, *Quality lesson plans for outdoor education* (Champaign, IL: Human Kinetics).

Activity 2: Bike Maintenance

It is crucial to keep bikes clean so that they stay in good working order. Participants must understand that a mountain ride is not completed until a bike is cleaned at some level—from hosed off to full bike cleaning.

Skill Cues

Participants clean the drivetrain (chain, sprockets, chainset, and derailleurs) in small groups:

- If the chain is dirty, place a little degreaser in a small pot. Dip a cleaning brush into the degreaser and scrub the chain clean (do not remove the chain).
- Degrease sprockets and chainsets next.
- After everything dries, relubricate the chain with drip oil or spray.
- Clean wheels and rims.
- Brakes need to be cleaned depending on the type (rim or disc).
- Clean and oil parts of cables normally in casing.
- Pull the front derailleur over to the largest chain ring, click the shifter as if to change into the smallest sprocket, and release the casing in the same way.

Teaching Cues

- Remind participants to rinse bikes thoroughly to remove all traces of degreaser.
- Demonstrate the cleaning process with a very dirty bike.
- Discuss procedures before and after cleaning.

Risk Management

- Participants must handle parts carefully because some might have sharp edges.
- Personal working areas must remain neat at all times so that no one trips over any equipment.

Lesson Closure

Before the session ends, give each group one index card. Participants are responsible for stating two reasons why bikes should be well maintained. On the other side of the card, participants should record one or two things that they do not understand about the lesson so that you can revisit the topic of bike parts and bike maintenance at the beginning of the next class.

LESSON 3

ABC Quick Check, Gear Changing, and Pedaling Technique

Overview

Changing gears and understanding how to pedal effectively will enable riders to bike faster, longer, and on varied terrain. Everyone can benefit from a deeper knowledge of how to change gears in order to use energy efficiently.

Learning Objectives

- To be able to perform an ABC quick check
- To be able to pedal using an efficient technique
- To know how to switch gears
- To understand what pedaling in a high or low gear means

Activity 1: ABC Quick Check

Riders will have a safer and more enjoyable ride if they perform an ABC quick check before riding. Many bike groups across North America take time to teach beginners the ABC quick check, and though they may differ a bit from one another, the following cues will help riders perform this check.

Skill Cues

- A—Air; check that there is air in the tires.
- B—Brakes; check front and rear brakes.
- C—Chain and cranks; check to see if the chain and cranks are set properly.
- Quick—The quick release is up.
- Check—Do a short ride to make sure the bike is running properly.

Teaching Cues

- Ask riders what ABC stands for.
- Ask why it is necessary to perform an ABC quick check before riding.

Risk Management

- A nonnegotiable rule is that all participants must have a properly fitted helmet before riding (reinforce this with a buddy check and a final check by the outdoor leader).
- Before riding, an ABC quick check must be conducted (leaving out the check, or short ride, this first time).

Activity 2: Pedaling

Once helmets have been fitted and ABC quick checks are complete, participants are ready to mount their bikes and begin learning efficient pedaling technique. It is important that participants have an opportunity to hear a bit about pedaling technique. Never assume that riders know how to properly pedal a bicycle.

Skill Cues

- Toes on the foot pushing downward on the pedal stroke should be slanted up slightly.
- Pedal smoothly and consistently.
- Look ahead at a point well out in front of the front wheel so that you can see if your pedal stroke needs to be modified (increased or decreased) depending on the obstacles.

If using cages or clipless pedals, do these additional skill cues:

- When the pedal stroke is at the bottom of the downstroke, be sure to use a movement similar to wiping dirt off the bottom of your shoe on carpet or grass.
- Lift the heel and drag the foot upward, generating power while the opposite foot is pushing downward.
- Simply move heels outward to clip out of clipless pedals.

Teaching Cues

- Point the toes upward more as they approach the end of the downstroke.
- Demonstrate the motion of cleaning dirt off your shoe.
- A hard burn in the muscles does not mean accurate pedaling, although it can be good depending on the purpose of the workout.

Risk Management

Clear boundaries in an empty parking lot or field should be marked, and participants should understand that they are to ride within the marked boundary lines.

Activity 3: Gear Changing

Set up a bike route that has clearly marked lines along the perimeter of an area at the program site. This bike path should have cones on either side with room for approximately four cyclists to ride next to each other (i.e., very wide; this is the first time some participants have been on a bike in several years).

Skill Cues

- The right-hand lever on the handlebar operates the rear gear (moving the chain across the sprockets).
- The left-hand lever on the handlebar operates the front mechanism (shifts the chain from one chainwheel to another).
- The big chainwheel is for riding along flats or downhill.
- The smaller chainwheels are for riding uphill, into a strong headwind, or with lots of stopping and starting.
- The biggest sprocket is the lowest gear and is for hill climbing and starting.
- Keep pedaling while changing gears.
- Shift the gear one to three notches at a time rather than directly from smallest to biggest.

Teaching Cues

- Remind participants they will have the opportunity to pedal at their own pace while changing gears. This way, instruction is individualized and everyone benefits from the session.
- Have participants practice shifting gears by isolating the proper levers and timing the change for efficient pedaling speed to match the terrain.
- Participants need to be praised for their mastery of the tasks at hand and not the speed at which they travel.
- Ask participants to
  - bike at a pace where they are in control at all times,
  - get into the heaviest gear ratio (big ring with smallest sprocket),
  - get into the lightest gear ratio (small ring with biggest sprocket),
  - shift the gear one to three notches up, and
  - shift the gear two notches down.
- An easy way to avoid participants' confusion when shifting gears is to call out, "Big three, little six," "Big one, little one," and so on.
- Remind participants to look over their left shoulder when making turns.
- Remind participants to announce forward moves to pass someone.
- Remind participants to maintain a safe riding speed—stress comfort and learning proper technique rather than going fast.
- While practicing pedaling strokes, it is best if participants have the opportunity to use platform pedals, cages, or clipless pedals.

Risk Management

Clear boundaries in an empty parking lot or field should be marked, and participants should understand that they are to ride within the marked boundary lines.

Lesson Closure

Figure 6.5 could be used while participants are biking along the perimeter after instruction on proper pedal technique and gear shifting has been given and riders are practicing in a group. You can use this assessment to rate performance so that you can easily identify skill-specific feedback and relay it to the participants. Check the appropriate box when a rider masters the required task (see key).

To close this session, it is helpful to know the success rate of the participants so that you can identify topics that should be revisited next session. Figure 6.6 allows you to examine how well participants have learned the objectives of this lesson.

Name	PEDALING IN A GROUP					GEAR SHIFTING				
	1	2	3	4	5	1	2	3	4	5

Key

Pedaling	Gear shifting
1. Toes are slanted up on the downstroke.	1. Able to shift on command.
2. Pedaling is smooth and consistent.	2. Shifts 1-3 notches at a time.
3. Looks ahead while pedaling.	3. Right hand changes rear gear.
4. Announces presence when passing.	4. Left hand changes front gear.
5. Looks over left shoulder when turning.	5. Shifts to speed up to pass.

Figure 6.5　Pedaling and gear-shifting assessment.

From K. Redmond, A. Foran, and S. Dwyer, 2010, *Quality lesson plans for outdoor education* (Champaign, IL: Human Kinetics).

Name: _____　Date: _____

1. Name two advantages of using clipless pedals.

   a. _____

   b. _____

2. On a scale of 1 (inexperienced) to 5 (experienced), rate your competence with gear shift-ing and pedaling. _____

3. State two things you could do to improve or maintain this self-rating.

   a. _____

   b. _____

4. Why should you shift gears only one to three notches at a time?

   _____

   _____

Figure 6.6　Pedaling and gear-shifting exit slip.

From K. Redmond, A. Foran, and S. Dwyer, 2010, *Quality lesson plans for outdoor education* (Champaign, IL: Human Kinetics).

Ascending and Descending Hills Without Obstacles

Overview

Because mountain bike trails consist of many hills, it is time for participants to be exposed to balance and pedaling techniques in order to ascend and descend hills efficiently. These activities require participants to be on the bikes for a large portion of the session, and they will be participating in several spurts of rigorous activity.

Learning Objectives

- To know how to ascend a hill safely and using proper technique while on a mountain bike
- To be able to descend a hill safely and in control while on a mountain bike

Activity 1: Ascending Hills

Because the heart rate skyrockets while ascending hills, have participants get into groups of two or three for some peer teaching. Once all the skill cues are established, participants break off into their groups and one rider attempts to ascend the hill at a time. When the first rider reaches the top, she waits for the next rider to join her. At this time, the two riders give each other feedback based on the skill cues.

Skill Cues

- Riders need to gain speed while approaching the base of the hill.
- Riders should be in a gear that allows for easy pedaling as they begin riding up the hill.
- Weight needs to be forward (figure 6.7).
- Keep elbows in close to the core of the body.
- Change gears only one notch at a time.
- Perform smooth pedal strokes (i.e., do not stop pedaling).
- Maintain a consistent breathing rate.

Figure 6.7   The rider keeps his weight forward while ascending this hill.

Teaching Cues

- Ask riders to explain the steps of ascending a hill (check for understanding).
- Remind riders to be in an easy gear as they begin ascending the hill.
- Point out to riders that, unlike biking on flats, it is important that they change gears only one notch at a time while going uphill.

Risk Management

- The ABC quick check should be done before riding the bike.
- Because riders will be in groups of two or three, participants should spread out so that groups have plenty of room.

Activity 2: Descending Hills

In this activity, teach participants the proper cues for descending and demonstrate proper technique as they wait at the bottom of the hill. Then, in the same groups as activity 1, participants ride to the top of a wide hill (not on a trail but on an open hill so that everyone can be monitored at the same time). Riders can then ride down the hill one at a time and should be given adequate time to practice. The peers and the outdoor leader should use the skill cues to give skill-specific feedback (both positive and corrective) to group members.

Skill Cues

- Fingers should cover the brake levers so the brakes are easily accessible.
- Riders should not pull the front lever too hard at once; this could cause them to tip over the handlebars.
- Balance weight according to the steepness of the descent (the steeper the descent, the more the rider will have to balance weight to the rear).

Teaching Cues

- Leaning too far forward could cause the rider to fly over the handlebars.
- Leaning too far backward could cause the front wheel to pull back and the rider to land on his back.
- Control speed and control the bike while descending. Encourage beginners to use the rear brakes first, supported with front brakes.
- Riders might want to lower their seat depending on the steepness of the hill.
- Consider using an area where the hill is steeper in some parts than others or only have beginners ride halfway up the hill (or as far as they can).
- Invite intermediate and advanced riders to attempt to ride farther up the hill.
- If desired, have participants perform a peer activity requiring riders to give feedback to one another on ascending and descending technique (see figure 6.8). This will help hold all riders accountable for the skills needed and also offers skill-specific feedback on what needs to be improved to reach mastery.

Risk Management

- The ABC quick check should be done before riding the bike.
- Extra attention should be paid to the brakes because riders will be descending.
- Because riders will be in groups of two or three, participants should spread out so that groups have plenty of room.

Name: _____   Partner: _____

Please check off the appropriate skills that your partner has mastered.

Ascending

☐ Gains speed while approaching hill.

☐ Weight is forward.

☐ Elbows are close to the body.

☐ Changes gears one notch at a time.

Descending

☐ Fingers cover brake levers.

☐ Appropriate balance is maintained.

Set a goal for your partner based on the skills you observed.

Goal: _____

Figure 6.8   Peer assessment.

From K. Redmond, A. Foran, and S. Dwyer, 2010, *Quality lesson plans for outdoor education* (Champaign, IL: Human Kinetics).

Lesson Closure

In the closure of this session, ask the participants the following questions:

- What steps are necessary to ascend a hill efficiently?
- What steps are necessary to descend a hill safely?
- How do you feel physically? Why do you think you feel that way?

LESSON 5

Environmental Awareness and Maneuvering Around Obstacles

Overview

Teaching riders to respect trails and the environment as well as preparing them to ride on trails and safely avoid obstacles (e.g., trees, other riders, hikers) is critical in a mountain biking unit. Activities in this lesson will help participants understand rules that need to be followed so that mountain bikers continue to be welcomed on the trails. In addition, steering technique must to be taught and practiced so that riders can avoid biking into obstacles while on the trails.

Learning Objectives

- To understand how to be an environmentally friendly mountain biker
- To know the techniques for maneuvering the mountain bike around obstacles
- To be able to maneuver a mountain bike at a slow speed around obstacles

Activity 1: Environment

In this lesson, participants will be asked to come up with group trail guidelines, and these should be posted so that they are clearly visible to everyone. These guidelines should remain posted throughout the duration of the unit so that everyone is reminded to be environmentally friendly riders (figure 6.9).

Skill Cues

- Never leave anything behind.
- Ride on open trails only.
- Never spook animals.
- Help keep trails maintained.
- Stay off wet trails.
- Avoid hard braking that tears up the trail.

Teaching Cues

- Quiz participants on their knowledge of skill cues.
- Encourage participants to organize a trail awareness campaign in their school or community.

Activity 2: Steering Around Obstacles

Bike trails vary greatly in the obstacles that exist on them. Whereas beginner trails may have none, others may have several. It is necessary for riders to learn how to maneuver their mountain bikes around obstacles so that they are prepared to ride safely on trails.

In this activity, participants should spread out along a perimeter that consists of two of the following (where possible): grass, gravel, or pavement. In doing so, riders will be exposed to steering around obstacles on varying terrain. All riders should start slowly through the obstacle course. Eventually you should invite those who are demonstrating confidence and success in the skill to speed up through the course. You may want to set up two obstacle courses, one with many obstacles and one with fewer obstacles. Then riders can choose which course they would like to attempt to ride through; typically beginner riders would choose the easier course.

Skill Cues

- Only turn handlebars at slow speeds.
- Lean your body to the side you want to steer (it's instinctive).
- Look ahead so you are aware of what is coming (just as when driving a vehicle).
- Stay focused.

Teaching Cues

- After placing pylons (large and small), balls of various sizes, and large diagrams of animals, participants maneuver around the obstacles.
- Remind participants to focus on maneuvering (i.e., mastery) and not on speed.
- Ask participants how they were able to move around these obstacles successfully.

Risk Management

- All riders must wear a helmet during the biking sessions.

Figure 6.9   The group has developed trail guidelines, and now they are ready to go on an environmentally friendly ride.

- Riders must perform the ABC quick check before riding.
- Encourage riders to focus on mastery of riding around obstacles rather than speed.
- A distance of at least four bike lengths must be maintained between each rider.

Lesson Closure

Upon completion of this session, ask participants the following:

- What was one aspect of steering that you improved on today?
- If a beginner cyclist asked you what are the most important aspects of steering to remember when steering around obstacles, what would you say? (Fill in any points that the group forgets to mention.)

LESSON 6

Ascending and Descending Hills With Obstacles

Overview

Now that proper technique for ascending and descending has been taught, riders need the opportunity to improve their skills because most trails will have obstacles (e.g., trees, hikers, sharp turns). Once riders warm up, direct them to the area where they learned how to ascend and descend hills. Here, riders should be given time to review ascending and descending and practice riding up and down the hill without obstacles. This entire lesson should be devoted to a long warm-up and then lots of practice time for the skills of riding up and down a hill with obstacles.

Learning Objectives

- To state the steps for properly maneuvering, ascending, and descending a hill on a mountain bike
- To effectively maneuver and ascend a hill at the same time
- To effectively maneuver and descend a hill at the same time

Risk Management

- Begin with an ABC quick check as well as a peer check on helmet sizing.
- Give adequate time to warm up on flat ground before taking part in the activities.
- All safety commands (e.g., announce when passing, looking over left shoulder when turning) must be followed at all times.

Activity: Ascending and Descending Hills With Obstacles

Place obstacles (football [soccer] corner flagpoles are ideal, but large cones and other taller objects work well also) in a zigzag formation on the side of the hill where participants are not warming up. In groups of two or three, participants practice riding up the hill one at a time and then descending the hill one at a time.

Skill Cues

- Look ahead approximately 1 meter (3 feet) so there is time to react to obstacles.
- Keep pedaling while ascending.
- Keep elbows close to the core of the body.
- Keep weight forward while ascending.
- Keep weight backward while descending.
- Maintain control while ascending.
- Use handlebars more to steer rather than balance if going at a slow speed.
- Keep hands on brake levers while descending (start slow when first learning to descend with obstacles).
- Keep feet equal on pedal descent (i.e., neither foot should be high or low on the pedal stroke because the rider is not pedaling) to decrease the risk of hitting obstacles.

Teaching Cues

- Invite riders who are more experienced to ride higher on the hill. Riders who are less confident should only be requested to ride up a shorter section.
- Although many obstacles should be placed, riders should only attempt to maneuver around the obstacles as they feel confident to do so. As confidence increases, riders should be required to weave through all obstacles just as they would have to if a tree or other obstacle were on a trail.
- Check for understanding on skill cues before starting
- Reinforce proper balance (see skill cues).
- Remind participants to gain speed before ascending the hill.
- Ask peers to give feedback to their groups and partners.
- This would be a good time to assess the group or use the skill-specific feedback chart (figure 6.10) to offer specific feedback to the riders.

Name	ASCENDING AROUND OBSTACLES					DESCENDING AROUND OBSTACLES				
	1	2	3	4	5	1	2	3	4	5

Key

Ascending around obstacles	Descending around obstacles
1. Gains speed when approaching hill.	1. Descends slowly enough to be in control.
2. Eyes are forward approximately .5-1 meter (2-3 feet).	2. Weight is balanced.
3. Weight is shifted forward.	3. Feet are level to avoid roots.
4. Uses handlebars to maneuver bike.	4. Hands are on brake levers.
5. Gears down one notch at a time.	5. Eyes are ahead to see upcoming obstacles.

Figure 6.10   Skill-specific feedback chart for ascending and descending around obstacles.

From K. Redmond, A. Foran, and S. Dwyer, 2010, *Quality lesson plans for outdoor education* (Champaign, IL: Human Kinetics).

Lesson Closure

- Hold a group discussion at the end of the session and ask the following questions.
  - Why is important to learn how to avoid obstacles on a trail?
  - What is the most important safety concern when descending a hill on a mountain bike?
  - What is one thing you feel you need to improve on while practicing these skills?
- The skill-specific feedback chart (figure 6.10) could be used while participants are practicing. You can use it to rate performance so that skill-specific feedback is easily identified and can be relayed to the participants. Check the appropriate box when a rider masters the required task.

LESSON 7

Hopping Logs and Other Obstacles

Overview

At this point in the unit, many group members will be excited about how much they have learned. To keep these participants from becoming bored, new skills need to be introduced. However, it is important to set up an alternative activity (i.e., an activity of your choice that some riders need more practice on) for those who might not want to attempt hopping obstacles. It is not necessary for participants to successfully hop a log upon completion of this lesson; rather, it is important that they know how to do it. If they do not feel comfortable, they should not try to hop the log.

Learning Objectives

- To state the steps of hopping a log successfully
- To understand the importance of timing in log hopping

Activity 1: Hopping Logs

Participants will learn proper hopping technique and practice the technique through an obstacle course. Participants are given an obstacle (fire logs are ideal) and asked to place it somewhere on the field where they have plenty of personal space. (The field should be dry so the bikes do not tear the ground.) Once skill cues are given, riders spread out and practice hopping the log.

Skill Cues

- Practice lifting the front wheel by riding forward. Just before lifting the front wheel, keep the pedals horizontal, knees slightly bent, and bottom out of the saddle and pull the bike upward in a popping motion. (Note: The log is not being used at all at this point.)
- Add the log.
- Ride to the log.
- Set the front tire on the front of the log by lifting the front wheel using the previous steps and then letting it fall back down on top of the log.
- Continue to pedal to move the front wheel on the log and to propel forward so the back wheel will move up and over the log.
- Try different speeds to determine what speed is best for hopping up on the log.

Teaching Cues

- Remind participants that lifting the front wheel too soon will cause it to hit the log but not allow them to hop onto the log.
- Participants should pedal immediately after setting the front wheel on the log so there is adequate momentum to move the back wheel up and over the log (especially when descending) (figure 6.11).

Risk Management

- ABC quick check and helmet fitting check must take place before riding.
- Introduce participants to hopping on dirt or dry grass so that if they do fall, they will have a softer landing than if they were on pavement.
- Riders should also be instructed to find personal space when necessary so that they avoid other riders.

Activity 2: Hopping Logs Throughout a Course

Participants who did not wish to learn how to hop a log during activity 1 were practicing all other skills through an obstacle course. At this point, all participants come together to the obstacle course, place their logs somewhere on the course, and practice all skills learned to date. The larger the perimeter of the course, the less boring it will be for the group, and it is best if there are some hills in the course so ascending and descending skills can be practiced. Additionally, this activity will afford participants a rigorous cardiorespiratory workout.

Skill Cues

- Reinforce skill cues for activity 1 of this lesson.
- Look over the left shoulder when making a turn.

Teaching Cues

Figure 6.11 After setting the front wheel on a log, pedal immediately to generate enough momentum to get the back wheel over the log, too.

- Set up two courses, one with more hills and many more obstacles than the other. Invite participants to ride through either course. To individualize instruction even more, color code some obstacles (e.g., blue cones are the most difficult) and challenge participants to ride along a particular color course.
- Check participants' understanding of skill cues through guided discovery (i.e., use prompting questions so that students can formulate the correct responses).
- Reinforce all skill cues throughout this lesson, providing skill-specific feedback to participants.
- Remind participants to ride safely and with adequate distance between them and their peers (three bike lengths).

Risk Management

- ABC quick check and helmet fitting check must take place before riding.
- Announce yourself when you're about to pass a peer.

Lesson Closure

Upon completion of this session, ask participants the following questions:

- Were you nervous before learning how to hop a log?
- Are you nervous now?

- What do you think you need to do to become more confident?
- Are you tired?
- On a scale of 1 to 10, how hard do you think you worked?

LESSON 8

Small-Group Ride and Etiquette

Overview

Understanding proper etiquette and being exposed to trails are a wonderful way to conclude a mountain biking unit. A group ride allows participants to demonstrate their respect for the environment and their ability to ride in a group.

Learning Objectives

- To practice skills in a group setting
- To know and practice proper group-ride etiquette

Activity: Group Ride

Throughout this session, the entire group will be placed into smaller groups of five or six riders based on experience. It is best if additional coleaders are available so that each group of riders has an experienced adult present. Once skill cues are given, riders are given time to ride and follow proper etiquette as a group (figure 6.12). Encourage riders to spend the last part of the session cleaning up any garbage that they find on the trail.

Skill Cues

Inform participants of the following information related to group rides so that they will be more confident joining such groups and so they will be positive members of the group.

- Be on time. Many people only have a little time to devote to group rides; respect their time!
- Research the group so that you do not end up with beginners if you are advanced or advanced riders when you are a beginner.
- Communicate in traffic (i.e., "Car back" or "Rider back" means a car or rider is approaching the group from the rear; "Car up" or "Rider up" means a car or rider is approaching from the front).
- "Walker up" means there is a pedestrian on the road or trail ahead; "On your left" means that a rider is about to pass.
- Stay alert at all times and focus on the rider ahead.
- Do not look back; this can cause swerving.
- Move to the back when tired.

Teaching Cues

- Before the ride, check for understanding of all the skill cues.

- Remind riders of the proper cues when approaching them on the trail and so on.
- It makes sense to place intermediate riders in the same group and so on. By placing participants in groups according to their experience and comfort, the pace of the ride will be comfortable and riders are less likely to become discouraged.

Risk Management

- The ABC quick check should be done once all helmets are properly fastened.
- You should be familiar with the trail system. Ideally the trail system would have various levels of trails (beginner and intermediate) and obstacles.
- Avoid rocky and rooted trails because most riders will likely be at the beginner level.
- If riders do come across rocks or roots that they do not feel confident passing through, encourage

Figure 6.12 Stay alert and focus on the rider ahead during a group ride.

them to stop, pick up their bike over one shoulder, and walk around or over the obstacles. Once through, they can remount the bike and continue the ride.

Lesson Closure

Ask riders the following questions to make sure that they understand safety and etiquette commands.

- What should you say if you know a car is coming up behind you?
- What do you say if a hiker is walking toward you on a trail?
- Are you tired? Did you find it difficult to stay alert the entire time?
- Did you remember to give group members cues? If not, why? How did you feel as a group member if a command was not passed along to you?

References and Resources

Allwood, M. 2005. *Mountain bike maintenance: The illustrated manual.* Ontario, Canada: Firefly Books.

League of American Bicyclists. 2008. Beginning cycling: ABC quick check. www.bikeleague.org/resources/better/beginningcycling.php.

National Highway Traffic Safety Administration (NHTSA). 2006. Easy steps to properly fit a bicycle helmet. www.nhtsa.dot.gov/people/injury/pedbimot/bike/EasyStepsWeb/index.htm.

Overend, N. 1999. *Mountain bike like a champion: Master the techniques of America's greatest rider.* New York: St. Martin's Press.

Worland, S. 2003. *The mountain bike book.* St. Paul, MN: Motorbooks International.

Flatwater Canoeing

▼ Kevin Redmond ▼

Wherever there is a
channel for water,
there is a road for
the canoe.

– Henry David Thoreau

Historically, the canoe was a primary mode of transport used by aboriginal people around the world. Today, the canoe is a source of recreational pleasure. Learning flatwater canoeing skills opens the door to exploring the natural world in a variety of settings and conditions. The challenges associated with navigating a canoe safely and with ease are increasingly minimized by developing strong paddling skills.

Flatwater canoeing refers to paddling a body of water that has no currents. When the wind ceases, the water is calm and still. In some areas flatwater canoeing may be called *lakewater canoeing.*

This unit offers a list of basic equipment, risk management tips, skill progressions, etiquette, and introductory lesson plans for flatwater canoeing that may be adapted to personal circumstances and experience. The lessons featured in this unit include the core skill set for flatwater paddling. Developing competency in these skills will enhance efficient paddling and pleasure.

Equipment

Group Equipment

- 1 canoe (5 meters [16 to 17 feet] long) for every two people
- 1 paddle per person
- 1 approved personal flotation device (PFD) with whistle attached per person
- 1 spare paddle per canoe
- 1 bailer per canoe
- 1 throw bag or rescue rope per canoe

Check your national coast guard regulations for a more detailed listing. For example, in the United States, visit the Coast Guard Office of Boating Safety Web site (www.uscgboating.org). In Canada, visit Transport Canada's Web site (www.tc.gc.ca/marinesafety/debs/obs/quick/quick_human_powered.htm).

Personal Equipment

- Spare set of clothes (for dressing in layers to make it easier to warm up or cool down)
- Personal survival kit (optional)
- Personal first aid kit
- Snacks
- Water
- Sunscreen
- Hat
- Sunglasses
- Rain gear
- Camera (optional)
- Kneeling pad (optional)

Equipment Care and Maintenance

- When not using a paddle, stand the paddle against a tree or vertical object so that it cannot be stepped on or broken.
- For extended storage, paddles should be stored hanging and out of direct sunlight and heat.
- Canoes should be stored upside down, preferably off the ground. For extended storage, canoes should be stored upside down on a rack out of direct sunlight.

Site Selection

A variety of teaching environments and methodologies are recommended to ensure success, such as the following:

- Teaching a J-stroke on land and then on a dock before going on the water
- Practicing portaging techniques or discussing hypothermia on land to give participants a physical break between on-water skill sessions
- Discussing a theory topic with canoes rafted up; participants sit up, giving their ankles and knees a break

All sites should minimize exposure to wind as much as possible. If there is wind, an onshore wind is safer because paddlers who are having difficulty will be blown back to their starting point rather than blown away down the lake. A sample listing of sites is as follows:

- Wet session—pool or warm-water lake
- Theory sessions—on land, at a quiet area near the water's edge, or with canoes rafted together on the water
- Flatwater paddling—protected area not severely affected by wind

Social Skills and Etiquette

It is important that all participants and outdoor leaders contribute to a positive learning environment. With this in mind, respect is the norm for all circumstances. Social skills and etiquette should reduce fear so that optimal learning may occur.

- If using private property such as access to water, dock, or beachfront, ask permission first.
- No splashing or horsing around.
- Communicate with your paddling partner before you move.
- Offer positive feedback to your paddling partner when he does something well.

Risk Management

Managing the risk associated with flatwater canoeing demands a thorough understanding of factors that may affect safety, such as participant skills and maturity, equipment, site, air temperature, water temperature, water conditions, and weather conditions. Risk management is a fluid process that must be continually monitored and the program adjusted accordingly.

- Before participants are accepted into the program, it is important to verify their comfort level in water over their head while wearing a PFD. This can be done by verifying swim credentials or holding a swim verification session in a pool or lake.
- Monitor participants' personal comfort and adjust the activity schedule to allow for water-in and water-out breaks, sunscreen, physical breaks for knees or ankles, dressing up or down, and any other relevant considerations.
- When in the canoe, paddlers should paddle on opposite sides of the canoe at all times unless directed otherwise.
- Canoes stay within the designated area. A designated area may be marked out with buoys or identified by features specific to the area (such as by saying "Between these three docks," "Within this cove," "Not past the two points of land," and so on). Participants should not go beyond the area where the leader can maintain voice contact and make a timely rescue in the event of upset. A general rule of thumb for beginning groups is approximately 6 to 10 canoe lengths (30 to 46 meters [100-150 feet]) from the outdoor leader. This distance is a guideline and may be adjusted depending upon the skill level

of the group and the wind and water conditions. For example, in cold water conditions cut the distance in half, thereby minimizing the distance required to carry out a rescue.

- When paddling from point A to point B, all canoes stay between the lead and sweep canoes. The lead and sweep canoes should contain the group, allowing for approximately one canoe length between canoes.
- Communication is the key to a dry and enjoyable paddling experience. Any movements or changes should be discussed with your paddling partner and initiated on a cue understood by both paddlers.
    - For example, paddler A is uncomfortable and wishes to shift her weight. She may say something to the effect of, "Shifting my weight to the left gunwale on three: One, two, shift."
    - Paddlers may wish to change paddling sides. An appropriate comment would be, "Change sides on three: One, two, change."
- Learn the whistle code:
    - One whistle blast = Stop! Wherever you are, stop, look, and listen.
    - Two whistle blasts = Stop! The person who blows the whistle can raise a paddle to indicate where to go.
    - Three whistle blasts = Stop! Emergency! Go quickly toward whoever blew the whistle and raft up together; there is an emergency at hand.
- Under no circumstances should participants in flatwater canoeing instruction be exposed to moving water (rivers) without adequate training by a qualified instructor.

Unit Organization

This unit is best presented with a wet session (lessons 2, 3, and 4) followed by an on-water skills and dry session. If you have additional outdoor leaders, it is efficient to organize lessons 2, 3, and 4 as stations that operate concurrently, with participants completing a station and then moving to the next station (see figure 7.1). For a group with up to 10 participants, lessons 1, 2, 3, and 4 are an average of 45 to 60 minutes long; lessons 2, 3, and 4 may be combined into a 1- to 2-hour pool or warm-water lake session.

When paddling for extended lengths of time, inject instructional information, demonstrations, or short theory sessions between paddling sessions and practice.

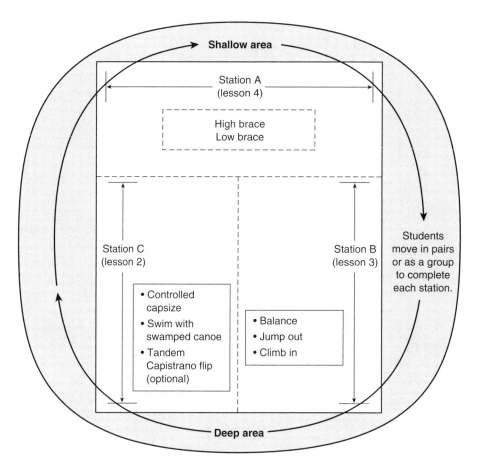

Figure 7.1   Participants can rotate clockwise from one station to the next.

If lessons 2, 3, and 4 (wet lessons) are not a reasonable option, doing lessons 1, 5, and 6 with the addition of a T-rescue demonstration (and practice if possible) in lesson 4 is a practical alternative.

Lessons 5 and 6 may last from 1 to 3 hours each depending on the detail and expectations. Lessons 1, 5, and 6 work well as a full-day field trip.

In the lessons on paddling skills (lessons 5 and 6), turning strokes are the first skills introduced. Rationale for this progression is that the canoe will turn naturally and hence introducing the turning strokes first offers the highest probability for success. This will work well if water conditions are good. In the event of significant wind, it may be necessary to introduce a combination of turning (for the bow paddler) and steering (for the stern) strokes at the start of the first on-water session.

Lesson Plans

Lesson 1: Equipment Fitting, Entries, and Exits. This is an introductory lesson for getting started.

It begins on land with proper equipment selection and fitting, essential terminology, and how to carry canoes to and from the waterfront, and it finishes with canoe entries, proper paddling position, and exits.

- PFD fitting
- Paddle selection and parts
- Canoe anatomy
- Tandem suitcase carry
- Tandem overhead carry
- Entering and exiting a canoe
- Three-point kneeling position

Lesson 2: Getting Wet to Get Comfortable. The focus of lesson 2 is a controlled capsize of the canoe. For most people, their first capsize is a frightening event. One of the main outcomes of this lesson is to help participants become comfortable with capsizing and to feel in some degree of control because they know what it feels like and they know what to do when it occurs.

- Controlled capsize
- Swim with swamped canoe
- Tandem Capistrano flip

Lesson 3: Balancing, Jumping Out, and Climbing In. The focus of lesson 3 is to become more comfortable with the limits of canoe stability by pushing the limits in a controlled environment. This is followed by jumping out of and reentering the canoe, the latter skill being essential in most rescue scenarios involving canoe capsize.

- Balancing a canoe
- Jumping out of a canoe
- Climbing back in a canoe

Lesson 4: Rescues. The focus of lesson 4 is first on self-rescue strokes used to avoid canoe capsizes. Should these strokes fail (resulting in capsize), then the self-rescue tandem Capistrano flip and assisted T-rescue are introduced. By the end of this lesson, all participants should be familiar with T-rescue victim procedures and protocols, and hopefully some participants will be comfortable performing the rescue for others.

- High brace and pry brace
- Low brace
- T-rescue

Lesson 5: Introductory Turns, Pivot Spins, and Sideways Displacement. The canoe has a natural tendency to turn. By introducing turning strokes first, participants are more likely to experience success. This lesson introduces stationary turning strokes. Once competency in these strokes is achieved, participants learn to move the canoe sideways using the same strokes in different combinations.

- Forward reverse paddle turn
- Standing draw
- Push-away
- Pry
- Sideways displacement
- Pivot spins
- Rafting up

Lesson 6: Paddling Circles and Straight Lines. This lesson introduces the strokes required to control the tendency of a moving canoe to turn and to keep the canoe going in a straight line.

Paddling in a straight line makes going between two points more efficient and less work for the paddlers.

- Stern sweep
- Stern J
- Paddling a straight line
- Canoe tour

Terminology

- **bailer**—Open-ended container used for removing water from a canoe, such as a bleach bottle with one end cut off.
- **beam**—Width of a canoe when measured at its widest point.
- **bilge**—The rounded portion of the hull joining the bottom and sides of the canoe.
- **blade**—The part of the paddle between the throat and tip that is normally used to move water and thus move the canoe.
- **bow**—Forward extremity of a canoe.
- **deck**—The enclosed area over the bow or stern of a canoe that increases the strength of the canoe.
- **displacement**—The amount of water displaced by a floating vessel.
- **freeboard**—The distance from the top of the water to the top of the gunwale at the lowest point of the gunwale (closest to the water); should be a minimum of 15 centimeters (6 inches).
- **grab loop**—Loop of rope on the bow or stern of a canoe that is useful for grabbing onto in an upset.
- **grip**—Top part of the paddle that the upper hand holds.
- **grip hand**—Hand holding the grip of the paddle.
- **keel**—A strip or extrusion along the bottom of a boat to prevent sideslipping. The keel makes it easier to keep the canoe going straight but also makes it more difficult to turn.
- **personal flotation device (PFD)**—Used to aid flotation when a person is immersed in water.
- **power face**—Face of the paddle blade that exerts pressure on the water.
- **shaft**—The rounded handle of the canoe paddle between the grip and the blade.
- **shaft hand**—The hand holding the shaft of the paddle.
- **stern**—The rear end of a canoe.

- **throat**—The area of the paddle where the shaft meets the blade.
- **thwart**—Narrow board that joins gunwales on opposite sides of the canoe.
- **tip**—Bottom edge of the paddle blade.

- **trim**—The angle at which a canoe rides in the water.
- **yaw**—When a canoe swerves from its course.
- **yoke**—A modified thwart in the center of the canoe used as a shoulder rest to carry a canoe.

LESSON 1

Equipment Fitting, Entries, and Exits

Overview

Before getting in a canoe or on the water, it is important to be properly geared up and have a basic understanding of canoe terminology. This lesson begins on land before moving to the waterfront or dockside. The purpose of this lesson is to get participants ready for on-water skills and maneuvers.

Learning Objectives

- To fit PFDs securely and check others for proper fit
- To select a paddle of the proper length and style
- To identify the parts of a paddle
- To identify the parts of a canoe
- To perform the tandem suitcase canoe carry
- To attempt to perform the tandem overhead lift and carry (depending on age and strength)
- To demonstrate proper canoe entry from dockside or waterfront
- To demonstrate the three-point kneeling position
- To demonstrate a proper exit from the canoe

Activity 1: PFD Fitting

PFDs are important to the safety of all participants. An improperly fitting PFD will not perform as intended, with potential consequences of panic and even drowning.

Skill Cues

- PFDs should be snug around the upper body when out of the water and when in the water.
- When in the water, if the PFD rides up in the user's face when all fasteners are fitted and secured, a smaller PFD is required.
- If not in the water, a partner should be able to pull up on the shoulder straps of the PFD without the PFD riding up in the wearer's face.

Teaching Cues

- Demonstrate the difference between a properly fitting PFD (can't pull it up in front of the paddler's face) and an improperly fitting PFD (can be pulled up in front of the paddler's face).

- Have participants check each other to ensure proper PFD fit by pulling up on the shoulder or collar of the PFD. If the PFD comes up in the user's face, it is too loose; readjust the PFD to fit correctly or seek the proper size.

Risk Management

- Do a visual and physical PFD fit check before going on the water.
- If time and conditions permit, have participants test their PFD fittings by going in water over their heads.

Activity 2: Paddle Parts, Selection, and Care

The paddle (in conjunction with the paddler) is the equivalent of the engine and rudder of a boat. Selecting the proper paddle should provide the best results for the least effort.

Skill Cues

Identify Parts of a Paddle

Refer to figure 7.2.

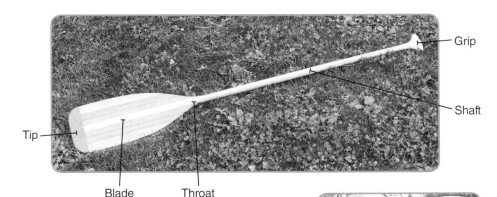

- Grip—top part of the paddle made comfortable for holding, pushing, and pulling
- Shaft—rounded part of the paddle between the grip and throat
- Throat—top, narrowing extension of the blade that joins the blade and shaft
- Blade—part of the paddle that exerts pressure on the water
- Tip—bottom edge of the paddle blade

Figure 7.2 Parts of the paddle.
© Human Kinetics

Select Paddle Length

There are two common methods for selecting the proper paddle length:

- Stand the tip on the ground. The grip should come between the chin and nose (figure 7.3).
- Holding the grip and throat of the paddle with the shaft resting on top of the head, the elbows should be at right angles (figure 7.4).

Storing Paddles

- Paddles should be stored upright and out of the sun when possible.
- For short amounts of time, they may be stored under an overturned canoe or standing against a tree or vertical object to ensure no one walks on them.
- When using the paddle, avoid pushing off the bottom with the grip, and only use the tip if it has additional protection for that purpose.

Teaching Cues

- Identify the parts of a paddle and then quiz participants.
- Demonstrate two ways of selecting proper paddle length before allowing participants to choose their paddle.
- Discuss ways to take care of paddles.

Figure 7.3 Standing a paddle on the ground (or your toe), the paddle should reach between your chin and nose. This is the most common method of selecting a paddle.

Figure 7.4 Selecting a paddle by holding it over your head ensures correct shaft length. Elbows should be at right angles for the best fit.

Risk Management

Space participants at least a liberal paddle length apart so that they may avoid being struck by a stray paddle.

Activity 3: Canoe Parts

Knowing the parts of the canoe is essential to understanding what is taught because the terms will be used throughout the unit.

Skill Cues

Review the main parts of the canoe shown in figure 7.5 and the following definitions.

- Bow—front of the canoe
- Stern—back of the canoe
- Gunwale—rail on the top edge of the sides of the canoe
- Bilge—rounded part of the canoe between the bottom and sides
- Keel—ridge along the center of the bottom that helps the canoe maintain a straight line (not present in all canoes)
- Bow seat—seat in the front of the canoe
- Stern seat—seat in the rear of the canoe
- Center thwart or yoke—perpendicularly connects the gunwales in the center of the canoe
- Bottom—the bottom of the canoe
- Ribs—small, riblike structures that go across the bottom of some canoes to maintain strength and structure of the hull

Teaching Cues

- Point out the parts of the canoe while on land.
- Point to the parts and have participants name them.

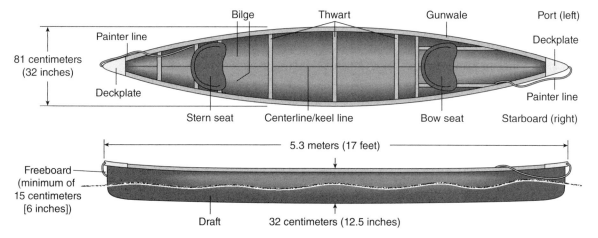

Figure 7.5 Basic parts of a flatwater canoe.

Adapted, by permission, from M. Wagstaff and A. Attarian, 2009, *Technical skills for adventure programming* (Champaign, IL: Human Kinetics), 500.

- Match every person in the group to one or two parts of the canoe and make them responsible for teaching others about their part and function. Participants could have their canoe parts as their nickname for the session.
- Play a game of What Am I? Group members ask leading questions to discover the identity of a part. The person who guesses correctly chooses the next part.
- Note that the normal length of canoes for tandem use is between 5 meters (16 feet) and 5.3 meters (17 feet).
- In addition to identifying the canoe parts, this is a good opportunity to compare types of canoes, especially if you are dealing with an older audience that may be interested in purchasing a canoe. Different canoes are available for different purposes.
  - Flatwater canoe: It's wider for carrying a load, has a flat bottom for stability, and sports a keel to ease straight-line travel.
  - Moving-water canoe (for rivers): Designed for ease of turning to avoid hazards; hence has a narrow, rounded bottom and no keel.
  - Multipurpose canoe: Suitable for use on flats and rivers.

Risk Management

Ensure adequate clearance to allow for tipping the canoes over when highlighting the canoe parts.

Activity 4: Tandem Suitcase Lift and Carry

Compared with most watercraft, the canoe is relatively lightweight with an average weight between 30 and 36 kilograms (65 and 80 pounds), allowing the canoe to be carried to the water's edge, around hazards, and between water systems. The purpose of lifts and carries is to portage the canoe with minimum risk and effort. The two basic carries in order of difficulty for this activity are the tandem suitcase and tandem overhead (activity 5). Select the carry best suited to your group and move quickly toward getting on the water.

Skill Cues

- Partners face the same direction (direction of intended travel).
- Partners are on opposite sides of the canoe.
- Partners are at opposite ends of the canoe.
- Placing the near hand under the deck, on cue (e.g., "One, two, three, lift") lift the canoe and walk.

Teaching Cues

- This carry is used for short distances.
- Give a quick demonstration and then let participants try it.
- The extension tandem suitcase lift and carry prevents the canoe from banging the leg near the canoe. Instead of lifting the deck, place the hand under the stem (near bottom of the canoe) and lift.
- If time is short, skip activity 5 (Tandem Overhead Lift and Carry) and go directly to activity 6.

Risk Management

Keep the side of the canoe against the thigh to prevent the canoe from striking or banging the knee or hip.

Activity 5: Tandem Overhead Lift and Carry

The tandem overhead carry is more energy efficient and comfortable than the suitcase carry, making it suitable for longer portages. Good technique and teamwork in lifting the canoe overhead are more important than strength, making the overhead lift and carry accessible to most participants.

Skill Cues

- Both partners stand on the same side of the canoe next to their paddling bay.
- Facing the paddling bay, lift the near gunwale up, resting the bottom of the canoe on the thighs.
- The arm toward the stern of the canoe goes between the legs and supports under the bilge.
- The hand toward the bow reaches across, holding the far gunwale with the thumb inside.
- On cue (e.g., "One, two, three, lift"), lift the arm on the bilge while pulling the far gunwale, rolling the canoe onto the back of the neck.
- Reverse the process for bringing the canoe down.

Teaching Cues

- The tandem overhead carry is used for carrying canoes over longer distances.
- Focus on technique to minimize the importance of strength.
- When bringing the canoe down, bring the canoe to the thighs to avoid dropping or damaging the canoe.

Risk Management

- Participants must have enough arm and shoulder strength to support the canoe overhead without the canoe falling on their heads (with the probable consequence of neck strain).
- Weak participants should use a light canoe to develop skill and technique; if a light canoe is not available, they should avoid the activity.

Activity 6: Entering and Exiting the Canoe

Getting in and out of a canoe comfortably is a refined skill due to the higher-than-desired center of gravity, which can cause instability. Performing this skill appropriately is important to stay dry and avoid injury.

Skill Cues

- Start with the canoe adjacent to the dock.
- The partner who is not entering the canoe holds the canoe as close as possible to the side of the dock where the person is entering or exiting the canoe.
- The partner in the canoe holds the canoe in place for the partner to enter or exit or has the paddle in the water at a low-brace ready position.
- To enter the canoe, hold the near gunwale with the same hand (i.e., left hand on left gunwale) and step to the center of the canoe, maintaining contact with the gunwale (figure 7.6).
- As the second foot steps in the canoe, the other hand should take hold of the other gunwale.

- Transfer weight to the hands holding the gunwales as weight is taken off the feet to shift into the three-point kneeling position.
- Use reverse procedure for exiting the canoe.

Teaching Cues

- Have stern paddlers enter the canoe first; they can see the bow paddler entering.
- Place the paddle across the gunwales the person enters, or if this is uncomfortable, on the bottom of the canoe and get the paddle once stabilized.
- Create a chain that moves forward—enter or exit stern and then move to enter or exit bow.
- Try having the bow person be the first in the canoe.
- Debrief participants on how it feels different when the bow person is first in the canoe and then the stern person enters. Ask what feels more comfortable.
- An extension of this activity is pushing away from the dock as the second paddler enters the canoe and when perpendicular to the shoreline.
- The second person practices getting in the canoe, holding the gunwales, one foot in the center of the canoe, and pushing away from the dock or shore with the other foot.
- Another extension of this activity is to place a butter tub filled with water on the center thwart (thwart must be flat, not round, for this to work) and challenge participants to enter and exit the canoe without spilling water.

Figure 7.6 Entering the canoe, place hands on the gunwales as the foot steps to the middle of the canoe.

Risk Management

- Due to the shallow water and adjacent hazards, a fall or capsize near the shore can be dangerous.
- Ensure the canoe is held in place as the paddler enters to avoid the splits and the person falling in the water or hitting the dock. Because the side of the canoe is rounded, it is safer if the person holding the canoe maneuvers the end of the canoe as close to the pool or dockside as possible while the partner gets in.

Activity 7: Tandem Three-Point Kneeling Position

A stable, comfortable paddling position is important for performing skills and minimizing the risk of capsizing.

Skill Cues

- Knees are spread and in the bilge of the canoe.
- Bottom is against the seat (figure 7.7).
- Keep a low center of gravity and wide base of support.

Figure 7.7 Tandem three-point kneeling position: The knees are positioned in the bilge as the bottom rests against the seat.

Teaching Cues

- The three-point kneeling position is so named because there are three points of contact between the paddler and the canoe.
- While in the three-point kneeling position, you should feel locked in with the boat.
- Practice rocking the canoe while holding the poolside or dockside; verify the stability of the position.
- If participants use a kneeling pad, ensure that the pad does not slide and destabilize them.
- Paddlers should always paddle on opposite sides of the canoe unless otherwise directed.
- If partners are going to change sides, they should communicate first and then change on cue, as in, "Change on three: One, two, change."
- As participants become more comfortable and begin to perform more advanced strokes and maneuvers, they may wish to put their hip against the gunwale on their paddling side while in the three-point kneeling position. This should be done by both paddlers at the same time so that the canoe is balanced.

Risk Management

When rocking the canoe while holding the poolside or dockside, make enough contact to avoid capsizing in shallow water and striking your head. This activity can be made safer by tethering the canoe, moving it to deep water away from obstacles.

Activity 8: Over-and-Under Balancing

Over-and-under balancing is not an essential activity for this lesson or unit, but it is a fun activity to finish a lesson with and it reinforces principles of balance.

Skill Cues

- Three or four paddlers in one canoe stand up and with their legs spread apart, they try to pass a ball alternating over the head and under the legs.
- Feet should be spread apart with one foot in each bilge of the canoe.
- Before beginning, make sure the canoe is in deep water and out of range of other canoes or hazards.

Teaching Cues

- Give a quick demonstration (on land or in canoe) and get participants going.
- Continually monitor canoes to ensure they are spread apart in deep water with no danger of participants striking anything in the event of capsizing.

Lesson Closure

Review the lesson with the participants. Use the following questions and topics to reinforce learning, verify understanding, and offer feedback.

- Why is it important to wear a properly fitted PFD?
- What should you look for when fitting a PFD?
- Identify five parts of the paddle.
- Identify the parts of the canoe (leader points and participants name the parts).
- What is the difference between the tandem suitcase carry and the tandem overhead carry, and when are they used?

- What are the steps for entering and exiting a canoe?
- Where do you think the three-point kneeling position gets its name?

After this lesson, participants should have a reasonable recall for basic terminology and be practiced in activities for getting geared up and on the water.

LESSON 2

Getting Wet to Get Comfortable

Overview

Lessons 2, 3, and 4 (the wet lesson sequence) are invaluable and stand on their own as a nonpaddling introduction to canoeing. These lessons are full of memorable experiences to last a lifetime.

The purpose of lesson 2 is to deliberately capsize a canoe and swim or hand-paddle a swamped canoe. In practicing these activities, participants learn how to put themselves back in control, thereby reducing the fear and anxiety associated with the loss of control experienced in a canoe capsize. For most people, capsizing a canoe for the first time is a scary or ambivalent feeling at best.

This lesson should be done in swimwear and a PFD to ensure participants maintain a basic comfort level. For people who are interested in a more realistic experience, the next progression is to do the activities wearing normal clothing or paddling apparel.

Learning Objectives

- To capsize a canoe
- To enter a swamped canoe
- To swim with a swamped canoe
- To attempt a Capistrano flip

Risk Management

- Establish a 3-meter (10-foot) safe zone around the canoe free of obstacles and hazards.
- If painters are attached to both ends of the canoe, they can be held to maneuver the canoe into a safe area.
- Encourage participants to maintain contact with the high gunwale to avoid being struck by the canoe when it flips.
- Remind participants to relax their legs, floating them out from under the seat. A panic exit often wedges feet and legs under the seat, increasing anxiety and risk.

Activity 1: Capsize Canoe

The anxiety associated with capsizing a canoe for the first time should be presented as a normal feeling. The purpose of practicing the canoe capsize is to reduce anxiety so that participants begin to initiate self-help and rescue procedures immediately instead of being frozen with fear!

Skill Cues

- Begin in standard three-point kneeling position.
- Hold gunwales and tip the canoe to one side after counting together: "One, two, tip to right (or left)."
- Increase tipping motion until the canoe flips over.
- Maintain contact with the upper gunwale to decrease the risk of being struck by the gunwale.

Teaching Cues

- Until participants have experienced numerous capsizes and are comfortable, any capsize should be strictly under the participants' control.
- Participants should plan which side they will tip toward and count, such as "Tip to the left on three: One, two, tip."
- Once participants are comfortable capsizing, extensions may include the following: Controlled swamping of the canoe, capsizing the canoe while maintaining contact, flipping the canoe quickly, capsizing the canoe while extending the body away from the canoe, and capsizing the canoe while keeping the head out of the water.
- Further extensions of this activity include the following:
  - Balancing (lesson 3, activity 1, on page 238) may be done before the capsize.
  - Climb in a swamped canoe and swim or arm paddle the canoe.
  - Some overturned canoes will maintain an air pocket with enough headroom for participants to breathe comfortably while under the overturned canoe.
  - See how many participants can fit in the canoe before it swamps or tips.
  - Once braces are learned, use braces to prevent capsizing.
  - Teach the freeboard concept: When paddling, there should always be a minimum of 15 centimeters (6 inches) freeboard, or distance from waterline to gunwale (see figure 7.8).
  - "Cramalotin," as in, cram a lot of people in a canoe (canoe should be strong and durable to avoid possible damage). The objective is to fill the canoe with people one at a time until it swamps or capsizes. Add up the total weight to illustrate what the canoe can hold before capsizing or being swamped.
  - With participants, calculate the safe payload of a canoe. (Hint: Load participants in the canoe to the minimum freeboard mark and add the total body weight in the canoe.)

Figure 7.8   Freeboard, the distance from waterline to gunwale, should be a minimum of 15 centimeters (6 inches).

Risk Management

- Establish a 3-meter (10-foot) safe zone around the canoe free of obstacles and hazards.
- If painters are attached to both ends of the canoe, they can be held to maneuver the canoe into a safe area.
- To avoid being struck by the canoe when it flips, encourage beginning participants to maintain contact with the high gunwale. Note that as students progress past the high and low brace, they will be asked to keep their hands on the paddle in the event of a potential capsize and use the paddle to actively attempt righting the capsized canoe.
- Remind participants to relax their legs, floating them out from under the seat. A panic exit often wedges feet and legs under the seat, increasing anxiety.

Activity 2: Swim With Swamped Canoe

Swimming with a swamped canoe exposes the characteristics of the canoe when it is full of water. Different canoes react differently when full of water. It is important to recognize and adapt to the characteristics associated with various canoe designs and materials. Knowing how design and material affect flotation when capsized can make rescues quicker and easier. This activity allows participants to learn these characteristics in a hands-on manner.

Skill Cues

- Approach the center bay entry point headfirst, keeping the legs and feet as close to the surface of the water as possible.
- Place one hand on the near bilge or bottom of the canoe to help drive the body in and over the gunwale.
- Once hips are inside the gunwale, roll over (to the same side as the hand that was placed on the bilge), planting the body in the bay.
- Once seated on the bottom in the canoe, spread arms and legs wide to stabilize the canoe for a partner to enter using same technique.
- Use arms and hands to paddle the canoe forward and backward.
- This technique is similar to but easier than climbing in a canoe (lesson 3, activity 3) when it is empty of water.

Teaching Cues

- Larger people may need to place a hand on the bilge or bottom of the canoe to help get in and over the gunwale.
- The canoe may be stabilized by the partner if necessary.
- When in the swamped canoe, practice paddling forward, paddling backward, and turning the canoe.
- An alternative method of swimming with a swamped canoe is for paddlers to stay outside the middle of the canoe. Reaching across the canoe, hold the wrist of the partner's opposite arm (e.g., left wrist of one partner and right wrist of the other partner); then use legs and the free arm to swim with the canoe. This method is useful when one partner is unconscious.
- Other extensions of this activity include the following:
  - Use paddles to paddle a swamped canoe.
  - Tip the canoe and roll out.

– If tipping over, roll out and under into the air pocket; this is the setup position for the tandem Capistrano flip (activity 3). This progression should only be done with canoes that contain enough flotation to afford an adequate air pocket.

– Have a tub race where swamped canoes paddle a distance or figure eight, competing for time.

Risk Management

• A canoe full of water has enough inertia when moving to seriously injure a person who is pinned between the end of the canoe and a wall or obstacle. All participants should stay away from the moving canoe.

• Participants practicing this activity have a responsibility to exercise good judgment and decision making as to what direction to paddle in, how far to paddle, and when to stop or slow down.

• If the outdoor leader is intending to practice tipping over, roll out and under into the air pocket; as a setup position for the tandem Capistrano flip (activity 3) it is recommended that the outdoor leader practice this skill in advance to ensure canoes that will be used by students contain adequate flotation to create a sufficient air pocket when upside down. If the air pocket is small or shallow and the bottom of the overturned canoe is pressuring the mouth or nose underwater, then the activity should be avoided or more adequate canoes should be sought for the activity.

Activity 3: Tandem Capistrano Flip

The tandem Capistrano flip is a quick and effective means of bailing and righting a swamped canoe when in water over your head. Although all participants may wish to give it a try, those with a strong, continuous kick are more likely to be successful.

Skill Cues

• Both partners are in the water facing each other, with the large center bays overhead.

• One gunwale must be above the waterline to break the air pocket (otherwise the canoe will act as a huge suction cup and the task will be impossible).

• Using a continuous egg beater or whip kick to project themselves as high as possible, partners count "One, two, three, push up" to a predetermined side and flip the canoe right side up.

Teaching Cues

• Emphasize the importance of trying the activity and understanding how to do it. It may be enough to talk another person through it. Not all participants will be successful.

• Have everyone try it. They may not get it, but they will learn the process.

• A fun competition is to flip with the least amount of water.

• Another fun competition is to free the canoe of all water.

• Once you do the Capistrano flip, climb in the canoe and then bail it empty.

• Try the flip solo from one end of the canoe; this will work best with canoes that have flotation in the stems.

• Compare the tandem Capistrano flip rescue with the T-rescue for effectiveness, time, and efficiency.

Risk Management

- Ensure an adequate air pocket can be created under the overturned canoe.
- Ensure participants are comfortable in the air pocket under the overturned canoe.
- While participants are in the air pocket, they should maintain a conversation (or tap the canoe at regular intervals) so onlookers know they are OK.

Activity 4: Sink the Navy

This is an optional activity that may be added if time and conditions permit. Water and air temperature should be warm, which makes this an ideal activity for a warm summer day at camp.

Skill Cues

- Using hands, bilge pumps, or containers such as jugs or bailers, get as much water in other canoes as fast as possible.
- Participants are not permitted to hold onto other canoes or bail water from their own canoe.
- Canoes must stay in the defined area (may be marked with buoys).
- Canoes may work together to focus efforts on the canoe with the least amount of water.
- Paddles may not be used to flick water.

Teaching Cues

- Demonstrate and explain the rules of the game.
- Monitor constantly for safety and rule adherence.
- Participants who are uncomfortable with water in their face or tipping over should be allowed to opt out of the activity in an honorable fashion; they may volunteer to help referee.
- Paddles may or may not be used to flick water; this is your call. If canoes are in close proximity, which is desired, it is safer to not use paddles.
- Set a time limit if necessary or play until the canoe swamps; this activity could last half an hour.

Lesson Closure

- The skills learned and practiced in this lesson have strong value even if they are not perfected.
- Reviewing this lesson may include what participants have learned, as well as how they could share this learning with others. For example, two young participants unable to perform the Capistrano flip may be able to explain the skill quickly to two physically mature paddlers who can perform the skill efficiently.
- Discussing the challenges, solutions, and relevance of these activities for oneself and others is important for participants as they learn that when they are in trouble, they can put themselves in some control of the situation by contributing to their own rescue.

LESSON 3

Balancing, Jumping Out, and Climbing In

Overview

This lesson helps participants develop an appreciation for the limits of the canoe and expand their comfort zone for what they can do in a canoe.

Learning Objectives

- To demonstrate proper balance from kneeling and standing positions
- To jump out of the canoe and maintain contact with it
- To climb back in the canoe without tipping it over or adding excessive water

Risk Management

Ensure there is a 3-meter (10-foot) safe zone around the canoe that is free of obstacles and hazards.

Figure 7.9 Balancing in the bow of the canoe by spreading the feet in the bilge and looking forward.

Activity 1: Balancing

Good balance in a canoe reduces the risk of unplanned capsize. Having a wide base and adjusting the center of gravity to manipulate balance are the foundations of maintaining stability when paddling. With experience, participants will continually and subconsciously fine-tune balance in their canoes, applying the principles learned in this activity.

Skill Cues

- One paddler gets in the three-point kneeling position.
- Partner moves from a kneeling to a standing position; holding gunwales may assist balance while standing up.
- Once standing, feet should be spread apart and in the bilge (rounded corner that joins the bottom and side of canoe) and arms may be held at the side or out (figure 7.9).
- Begin rocking the canoe by applying pressure from one foot to the other, and as comfort level improves, increase the rocking motion.
- Eyes should focus on a distant spot (e.g., horizon line or spot on a wall).

- The upper body should remain vertical over the center of gravity while the legs move to apply pressure for rocking and maintaining balance.

Teaching Cues

- Encourage communication (e.g., standing on three: "One, two, standing"; rocking canoe on three: "One, two, rocking").
- Arms may be spread for balance.
- People in the standing position look at a fixed point for reference to aid balance.
- Try to keep the upper body in position and absorb rocking motion with the legs.
- Take turns balancing the canoe.
- Do the activity with and without paddles for the person not balancing.
- Compare the comfort level of standing (in control) versus kneeling (reactionary).
- If participants have completed braces (lesson 4), have the person in the kneeling position hold a paddle, ready to brace if necessary.
- Balancing, jumping out, and climbing back in the canoe can all be linked into one activity.

Activity 2: Jumping Out of the Canoe

Jumping out of the canoe teaches participants how to properly exit a canoe in deep water.

Skill Cues

- Move one step ahead of the seat.
- Feet are in the middle of the canoe, a comfortable distance apart for a jump.
- Both hands are on the gunwales.
- If jumping to the right side, the thumb on the right side must point out (away from the canoe).
- When turning the thumb out, ensure it follows the direction (in front of the arm or behind the arm) in which the person intends to jump. The "rule of thumb" is that the body has to follow the thumb. The starting thumb position for both hands is on the inside of the gunwale. If the participant is jumping out of the canoe on the right side, then the right thumb must be on the outside of the gunwale when they jump. To get the thumb from the inside of the gunwale to the outside of the gunwale, the jumper has two choices: either turn the right thumb clockwise (forward) or counterclockwise (backward). If the thumb is moved in a clockwise direction, then the jumper's body must follow in the same clockwise direction, which means the body will jump ahead or forward of the right arm or hand as it maintains contact with the canoe throughout the jump. Alternately, if the thumb is moved in a counterclockwise direction, then the jumper's body must follow in the same counterclockwise direction, which means the body will jump behind or backward of the right arm or hand as it maintains contact with the canoe throughout the jump.
- Both jumpers agree to which side of the canoe they will exit (should be opposite sides).
- Both people jump at the same time on cue: "One, two, jump."
- Once in the water, use voice communication to make sure the other person is OK.

Teaching Cues

- When turning the thumb out, ensure it follows (in front of the arm or behind the arm) the direction in which the person intends to jump.

- For clarification, the thumb position and jump direction should be rehearsed before getting in the canoe.
- To maintain contact with the gunwale, the body must follow the direction the thumb took when it was turned out (figure 7.10).
- Challenge participants to execute the jump so that they maintain contact with the canoe and keep their heads out of the water.

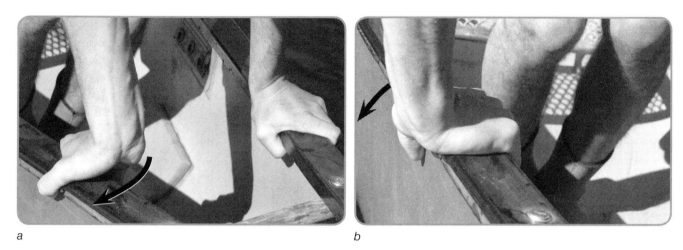

a   b

Figure 7.10   Jumping *(a)* in front of the forearm and *(b)* behind the forearm. The body must follow the direction in which the thumb turned.

Risk Management

It is critical that the jumpers be one step ahead of their seat to avoid kicking the seat with their heels when they jump. Practice jumping straight up and down (staying in the same position inside the canoe) while keeping contact with the gunwales and ensure distance is adequate.

Activity 3: Climbing Back in the Canoe

This activity teaches participants how to climb in a canoe when in deep water. This is an important skill for getting back in the canoe after capsizing.

Skill Cues

- Approach the center bay entry point headfirst, keeping legs and feet as close to the surface of the water as possible.
- Place one hand on the near bilge or bottom of the canoe to help drive the body in and over the gunwale.
- Once hips are inside the gunwale, roll over (to the same side as the hand that was placed on the bilge), planting the body in the bay.
- When both partners are in the water, the role of the person not climbing in is to control the high gunwale to make it easy for the other person to climb in without the canoe swamping.
- Once in the canoe, maneuver into a comfortable, stable position, supporting the canoe as the second person reenters the canoe.

Teaching Cues

- If possible, have participants grab the far gunwale of the canoe to help pull themselves into the canoe.

- Larger people may need to place a hand on the near bilge or bottom of the canoe to help them get in and over the gunwale.
- There are two ways of expressing the essential skill cues: Climb in over the gunwale (associated with reaching the far gunwale), or bring the gunwale in under your hip (associated with placing a hand on the near bilge or bottom of the canoe).
- Whatever hand is farthest into the canoe, roll to the opposite side.
- A good progression is to practice with a swamped canoe (lesson 2, activity 2) for anyone that may have difficulty.

Risk Management

It is not unusual for this activity to result in bruises on the hip or thigh from making contact with the canoe upon reentry. Anyone with a medical condition exasperated by bruising (e.g., anyone on blood thinners, hemophiliacs) should be excluded from or have the option of sitting out this activity.

Lesson Closure

With a little practice, entry-level paddlers can become adept at the skills of balancing, jumping out, and climbing in a canoe. As confidence grows with these activities, participants become more willing to extend their paddling positions and stroke techniques.

- Have participants share strategies that worked for balancing, jumping out, and climbing back in the canoe.
- As other skills are taught, ask participants to relate the value of these skills to further learning. For example, learning the limits of the canoe through the balancing activity may lead a participant to comfortably extend a draw stroke outside the canoe, keeping the paddle shaft vertical longer and making the stroke more efficient and effective.

LESSON 4

Rescues

Overview

Rescues are an effective means of recovering from the unexpected. It is important that participants take responsibility for themselves by initiating self-rescue procedures in the event of a mishap. Creating a proactive mentality helps eliminate dependence on others and being a victim. The high and low braces are self-rescue righting strokes that avoid the need for assisted rescue.

Learning Objectives

- To demonstrate proper technique for the high brace and pry brace
- To use the high or pry brace automatically when the canoe tips away from the paddling side (pry brace may be referred to as a *righting pry*)
- To demonstrate proper low-brace technique

- To use the low brace automatically when the canoe tips toward the paddling side
- To perform the T-rescue as victim and rescuer

Activity 1: High Brace and Pry Brace

The high brace and pry brace are used to stabilize the canoe when it tips toward the nonpaddling side. Either stroke may be used; the high brace is more traditional and the pry brace is a more recent skill (and is considered more effective by some experts). Participants may be introduced to one or both of these strokes, but the ultimate goal is to become competent with at least one of the strokes.

Skill Cues

High Brace

- Begin the stroke as for a standard draw with longer reach and lean.
- Paddler leans out to the paddling side, grabbing water in a pulling motion.
- The paddle is as vertical as possible.
- Pulling in on the blade should tilt the canoe hull back to the desired position.
- The paddle remains in the water until the canoe is stabilized.

Pry Brace

- Hips and legs flex with boat movement and the upper body remains vertical over center of gravity—no exaggerated leans with this stroke.
- As the canoe tips away from the paddling side, knife the paddle, placing the blade flat and deep against the bilge.
- Pry the shaft off the gunwale to right or stabilize the canoe (figure 7.11).

Teaching Cues

High Brace

- A high brace is similar to an outrigger.
- Emphasize keeping the upper body outside the canoe if possible.
- Demonstrate the stroke with exaggerated body lean.
- Participants learn first in a three-point kneeling solo position with the outdoor leader tipping the canoe from behind and the paddler reacting with the appropriate brace.
- When the canoe hull tips away from the paddler, the leader calls "High" or "Pry" (depending on the brace being used).
- Once both paddlers know high and low braces, practice and repeat together on cue ("One, two, three, brace"), with one paddler initiating with

a

b

Figure 7.11 Stabilize the canoe by *(a)* initiating the pry brace and *(b)* completing the pry brace as the canoe returns to stable position.

low braces and the other responding with the high or pry brace. They then play a game where at any point one paddler initiates a low brace and the partner must react with a high or pry brace.

- Encourage frequent practice of these strokes to make them automatic reactions.
- Entertain the possibility of the air brace, which occurs in big waves or radical tips where the paddler attempting to execute the high brace catches nothing but air, often resulting in a wet wake-up! The air brace introduces the possibility that in some situations a pry brace might have worked.
- A whitewater paddle may be used when learning braces to minimize risk of paddle damage or breakage.

Pry Brace

- Participants learn first in a three-point kneeling solo position, with the outdoor leader tipping the canoe from behind and the paddler reacting with the appropriate brace.
- When the canoe hull tips away from the paddler, the leader calls "High" or "Pry" (depending on the brace being used).
- Once both paddlers know high and low braces, practice and repeat together on cue ("One, two, three, brace"), with one paddler initiating with low braces and the other responding with the high or pry brace. Then they play a game where at any point one paddler initiates a low brace and the other must react with a high or pry brace.
- Practice both the high and pry brace so participants can choose for themselves later.
- Encourage frequent practice of these strokes to make them automatic reactions in real situations.
- Entertain the possibility of the air brace, which occurs in big waves or radical tips where the paddler attempting to execute the high brace catches nothing but air, often resulting in a wet wake-up! The air brace introduces the possibility that in some situations a pry brace might have worked.

Activity 2: Low Brace

The low brace is used to stabilize the canoe when it tips to the paddler's side. It is a wonderful realization for participants when they believe that this stroke actually works and can save them from complete capsize.

Skill Cues

- The paddle strikes the water nearly horizontal, with knuckles facedown (figure 7.12).
- The force is applied to the back face of the paddle by the shaft arm after the grip hand hits the water.
- The shaft of the paddle should be perpendicular to the keel line of the canoe.
- The paddle slices out of the water after the canoe is stabilized.

Teaching Cues

- Start with a simple slap brace.
- Make sure the grip hand touches the water before the shaft hand.

Figure 7.12 Knuckles down and the paddle flat to apply pressure for the low brace.

- Place the paddler in the canoe solo. The outdoor leader tips the canoe from behind and the paddler reacts to the tip with the appropriate brace.
- Some water entering the canoe is acceptable.
- Teach and practice the technique in waist-deep water before trying it in the canoe. This is a good progression if weather and water conditions permit.
- After the paddle sinks, bring it back to the surface (can alternate low and high brace).
- Progress into a sculling low brace.
- Use whitewater paddles for learning the low brace to minimize the risk of paddle damage or breakage.

Activity 3: T-Rescue

The T-rescue (also called *canoe-over-canoe rescue*) rights an overturned or swamped canoe and helps victims reenter their canoe.

Skill Cues

- Confirm that victims are OK.
- If possible, victims aid the rescue by helping get the canoes in the T-position.
- If victims are not aiding the rescue, they go to opposite ends of the rescue boat and talk back and forth such that rescuers can hear them and know they are OK.
- Maneuver the rescue boat into a T-position with the victim canoe (figure 7.13).
- Turn the victim canoe upside down.
- Tip the victim canoe slightly to one side to break the air pocket.
- Pull the victim canoe's deck up near the gunwale of the rescue canoe.
- Continue to slide the victim canoe across the gunwales of the rescue canoe until it is halfway across.
- Rescuers pull and lift the near gunwale of the victim canoe toward themselves.

Teaching Cues

- During the demonstration, take time to break down each stage: Establish the T-position, break the air seal, set the deck of the victim boat on the gunwale of the rescue boat, pull the victim canoe (upside down) across the rescue canoe gunwales, right the canoe, and slide it back into the water.
- Place the victim canoe adjacent (parallel) to the rescue canoe.
- Victims climb back in the canoe one at a time while the victim canoe is supported by rescuers.
- If paddlers are young or lacking strength, practice together to effect the rescue.
- Work toward practicing rescues for efficiency and speed.
- Progression is to work toward the victims assisting the rescue where possible at the request of and discretion of the rescuers.
- If flotation is in the stem of the victim canoe, the rescuer may stand, lifting near the stem, and right the victim canoe without pulling it in over the rescue canoe. This is higher risk but faster.

Risk Management

Victims should stay at the end of the rescue canoe while it is being emptied of water so as to avoid being caught in between canoes.

a

b

c

d

e

Figure 7.13   T-rescue: *(a)* Form the *T* and break the seal. *(b)* Pull the canoe across the rescue boat. *(c)* Turn the canoe right side up. *(d)* Return the canoe to the water. *(e)* Support the canoe for re-entry.

© Human Kinetics

Lesson Closure

Rescues are important to canoeing safety. In a controlled learning environment, participants are often encouraged to push the envelope in an effort to facilitate greater learning. Effective rescues minimize the risk associated with making mistakes throughout the learning process, and those making mistakes provide practical learning opportunities for others as they practice and refine rescue skills in a variety of real situations.

From the beginning, encourage participants to initiate self-rescue techniques such as bracing in unstable conditions. In the event of capsize, victims should demonstrate proactive procedures (e.g., get the victim canoe ready for the rescue canoe) and a positive mentality: "If it is to be, then it's up to me!"

LESSON 5

Introductory Turns, Pivot Spins, and Sideways Displacement

Overview

The canoe has a natural tendency to turn. Introducing turning strokes in the first on-water session improves the likelihood of participant success. Furthermore, the strokes in this lesson are performed while the canoe is stationary, creating a more controlled and defined learning environment.

Stationary turns are used to turn the canoe when it is not moving. These turns help beginning paddlers line up the canoe in any desired direction or intended line of travel. The skills in this lesson will not only allow participants to turn their canoe but also increase their repertoire of skills for making the canoe move sideways.

Learning Objectives

- To demonstrate the forward reverse paddle turn from both ends of the canoe
- To demonstrate the standing draw and push-away or pry
- To demonstrate stationary pivot spins
- To demonstrate sideways displacement, keeping the canoe parallel with the starting position
- To raft up canoes on cue so they are all pointing in the same direction

Risk Management

With the pry, if the thumb and forefinger hold the shaft to the gunwale, there is a risk of skin being pinched. The alternative is to keep the shaft hand above the gunwale, but this increases the degree of difficulty.

Activity 1: Forward Reverse Paddle Turn

The forward reverse paddle turn turns the canoe quickly and easily toward the stern paddler's paddling side. This is the easiest and quickest turn for beginning paddlers to learn. If conditions are less than ideal (windy), this turn should be introduced first. If calm conditions exist, the forward reverse paddle turn may be introduced before or after draw and pry strokes.

Skill Cues

- Bow paddler paddles forward.
- Stern paddler reverse paddles (figure 7.14).
- Open the power face of the paddle for greater boat reaction.

Teaching Cues

Figure 7.14 To turn the canoe, the bow paddler paddles forward, and the stern paddler paddles in reverse.

- Give instructions and a demonstration; then get participants performing the maneuver as soon as possible.
- Turn the canoe a full circle using the forward reverse paddle turn.
- To improve efficiency and effectiveness of the turn, both paddlers can open the power face of the paddle.
- As participants become more proficient, they can try this maneuver while moving.

Activity 2: Standing Draw

The standing draw moves the canoe toward the paddler's side. Some use the analogy that the paddle is planted in concrete and the canoe is pulled to the paddle.

Skill Cues

- The grip hand remains relatively stationary and extended outside the gunwale (the farther outside, the greater the boat reaction).
- The paddle is planted outward from the hip with the paddle face facing the paddler.
- Keep the paddle shaft as vertical as possible (figure 7.15).
- Pull the paddle smoothly toward the side of the canoe, keeping the blade parallel with the keel line of the canoe.
- Rotate the blade 90 degrees before it reaches the side of the canoe. Slide the blade outward toward the extended position (grip thumb should be turned outward, away from the face).
- Full blade should be in the water in the power phase of the stroke.
- Rotate the blade 90 degrees to original position; the blade may be half out of the water in this recovery phase.
- The canoe should move smoothly toward the paddler's side without forward or backward movement.

Figure 7.15 A vertical paddle shaft ensures efficient power in the draw.

Teaching Cues

- Encourage a long reach out with the top hand (make a window or box with torso, arms, and paddle shaft).
- Stroke should be rhythmic and dynamic.

- There should be no significant disturbance on the surface of the water if the full blade is in the water.
- If the stroke is done correctly, bubbles will appear on the nonpaddling side of the canoe; water should go under the canoe rather than splash against the side.
- If both paddlers draw simultaneously, the canoe should do a stationary pivot spin without rocking.
- The grip hand should be loose, relaxed, and stationary (acting as a pivot point) outside the gunwale.
- Both the draw and push-away use an equal distance, stroke, and pressure from the pivot point.
- If the canoe is rocking, paddlers check to ensure that they both initiate the draw at the same time, they soften the power phase until the paddles are close to vertical, and their grip hands are stationary outside the gunwale.
- If the grip hand is moving, look at the grip hand and keep it stationary outside the gunwale.
- If the stroke is weak, make sure the whole blade is in the water.
- Practice spinning the canoe in one place with both paddlers performing the same stroke. This can be confirmed by a stationary person on shore who extends an arm, pointing the index finger at the middle of the canoe. If the finger remains pointing at the middle of the canoe as the canoe spins, then it is a perfect stationary pivot.
- Do a rosette—raft all canoes together, pointing in the same direction.
    - All the stern paddlers put their paddles aside and hold the two canoes on either side until they complete a circle.
    - All bow paddlers draw on the same side (left or right) and the rosette containing all the canoes should spin in the direction of the paddling side.

Activity 3: Push-Away and Pry

The purpose of the push-away and pry is to move the canoe away from the paddling side. Both strokes create the same boat reaction. The push-away is an elementary stroke that should only be introduced to weak beginners. The pry is a much more efficient stroke that can be introduced directly to most participants.

Skill Cues

Push-Away

- The push-away is the exact opposite of the draw.
- The grip hand remains relatively stationary and extended outside the gunwale.
- The paddle is planted outward from the hip with the power face facing away from the paddler.
- Keep the paddle shaft as vertical as possible.
- Extend the paddle smoothly away from the side of the canoe, keeping the blade parallel with the keel line of the canoe.
- On completing comfortable extension, rotate the blade 90 degrees. Slide the blade inward toward the extended position (grip thumb should be turned outward, away from the face).
- Rotate the blade 90 degrees to original position.

Pry

- The paddle is placed in a vertical position with the shaft against the gunwale and the blade parallel with the keel line of the canoe (figure 7.16).

- The thumb of the lower hand may be hooked over the gunwale.
- The grip end of the paddle is then pulled inward, using the gunwale as a fulcrum, until the grip hand reaches the body midline.
- At this point, the underwater recovery commences with the blade turning 90 degrees and slicing inward, returning it to its starting position where the blade again turns 90 degrees and the stroke is repeated.
- The grip thumb should be turned outward (away from the gunwale) in the recovery phase of the stroke.
- The thumb of the lower hand may be hooked over the gunwale and the forefinger around the paddle shaft to perform an oarlock-like function.

Teaching Cues

Push-Away

- The push-away is an easy stroke to learn after learning the standing draw and may be introduced as the exact opposite of the draw.
- This is an ideal stroke for teaching whole–part, where participants perform the skill and refine it through your correction.

Figure 7.16 Prying the paddle off the gunwale to move the canoe away from the paddling side.

Pry

- Confining the power phase of the stroke to approximately the first 30 degrees off the gunwale provides a powerful and smooth stroke; a general rule of thumb is that the grip hand should not cross the centerline of chest. Extending the power phase past this 30-degree angle pushes water up and the gunwale down, resulting in a rocking action.
- Emphasize importance of the paddle blade being perpendicular to the keel line in the recovery phase; if it is not, the paddle shaft will travel along the gunwale and the paddler will have difficulty getting the blade back to proper starting position for next stroke.
- If pry action is weak, try getting the blade deeper in the water. Get the blade in under the bilge to start.
- Practice spinning the canoe in one place with both paddlers performing the same stroke. This can be confirmed by a stationary person on shore who extends an arm, pointing the index finger at the middle of the canoe. If the finger remains pointing at the middle of the canoe as the canoe spins, then it is a perfect stationary pivot.
- Do a rosette—raft all canoes together pointing in the same direction.
  - All the stern paddlers put their paddles aside and hold the two canoes on either side until they complete a circle.
  - All bow paddlers push away or pry on the same side (left or right), and the rosette containing all the canoes should spin in the direction of the paddling side.

Risk Management

When the thumb of the lower hand is hooked over the gunwale, the thumb may become pinched by the action of the paddle shaft. Participants should be made aware of this hazard and given the choice to place their shaft hand on the paddle shaft and keep it slightly above the gunwale.

Activity 4: Sideways Displacement

Sideways displacement moves the canoe sideways without changing the orientation of the canoe. It uses the skills previously taught in this lesson.

Skill Cues

- One paddler does a pry stroke as the other paddler draws.
- It is important to balance the power of the strokes between the paddlers to maintain sideways displacement parallel with the starting position.

Teaching Cues

- After participants are competent in the draw and pry, discovery learning works well for teaching sideways displacement.
- Challenge canoes to move laterally in one imaginary or defined corridor.

Activity 5: Pivot Spins

Pivot spins are a precise maneuver. With good communication and a little refinement of the draw and pry, beginners can perform these spins at a high level in a short time.

Skill Cues

- Spin the canoe on a dime in one direction (both paddlers using draws), stop (sometimes called *check*) the momentum of the canoe (by holding the paddles in the water with blades parallel with the keel line), and then spin the opposite direction (using pry strokes).
- Perform three revolutions in one direction, check, and then three revolutions in the opposite direction, maintaining consistent momentum when turning and coming to a complete stop in the check phase. Use splashless strokes, minimal rocking of the canoe, and consistent, positive communication between paddlers.

Teaching Cues

- Both paddlers draw for three pivot spins, stop (stop paddling and hold paddle blades vertical and parallel with the keel line), and then pry for three pivot spins.
- Challenge canoes to perform pivot spins smoothly, rhythmically, and dynamically.
- Once tandem pivot skills are mastered, consider challenging canoes to do as many pivots as possible within a set time to improve efficiency.

Activity 6: Rafting Up

Rafting up is a practical skill that can be used as a physical break to allow paddlers a chance to sit rather than kneel. It also provides a suitable teaching platform for instruction and demonstrations.

Skill Cues

Using a combination of the skills taught in this lesson, raft all canoes up to one canoe. They should all finish side by side and facing the same direction.

Teaching Cues

- Rafting up is an ideal application of the skills taught in this lesson. It gets all the canoes together facing one direction, an effective formation for teaching other skills.

- Rafting up provides a good problem-solving and communication activity for participants.

Activity 7: Simon Says

This is an optional activity to review and practice skills on demand. This activity may be inserted at any point in the unit and is best suited to younger age groups, although it may be used with participants of all ages.

Skill Cues

Follow the leader's directions.

Teaching Cues

- Adapt Simon Says to canoeing; for example, "Simon says 'Stand up,'" or "Simon says, 'Five draw strokes.'"
- This activity can be used with tandem or solo paddlers.
- This activity can be used as a break during a lesson or to review skills and maneuvers already taught.

Lesson Closure

- After completion of these skills and maneuvers, participants should be able to point the canoe in any direction.
- It is appropriate to compare the efficiency and effectiveness of the strokes covered in this lesson, especially the pry and the push-away.
- Using the skills taught in this lesson, participants can apply their problem-solving and communication skills to a wide variety of challenges.

LESSON 6

Paddling Circles and Straight Lines

Overview

This lesson completes the skill set necessary for canoe touring, a natural goal for any paddler. The ability to paddle from point A to point B or around a lake under control despite wind, waves, or other challenges is a desired skill. This lesson focuses on the ability of the stern paddler to turn the canoe or keep it in a straight line when the canoe is moving. Competency in these skills will help the paddlers be in control, and with a little experience, they will develop the ability to exercise good judgment in adverse conditions.

Learning Objectives

- To demonstrate the stern sweep stroke
- To demonstrate the J-stroke with all components
- To perform the figure-eight maneuver to practice turning strokes

- To know which strokes are appropriate in various situations
- To perform straight-line paddling, keeping the canoe in the designated corridor
- To participate in a canoe tour

Activity 1: Stern Sweep Stroke

The purpose of the stern sweep stroke is to turn the canoe away from the stern paddler's paddling side.

Skill Cues

- The blade is planted opposite the hips at a right angle to the keel.
- The shaft should be slanted down 30 to 45 degrees, full blade in the water.
- The paddle starts at the hip and continues until it almost touches the stern, scribing an arc from 3 o'clock to 6 o'clock (right side) or 9 o'clock to 6 o'clock (left side) (figure 7.17).
- The paddle blade slices vertically out of the water, parallel with the side of the canoe.
- Feather the paddle back to the catch position, pointing the thumb of the upper hand forward.

a   *b*

Figure 7.17   The sweep stroke: *(a)* turning portion; *(b)* nearing completion.

Teaching Cues

- Paddle circles using only sweep strokes. As the stroke improves, the circle should become tighter.
- Try the stroke with the shaft hand farther up the shaft, thereby extending the reach of the paddle.
- Lean out and twist the upper body with the stroke.
- When using the sweep as a corrective stroke (e.g., to maintain a straight line), stop correction slightly before the canoe is pointing in the desired direction. The corrective momentum will continue after the paddle is taken out of the water.
- To increase turning action, initiate the stroke at 4:30 right or 7:30 left.

Activity 2: J-Stroke

The purpose of the J-stroke is to turn the canoe toward the stern paddler's paddling side.

Skill Cues

- The catch is a comfortable reach forward.
- The power phase of the stroke is a bow or power stroke.
- The correction phase of the stroke begins when the power phase reaches the paddler's hip. The paddle blade should go from vertical and perpendicular to the side to scribing a *J*, staying close to and parallel to the side of the canoe as it moves back. The grip thumb turns down in this portion of the stroke, maintaining the same power face, and corrective momentum will continue after the paddle is taken out of the water (figure 7.18). (Note: The paddle shaft should rotate freely between the thumb and index finger of the shaft hand in transition from the power to the corrective phase.)
- As the paddle approaches its natural extension, the paddle should be pried off the gunwale as determined by the amount of correction required.
- For the recovery, the blade is feathered ahead (in position to cut through wind) parallel with the water, grip thumb forward.
- The J-stroke is used to turn the canoe toward the stern paddler's paddling side.
- Under most conditions, a small correction (J-stroke) is needed to counteract the tendency of the boat to turn away from the stern paddler's paddling side.

Figure 7.18   In the correction phase of the J-stroke, point the grip thumb down.

Teaching Cues

- This is the most challenging basic stroke for most paddlers. It is worth spending time on land using the part–whole teaching strategy before trying the stroke on the water.
- The land boat (or dock) is a useful place to start when teaching this stroke. Have the participants apply pressure against your hand during the correction phase.
- Have participants experiment with forward paddling (no J-stroke) and see what happens to the canoe.
- Next, have participants perform a 360-degree inside turn (toward the stern paddler's side of the boat) using only J-strokes.
- As participants become more acquainted with the stroke, have them try focusing on a distant object, lining up the bow of the boat with this object, and then paddling in a straight line, allowing the bow to deviate from the course as little as possible.
- Assistance can be provided to individual participants by sitting in the canoe directly in front of and facing the stern paddler. Have the participant perform the stroke. Adjust the blade pitch as necessary by placing a hand on top of the participant's grip hand and applying pressure until the paddle is pitched and angled into the proper position.
- The long-term goal is to apply the J-stroke more frequently (same paddling pace as bow paddler), requiring only minimal corrections.

Activity 3: Figure Eight

The figure eight is ideal for practicing and perfecting the stern sweep and J turning strokes. Participants who can paddle the figure eight scribing a consistent 5- to 8-meter (5.5- to 9-yard) radius will find that their strokes for paddling straight lines are more effective and efficient after achieving competency in the figure-eight maneuver.

Skill Cues

- Paddle the figure eight around two buoys in the middle of each circle.
- Try to stay equidistant from the buoy at all times.
- A good reference for paddlers is to keep the center thwart or yoke pointed at the buoy at all times throughout the maneuver.

Teaching Cues

- A good reference is to keep the center thwart or yoke pointed at the buoy throughout the maneuver.
- Let the bow paddler try a J-stroke in the bow without extending the blade back in the correction phase. The bow J-stroke is an effective strategy for the bow paddler to use when the wind is blowing on the bow paddler's nonpaddling side. It can also aid the stern paddler when doing the inside circle portion (stern paddler's paddle on the inside of the circle) of the figure eight.
- Paddling a figure eight offers excellent practice to refine the stern sweep and J-stroke.
- The bow paddler must paddle at a normal pace to maintain the momentum of the canoe.

Activity 4: Paddling a Straight Line

The ability to paddle a straight line makes for efficient and safe paddling. It minimizes the distance between two points and in the event of a rescue, paddling a straight line brings rescuers to the victims in the timeliest fashion possible. Furthermore, paddling a straight line minimizes the effort required to bring the canoe back on course, which can be especially challenging in windy conditions. Being able to stay on course affords paddlers the opportunity to use wind as an aid and minimize energy output.

Skill Cues

- Paddle the canoe within a predetermined corridor using an appropriate combination of steering strokes.
- As skill improves, the corridor should become narrower. For example, begin with a 4-meter (4-yard) corridor and work toward a 1-meter (1-yard) corridor.
- All correction strokes must be stopped slightly before the canoe is pointing in the desired direction because the turning momentum will continue after the paddle is out of the water.

Teaching Cues

- Paddlers line up two objects in the distance. If they keep them in line, they will be going straight (figure 7.19).
- When paddling a straight line, the bow of the canoe will naturally yaw left and right. If the bow yaws too far, the forward momentum of the canoe shifts to a turning momentum, which is difficult to check and creates a snakelike trail instead

of a straight line. The solution is to establish two imaginary goalposts and keep the bow within these two goalposts.

- All correction strokes must be stopped slightly before the canoe is pointing in the desired direction because the turning momentum will continue after the paddle is out of the water.
- Learning to paddle a straight line minimizes the effort and distance in traveling between two points.

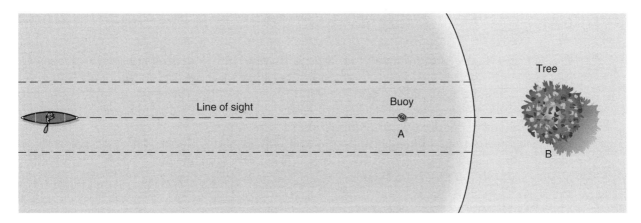

Figure 7.19 To travel in a straight direction, the paddler should line up A and B.

Activity 5: Blind Person's Bluff

Blind Person's Bluff is an optional activity that emphasizes communication skills and proprioceptive awareness. It incorporates skills already covered in the unit.

Skill Cues

- The seeing partner communicates clearly to the blindfolded partner what strokes to do, how hard, and how often, using specific commands such as "Forward stroke, forward stroke, J-stroke, smaller J-stroke."
- The blindfolded paddler follows the directions of the seeing paddler.
- After a defined time, switch roles.
- The objective is to navigate the designated course or distance as efficiently as possible.

Teaching Cues

- Designate a specific course or distance to be maneuvered. At this point in the unit it is not unreasonable to set out buoys and include a combination of basic paddling skills in the course, such as forward paddle, stop, sideways displacement, and pivot spin.
- Emphasize that specific communication is more effective than general comments.
- Emphasize that positive reinforcement is important.
- Emphasize that the objective is for the canoe to navigate the designated course or distance as efficiently as possible.

Activity 6: Canoe Tour

The canoe tour should be a primary objective for anyone learning to paddle. The tour is an opportunity to apply, practice, and refine the skills in an unthreatening, relaxed, and pleasurable environment. It affords learners the opportunity to mentally and physically process all skills through practical application and internalize effective and efficient paddling skills and habits. Last but not least it provides the opportunity to associate the outdoors with pleasurable activity, paddling!

Skill Cues

- Partake in a canoe tour.
- Stay behind the designated lead canoe and in front of the designated sweep canoe.

Teaching Cues

- The canoe tour offers a practical application of the strokes taught in this lesson, and oftentimes this is where paddlers refine their strokes to the point that good mechanics are natural and they don't have to think, they just do it!
- Once these essential strokes are learned, do a short canoe tour—paddle around the lake or the cove, staying parallel to the shore.
- If participants have solid map and compass navigational skills and are mature, this activity can be followed by night orienteering in an area bordered by shoreline and under calm conditions.

Activity 7: Sponge Tag

Sponge Tag is an optional fun activity to conclude the unit or any lesson when water and air temperatures are warm.

Skill Cues

- If your canoe has the sponge, your objective is to throw it so it hits another canoe or paddler, making that canoe It.
- If your canoe does not have the sponge (not It), then you must stay within the defined area and avoid being hit by the sponge.
- Use any appropriate skills to maneuver the canoe to avoid being hit or hitting others.
- Consider dipping the sponge in water before throwing it to make it travel farther.

Teaching Cues

- Define the boundary for the game using a combination of shoreline and buoys.
- Explain the game and get it started quickly.
- Consider being part of the game. Participants will derive a little extra pleasure from making you It or hitting you with a wet sponge.

Lesson Closure

The high point of this lesson should be a canoe tour, even if it is only half an hour, going for an organized paddle that includes starting point, end point, and some basic structures such as a lead boat and sweep boat designed to keep the group together. Everything in this lesson should build toward the canoe tour. With this in mind, it is important to end this lesson with some high points or memorable moments. One such possibility is rafting up all the canoes near the end of the trip and sharing snacks, personal highlights, and maybe a joke or two. It is a time when you have a captive audience, making it a good opportunity for reinforcing whatever you feel is important.

References and Resources

Dillon, P.S., and J. Oyen. 2008. *Canoeing*. Champaign, IL: Human Kinetics.

Mason, B. 1984. *Path of the paddle*. Toronto: Key Porter Books.

Whitewater Canoeing

▼ Kevin Redmond ▼

It is difficult to find in life any event which so effectually condenses nervous sensation into the shortest possible space of time as does the work of shooting, or running an immense rapid. There is no toil, no heart-breaking labor about it, but as much coolness, dexterity, and skill as a man can throw into the work of hand, eye, and head; knowledge of when to strike and how to do it; knowledge of water and rock, and of the one hundred combinations which rock and water can assume—for these two things, rock and water, taken in the abstract, fail as completely to convey any idea of their fierce embracings in the throes of a rapid as the fire burning quietly in a drawing-room fireplace fails to convey the idea of a house wrapped and sheeted in flames.

– Sir William Francis Butler, *The Great Lone Land: A Narrative of Travel and Adventure in the North-West of America* (1872)

Rivers and lakes were the roads used by early settlers and voyageurs in North America as they explored the North in search of furs and subsequent development. The canoe offered fast means of travel and the ability to carry a load with relative ease. Yet the fast-moving water and rapids were not without risk. Lacking modern safety equipment such as PFDs and even skills such as swift-water rescue, many voyageurs lost their lives in rapids. Although that risk still exists today, it is greatly minimized with use of proper equipment, safety procedures, and skill development through organized programs.

This unit covers basic whitewater (also called *moving-water*) canoeing skills and progressions essential for safety, learning, and performance. The unit includes basic equipment, risk identification and management, skill progressions, etiquette, and introductory lesson plans for whitewater canoeing. The program is a guide that you can adapt to your program needs and circumstances.

The major objective of this unit is facilitate participants' skill development, knowledge, and confidence so that they can navigate moving water, rapids, and hazards without the overbearing fear that inhibits learning and enjoyment but with enough apprehension and knowledge to engender respect and good judgment in challenging circumstances.

Equipment

Group Equipment

- 1 canoe (5 meters [16 to 17 feet] long) outfitted for moving water, which should include grab loops and flotation such as secured air bags inside canoe, for every two people
- 1 whitewater paddle per person
- 1 approved PFD with whistle attached per person
- 1 spare paddle per canoe
- 1 bailer per canoe
- 1 throw bag or rescue rope per canoe
- First aid kit
- Means of communication, such as cell phone or very high frequency (VHF) radio

Personal Equipment

- Wet or dry suit if needed
- Helmet
- Paddling gloves (optional)
- Spare layers of clothing secured in a dry bag
- Sunscreen
- Sunglasses

Equipment Care and Maintenance

- When not using a paddle, stand the paddle against a vertical object.
- For extended storage, paddles should be stored hanging and out of direct sunlight and heat.
- Canoes should be stored upside down. For extended storage, canoes should be stored upside down on a rack out of direct sunlight.
- Modern canoes specifically made for rivers are designed to take abuse on the river such as sliding over rock. When on land, avoid dragging canoes over rough surfaces such as rock when possible.
- Treat helmets with care. Avoid tossing them on hard surfaces.

Site Selection

Several sites are required to teach this unit effectively. Sites should minimize participants' exposure to wind as much as possible.

- Lessons 1, 2, and 3 may be done on a warm-water lake or a river section with slow-moving, hazard-free current and no hazards below the teaching area. A measure of slow-moving current is if participants are capable of paddling upstream with relative ease.
- Theory sessions can be held on land or a quiet area near the edge of the water, and some sessions can be done with canoes rafted together on the water.
- A small creek suitable for wading is an ideal site for teaching river features and topography.

Social Skills and Etiquette

- If using private property such as access to water, dock, or beachfront, ask permission first.
- Communicate with your paddling partner on all maneuvers.
- When sharing a section of river with other canoes, keep movement orderly so everyone gets relatively equal time practicing and performing skills.

- The first canoe to shore should help other canoes as they land.
- Offer praise (e.g., "Nice crisp paddle plant!"), support, and encouragement to fellow paddlers.

Risk Management

- If painters are attached to the ends of the canoe, they should be secured (e.g., with a bungee cord) to avoid entanglement with body parts. A loose rope in current that wraps an arm or leg once can result in serious injury or death. There should never be any loose ropes in or dangling from the canoe!
- Before participants are accepted to the program, it is important to verify their comfort level in water over their heads while wearing a PFD. This can be done by verifying swim credentials or holding a swim verification session in a pool or lake.
- Canoes stay within the designated area identified by the outdoor leader. This area should be contained so that rescues can be made quickly with minimum risk to participants.
- When paddlers are walking on shore, they must keep the helmet on and their paddle with them at all times. Helmets protect in case of a fall, and paddles are useful if participants slip in the river or as a reach assist for helping someone else.
- When a paddle is inserted in moving water, it is not always possible to anticipate a rock just beneath the surface. This is compounded by the fact that whitewater paddles are rigid. Paddlers must never lock their elbows when performing strokes on a river. Locking elbows significantly increases the risk of shoulder dislocation. Paddlers should maintain at least a slight bend in the elbows when learning and practicing whitewater strokes and maneuvers.
- If possible, all canoes should be outfitted with the following:
  - Grab loops at both ends of the canoe
  - A 3-meter (10-foot) painter at each end secured by bungee cord, with the short end of the rope extended a few centimeters for easy identification and access
  - Additional flotation in the bow and stern end of the canoe as well as the center bay
- Having all boats outfitted the same ensures that in the event of a rescue, the rescuers know exactly what to expect. In the event that all boats are not outfitted similarly, leaders and participants should be aware of differences and how best to deal with them.
- Learn the whistle code:
  - One whistle blast = Stop! Wherever you are, stop, look, and listen.
  - Two whistle blasts = Stop! The person who blows the whistle can raise a paddle to indicate where to go.
  - Three whistle blasts = Stop! Emergency! Go quickly toward whoever blew the whistle and raft up together—there is an emergency at hand.
- Review paddle signals before going on the river (see lesson 4 on page 282).

Unit Organization

When paddling for extended lengths of time, inject instruction, demonstrations, and short theory sessions between paddling and practice sessions.

Lesson Plans

Lesson 1: Gearing Up and Rescues. This introductory lesson covers equipment terminology and selection before moving to self-rescues, such as how to swim rapids. Finally, it covers assisted rescues, such as the T-rescue, which is similar to the T-rescue introduced in the flatwater canoeing unit.

Lesson 2: Basic Whitewater Strokes and Maneuvers. This lesson introduces basic whitewater strokes and maneuvers in controlled conditions where the participants can focus on learning the proper techniques without distraction. The lesson begins with strokes learned in flatwater canoeing and their application and nuances for moving water. Then it moves into strokes and basic whitewater maneuvers.

Lesson 3: Intermediate Whitewater Strokes and Maneuvers. In this lesson, more complex river strokes and maneuvers are introduced. Many of the skills include components of strokes and maneuvers from lesson 2 but take them to the next level. By the end of this lesson, strokes and maneuvers from lessons 2 and 3 should be reasonably fluid and ready for application on the river in lesson 4.

Lesson 4: Introduction to the River. Participants must be able to recognize the hazards on the river and know how to navigate these hazards safely before they are introduced to the river. In this lesson, participants will also be introduced to and practice all basic whitewater skills in preparation for lesson 5—the river run.

Lesson 5: River Running. The river run should be a highlight for participants as they apply their skills in a practical environment. This lesson puts participants to the test as they gain experience not only in developing their physical skills but also in decision making, judgment, and communication with their paddling partner and peers.

Terminology

- **grip hand**—The hand holding the grip of the paddle.
- **power face**—The face of the paddle blade that exerts pressure on the water.
- **shaft hand**—The hand holding the shaft of the paddle.

Parts of the Paddle

- **T-grip**—The top part of the paddle made comfortable for holding, pushing, and pulling.
- **shaft**—Rounded or oval shaft between the grip and throat.
- **throat**—The top narrowing extension of the blade that joins the blade and shaft.
- **blade**—Part of the paddle that exerts pressure on the water.
- **tip**—Bottom edge of the paddle blade.

Parts of the Canoe and Canoe Outfitting

- **air bags**—Bags that contain air to displace water in the event of capsizing, swamping, or partial swamping; air bags are normally in the bow, center, and stern of the tandem boat.
- **bilge**—Rounded part of the canoe between the bottom and sides.
- **bottom**—Bottom of the canoe.
- **bow**—Front of the canoe.
- **bow seat**—Seat in the front of the canoe.
- **center thwart or yoke**—Perpendicularly connects the gunwales in the center of the canoe.
- **gunwale**—Rail on the top edge of the canoe sides.
- **keel line**—Imaginary line that runs longitudinally along the center of the bottom that helps the canoe maintain a straight line.
- **ribs**—Small, riblike structures that go across the bottom of some canoe designs; they maintain strength and structure of the hull.
- **skid plate**—Kevlar strip protecting stems of the canoe from wear and tear; not present in all canoes.
- **stem**—The extreme pointed ends of the canoe where the sides meet.
- **stern**—Back of the canoe.
- **stern seat**—Seat in the back of the canoe.
- **thigh straps**—Straps that cross the paddler's thighs, securing the paddler in a solid paddling position.
- **throw bag**—Bag of rope used to aid rescue of swimmers or boats.

Gearing Up and Rescues

Overview

This first lesson introduces participants to whitewater canoeing equipment and relevant terminology before moving on to capsizing, basic self-rescue skills, and assisted-rescue skills.

Learning Objectives

- To be able to identify and understand whitewater equipment
- To demonstrate proper paddle and PFD selection and fitting
- To enter and exit a canoe at shoreline or dockside (preferably shoreline)
- To participate in a canoe capsize
- To apply the high brace or pry brace
- To apply the low brace
- To demonstrate the appropriate brace in reaction to unpredictable tipping motion of the canoe
- To participate in a T-rescue as victim and rescuer

Risk Management

- Because of the risk associated with moving water, this lesson is best done in quiet or nonmoving water.
- When performing canoe entries and exits, ensure that the canoe is held in place as each paddler enters and exits to avoid the splits or falls.
- When performing controlled capsizes, establish a 3-meter (10-foot) safe zone around the canoe that is free of obstacles and hazards.
- If painters are attached to the ends of the canoe, they should be secured (e.g., with a bungee cord) to avoid entanglement with body parts. A loose rope in current that wraps an arm or leg once can result in serious injury or death. There should never be any loose ropes in or dangling from the canoe!
- Remind participants to relax their legs, floating them out from under the seat. A panic exit often wedges feet and legs under the seat, increasing anxiety.
- Wear helmets when capsizing canoes.
- When performing the T-rescue, practice in quiet water free of obstacles before practicing in moving water. This rescue should not be performed in a boulder garden on the river.

Activity 1: Canoe Selection and Boat Outfitting

It is important for whitewater paddlers to select a canoe that is adequately designed and outfitted for moving water. Most design and outfitting features in a whitewater canoe not only enhance paddler safety and success in moving water but also facilitate ease of rescue (figure 8.1).

Skill Cues

Select a whitewater canoe based on the following criteria:

- Rocker: Allows boat to turn easily and offer minimum resistance to current.
- Durable construction: Able to withstand collisions with hard obstacles such as rocks without damaging the canoe.
- Skid plates: Kevlar strips protecting the stems of the canoe.
- Grab loops at both ends of the canoe: Used for rescues and attaching throw bags.
- Painters: Ropes approximately 3 meters (10 feet) secured to the canoe and stored (e.g., under bungee cord) on the deck plate with no loose rope but the end of the rope easily available. Painters are used for tying canoes, lining, and in some instances assisting rescues.
- Quick-release thigh straps: Used to secure paddlers in canoes, providing a quick-release option in the event of capsizing and exiting the canoe.
- Kneelers: Foam kneelers in the bilge help lock paddlers in the canoe, help prevent slipping, and are comfortable.
- Air bags or flotation: Canoes should be outfitted with flotation secured in the center bay and both ends of the canoe. This allows the canoe to ride higher in the water when swamped and significantly decreases the risk of the canoe being wrapped (pinned on a rock underwater).
- Length: Canoes should be 5 to 5.5 meters (16 to 18 feet) for tandem paddling.

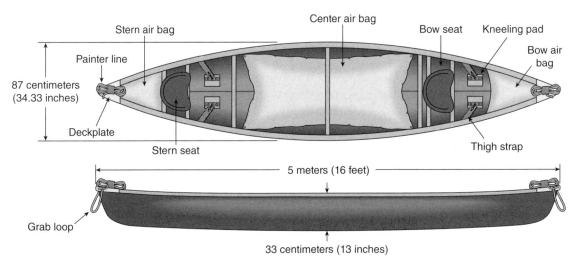

Figure 8.1   Parts of a whitewater canoe.

Adapted, by permission, from M. Wagstaff and A. Attarian, 2009, *Technical skills for adventure programming* (Champaign, IL: Human Kinetics), 500.

Teaching Cues

- After explaining canoe parts, construction, and outfitting, ask the group to identify and give the functions of the same.
- Have participants choose a good whitewater canoe from a selection of canoes and offer rationale for their choice.

Activity 2: Paddle Selection

Selecting a paddle that fits the paddler and can withstand the power and hazards of the river is essential for success.

Skill Cues

Select a whitewater paddle (figure 8.2) based on the following criteria:

- Length: With the tip on the ground, the grip should come between the chin and nose.
- Durable construction: Should be able to withstand collisions with hard obstacles such as rocks without damaging the paddle.
- Rigid shaft: Allows immediate reaction when water is pulled or pushed.
- Protective paddle tip: Prevents blade from splitting.
- Short, wide blade: Allows for quick grab of water.
- T-grip: Permits full finger grip and may be used in snagging rope, boats, or other objects.

Grip   Shaft   Throat   Blade   Tip

Figure 8.2   Parts of the whitewater canoe paddle.

Teaching Cues

- After explaining paddle parts and construction, ask the group to identify and give the functions of the same.
- Have participants select a good whitewater paddle from a selection and offer rationale for their choice.

Activity 3: PFD Selection

Proper PFD selection is important for the paddler's comfort and safety. There are a wide range of PFD styles that will work, but serious whitewater paddlers should consider a PFD specifically designed for the activity to facilitate ease of rescue.

Skill Cues

- Locate and read the PFD label for sizing and other relevant data.
- Locate and identify the function of each adjustor on the PFD.
- Try on the PFD, ensuring a snug but comfortable fit when all adjustments are made.
- When floating in deep water, keep the PFD snug to the torso without it riding up in your face.

Teaching Cues

- Have participants select a good personal PFD from a selection of PFDs and offer rationale for their choice.
- Demonstrate and explain the consequences of an improperly fitting PFD: If it's too small, it may not support the person sufficiently to be effective and it restricts movement; when it's too large, it floats up around the face when in deep water.
- After explaining PFD adjustors, ask the group to identify and give the function of the same.

Activity 4: Entering and Exiting the Canoe From Dock or Shoreline

Learning to enter and exit a canoe in moving water requires precision and cooperation, and if done improperly, it can have dastardly consequences. Practicing this skill from a dock or shoreline is an effective progression that enhances confidence and ability to perform the skill once on the river.

Skill Cues

- The partner who is not entering the canoe should hold the canoe as close as possible to the shoreline or dock.
- To enter the canoe, hold the near gunwale with the same hand (i.e., left hand on left gunwale) and step to the center of the canoe, maintaining contact with the gunwale.
- As the second foot steps in the canoe, the other hand should take hold of the other gunwale.
- Transfer weight to the hands holding the gunwales as weight is taken off the feet to shift into the three-point kneeling position.
- The person in the canoe now holds the canoe in place for the partner to enter and may stabilize the canoe with a low brace.

Teaching Cues

- Have stern paddlers enter the canoe first; they are in a more stable position and can see the bow paddler entering.
- Place the paddle across the gunwales while entering, or if this is uncomfortable, on the bottom of the canoe. Once stabilized, get the paddle.
- Use the reverse procedure for exiting the canoe.
- Once in the current, hold the upstream end of the canoe in toward the shore while the person holding the upstream end of the canoe gets in the canoe second. This prevents the current from pushing the upstream end of the canoe into the current before the paddlers are in position.

Activity 5: Controlled Capsize

The anxiety associated with capsizing a canoe for the first time should be presented as being normal. The purpose of practicing the canoe capsize is to reduce anxiety so that participants begin to initiate self-help and rescue procedures immediately rather than being frozen with fear! This proactive approach on the river can make the difference between a safe rescue or serious injury and possible death.

Skill Cues

- Begin in the standard three-point kneeling position.
- Increase tipping or rocking motion until the canoe flips over.

Teaching Cues

- Until participants have experienced numerous capsizes and are comfortable, any capsize should be strictly under the participants' control.
- Participants should plan which side they will tip toward and count, such as "Tip to the left on three: One, two, tip."
- Encourage participants to hold onto their paddle (not the sides of the canoe) when they capsize. This sets them up to use their braces later in the lesson.

• An extension of this activity to prepare participants for the river is having paddlers hold onto their paddles throughout the controlled capsize and, once in the water, move to the designated upstream end of the canoe. Because the activity is being practiced in still water, designating a current direction is necessary to simulate water flow on the river.

Risk Management

Consider having participants wear a helmet for this activity in case the gunwale strikes their head.

Activity 6: High Brace

The high brace is used to stabilize the canoe when it is tipping away from the paddler's paddling side. The pry brace may be used in place of the high brace. Skill and teaching cues for the high brace can be found on pages 242 to 243.

Skill Cues

• The paddler leans out toward the paddling side in standard draw position.
• Keep the paddle as vertical as possible and grab as much water as possible.
• Release water as the canoe stabilizes.

Teaching Cues

• This brace is effectively taught in shallow (waist-deep) water, with the paddler in the bow and the instructor or partner standing in the water on the opposite side from the paddler and near the stern of the canoe.
• The partner presses down on the gunwale, tipping the canoe away from the paddler's side.
• When the canoe tips away from the paddling side, the paddler reacts with a high brace.
• When first learning, the partner may give a cue by calling "High brace" while tipping the canoe. When the technique is mastered and the paddler is comfortable, the canoe may be tipped without cue.
• This skill can be introduced and practiced with students standing in thigh-deep water.

Activity 7: Low Brace

The low brace is used to stabilize the canoe when it is tipping toward the paddler's paddling side (figure 8.3).

Skill Cues

• The paddle is extended so that it is horizontal over the water (power face up) and perpendicular to the keel line of the canoe.
• The paddler leans out toward the paddling side with knuckles down.
• The grip hand hits the water first.
• The shaft elbow will be at a near right angle as pressure is applied to the paddle, pressing on the water and righting the canoe.

Teaching Cues

• This brace is effectively taught in shallow (waist-deep) water, with the paddler in the bow and the instructor or partner standing in the water on the opposite side from the paddler and near the stern of the canoe.

a

b

c

Figure 8.3 Low brace technique: Keep the knuckles down as the paddle slaps the water for support.

- The partner lifts near the gunwale, tipping the canoe toward the paddler's side.
- When the canoe tips toward the paddling side, the paddler reacts with a low brace.
- When first learning, the partner may give a cue by calling "Low brace" while tipping the canoe. When the technique is mastered and the paddler is comfortable, the canoe may be tipped without cue.
- This skill can be introduced and practiced with students standing in thigh-deep water.

Activity 8: Applying the High and Low Braces in Pairs on the Water

For bracing to be effective, the proper brace must be applied instinctively to avoid capsizing. Applying the high and low brace in pairs on the water is an ideal activity to help facilitate instinctive braces.

Skill Cues

- One paddler initiates with a low brace, causing the canoe to tip away from the other paddler's paddling side.
- The other paddler instinctively reacts with a high brace.

Teaching Cues

- Introduce this activity after technique for the high and low braces is mastered.
- Practice this activity in both ends of the canoe.
- This activity can be used throughout all subsequent lessons, making bracing an instinctive reaction to unstable conditions.

Activity 9: T-Rescue (Canoe Over Canoe)

The T-rescue (also called *canoe-over-canoe rescue*) rights an overturned or swamped canoe and helps victims reenter the canoe.

Skill Cues

- Swimmers should always be upstream of a swamped canoe to avoid being pinned between a rock and swamped canoe (force equivalent to approximately 900 kilograms [2,000 pounds]). If practicing on a lake, swimmers should be upwind to avoid being struck by the canoe.
- Ensure swimmers are OK and no other hazards (rapids, hypothermia) exist, and then collect any loose gear in the immediate area. If other hazards exist, proceed directly to the rescue.

- Form a *T*, with the rescue canoe forming the top of the *T* and the swamped canoe forming the trunk. (See figure 7.13 on page 245 for the sequence.)
- Lift and twist the near stem of the swamped canoe, breaking the air seal.
- Place the deck of the swamped canoe on the near gunwale of the rescue canoe.
- Slide the upside-down canoe across the gunwales of the rescue canoe until it is balanced and all the water is out.
- Turn the canoe right side up and slide the canoe back in the water.
- Stabilize the victim canoe while paddlers reenter it.
- The speed of rescue correlates highly with risk. The faster the rescue, the less risk of injury or equipment damage.

Teaching Cues

- Introduce this activity as early as is practical to give participants the opportunity to effect a real rescue in the event of an unplanned capsize.
- Speed of rescue is important on the river. When technique is competent, time rescues from the point of contact with the swamped canoe until the canoe is back in the water with all or most water removed.
- After basics are competent, introduce the quickie option: After contact is made with the swamped canoe, the near end of the swamped canoe is lifted as high as possible (with the far end being floated by the air bag) to drain water. Then it is tipped right side up and ready to go. If the swamped canoe contains adequate flotation, this will leave some water but the canoe will be functional for getting out of trouble.
- A further extension is to stand and lift the stem of the victim canoe. This latter variation should only be performed by those who are able to perform the task without creating more victims.

Lesson Closure

The water in a river moves much faster than the water in a lake. The water speed coupled with the hazards of rivers (e.g., rocks, holes, falls) exponentially increase the urgency of river rescue over flatwater rescues. Hence, competency, communication, and speed of rescues are paramount. Furthermore, from the beginning victims should be taught protocols for initiating self-rescue procedures to minimize risk before assisted rescue arrives. Although this lesson takes place in slow-moving water, refining the skills introduced in this lesson will make later lessons safer and more enjoyable.

LESSON 2

Basic Whitewater Strokes and Maneuvers

Overview

This purpose of this lesson is to introduce the basic strokes: forward power, draw, pry, river J, stern sweep, reverse stern sweep with low brace, and some maneuvers that combine these strokes. Participants should not be disappointed they are not on the river for lessons 2 and 3; remind them that many world-class whitewater paddlers train on lakes, perfecting their skills and using wind as their current.

Learning Objectives

- To demonstrate the forward power stroke
- To demonstrate the draw and pry strokes
- To demonstrate the pivot spin with one paddler using a pry and the other using a draw
- To demonstrate sideways displacement with both paddlers using the same stroke
- To demonstrate the river J-stroke
- To demonstrate the stern sweep stroke
- To demonstrate the quick turn variations with the bow paddler paddling forward and the stern paddler using a reverse stroke or reverse stern sweep with low brace

Risk Management

With the pry, if the thumb and forefinger hold the shaft to the gunwale, there is a risk of skin being pinched. The alternative is to keep the shaft hand above the gunwale, but this increases the degree of difficulty.

Activity 1: Forward Power Stroke

Forward power on the river is essential for all strokes to work. The greater the canoe's momentum, the easier and more effective the performance of corrective strokes is.

Skill Cues

- The shoulder nearest the paddle rotates forward as the torso winds up, placing the paddle near vertical at a comfortable reach forward and with hands outside the gunwale.
- The paddle and arms remain relatively locked as the torso unwinds, providing power in the stroke.
- The elbows maintain a slight flex throughout the complete stroke.
- The range of the stroke is approximately knee to hip, assuming the paddler is kneeling.
- The paddler should feel the abdominal muscles contract during this stroke.

Teaching Cues

- In moving water, the forward power stroke provides aggressive forward propulsion as needed.
- As a warm-up to this stroke, have participants place the paddle across their shoulders and rotate the torso. This twisting motion is the same motion used in the forward power stroke.
- The forward power stroke may be effectively introduced and practiced in thigh-deep water.
- Have participants practice this stroke in bursts of four to eight aggressive strokes followed by a rest to simulate actual usage on the river.

Activity 2: Draw Stroke

The draw moves the canoe toward the paddler's side. Some use the analogy that the paddle is planted in concrete and the canoe is pulled to the paddle.

Skill Cues

- The paddler turns the shoulder toward the paddling side with the grip hand stationary and extended outside the gunwale (the farther outside the gunwale, the greater the boat reaction).
- Paddle outward from the hip, keeping the paddle shaft as vertical as possible.
- Pull the paddle smoothly toward the side of the canoe, keeping the blade parallel with the keel line of the canoe.
- For recovery, rotate the blade 90 degrees before it reaches the side of the canoe. Slide the blade outward toward the extended position (grip thumb should be turned outward, away from the face).
- Rotate the blade 90 degrees to the original position.

Teaching Cues

- The purpose of the draw is to move the canoe toward the paddler's side.
- Encourage a long reach out with the top hand (make a window with paddle and arms).
- Stroke should be rhythmic and dynamic.
- Both paddlers should lean out as far as possible and draw at the same time. Their paddles work as outriggers, stabilizing the canoe while providing great boat reaction (figure 8.4).
- If both paddlers draw simultaneously, the canoe should do a stationary pivot spin.

Activity 3: Pry Stroke

The purpose of the pry is to move the canoe away from the paddling side.

Skill Cues

- The paddle is placed in a vertical position with the shaft against the gunwale and the blade parallel with the keel line of the canoe.
- The grip end of the paddle is then pulled inward, using the gunwale as a fulcrum, until the grip hand reaches the body midline (figure 8.5).
- At this point the underwater recovery commences, with the blade turning 90 degrees and slicing inward, returning to its starting position where the blade again turns 90 degrees and the stroke is repeated.
- The grip thumb should be turned outward away from the gunwale in the recovery phase of the stroke.
- The thumb of the lower hand may be hooked over the gunwale and the forefinger around the paddle shaft to perform an oarlock-like function.
- For additional power, extend the paddle blade deeper in the water by lowering the grip hand (relative to the body) and raise the shaft hand on the paddle shaft (referred to as *shortening the shaft*).

a

b

Figure 8.4 The *(a)* start and *(b)* finish of the draw stroke.

a

b

Figure 8.5 The *(a)* start and *(b)* finish of the pry stroke.

Teaching Cues

- Confining the power phase of the stroke to approximately the first 30 degrees off the gunwale provides a powerful, smooth stroke. A general rule of thumb is that the grip hand should not cross the centerline of the chest. Extending the power phase past this 30-degree angle pushes water up and the gunwale down, resulting in a rocking action of the canoe.
- Emphasize the importance of the paddle blade being perpendicular to the keel line in the recovery phase. If it is not, the paddle shaft will travel along the gunwale and the paddler will have difficulty getting the blade back to the proper starting position for the next stroke.
- If the pry action is weak, try getting the blade deeper in the water. Get the blade in under the bilge to start.
- Practice spinning the canoe in place with both paddlers performing the same stroke.

Risk Management

With the pry, if the thumb and forefinger hold the shaft to the gunwale, there is a risk of skin being pinched. The alternative is to keep the shaft hand above the gunwale, but this increases the degree of difficulty.

Activity 4: Sideways Displacement

Sideways displacement moves the canoe sideways without changing the orientation of the canoe. It uses the skills already taught in this lesson. It is an important maneuver on the river because it allows paddlers to sideslip to avoid obstacles and hazards.

Skill Cues

- The objective is to move the canoe sideways with control while avoiding excessive yaw.
- One paddler uses the draw and the other uses the pry. To go in the opposite direction, both paddlers switch strokes.
- Paddlers must adjust the power of their strokes so they provide equal boat reaction.

Teaching Cues

- The purpose of sideways displacement is to move the canoe sideways for a specific purpose (e.g., rafting up) or to avoid an obstacle such as a rock.
- Challenge canoes to move laterally in one imaginary or defined corridor.
- Once competency is achieved with stationary sideways displacement, challenge participants to try it when they are moving forward. Paddle forward three strokes, sideslip 3 seconds, and repeat.

Activity 5: River J-Stroke

The river J-stroke is the equivalent of a forward power stroke and a rudder or pry. It is more effective than the flatwater J-stroke on the river because the prying action is more active and vertical, resulting in better boat reaction.

Skill Cues

- The first phase of the river J-stroke is the forward power stroke.
- When the paddle reaches the hip, the grip knuckles remain facing the sky (figure 8.6).
- The paddle is pried off the gunwale. Note that the power face of the paddle is different for the power and pry phases of the stroke.

Teaching Cues

- The purpose of the river J is to move the canoe away from the paddler's paddling side.
- Smaller, more frequent corrections are preferred to longer, exaggerated corrections.
- Emphasize similar cadence between the bow and stern paddlers where possible.
- The river J-stroke is best suited to quick, aggressive corrections that help maintain forward momentum; less frequent, large corrections tend to slow the canoe and diminish the effectiveness of the corrective stroke.

Figure 8.6   The grip knuckles face up for the river J-stroke.

Activity 6: Stern Sweep

The purpose of the stern sweep is to turn the canoe away from the stern paddler's paddling side. The stern sweep will be used in lesson 3 for initiating eddy turns on the stern paddler's nonpaddling side.

Skill Cues

- The blade is planted opposite the hips at a right angle to the keel line.
- The shaft should be slanted down 30 to 45 degrees, full blade in the water.
- The paddle starts at the hip and continues until it almost touches the stern, scribing an arc from 3 o'clock to 6 o'clock (right side) or 9 o'clock to 6 o'clock (left side), with the torso rotating with the paddle (figure 8.7). For greater turning motion and less forward power, initiate the stroke at 4:30 or 7:30.
- The paddle blade slices vertically out of the water parallel to the side of the canoe.
- Feather the paddle back to the catch position, pointing the thumb of the upper hand forward.

a

b

c

Figure 8.7   Three phases of the stern sweep: *(a)* start, *(b)* correction, and *(c)* completion.

Teaching Cues

- The purpose of the stern sweep is to turn the canoe away from the stern paddler's paddling side.
- To increase turning action, initiate the stroke at 4:30 right or 7:30 left.
- Practice paddling circles. As the stroke improves, the circle should become tighter.
- When participants are competent, have them try the stroke with the shaft hand further up the shaft, thereby extending the reach of the paddle.

Activity 7: Reverse Stern Sweep With Low Brace

The reverse stern sweep with low brace is an important stroke for the stern paddler when initiating eddy turns on the stern paddler's side. The low-brace portion of the stroke combination is important in maintaining canoe stability as the paddlers lean to present the bottom of the canoe to current. The more refined and comfortable paddlers' skills are after this lesson, the greater success they will have in subsequent maneuvers.

Skill Cues

- Paddle hands are close to the water and the shaft hand is choked up (shortened shaft) throughout the stroke.
- Insert the blade near the stern of the canoe with a slightly closed or climbing angle for stabilization.
- Scribe a 90-degree arc going forward from the stern, with the torso rotating with the paddle arc (figure 8.8).

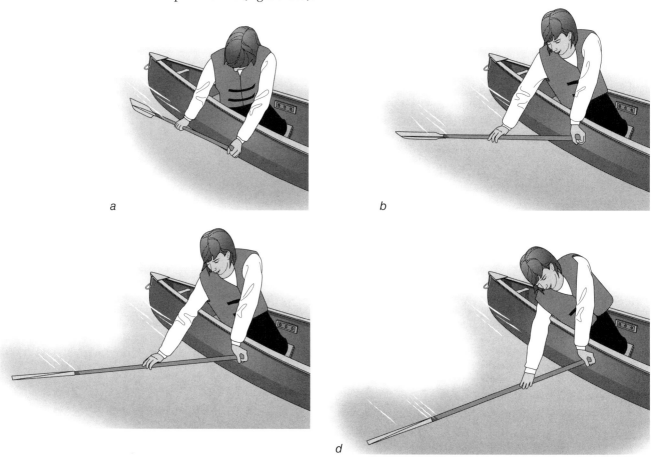

a

b

c

d

Figure 8.8 The leading edge of the paddle is higher than the trailing edge throughout the reverse stern sweep with low brace.

Teaching Cues

- Develop this stroke in comfortable conditions or at the end of the lesson, encouraging participants to lean on their paddle and create boat tilt toward the stern paddler's paddling side.
- The leading blade edge must be higher than the trailing blade edge to provide stability.
- If the stroke is used for or in preparation for eddy turns, after completing the 90-degree arc the paddle is in position for a forward power stroke.
- The stern paddler can experiment with blade angle. A perpendicular blade angle provides increased turning motion and less stability, whereas a horizontal blade angle provides less turning motion and more stability.

Activity 8: Reverse Stern Sweep With Forward-Power Quick Turn

The reverse stern sweep combined with forward power in the bow turns the canoe quickly and easily toward the stern paddler's paddling side. This is an easy and quick turn for beginning paddlers to learn and perfect.

Skill Cues

- The bow paddler paddles forward at the same time as the stern paddler performs the reverse stern sweep.
- The canoe turns away from the bow paddler's paddling side.
- To increase turning motion, paddlers open the power face throughout the stroke.

Teaching Cues

- Teach this stroke with the canoe stationary before trying it when the canoe is moving.
- A reverse power stroke may be used in the stern as a leadup to using the reverse stern sweep.
- Stern paddlers may vary the power face of their blade in the reverse stern sweep from completely open (to catch all possible water) to partially closed (to catch less water and offer some bracing support throughout the stroke).

Lesson Closure

Most skills introduced in this lesson have static origins. As participants progress, adding momentum to these skills increases the degree of difficulty and simulates whitewater conditions, and it also increases the boat reaction positively or negatively, both of which are equally important at this stage of learning. In many cases participants will learn just as much from the reaction of the boat as they do from the outdoor leader.

LESSON 3

Intermediate Whitewater Strokes and Maneuvers

Overview

This lesson builds on previous skills and introduces more advanced skills and maneuvers that require competency before getting on the river.

Learning Objectives

- To demonstrate the reverse power stroke
- To demonstrate the reverse J-stroke and draw steering strokes
- To demonstrate the cross-bow cut
- To demonstrate the cross-bow cut with reverse stern sweep turn
- To demonstrate the running draw with forward stern sweep turn
- To demonstrate sideslipping

Activity 1: Reverse Power Stroke

The reverse power stroke is an important stroke used to slow forward progress, buying time to avoid hazards or choose a safe route. It is also combined with more complex strokes and maneuvers.

Skill Cues

- Use a normal paddling grip.
- The paddler leans back, rotating the torso toward the paddling side.
- The paddle is planted in the water as far back as comfortable, with the blade perpendicular in the water and to the keel line.
- Power comes as the torso rotates forward from the paddle catch postion, with the paddle being held in a vertical position as long as possible and extending a comfortable reach forward (figure 8.9).

a   b

Figure 8.9   Reverse power stroke: *(a)* Applying reverse power; *(b)* side view.

Teaching Cues

- The back muscles are the main movers.
- Paddlers should look backward on their paddling side to make sure they are going in the desired direction and speed.
- Advanced progression of this stroke is the compound reverse stroke, which begins with a reverse draw, changes power face, and continues with the reverse power stroke. This progression may be presented if appropriate for participants' skill levels.
- The reverse power stroke moves the canoe backward to slow descent on a downstream run, as in the downstream ferry of lesson 5 on page 289.

Activity 2: Reverse J-Stroke or Draw Steering Stroke

The purpose of the reverse J-stroke is to provide directional control from the bow when reverse paddling.

Skill Cues

- The power phase is a standard reverse stroke.
- At the end of the power phase, the shaft is shortened as the paddle extends as far forward as comfortable with the grip thumb pointing down, making the blade parallel with the keel line.
- The paddle is now in a neutral steering position where it can pivot in the shaft hand while the blade is being drawn in toward the bow (equivalent of reverse draw or sweep) or pushed out away from the bow (reverse J-stroke) to turn the canoe in the desired direction (figure 8.10).

Teaching Cues

- When first teaching this stroke, have the bow paddler begin in the neutral position and make corrections using the blade as if it were a rudder while the stern paddler provides the power.
- After bow paddlers are competent, have them add the power phase to their stroke with the long-term goal of synchronizing their strokes with the stern paddler.

a b c

Figure 8.10 The reverse J-stroke (draw steering stroke): *(a)* Neutral position—transition from reverse power to reverse steering; *(b)* reverse draw option; *(c)* reverse J option.

- When learning this stroke on flat water, momentum is essential for the paddler to see the stroke work. On the river, the more upstream momentum there is, the less effort is required for positive results.
- Practice paddling a reverse figure eight and a straight line on flat water.
- On the river, practice downstream ferries (lesson 5, p. 289) in slow-moving current.

Activity 3: Cross-Bow Cut

The purpose of the cross-bow cut is to move the canoe to the bow paddler's off side.

Skill Cues

- Paddlers paddle forward one stroke, two strokes, three strokes (stern paddler ensures bow is moving away from stern paddler's side), and four strokes (bow paddler initiates cross-bow cut). During initial learning, the stern paddler does nothing on the fourth stroke so the bow paddler can see the effects of the cut.
- From the neutral paddling stance, the bow paddler rotates the torso to the off side.
- The paddle follows the torso and is planted at a comfortable reach forward at a 30- to 40-degree angle from the keel line of the canoe (figure 8.11).
- Although there is a slight weight shift toward the bow paddler's off side, the paddler should maintain a three-point kneeling position, with the third point more likely being the off-side cheek (buttock).
- The paddle shaft may be shortened to extend the reach of the blade and minimize lean.

Figure 8.11 Cross-bow cut. The bow paddler's paddle is at a 30- to 40-degree angle from the keel line of the canoe.

Teaching Cues

- Practice first on flat or quiet water but with some momentum.
- Encourage bow and stern paddlers to communicate on the degree of boat tilt because both paddles will be on the same side, making instability more probable and capsize possible.
- This is a good opportunity for the stern paddler to use a reverse sweep or low brace (only after the bow paddler has achieved relative competency with the cross-bow cut), which aids stability and sets up one of the stroke combinations for the eddy turn.

Activity 4: Cross-Bow Cut With Reverse Stern Sweep Turn

This maneuver will be used for eddy turns to the stern paddler's side.

Skill Cues

Paddlers paddle two or three forward power strokes followed by simultaneous strokes:

- The bow paddler uses a cross-bow cut.
- The stern paddler uses a reverse stern sweep with low brace.

Teaching Cues

- The purpose of this stroke combination is to radically turn the canoe to the bow paddler's off side.
- Begin with moderated momentum, lean, and bracing.
- As competence improves, increase speed, boat tilt, and bracing.

Activity 5: Running Draw With Forward Stern Sweep Turn

This maneuver is used on the river for eddy turns toward the stern paddler's paddling side. (The running draw may also be called a *hanging draw*.)

Skill Cues

- Create forward momentum by paddling forward two or three strokes, with the stern paddler performing a stern sweep on the last stroke before the bow paddler plants the running draw.
- To turn the canoe hard toward the bow paddler's paddling side, on cue the bow paddler plants the paddle in the water for a draw with the leading blade edge pointing slightly away from the canoe, making the power face open to oncoming water (figure 8.12).
- As this position is held, slight adjustments may be made to increase or decrease the amount of water caught by the blade, the effort required to hold the paddle in position, and the reaction of the boat to the paddle.
- Hold this position (hanging draw) until the momentum of the canoe begins to slow and then begin a series of draws (running draw, or drawing when the canoe is moving) to continue the turning action if desired.

Teaching Cues

- Begin this activity at slow speeds, emphasizing proper blade angle.
- As participants become proficient, add more momentum.
- Place obstacles (buoys) in the water to simulate rocks in the river and eddy turns.

Figure 8.12 Bow paddler practicing the running draw.

Activity 6: Sideslipping

Sideslipping is moving the canoe laterally while the canoe has forward momentum.

Skill Cues

- When paddling with momentum, one paddler uses a continuous draw as the other uses a pry.
- The canoe should move forward and laterally toward the draw side.
- The force of the draws and pry strokes must be relatively equal and at a right angle to the canoe to keep the canoe parallel to the current.

Teaching Cues

- The purpose of sideslipping is to move the canoe laterally while maintaining some forward momentum (figure 8.13).
- Practice paddling forward to an obstacle and sideslipping by it.
- If learning this maneuver in calm water, forward momentum is required to achieve the desired boat reaction.

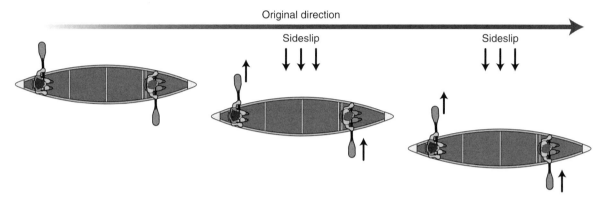

Figure 8.13   Sideslipping to the bow paddler's paddling side.

Lesson Closure

Participants should now have enough practical experience to discuss how boat speed and blade angles influence the ease and effectiveness of the strokes and maneuvers taught to date. Such a discussion before they head to the river is important in validating their learning thus far.

LESSON 4

Introduction to the River

Overview

This lesson introduces participants to paddling in moving water, but more importantly, it teaches them to recognize hazards on the river and apply their skills to minimize the risks of these hazards. Activities 1 through 7 could be placed in their own separate risk management section, but to avoid duplication and to include relevant skill and teaching cues to facilitate greater learning, these activities are presented independently within this lesson.

Although activities are presented individually in this lesson, it may be best to combine some activities as participants become competent, depending on your local river characteristics and circumstances. Ferries and eddy turns can be easily and effectively combined.

Learning Objectives

- To demonstrate how to read a river
- To demonstrate understanding of and recognition of basic river hazards

- To demonstrate how to communicate on the river
- To demonstrate appropriate river protocols
- To demonstrate rope rescues as a rescuer and a victim
- To demonstrate how to swim a rapid or current
- To demonstrate launching and landing in river current
- To demonstrate the upstream ferry
- To demonstrate the eddy-out
- To demonstrate the eddy-in
- To demonstrate broaching on a rock

Activity 1: Introduction to River Reading

A river can be likened to a road; all you have to do is read the signs. River reading is a skill that comes with practice. Knowing what to look for is the basis of good river reading, and this activity should aid participants in their observations.

Skill Cues

Participants should be able to recognize the following topographical features of rivers (figure 8.14):

- Upstream Vs—normally mark an obstacle to be avoided.
- Downstream Vs—created by river current flowing between two obstacles such as rocks. Downstream Vs are normally the preferred feature in identifying a navigable safe route through a rapid, as long as the downstream V does not lead to a hazard.
- Eddies—areas of upstream current located immediately downstream of obstacles. These are normally safe areas for taking a break or scouting the rapid ahead.
- Eddy line—the line at the edge of the eddy that marks the current differential between the current moving downstream and the upstream current of the eddy.
- Standing waves—waves that dance (move position), created by obstacles deep underwater. They're normally safe unless they are extremely large, where they present a risk of swamping, or unless the current is very slow, in which case they mark a shallow area of the river. It is not uncommon to see standing waves at the bottom of a downstream V caused by the two colliding currents.
- Pillow—an area of white turbulence on the surface of the water that does not move, indicating an obstacle under water. Normally pillows are to be avoided.
- Holes—caused by water falling over a drop or ledge, going deep under water, and then recirculating upstream. Generally, the deeper the water goes, the less turbulence is on the surface. The surface often appears similar to aerated ginger ale and offers less buoyancy to the canoe. Safer holes smile downstream, offering two possible exits.
- Keeper—hole with no exit. Anything that goes in a keeper will be Maytagged, or will spin around and around, continuing to go back and forth from one side to the other. Keepers smile upstream and offer no opportunity of being flushed out. Keepers are deadly! Stay out!

Teaching Cues

- Scout a rapid from shore and have participants identify and justify their route plan.
- Wade a small stream (water level below the knee) and identify various features described previously.
- While wading, take a bunch of small sticks to simulate canoe reaction with the features.
- Have a portable whiteboard available for explaining features or use sand or rock as a drawing board.

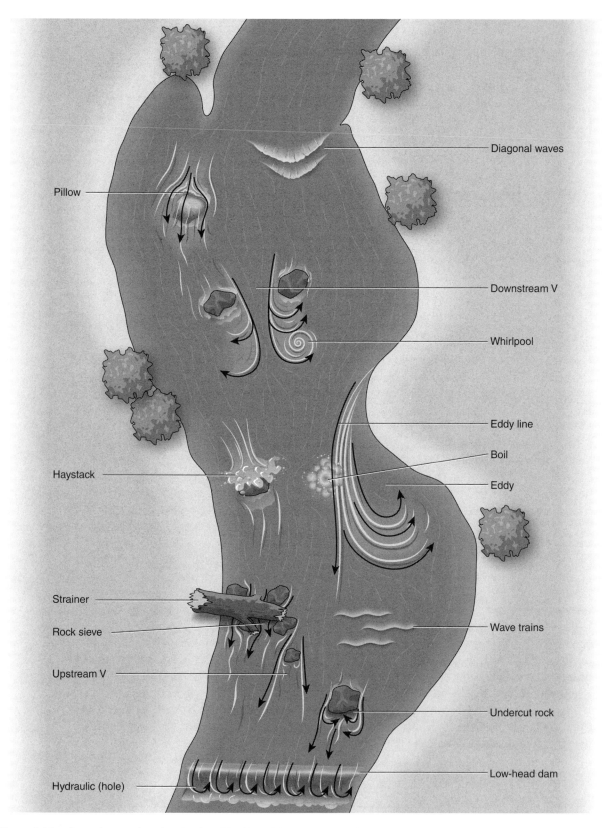

Figure 8.14 Some features found on the river. Identify which features a paddler can use and which should be avoided.

Activity 2: Introduction to River Hazards

River hazards presented in this activity can be fatal. Under no circumstances should participants be intentionally exposed to these hazards. The risk of serious injury or death is very real, and any rescue attempts will endanger the lives of others.

Skill Cues

Participants should be able to recognize and know how to avoid the basic river hazards:

- Reversals—similar to vertical eddies caused by sizeable obstructions underwater. The most dangerous reversals are created by weirs (low-head dams) or ledges. Holes and keepers mentioned previously feature similar hydrology. The only possible exit is by swimming toward the bottom of the river to find some water escaping downstream.
- Sweepers—trees that are in the water (normally on an outside bend) with the river current flowing through the tree. These are not usually seen until the last minute, and with most of the current pushing toward the outside bend, canoes tend to be pushed into the sweeper. On striking a sweeper, the current may tip the canoe and swimmers may be trapped among the branches underwater. Climbing on top of the sweeper is the only escape. When paddling sharp bends in a river, entering the bend from the inside center normally offers more route options and a weaker current than the outside bend.
- Undercuts—vertical rock face where the underwater portion is eroded, creating a cavernlike path for water to flow. Undercuts are to be avoided because there may be no air pocket (only rock) above the water and because where current flows into an undercut, canoes or swimmers may become trapped.
- Cold water—increases the difficulty rating. Cold water is a significant limitation in self- and assisted rescues.
- Debris—may come from floods, logging, or construction and is often unexpected and dangerous. Be aware of flooding cycles and old or new construction in your paddling area.

Other hazards that will be explained in more advanced lessons or depending on local conditions include whirlpools, big water, varying flow rates, log jams, and low-head dams or weirs.

Teaching Cues

- Scout a rapid from the shore and have participants identify the hazards to be avoided.
- Wade a small stream (water level below the knee) and identify various hazards.
- While wading, use rocks to create hazards and use a small stick to simulate the reaction of a canoe to the hazard.
- Have a portable whiteboard available for explaining various features or use sand or rock as a drawing board.

Activity 3: River Communication

Communication is the key to a healthy and happy relationship, and the same is true for paddlers on the river. The only difference is that distance and roaring rapids on the river impede verbal communication; hence the communication system presented in this activity should be well known by every person in the group.

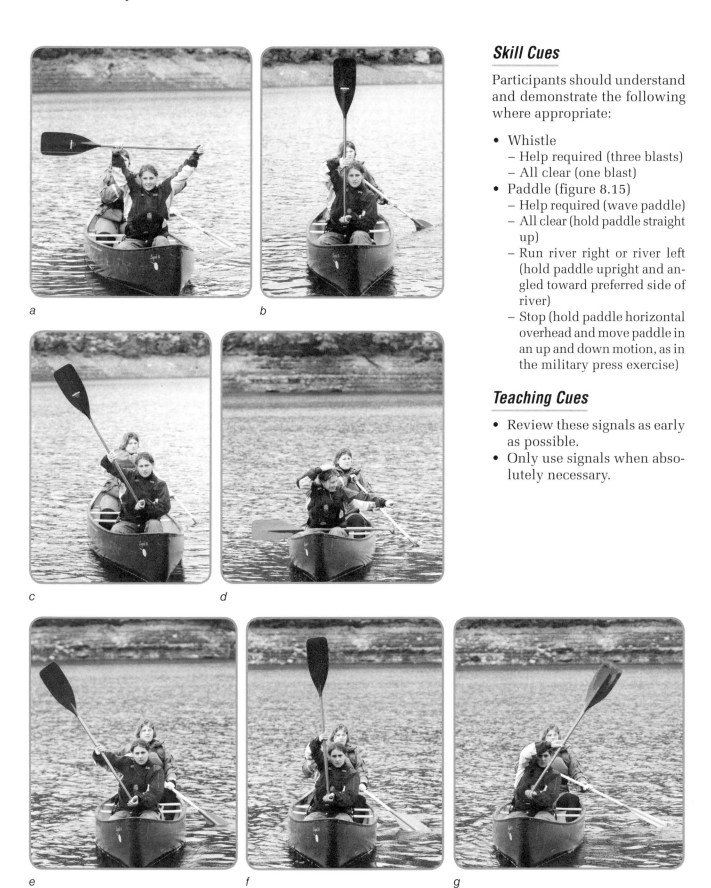

Skill Cues

Participants should understand and demonstrate the following where appropriate:

- Whistle
  - Help required (three blasts)
  - All clear (one blast)
- Paddle (figure 8.15)
  - Help required (wave paddle)
  - All clear (hold paddle straight up)
  - Run river right or river left (hold paddle upright and angled toward preferred side of river)
  - Stop (hold paddle horizontal overhead and move paddle in an up and down motion, as in the military press exercise)

Teaching Cues

- Review these signals as early as possible.
- Only use signals when absolutely necessary.

Figure 8.15 International paddle signals: *(a)* Stop; *(b)* all clear; *(c)* go this way; *(d)* are you OK?; *(e-g)* help.

Activity 4: River Protocols

This activity presents fundamental protocols while on or around the river to minimize risk associated with specific hazards.

Skill Cues

- Rocks and obstacles: Avoid rocks and obstacles. A general rule of thumb is to have the canoe parallel to the current to minimize the risk of encountering obstacles; even if that means going backward, it is better than going broadside or perpendicular to the current.
- Broach: If a canoe broaches a rock, paddlers must lean downstream into (hug) the rock. Failure to comply often results in capsizing and the canoe wrapping around the rock.
- Foot entrapment: When a foot gets trapped between two rocks in the river bottom, it can be deadly in fast-moving water at the upper thigh or above. It can be avoided by keeping feet pointing downstream near the surface and not standing until in shallow or slow-moving water.
- Falling: Be careful when walking the shore, especially after rain, in high humidity, or over moss- or lichen-covered rock. Participants should always wear their helmets and PFDs and carry their paddles when walking the shoreline. The helmet is worn for protection in case of a fall and the paddle is carried to aid stability on shore or to assist self-rescue in case of an accidental fall in the river.

Teaching Cues

- Review and reinforce protocols before going on moving water.
- Have participants follow and practice protocols where possible to make the appropriate reaction a natural response.

Activity 5: Rope Rescues

The purpose of rope rescue is to rescue swimmers in the water. When executed properly, rope rescues increase learning time and decrease risk by preventing exposure to downstream hazards.

Skill Cues

- The rescuer anticipates the path of the swimmer.
- The rescuer gets the swimmer's attention by yelling "Rope!"
- The swimmer should acknowledge the rope call with a hand wave or eye contact (latter preferred).
- The rescuer throws the rope to the swimmer and secures belay position.
- The swimmer grabs the rope and secures it over the outside shoulder.
- The swimmer swims on back with feet near or on the surface and downstream (figure 8.16).
- The swimmer does not stand until in slow-moving, shallow (below-knee) water.
- Once on shore, the swimmer stuffs the rope in the throw bag so it's available for another rescue.

Teaching Cues

- Rope-throwing practice may begin on land before trying it on the river.
- When practicing on land, lay out targets in concentric circles.
- Once competency is achieved on land, this activity may be practiced concurrently with activity 6.

Figure 8.16 Classic rope rescue of a swimmer.

Activity 6: Swimming a Rapid or Current

Paddling moving water means getting wet. Improving skills often means pushing the envelope, resulting in the boat capsizing. Given that swimming in rapids is inevitable, this activity teaches participants how to swim a rapid safely and proactively.

Skill Cues

- On immersion, float on your back with feet near or on the surface and pointing downstream.
- Slow downstream progress with your arms using the backstroke or with the paddle by reverse paddling.
- Angle the body such that the head is closer than the feet to the desired shore to help ferry yourself to shore.
- Stay in a floating or swimming position until in slow-moving water below knee depth.
- In the event of an approaching hazard such as a log jam or sweeper, roll over and aggressively swim with the front crawl and climb on top of the hazard. This is only used in life-threatening situations.

Teaching Cues

- The purpose of the swim in a rapid is to minimize the swimmer's risk.
- For the first time, this activity should be done in a deep, clear channel near shore.
- The outdoor leader should swim with nervous participants if necessary.
- When participants' competency increases, the swim may be combined with the rope rescue.
- Encourage participants to actively work toward bettering their circumstances by initiating self-rescue procedures. This puts the victim in some control while promoting a proactive mindset.
  – Appropriate body position with feet downstream and near the surface
  – Good body ferry toward the desired shore
  – Use of the hands or paddle to slow downstream movement

Activity 7: Launching and Landing in River Current

The purpose of launching and landing in river current is to safely enter or exit a river shoreline with control. Launching and landing a canoe on a river shoreline may seem a simple task, but if done improperly it can leave one partner on shore and the other going helplessly downriver.

Skill Cues

- Launching
  - The paddler in the downstream end of the canoe enters first while the upstream paddler steadies the canoe and keeps the upstream end of the canoe closer to the shoreline than the downstream end (figure 8.17).
  - After the first paddler is secured, the second paddler enters the canoe.
- Landing:
  - The paddler in the upstream end of the canoe exits first, making sure no significant current comes between the upstream end of the canoe and the shoreline.
  - Once on shore, the first paddler secures and steadies the canoe for the second paddler to exit.

Teaching Cues

Throughout both launching and landing, paddlers must make sure no significant current comes between the upstream end of the canoe and the shoreline. Failure to do so results in the upstream end of the canoe spinning out of control and into the current.

Activity 8: Upstream Ferry

The purpose of the upstream ferry is to move across current with control. This is the easiest means for beginner paddlers to safely traverse moving water.

Skill Cues

- With bow pointing upstream, the canoe should enter the current on a shallow angle.
- In setting the angle, the bow (upstream end of canoe) must be angled toward the desired destination (figure 8.18).
- Adjust the angle to the current. A general rule of thumb is that slower current can accommodate wider angles, whereas stronger current demands smaller angles to avoid being blown off course.

Teaching Cues

- Begin this activity in slow-moving current free of obstacles.
- In current, have participants ferry across a river channel and back to the starting point without losing ground or moving downriver.

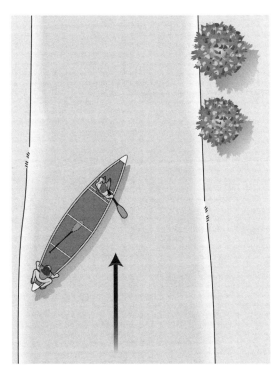

Figure 8.17   In a proper launch of a whitewater canoe, the upstream end of the canoe angles in toward the shore.

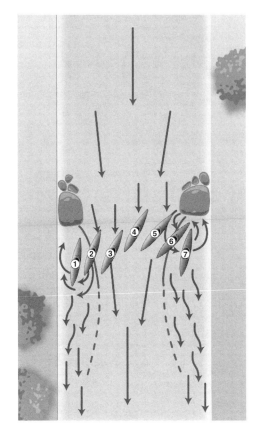

Figure 8.18   In an upstream ferry, the bow angles toward the target shore.

Reprinted, by permission, from ACA, 2008, *Kayaking* (Champaign, IL: Human Kinetics), 179.

- Where possible, the upstream end of the canoe (in this case, the bow) should be lighter than the downstream end, making it easier to adjust and hold the desired angle.
- The concept and skills for the upstream ferry may be taught with wind on a lake with the bow pointing into the wind (wind ferry).
- A general rule of thumb is that the upstream paddler (bow paddler) provides power while the downstream paddler (stern in this case) provides directional control of the canoe and additional power where possible.

Activity 9: Eddy-Out

The eddy-out is used to move the canoe into the main downstream river current from the safety of an eddy (figure 8.19).

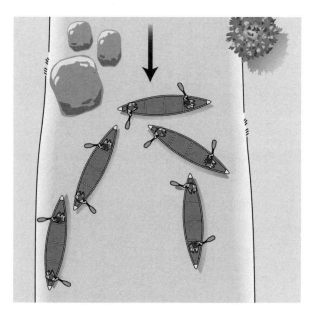

Figure 8.19   Eddying out.

Skill Cues

- M—Momentum must be faster than the current you are exiting. Two to three accelerating strokes before entry are normally sufficient.
- L—Lean into the turn as if on a bicycle, presenting the bottom of the canoe to the oncoming downstream current.
- A—Angle of approach to the eddy line is 30 to 45 degrees.
- P—Plant. The bow paddler plants the paddle for the appropriate stroke as the hips cross the eddy line into the downstream current.
- Stroke combinations are one of the following:
  - Bow draw and stern forward sweep
  - Bow pry (or cross-bow cut) and stern reverse sweep with low brace

Teaching Cues

- Emphasize MLAP (momentum, lean, angle, plant). All four of these components should be demonstrated by participants on every eddy-out.
- Simulate on land using rope as the eddy line.
- Simulate on flat water using obstacles (buoys or ropes).
- Further upstream toward obstacles is the strongest current differential; current differential diminishes with distance from obstacles.
- A small river with deep water, well-defined eddies, and minimal hazards is an ideal site.
- If limited eddies are available, teach eddy-in, eddy-out, and upstream ferry, and then do S-turns.

Activity 10: Eddy-In

The eddy-in is used to move the canoe out of the main downstream river current and into the safety of an eddy.

Skill Cues

- M—Momentum must be faster than the current you are exiting. Two to three accelerating strokes before crossing the eddy line are normally sufficient.

- L—Lean into the turn as if on a bicycle, presenting the bottom of the canoe to the oncoming downstream current.
- A—Angle of approach to the eddy line is 30 to 45 degrees.
- P—Plant. The bow paddler plants the paddle for the appropriate stroke as the hips cross the eddy line into the downstream current.
- Stroke combinations are one of the following:
  – Bow draw and stern forward sweep
  – Bow pry (or cross-bow cut) and stern reverse sweep with low brace

Teaching Cues

- Emphasize MLAP (momentum, lean, angle, plant). All four of these components should be demonstrated by participants on every eddy-in.
- Simulate on land using rope as the eddy line.
- Simulate on flat water using obstacles (buoys or ropes).
- Further upstream toward obstacles is the strongest current differential; current differential diminishes with distance from obstacles.
- A small river with deep water, well-defined eddies, and minimal hazards is an ideal site.
- If limited eddies are available, teach eddy-in, eddy-out, and upstream ferry, and then do S-turns.

Activity 11: Broaching on a Rock

When a canoe broaches on a rock, one of two things happens. Either the paddlers lean into the rock and jimmy the canoe off the obstacle, or they lean away from the rock, resulting in the canoe filling with water and then folding backward downstream around the rock in what is commonly called a *wrap*.

Skill Cues

- Lean the canoe into the rock (figure 8.20).
- Present the bottom of the canoe to downstream current.
- Downstream paddlers plant the paddle in the downstream current, drawing that end of the canoe into the current and off the rock.
- Maintain good downstream lean at all times throughout this maneuver.

Figure 8.20 When broached on a rock, lean downstream or hug the rock.

Teaching Cues

- Introduce this skill in water that is class I or lower.
- Explain how improper broaching reactions lead to wrapped canoes.
- Demonstrate proper technique on the river.
- Introduce and practice on shore to minimize risk and potential equipment damage.

Lesson Closure

Now that participants are on the moving water, it is valuable to debrief and compare performance of skills in quiet versus moving water. Discuss ways paddlers can use the river to their advantage, such as how the current differential on the eddy line spins the boat (downstream current ferries the canoe with a good angle across the river with minimal effort).

LESSON 5

River Running

Overview

There are two approaches to paddling moving water. The first is to stay and play in one location (as applied in lessons 1 through 4), and the second is to run a section of river, as in this lesson. All the activities in this lesson can be practiced at appropriate sites as your group descends the river. The order of the activities in this lesson may need to be adjusted to reflect the characteristics of your local river.

Learning Objectives

- To demonstrate S-turns
- To demonstrate sideslipping
- To demonstrate the downstream ferry
- To participate in a river run
- To demonstrate understanding of the International Scale of River Difficulty

Risk Management

- Designate lead and sweep canoes; all canoes stay behind the lead boat and in front of the sweep boat.
- The lead boat should be familiar with the river to avoid dangerous hazards.
- The sweep boat should carry a first aid kit and be competent in rescues.

Activity 1: S-Turns

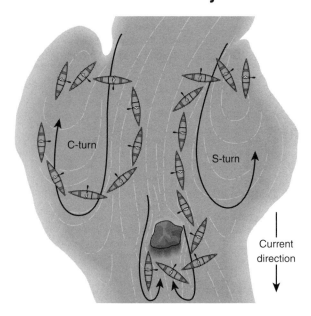

S-turns are a natural means of using obstacles in the river to the paddler's advantage (figure 8.21). These eddies provide protection from hazards, opportunities for breaks and to scout downriver, and a natural means to descend the river.

Skill Cues

Paddlers eddy out of one eddy, paddle a short distance downstream, and eddy in on the opposite side.

Teaching Cues

- This activity is an ideal way to practice and perfect inside and outside eddy turns.
- Begin in slower-moving current. As competency improves, use a site with stronger current.
- After eddying in the lower eddy, have participants ferry across and up into the starting eddy. This makes for plenty of practice at one site.

Figure 8.21 S-turns and C-turns.

Reprinted, by permission, from M. Wagstaff and A. Attarian, 2009, *Technical skills for adventure programming* (Champaign, IL: Human Kinetics), 525.

Activity 2: Sideslipping in Current

Sideslipping is an important maneuver on the river that paddlers use to avoid obstacles and hazards while maintaining forward momentum and staying parallel to the current.

Skill Cues

- Practice sideslipping by obstacles in the river.
- Ensure the canoe stays parallel to the current.
- One paddler will draw and the other paddler will pry.

Teaching Cues

- Use sideslipping as a warm-up to the next activity: the downstream ferry.
- Make sure both paddlers' strokes are equally effective; if one paddler is overpowering the other, they must adjust their strokes to be as close to equal as possible.

Activity 3: Downstream Ferry

The purpose of the downstream ferry is to move across current with control while the canoe is facing downstream. The downstream ferry is a difficult maneuver to master. When performing this maneuver, paddlers should err on the side of caution (begin with a narrow or shallow angle) to avoid being pushed off and broadside to the current.

Skill Cues

- Begin with the stern of the canoe upstream and enter the current on a shallow angle.
- In setting the angle, the stern (upstream end of canoe) must be angled toward the desired destination.
- Adjust the angle to the current. A general rule of thumb is that slower current can accommodate wider angles, whereas stronger current demands smaller angles to avoid being pushed off course.
- The downstream ferry will be easier to perform and control if the stern (upstream end) of the canoe is slightly lighter than the bow (downstream end) of the canoe.

Teaching Cues

- Where possible, have the upstream end of the canoe (in this case, the stern) be lighter than the downstream end, making it easier to adjust and hold the desired angle.
- In current, have participants ferry across a river channel and back to the starting point without losing much ground or moving downriver. It is normal to lose some ground with the downstream ferry because the paddlers are not in as strong of a paddling position compared with the upstream ferry.
- Begin in slow-moving current free of obstacles.
- A general rule of thumb is for the upstream paddler (stern paddler) to provide power while the downstream paddler (bow in this case) provides directional control of the canoe and additional power where possible. Reference activity 2 in lesson 3 (page 275) for the bow paddler if necessary.
- The concept and skills for the downstream ferry may be taught and practiced with wind on a lake with the stern pointing into the wind.

Activity 4: Short River Run

The river run is an opportunity to apply all the skills learned in this unit. In some ways it is a further test for participants as skills refined in one play area are applied to new areas of the river, forcing participants to adapt their thinking and judgment to challenging circumstances.

Skill Cues

- Review river communication and protocols.
- Establish lead and sweep canoes that all participants are expected to stay in between.
- Play Follow the Leader, with the lead canoe setting the route for others to follow.

Teaching Cues

- Review lead and sweep boats, signals, rescue procedures, emergency procedures, leader, rescue leader, route overview, and etiquette before going on the water.
- The pace of the group should be that of the slowest boat; if fatigue is a factor, place slow boats near the front of the group behind the lead boat.
- Highlight hazards and major obstacles as they arrive. Encourage participants to contribute to river reading.

Activity 5: International Scale of River Difficulty

Rivers are rated for their difficulty using this internationally recognized rating scale (figure 8.22). Individual rapids are rated by class, ranging from class I to class VI. Where two ratings are indicated for a specific rapid, the first rating applies to high water conditions and the second to medium-low water. Furthermore, rapid classifications are normally increased one level of difficulty in remote wilderness and extreme cold water.

Skill Cues

- Know and learn to recognize the rapid classifications.
- Practice assessing the level of difficulty of rapids according to the scale.

Teaching Cues

- Discuss rapid features and classifications.
- Once participants begin to understand classification system, have them rate rapids and justify their ratings.

Lesson Closure

Paddling moving water requires a mental edge. This state of mental readiness can change from hour to hour or day to day. Paddlers should be respected no matter whether they decide to run a rapid or take a pass. If they do not feel they have that mental edge at a given time, that choice should be respected rather than forcing them to run a rapid they are not mentally prepared for, thereby putting themselves and others at risk. Reinforcing this concept while scouting a rapid early in your river run would be most appropriate.

References and Resources

Dillon, P.S., and J. Oyen. 2008. *Canoeing*. Champaign, IL: Human Kinetics.
Mason, B. 1984. *Path of the paddle*. Toronto: Key Porter Books.

Class I Rapids

Fast-moving water with riffles and small waves. Few obstructions, all obvious and easily missed with little training. Risk to swimmers is slight; self-rescue is easy.

Class II Rapids: Novice

Straightforward rapids with wide, clear channels that are evident without scouting. Occasional maneuvering may be required, but rocks and medium-sized waves are easily missed by trained paddlers. Swimmers are seldom injured and group assistance, while helpful, is seldom needed. Rapids that are at the upper end of this difficulty range are designated class II+.

Class III: Intermediate

Rapids with moderate, irregular waves that may be difficult to avoid and that can swamp an open canoe. Complex maneuvers in fast current and good boat control in tight passages or around ledges are often required; large waves or strainers may be present but are easily avoided. Strong eddies and powerful current effects can be found, particularly on large-volume rivers. Scouting is advisable for inexperienced parties. Injuries while swimming are rare; self-rescue is usually easy but group assistance may be required to avoid long swims. Rapids that are at the lower or upper end of this difficulty range are designated class III– or class III+, respectively.

Class IV: Advanced

Intense, powerful, but predictable rapids requiring precise boat handling in turbulent water. Depending on the character of the river, it may feature large, unavoidable waves and holes or constricted passages demanding fast maneuvers under pressure. A fast, reliable eddy turn may be needed to initiate maneuvers, scout rapids, or rest. Rapids may require "must" moves above dangerous hazards. Scouting may be necessary the first time down. Risk of injury to swimmers is moderate to high, and water conditions may make self-rescue difficult. Group assistance for rescue is often essential but requires practiced skills. A strong Eskimo roll is highly recommended. Rapids that are at the lower or upper end of this difficulty range are designated class IV– or class IV+, respectively.

Class V: Expert

Extremely long, obstructed, or very violent rapids that expose a paddler to added risk. Drops may contain large, unavoidable waves and holes or steep, congested chutes with complex, demanding routes. Rapids may continue for long distances between pools, demanding a high level of fitness. What eddies exist may be small, turbulent, or difficult to reach. At the high end of the scale, several of these factors may be combined. Scouting is recommended but may be difficult. Swims are dangerous, and rescue is often difficult even for experts. A very reliable Eskimo roll, proper equipment, extensive experience, and practiced rescue skills are essential. Because of the large range of difficulty that exists beyond class IV, class V is an open-ended, multiple-level scale designated by class 5.0, 5.1, 5.2, and so on. Each of these levels is an order of magnitude more difficult than the last. For example, increasing difficulty from class 5.0 to class 5.1 is a similar order of magnitude as increasing from class IV to class 5.0.

Class VI: Extreme and Exploratory Rapids

These runs have almost never been attempted and often exemplify the extremes of difficulty, unpredictability, and danger. The consequences of errors are very severe and rescue may be impossible. For teams of experts only, at favorable water levels, after close personal inspection and taking all precautions. After a class VI rapids has been run many times, its rating may be changed to an appropriate class 5.x rating.

Figure 8.22 American Whitewater's International Scale of River Difficulty.

Sea Kayaking

▼ **Mark Dykeman and Kevin Redmond** ▼

A man who is not afraid of the sea will soon be drowned, for he will be going out on a day he shouldn't. But we do be afraid of the sea, and we only do be drowned now and again.

– John Millington Synge (1907)

Archeological evidence has revealed that the kayak has been with us for close to 4,000 years. Most commonly fashioned with a wooden frame covered by animal skins and in some cases dug out from driftwood, the earliest kayak was primarily a hunting vessel; when translated, *kayak* means "hunter's boat."

By the early 1900s, modern cultures, fascinated with the paddling exploits of native cultures, began building wood and wood–fabric kayaks, which remained common until the 1950s, when fiberglass was introduced. The greatest revolution in sea kayaks was the introduction of plastic-hull sea kayaks in 1984. These mass-produced, relatively inexpensive, rotomolded boats made sea kayaking accessible to the larger population, leading to the explosion of sea kayaking popularity evidenced throughout the world.

Today, the kayak is a source of recreational pleasure and a means of adventure travel. The sea kayak offers easy access to the large bodies of water, oceans, and the intertidal zone, the most nutrient-rich ecosystem on the planet.

Sea kayaking offers a unique combination of relaxation and exhilaration. Exploring the nooks and crannies of a quiet archipelago coastline is a sharp contrast to surfing large ocean waves. Feeling comfortable enough to appreciate each situation without the overbearing fear that inhibits learning and enjoyment but enough fear to engender respect requires knowledge, skill, and experience.

This unit covers basic sea kayaking progressions essential for performance and appreciation of surrounding natural wonders. In this unit, *sea kayaking* refers to paddling a sea kayak, whether in freshwater or saltwater. The rationale for including the possibility of freshwater paddling in a sea kayaking unit is that some large bodies of freshwater may present oceanlike conditions, making the sea kayak the ideal craft in these areas. Furthermore, introductory sea kayaking skills may be introduced and practiced by all levels of paddlers on freshwater.

A variety of teaching environments (e.g., shoreline, beachfront, warm freshwater, saltwater bay) and methodologies (e.g., whole–part, part–whole, guided discovery) are recommended where appropriate to ensure success.

This unit offers a list of basic equipment, risk identification and management, skill progressions, etiquette, and introductory lesson plans for sea kayaking. The program presented in this unit is a guide that you can adapt to your personal circumstances and experience.

Equipment

Group Equipment

- 1 kayak per person or double kayak per two people
- 1 paddle per person
- 1 approved PFD with whistle attached per person
- 1 bailer or bilge pump per kayak
- 1 properly fitting spray skirt per paddler
- 1 tow rope for every two boats
- First aid kit
- 1 spare paddle for every two boats
- Map or chart (if touring)
- Compass, preferably mounted on kayak deck

For a detailed explanation of current regulations and requirements, check the Coast Guard governing your paddling area. For example, in Canada visit www.tc.gc.ca/marinesafety/debs/obs/quick/quick_human_powered.htm.

Personal Equipment

- Spare set of clothes (for dressing in layers to make it easier to warm up or cool down depending on the conditions)
- Personal survival kit
- Personal first aid kit
- Snacks
- Water
- Sunscreen and lip balm
- Hat
- Sunglasses
- Rain gear
- Camera (optional)
- Appropriate paddling dress (dry suit, wet suit, paddling or splash jacket, insulation fleece layers, polypropylene wicking layer)

Wet suits and dry suits provide the best protection in the water. The alternative is applying common layering principles: Next to the skin is a layer of polypropylene that wicks moisture away, outside the polypropylene is a layer of insulation (i.e., pile), and the exterior layer is the outer shell that prevents the outer elements (wind and moisture) from penetrating the insulating layer.

Equipment Care and Maintenance

- After use, all equipment should be rinsed with freshwater, dried completely, and stored in a dry area out of direct sunlight.
- Rudders and skegs should be in the up position when paddling in reverse or launching and landing onshore.
- Check rudders, skegs, and associated parts (cables, hardware, and so on) regularly to ensure they are functioning properly. Clean all surfaces, remove sand and grit, and lubricate moving parts.
- All water-sensitive items (e.g., camera, spare clothes, GPS) should be secured in waterproof bags of some sort, even if they are stored in bulkheads.
- Fiberglass and Kevlar kayaks require greater care and maintenance and should only be given to skilled participants prepared to take on the responsibility. This includes ensuring that the kayak is fully floating in water for entries and exits (except in extreme surf conditions).
- Coating the water-displacement area of the hull (two or three times a year depending on use) with a protectant such as Armor All decreases water resistance.

Site Selection

Several sites are required to teach this unit effectively. All sites should minimize exposure to wind as much as possible. In case of wind, an onshore wind is safer because paddlers who are having difficulty will be blown back to their starting point rather than blown away from shore. A sample listing of sites is as follows:

- Wet sessions can be held in a pool or warm body of water (lake or ocean).
- Theory sessions can be held on land or a quiet area near the water, and some sessions can be done with kayaks rafted together on the water.
- Dry or skill sessions can be held at a dock or beachfront for launching and landing.
- The introductory paddling area should be a protected area not severely affected by wind, current, or wave action.

Social Skills and Etiquette

- If using private property such as access to water, dock, or beachfront, ask permission first.

- Do not deliberately splash others.
- Keep a safe distance from other boats, especially in rough conditions, to avoid contact.
- Keep close enough to other boats to facilitate effective communication and timely rescue as needed.
- Follow the sea kayaker's code of ethics in lesson 5, activity 2 (page 319).

Risk Management

- One major risk issue facing sea kayakers paddling cold or cool water is clothing. Clothing for water temperature, air temperature, skill level, and projected paddling conditions must be considered before determining the dress code. For example, a novice paddling in calm, cold ocean water should wear a wet or dry suit, with the latter preferred. An expert paddler in the same conditions may wear layered clothing covered with a splash jacket. The general rule of thumb is that unless paddlers are highly skilled with a bombproof roll, all paddlers should dress for the water temperature.
- Before participants are accepted in the program, it is important to verify their comfort level in water over their head and with their head underwater while wearing a PFD. This can be done through verifying swim credentials or holding a swim verification session in a pool, lake, or oceanfront.
- Kayaks should stay within a clearly defined area. The designated area may be marked with buoys or be specific to the location (such as "Between these three docks," "Within this cove," or "Not past the two points of land"). Participants should not go beyond the area where the outdoor leader can maintain voice contact and perform a timely rescue in the event of upset. A general rule of thumb in good conditions is approximately 6 to 10 boat lengths, or 30 to 46 meters (100-150 feet) from the leader. This distance is a guideline and may be adjusted depending upon the skill level of the group and the wind and water conditions. In adverse conditions it is wise for kayaks to paddle close together in two offset rows such that kayaks bringing up the rear point in between two kayaks in the lead row, making it improbable for the trail kayak to land on the lead kayaks in big-wave or swell conditions.

- When paddling from point A to point B, all kayaks should stay between the designated lead and sweep boats. The lead and sweep kayaks should contain the group, allowing for approximately one to two boat lengths between kayaks.
- If possible, all kayaks should be outfitted in a similar manner, with leaders and participants surveying all boat outfitting before going on the water. Having boats outfitted the same ensures that in the event of a rescue, the rescuers know exactly what to expect. In the event that all boats are not outfitted similarly, leaders and participants should be aware of differences and how best to deal with them.
- Sea kayaks should contain watertight bulkheads in the bow and stern. If the kayak includes only one watertight bulkhead, flotation in the form of an airbag should be in the end without the bulkhead. Otherwise assisted rescue is nearly impossible because the end without the bulkhead becomes water laden and difficult to elevate to a rescue position.
- Learn the whistle code:
  - One whistle blast = Stop! Wherever you are, stop, look, and listen.
  - Two whistle blasts = Stop! The person who blows the whistle can raise a paddle to indicate where to go.
  - Three whistle blasts = Stop! Emergency! Go quickly toward whoever blew the whistle and raft up together; there is an emergency at hand.

Unit Organization

Ideally, a wet session in a pool or warm lake or pond will precede the on-water skills sessions. The wet session focuses on participants becoming comfortable in the boat, tipping over the boat, exiting the boat, and partaking in basic self-rescue and assisted procedures. Following the wet sessions, basic paddling skills and maneuvers such as forward strokes, reverse strokes, and turning strokes are introduced.

When paddling for extended lengths of time, inject instructions, demonstrations, and short theory sessions between paddling sessions and practice.

Lesson Plans

Lesson 1: Getting Started. This introductory lesson prepares participants for paddling. It includes terminology, equipment selection and adjustment, and carrying a kayak to the water. At the shoreline, participants are introduced to kayak entries and exits. The lesson concludes with kayak capsize (commonly referred to as *wet exit*) and assisted rescue.

Lesson 2: Kayak Feel, Tilt, and Strokes. The second lesson reviews important skills covered in the first lesson before introducing basic paddling strokes. It concludes with some self- and assisted-rescue practice.

Lesson 3: Kayak Rolling. The focus of lesson 3 is assisted bow rescue and rolling progressions. Although participants may not achieve immediate success with the roll, this lesson lays the foundation for future success.

Lesson 4: Paddle Strokes. This lesson concludes the entry-level paddling strokes and includes the self-rescue and righting low brace.

Lesson 5: Sea Kayak Tour. The final lesson should be a highlight where participants apply what they have learned. It includes the sea kayaker's code of ethics and an on-water tour.

Terminology

Terms that are *italicized* should be covered in the first lesson.

- **adrift**—Not made fast; floating loose, at mercy of wind and current.
- **aft**—A directional term indicating the back area of the kayak.
- **aground**—Touching or stuck on the bottom.
- **beacon**—A marked post located on a shoal or bank to warn of danger or to mark a channel; a signal mark on land that could be a light or radio signal.
- **beam**—The widest part of the kayak, typically 56 to 61 centimeters (22-24 inches).
- *bilge pump*—Device used for pumping water out of the kayak.
- *bow*—The front end of the kayak; the end that usually goes first.
- **broach**—Turning of the sea kayak broadside to the wind or waves, normally increasing risk of capsize.
- *bulkhead*—Vertical wall (preferably watertight) partitioning the kayak behind or in front of the paddler.
- **buoy**—An anchored float used for marking a position on the water or a hazard, shoal, or mooring.

- **capsize**—To turn over; usually followed by a wet exit, assisted righting, or roll.
- **center of gravity**—The average spatial location of the force of gravity acting upon an object. In a singles kayak, it is normally somewhere around the lower area of the paddler's torso, at the same location as the center of mass.
- *cleat*—A fitting with two projection horns that hold a line from slipping, as in many popular seat-back adjusters. (Note: Only cover this in lesson 1 if kayaks have cleats.)
- **Cleopatra's needle**—Position of the kayak when one end fills with water and the other end sticks up in the air, rendering the kayak useless. This explains the need for watertight bulkheads and flotation in both ends of the kayak!
- *cockpit*—The semienclosed area where the paddler sits.
- *combing*—The raised edge around the cockpit to which the spray skirt is attached.
- **compass**—Should be a spherical marine compass, which is equipped with a magnet that floats freely in a sphere and a lubber line that lets you keep track of your heading at all times. The compass should be deck mounted. Note that the farther forward from the paddler the compass is mounted, the less the risk of sea sickness.
- **contact points**—The paddler's feet, thighs, and hips should make comfortable contact with the kayak, ensuring a snug fit (sometimes referred to as being "as one") with the kayak.
- **cross section**—The cross section is the shape of the kayak from one side to the other, perpendicular to its centerline. Round hulls are fast but unstable compared with flat hulls, which are initially stable but slow while flared sides offer comfortable secondary stability.
- *deck*—The top of the kayak.
- **deck bag**—Bag attached to the kayak deck in front of the cockpit; contains items required when paddling or in an emergency. The deck bag offers easy access to frequently used items (sunscreen, snacks, and so on) or emergency items (flares, strobe light, and so on).
- *deck rigging*—The rope and attachments on the deck of the kayak.
- **draft**—The depth the kayak sinks when afloat, as measured vertically from the waterline to the lowest point. The kayak requires this much water depth or it will run aground.
- **ebb**—Receding tide or current.
- **edging**—Leaning the kayak to one side while paddling to add turning motion.
- **flare**—(1) The outward angle of the kayak sides that gets wider as they get higher. (2) A signaling device to attract rescuers' attention; only used in an emergency.
- **flood**—Incoming tide or current.
- **following sea**—An overtaking sea that comes from astern.
- *foot braces or pegs*—Small, adjustable plates in the forward part of the cockpit for resting or supporting feet. In kayaks without rudders, they are adjustable for length but fixed when adjusted. In kayaks with rudders, they are adjustable for length and flexible to control steering for the rudders.
- **fore**—Directional term indicating the front area of the kayak.
- **freeboard**—The distance between the waterline and the lowest point of the deck.
- *grab loop (kayak)*—Loop or toggle at the end of the kayak used for carrying.
- *grab loop (spray deck)*—Loop on the front of the spray skirt used for detaching spray skirt from combing.
- *hatch*—An opening in the deck fitted with a watertight cover.
- *hull*—The main body of the kayak (bottom and sides).
- **knot**—Measure of speed in nautical miles. A nautical mile is approximately 6,076 feet (1,852 meters), whereas a statute mile is 5,280 feet (1,609 meters).
- **lee**—Calm area behind an object that blocks the wind.
- **lee shore**—Shore that offers protection from the wind or current.
- **leeward**—Direction away from the wind.
- **locked in**—Refers to being one with the kayak; points of contact are feet on foot braces, thighs snug on thigh rests, and bum on seat.
- **midship**—Location equidistant from the bow and stern.
- **nautical mile**—Unit of distance equal to 6,076 feet (1,852 meters). Originally intended to be 1/24,000 of the circumference of the earth at the equator.
- *paddle float*—Floatable object that attaches to the outer end of the paddle after a capsize, helping the paddler get back into the kayak without help.
- **paddle leash**—Device that attaches the paddle shaft to the deck rigging.

- **port**—The left side of the kayak when looking forward; opposite of starboard.
- **rocker**—The curvature of the kayak bottom along the centerline from the bow to the stern. Most sea kayaks have little rocker along the bottom, allowing them to paddle long, straight courses. When a turn is required, paddlers lean the kayak, producing rocker from the curve on the kayak side.
- *rudder*—Adjustable vertical projection located at the stern used to assist in steering the kayak.
- **sea anchor**—Used for slowing the speed of the kayak.
- *skeg*—A vertical projection under the stern of the hull used to keep the kayak going in a straight line.
- **slack water**—Minimum velocity of tidal current.
- *spray skirt*—Provides a watertight seal around the kayaker, preventing water from getting in the kayak. Spray skirts are made out of coated nylon or neoprene and must be well fitted on the cockpit rim and around the waist. Certain models come with a mesh storage pocket. Sometimes referred to as a *spray deck*.
- **starboard**—The right side of the kayak when facing forward.
- *stern*—The end of the kayak behind the paddler's back.
- *thigh rests*—The underside of the deck adjacent to frontal cockpit combing where the thighs apply pressure for support.
- **tide**—The diurnal rise and fall of water level in the oceans due to gravitational forces exerted at different parts of the earth by the moon or sun.
- **tow rope**—Rope with belt or attachment (secured to rescuer or rescue boat) used for towing another kayak.
- **tracking**—The ability of a kayak to go straight without compensation from the paddler.
- **trim**—The longitudinal balance of a vessel described as even (level), bow heavy, or stern heavy.
- **very high frequency (VHF) radio**—One of the best ways of communicating with other ships. Smaller kayak models have a range of several kilometers and also receive weather channels. A watertight model is best suited to kayaking.
- *volume*—A measure of the gear and paddler carrying capacity of a kayak. A large person will likely require a boat with a higher volume than a very slight person will require.
- **wake**—The disturbed water following a moving kayak or boat.
- **wash**—The rush of waves on a bank, shore, or boat vessel.
- **waterline**—The line on the hull of the kayak that the surface of the water marks in calm conditions when the kayak is motionless.
- **weather cocking**—Turning of the kayak caused by wind.
- **windward**—The direction from which the wind is blowing.
- **yaw**—To swing off course, caused by wave action or poor steering.

Getting Started

Overview

The purpose of this first lesson is to introduce participants to the types of sea kayaks and basic safety equipment available; selecting the right boat for the individual; achieving the correct fit; and most importantly, performing a relaxed wet exit.

Learning Objectives

- To understand features and designs of sea kayaks
- To understand principles of paddle selection
- To learn how to select and wear a spray skirt
- To learn how to select and fit a PFD
- To learn how to carry a kayak
- To understand the principles of a proper warm-up
- To enter and exit the kayak from the poolside or shoreline
- To exercise good balance in a kayak
- To learn how to raft up two kayaks
- To understand the principles of and demonstrate competency in wet exits
- To understand the principles of and take part in deep-water T-rescues

Activity 1: Features and Designs of Sea Kayaks

This activity introduces the sea kayak (figure 9.1), its features and design characteristics, and associated terminology. Most terms used in this activity will become part of each paddler's working vocabulary throughout this unit.

Skill Cues

- Length of kayaks: Shorter means better turning, longer means better tracking.

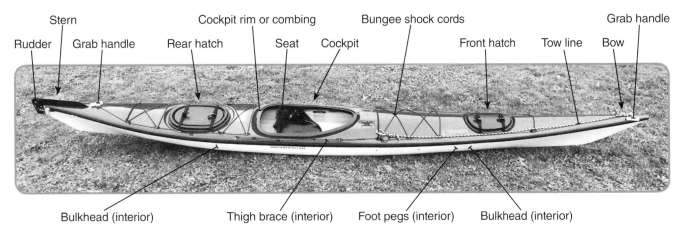

Figure 9.1   The basic parts of a sea kayak.

© Human Kinetics

- Seat adjustments can be made to suit the paddler.
- Identify and explaining the following parts of the kayak:
  - Rocker: More rocker means the kayak is easier turn and harder to track.
  - Edges: These affect primary and secondary stability.
  - Thigh rests: This padded area for resting the thighs helps make the paddler one with the boat.
  - Foot braces: Braces for the feet help make the paddler one with the boat.
  - Grab loop (spray deck): The loops on the spray deck are used for its removal; they should always be on the outside.
  - Grab loop (kayak): The loops at the ends of the kayak are used for carrying the kayak.
  - Rudders: Used to aid in steering the kayak.

Teaching Cues

- Participants should each select a kayak. For proper fitting, they should sit in the kayak with the footwear they plan to use when paddling.
- Foot pegs should be adjusted such that when the thighs are braced against the outside lower cockpit surfaces, the legs are comfortable. Foot pegs that are too loose result in less boat control, and those that are too tight will cause feet and legs to fall asleep.
- Participants should rock the kayak from side to side on the ground to ensure they have a proper fit and control of the kayak angles. If glass kayaks are used, this should be done on a soft surface such as grass.
- Ideally, this first lesson should be performed in warm, still water in a small lake with a good beach or even an indoor heated pool. A quiet place that allows a good visual and hearing connection between participants and outdoor leader is ideal.
- At this point, most participants new to the sport will feel uncomfortable thinking of what it will be like to go upside down in the water. Reassure participants that although the kayaks may feel tight on shore, if they can get into the kayak, they can get out.
- Demonstrate the forward tumble to be used for a wet exit.

Activity 2: Paddle Selection

Using the proper size of paddle is not only important for personal comfort but also for safety. A paddle that is too large increases the risk of injury and decreases paddling efficiency. An appropriate paddle ensures paddling efficiency with minimal risk of strains or muscle tears. Refer to figure 9.2 for the parts of a paddle.

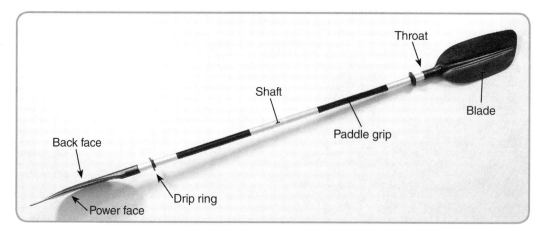

Figure 9.2   The parts of a sea kayak paddle.

Skill Cues

- Length: Standing the paddle on end, the top edge of the blade should fit in the grooves of the fingers with the arm extended. Paddle length may vary depending on kayak width and whether the person paddles with a high or low angle. If in doubt, go shorter.
- Size of blades: A small blade pulls less water and is less tiring; a big blade pulls more water and is more tiring.
- Twist angles (0, 30, 45, and 60 degrees): Zero-degree blades are usually reserved for traditional paddles, whereas 45- and 60-degree twist angles are more popular with modern paddles because the nonpaddling blade cuts through the wind, thereby requiring less effort.

Teaching Cues

- Review the optimal length of paddles.
- After paddle selection, ask the group to hold the paddles properly and to test the grip by placing the paddle on top of the head with the forearm and elbows at a 90-degree angle. Figure 9.3 shows the correct paddle length in a proper paddling position.

Figure 9.3   The appropriate paddle length as it appears in a proper paddling position.

Activity 3: Spray-Skirt Selection

A properly fitting spray skirt must fit the paddler's waist snugly and the kayak's combing securely enough to prevent implosion in rough seas, but there should be enough slack to facilitate removal in a wet exit. Improperly fitted spray skirts increase risk for individual paddlers and the group at large.

Skill Cues

- Look at different types of spray skirts (e.g., fixed waist sizes versus adjustable).
- Spray skirts are made to fit the boat.
- Look at factors that affect water tightness at the waist such as types of jacket edges.
- Participants step into and wear a spray deck. (Note: This is always done before putting on PFDs.)
- Put a spray deck on the kayak by starting from the back of the spray deck and working it forward with the all-important grab loop on the outside.
- Participants now remove the spray deck by pulling forward and up on the grab loop; repeat.

- Emergency exits can be done by popping the knees or using the hands on the side of the spray deck to remove it, simulating emergency procedure if the grab loop is not showing.

Teaching Cues

- Demonstrate stepping into the spray deck (always done before putting on a PFD).
- Monitor and verify the fit of skirts on participants and kayaks.
- Demonstrate putting a spray deck on the kayak by starting from the back of the spray deck and working it forward with the all-important grab loop on the outside.
- Explain to participants how to remove the spray deck (in case of emergency) if the grab loop is not showing. This can be done using the knee or using the hands on the side of the spray deck.
- Practice removing the spray deck with eyes closed.

Activity 4: PFD Selection

The primary function of the PFD is to aid the paddler when immersed in water. It also provides secondary benefits of heat insulation and cushioning impact. Improperly fitted PFDs increase risk to paddlers because the PFD does not provide the expected support. When improperly fitted, it is a dangerous distraction to the victim in the water, obstructing vision as well as rescue efforts. Furthermore, an improperly fitted PFD makes for uncomfortable paddling to the point that many are prone to take it off! A properly fitted PFD is inconspicuous to the paddler.

Skill Cues

- PFDs for kayaking should have a shorter waist. When sitting in the kayak, the PFD should be comfortable and above the spray skirt; the bottom of the PFD fits roughly at the bottom of the rib cage.
- Try on the PFD, ensuring a snug but comfortable fit; when floating in deep water, the PFD should remain in position and not ride up.
- Locate and read the PFD label for sizing and other appropriate data.
- Locate and identify the function of each adjustor on the PFD.

Teaching Cues

- Demonstrate and explain how to make a PFD fit using adjustors.
- Have participants select a personal PFD from a selection, fit the PFD on themselves, and offer rationale for their choice to a partner, who then tests the fit by tugging gently on the waist, armpits, and shoulders of the PFD.
- Have participants float in shallow or deep water (depending on their comfort level) wearing the PFD to ensure proper fit. This activity may be extended to putting the PFD on in deep water and making all adjustments while in the water.
- Ask questions of the group to identify and give the function of various PFD adjusters.
- Demonstrate the consequences of an improperly fitting PFD: If it's too small, it may not support the person sufficiently to be effective and it restricts movement; when it's too large, it floats up around the face in deep water; when it's too long, it interferes with the spray-deck fitting and rides up in the armpits and face.

Activity 5: Carrying the Kayak

Because kayaks are normally stored on land and used on the water, some form of carry is required to move the kayak from storage area to the shoreline. Carrying a kayak is an essential skill for all paddlers.

Skill Cues

- Participants practice the two-person suitcase carry, on opposite sides and ends of the boat (figure 9.4).
- Participants try the short one-person carry with two hands on the cockpit combing and the kayak resting on the thigh.
- The solo carry for longer distances is performed by carrying the kayak on the shoulder. To get the kayak onto the shoulder, use the upper leg to lift the kayak, not the wrist and shoulder.

Figure 9.4   The suitcase method of carrying a sea kayak.

Teaching Cues

- Demonstrate the one- and two-person carries.
- Ask participants to avoid dragging kayaks on the ground.
- Introduce the solo carry for longer distances if time and skill set permit. Consider introducing this carry at the end of the lesson to return kayaks to their racks after a paddling session.

Activity 6: Warm-Up

A proper warm-up for paddling is important for minimizing injury and improving paddling efficiency. Participants should come to view their warm-up as a personal responsibility.

Skill Cues

- A short warm-up of 3 to 5 minutes should be spent doing some exercises to loosen up and stretch the paddling muscles. Begin by making the same motions you'll be using on the water. Rotate your shoulders forward and back, twist and lean your torso, and move your body forward and back, simulating paddling motions. Repeat the motions until you feel the muscles loosen up.
- Once you're on the water paddling, start easy and work up to intense paddling.
- Once muscles are loosened, stretch muscles in the neck, chest, arms, shoulders, abdomen, and upper and lower back, holding each stretch 15 to 30 seconds.
- Stretch during breaks throughout the paddling day if necessary.
- A swim should be done if the water and weather are suitable.

- Perform a complete body stretch at the end of the paddling day that includes ankles, calves, knees, thighs, hips, abdomen, chest, neck, shoulders, biceps, forearms, wrists, and upper and lower back.

Teaching Cues

- Loosening and stretching muscles and tendons improves flexibility, muscle elasticity, and injury prevention. When stretching, paddlers should feel tension but never pain.
- Once the warm-up is understood, make it a personal responsibility for future sessions or let participants take the lead role for group warm-ups.

a

b

c

Figure 9.5   When entering a sea kayak, always lean the kayak toward the supporting side.

© Human Kinetics

- Paddlers who are more advanced may supplement dry-land routines with a personal on-water warm-up from their kayaks that may include graduated intensities (slow, moderate, and intense performance and water conditions) in performing a variety of strokes, maneuvers, and combinations.

Activity 7: Entering and Exiting the Kayak From Poolside or Shoreline

Learning to enter and exit a kayak ensures a good start and finish to any paddling session.

Skill Cues

- Dock, poolside, or shallow water are appropriate settings for entries and exits using the paddle as an outrigger. The paddle straddles a solid object (dock, pool deck, or bottom of water) and the back of the kayak combing. With hands on the paddle shaft, keep weight on the side of entry or exit as feet and legs enter or exit the cockpit (figure 9.5).
- A beach location can be used to perform the seal entry, which places the kayak bow forward in the water but not enough to have the kayak float away.

Teaching Cues

- The outrigger entry and exit should be used with all fiberglass boats, with the kayak fully floating in shallow water.
- The seal entry provides the opportunity to enter the kayak and ensure proper spray-deck fitting before leaving the shoreline.
- When participants are in the kayak with the spray skirt, have them practice reaching for the skirt, grabbing the loop first with eyes open and then with eyes closed.

Risk Management

- All participants should wear their PFDs and spray decks, as well as footwear that will stay on in the water but that is not so large as to cause jamming in the boat.
- Ask participants if they have any medical conditions that could affect their performance.

Activity 8: Kayak Balance

Maintaining balance in a kayak is essential to staying upright. Practicing balance under controlled conditions prepares paddlers for more challenging conditions such as wind and waves.

Skill Cues

- Start with the basic forward stroke, emphasizing the twist of the torso for each stroke.
- Rock the kayak from side to side by applying pressure on alternating thighs while keeping the upper body and the head silent and in a balanced, central location.
- While performing the rocking motion, focus eyes on a distant fixed object.

Teaching Cues

- Keep all the participants in a small area so they can be observed.
- Participants may become frustrated with not being able to control the direction of the kayak, and this is normal. Keeping the group in a small area alleviates some of the concerns.
- A fun balance activity is to discard paddles and paddle with the hands.

Activity 9: Rafting Up Two Kayaks

Rafting up is used for watching instruction, adjusting the boat and personal paraphernalia, providing safety and stability during rescue, or just taking a break from paddling.

Skill Cues

Kayaks Going in Same Direction
- Two kayaks paddle side by side in the same direction, with similar but slowing speed, and less than parallel where bows will glide by each other softly without heavy impact.
- Once paddles are in danger of interference from the other kayak, paddles are removed from the water and may be used to pull the two kayaks together.
- Once kayaks are together, paddles are laid across the two kayaks and paddlers can safely lean on the middle of the paddle or the opposite kayak.
- To break up a raft, do not push! Draw away from each other or slide where one kayak goes forward while the other goes back.

Kayaks Approaching Each Other From Opposing Directions
- Two kayaks paddle toward each other in opposing directions, with slowing speed, and less than parallel, aiming kayaks toward the desired position where bows will gently meet sterns.
- As the bow of one kayak approaches the cockpit of the other kayak, paddlers take hold of the opposite kayak, moving forward until the two cockpits are roughly side by side.

- Once kayaks are together, paddles are laid across the two kayaks and paddlers can safely lean on the middle of the paddle or the opposite kayak.
- To break up a raft, do not push! Draw away from each other or slide where one kayak goes forward while the other goes back.

Teaching Cues

- Demonstrate both methods of rafting up.
- In rough seas, emphasize flat-angle approaches to prevent one kayak from landing on the other.
- Draw strokes (if they have been taught) work well here, with the last draw stroke over the other kayak.
- It is critical not to put hands in between kayaks when rafted.
- Have participants lean full upper-body weight across the opposite kayak to discover the full effect of the maneuver.
- Discuss situations for rafting up in the same versus different directions.
- The two-kayak raft may be extended to any number of kayaks in a raft—even the whole group.
- Depending on the situation, rafting up may be better introduced after strokes are taught in lesson 3 or 4.

Activity 10: Wet Exit

The wet exit is an important safety skill that all paddlers should master in a wide variety of conditions. This skill should be practiced until it is automatic and the paddler is able to keep her wits while performing it.

Skill Cues

- Before doing the wet exit, practice finding the skirt grab loop with eyes closed.
- Tip the kayak to one side.
- Once underwater, pull the grab loop of the spray deck, separating the spray deck from the kayak.
- Tumble forward without kicking the legs; the legs must be relaxed to avoid jamming.
- Participants should do a wet exit and move to either the bow or stern and swim both kayak and paddle to shore. This is the ideal wet exit.

Teaching Cues

- First talk through the procedure and then perform at least one wet exit while maintaining contact with the kayak and paddle.
- If participants are very apprehensive, allow them to perform the first wet exit with the spray deck not in place and without a paddle.
- Participants should maintain contact with both kayak and paddle upon wet exiting, moving to the end of the kayak and swimming to shore.
- You may also facilitate the first wet exits by standing in shallow water next to the participant.
- Make sure participants know how to drain water from a swamped kayak so as not to cause back injuries (use legs to lift the bow first and then the stern).
- Explain that regardless of their skill level, they will swim from time to time and the best option to stay in their kayak will be a solid roll. Water in the eyes and sinuses is just part of the sport.

Risk Management

Carefully question participants with regard to their swimming ability. Experience has shown that even strong swimmers can become disoriented and uncomfortable when upside down in a kayak. This is an activity that must be learned.

Activity 11: Deep-Water T-Rescue

All paddlers should develop proficiency in deep-water rescue skills. If conditions permit, these skills should be practiced throughout the unit by participants performing any required rescues.

Skill Cues

- The victim moves to the bow of the rescue boat, holding onto his paddle.
- The rescuer stows her paddle blade under bungee cords.
- Throughout this process, the victim should talk, count, sing, or do anything that continues to let the rescuer know he is OK.
- The rescuer takes hold of the bow of the victim's kayak so a *T* is formed by the two boats.
- If the victim's boat is upside down, break the seal (air pocket caused by cockpit) by lifting (victim boat tipped slightly to one side) or using edges of the rescue boat to assist; pull the kayak up, draining water as it is pulled up (figure 9.6); and flip it right side up, ready for reentry.
- If the victim's kayak is right side up (and full of water), roll it over so it is upside down and complete the process described previously.
- In many cases, because of paraphernalia on the bow deck it may be simpler to keep the victim boat right side up, haul it on top of the rescue boat, flip it over to drain the water, and prepare for reentry.

Figure 9.6   Beginner paddlers practice a deep-water T-rescue.
Courtesy of Neil Burgess.

- With both kayaks parallel and facing opposite directions, the rescuer puts both paddles across both kayaks, leaning on the paddles and holding the victim boat in place for reentry.
- The victim comes from behind the cockpit of his boat and uses the buoyancy of the two kayaks (relatively equally, one arm on each kayak) to lift and slide his legs back into cockpit of his kayak.
- Alternatively, some may find it easier to reenter over the outside of the empty kayak.
- There should be constant communication between victim and rescuer.

Teaching Cues

- Demonstrate full rescue procedures before participants practice.
- Demonstrate the stability of the T-position.
- Emphasize that when performing a rescue, paddlers should always pick up the bow.
- Have participants practice being a rescuer and a victim.
- Have victims practice getting back in their kayak with kayaks rafted in opposite directions.

- Discuss rescue and victim variations, challenges, and solutions for each.
- Depending on the situation, the T-rescue may be better introduced in lesson 3 combined with the (unsuccessful) kayak roll. If the T-rescue is taught here, it can be practiced and reinforced in lesson 3 with some unsuccessful kayak rolls.

Lesson Closure

This first lesson is the foundation of future learning. With a little practice, all of the skills in this lesson should become second nature. Wet exits should be repeated enough so that participants are comfortable with tapping both hands on the bottom of a capsized kayak before the wet exit.

LESSON 2

Kayak Feel, Tilt, and Strokes

Overview

The purpose of this lesson is to make sure the participant is comfortable with the kayak fit and can feel and start controlling the motions of the kayak with paddle strokes.

Learning Objectives

- To improve proficiency in adjusting kayaks on the beach and entering and exiting techniques
- To improve proficiency in wet exits
- To be at one with the boat through understanding boat feel and boat tilt
- To understand and demonstrate kayak edging
- To understand and demonstrate the forward sweep stroke
- To understand and demonstrate the forward stroke
- To understand and demonstrate the reverse stroke
- To understand and demonstrate towing

Activity 1: Review

Review adjusting kayaks on the beach and entering and exiting techniques.

Skill Cues

- Participants select their kayaks, paddles, and spray decks and sit at the edge of the water, ready to go.
- Participants then flick their kayaks from side to side to ensure they are properly fitted.

Teaching Cues

Check all safety equipment at this stage—that is, all PFDs are adjusted and zipped up, skirts are properly fitted and cover complete combing, and most importantly, the spray-skirt grab loops are in the correct exposed position.

Activity 2: Wet Exit Reviewed

As noted in the closure of lesson 1, wet exits should be practiced to the point that participants are completely comfortable in the upside-down capsize position.

Skill Cues

- Participants verbally describe the technique and demonstrate the wet exit on dry land before performing it on the water.
- While performing the wet exit, participants maintain contact with the kayak and paddle.
- After exiting the kayak, swim the kayak to the shoreline and empty water from the kayak.

Teaching Cues

- If possible, you should be the first on the water.
- Once all participants are on the water in a safe and secure place, you should demonstrate a wet exit maintaining contact with the kayak and paddle, swim the kayak to the shoreline, and demonstrate the emptying technique.

Activity 3: Boat Feel and Boat Tilt

A large part of feeling stable and in control of the kayak comes from the paddler and kayak being one: The paddler's body is locked in the kayak and paddler movement in the kayak causes boat movement. Hence the paddler is able to feel boat action and reaction and tilt the kayak using the lower half of the body inside the cockpit.

Skill Cues

- Paddlers should feel snug in the kayak with feet, thighs, and hips "as one" with the kayak.
- Maintain correct body position for boat tilt, with chin up and chest slightly forward; to tilt the kayak, apply upward pressure with the opposite knee.
- To perform the hip flick, hold the paddle horizontally while the boat is being tilted from side to side, leaving the head in a neutral position.

Teaching Cues

- Discuss the contact points (feet, thighs, hips) between the paddler and the kayak.
- Body and kayak should be one.
- Introduce the hip flick (holding the paddle horizontally while the boat is tilting from side to side, keeping the head in a neutral position).

Activity 4: Kayak Edging

Edging a kayak is one of three options for turning the boat. Performing this skill requires good balance and positional control. One advantage of edging is that it allows the paddler to turn the kayak while maintaining forward momentum.

Skill Cues

- Put the boat on edge while keeping the upper body centrally positioned over the kayak.

- To edge the kayak, shift the weight in the seat to one side while applying upward pressure on the opposite knee to fine-tune the edge.
- Aim to edge the kayak to point the cockpit combing so that the spray-skirt edge gets wet.
- Participants paddle 5 to 10 boat lengths edging right and then 5 to 10 boat lengths edging left.

Teaching Cues

- Emphasize that the two phases of edging a kayak are (1) shifting weight in the seat to one side while (2) applying upward pressure on the opposite knee to fine-tune the edge.
- Participants should hold the kayaks on edge to a point where the spray decks are almost wet for approximately 10 seconds on each side.

Activity 5: Forward Sweep Stoke

This stroke is used to turn the kayak or control the direction of the turn while maintaining forward momentum.

Skill Cues

- The torso is wound up and the head and eyes are turned in the direction of the desired turn.
- The paddle is maintained in an almost horizontal position with the lower arm fully extended throughout the entire stroke.
- Participants first follow the forward blade of the paddle through the entire stroke by turning their head. This ensures a full 180-degree twist in the torso.
- Perform the stroke on each side a number of times while keeping the kayak in a neutral (flat) position.

Teaching Cues

- The forward sweep stroke is often taught before the forward stroke because it emphasizes torso rotation. Good torso rotation is the key to most paddling strokes.
- Though the optimal method is to demonstrate the torso winding up while looking in the direction of the turn, it is sometimes useful to have the participants first follow the forward blade of the paddle through the entire stroke by turning their head. This will ensure a full 180-degree twist in the torso.
- Have participants perform the stroke on each side a number of times while keeping the kayak in a neutral (flat) position.
- As a refinement of the stroke, have participants edge their kayaks in both directions using the carving turn techniques for edging the kayak.

Activity 6: Forward Stroke

The forward stroke drives the kayak forward. Good forward power not only moves the kayak but also makes turning strokes easier and more effective (figure 9.7).

Skill Cues

- As with all paddling strokes, the participant must first hold the paddle in the balance position. The balance position involves placing the paddle on top of the head with forearms and elbows bent at exactly 90 degrees and symmetrical on the paddle shaft.

- Select either high-angle paddling that has the top hand at eye level or low-angle paddling where the top hand is at shoulder level. A general rule of thumb is that high-angle paddling provides more power and consumes more energy, whereas low-angle paddling provides less power with less energy requirements.
- To start the stroke, the forward arm should be straight out for full extension to the toes while the upper arm allows the torso twist to put equal power onto the paddle blade.
- Forward paddling power is not critical at this stage; proper technique is the objective for the beginning paddler.

Teaching Cues

- With the forward stroke, the torso twist is important. However, the range of motion of the blade is from the toes to the hips.
- Participants should not move the paddle blade beyond the hips.
- The forward stroke emphasizes torso rotation for power and stamina and does not use arm muscles for power.

Figure 9.7   The forward stroke provides forward power.

Activity 7: Reverse Stroke

Reverse paddling may be used to slow the kayak's forward momentum or move it backward (figure 9.8).

Figure 9.8   The reverse stroke slows the kayak or moves it backward.

Skill Cues

- Select either high-angle paddling (top hand at eye level) or low-angle paddling (top hand at shoulder level). A general rule of thumb is that high-angle paddling provides more power and consumes more energy, whereas low-angle paddling provides less power with less energy requirements.
- The torso twist is important to provide power.
- Range of motion of the blade is from the hips to the knees.
- Reverse paddling power is not critical at this stage; proper technique is the objective.
- To start the stroke, the power arm should begin with the elbow at a right angle.
- Most power comes from reverse torso rotation, maintaining a bent elbow through the primary power phase.
- The power arm is extended to complete the power phase of the stroke.
- Twist the torso to the other side of the kayak and repeat on the opposite side.

Teaching Cues

- All rudders should be out of the water.
- In the reverse stroke, emphasize the torso twist for primary power.
- As with all paddling strokes, the participant must first hold the paddle in the balance position. The balance position involves placing the paddle on top of the head with forearms and elbows bent at exactly 90 degrees and symmetrical on the paddle shaft.

Activity 8: Towing

Contact towing (without a rope) is used to move a paddler quickly away from danger. Long tows using a rope work well for fatigued paddlers over longer distances.

Skill Cues

Contact Towing
- Contact towing can be done from the front or stern of the kayak.
- With kayaks offset parallel such that the rescuer is free to paddle, the victim holds the bow or stern of the rescue boat.
- The rescuer tows the kayak to the desired area.
- A short cow tail (a piece of nylon tubing with a shock cord core and carabiner used for short tows) may be attached for support if necessary.
- Practicing towing is a good activity to reinforce technique and the importance of forward or reverse power strokes.

Long Tow Using a Rope
- Long tows using a rope take a little longer to set up but work well for long distances.
- The tow rope must have some type of quick release so it can break free of the tow if required.
- The quick release can be attached to the lead kayak or lead kayaker.
- The length of the tow rope should be adjustable and will depend on the sea state. Rougher seas dictate longer rather than shorter rope.
- If the person being towed is unstable (e.g., seasickness) and if a third kayak is available, then a raft can be set up and the lead kayak can tow the raft. This is difficult and should only be done for short distances.

Teaching Cues

- Timing can be everything, and participants should be able to set up and go quickly. Have everything set up on shore before you are on the water; on the water is not the best time to rig a tow system.
- The person being towed should paddle if possible.
- If the kayak being towed has a rudder, the paddler should use it to keep the kayak going in a straight line.
- Discuss when to use short and long tows.

Activity 9: Wet Exit and Swim to Shore

This is the same as activity 10 in lesson 1 (page 306). It is repeated in lesson 2 to provide participants with an opportunity to do it right and to boost their confidence.

Lesson Closure

Participants should understand that forward and reverse strokes are the fundamental strokes of sea kayaking. Additional skills such as edging demonstrate precision paddling where small adjustments provide great results.

Kayak Rolling

Overview

In some schools it is now thought that introducing participants early to rolling will accelerate their progression as they move on to challenging water. To a large extent this will depend on the participants and the environment for teaching the roll. The ideal location is warm, clear water.

The rolling technique presented here is one of many methods, all of which will work for some people and circumstances. The more paddlers learn, the better they can fine-tune and adapt to their individual strengths and paddling scenarios.

Learning Objectives

- To understand and refine the hip flick
- To understand and practice the bow rescue as a victim and as a rescuer
- To understand the principles of the C-to-C roll

Activity 1: Introduction to the Hip Flick

The better the hip flick, the easier the roll. A solid, well-timed hip flick makes learning the roll simply a question of sequence and timing (figure 9.9).

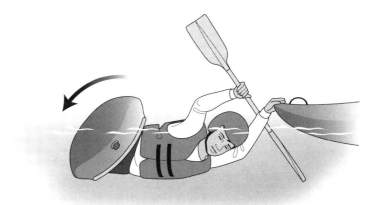

a

Skill Cues

- The paddler should maintain an upright or slightly forward chest at all times during the hip flick.
- Participants place one ear on top of the bow of another kayak and rotate the kayak back and forth at least three times.
- Practice the hip flick equally on both sides.
- Any leaning back to the stern should be discouraged at this stage.
- Boat tilt can be performed using the bow of another kayak, a paddle held by an outdoor leader standing in the water, or the edge of a pool or dock.

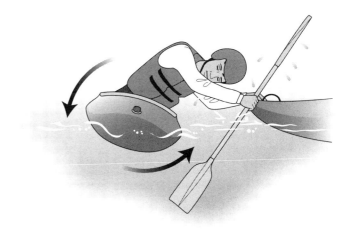

b

Figure 9.9   The hip flick is the same for the sea kayak and whitewater kayak.

Teaching Cues

- Look for a full range of motion in the C-to-C roll, which is bending the spine laterally to a full extension from one side to the other.
- Participants place one ear on top of the bow of another kayak and rotate the kayak back and forth at least three times.

- All of this practice should be done on both sides.
- Using the edge of the pool or dock is less desirable because there is no immediate feedback on the amount of pressure the participant is applying to get up.

Activity 2: Bow Rescue

For participants who have not perfected the Eskimo roll, the bow rescue is the next best method of righting an overturned kayak and avoiding a wet exit.

Skill Cues

- Participants should be in a relaxed position while upside down and remaining braced in the kayak.
- Both left and right hands are extended upward on each side of the kayak, first banging on the bottom of the kayak three times to get attention and moving back and forth approximately 10 centimeters (4 inches) from the side of the kayak.
- Once contact is made with the bow of another kayak, the second hand is placed on top of the bow, allowing the participant enough leverage to lift the head out of the water.
- At this point, most of the remaining rescue is performing a proper hip flick and follow-up (see figure 9.9).
- A check for a good hip flick is less pressure applied to the bow of the rescue boat.
- Proper follow-up includes the head coming up last and as close to the deck as possible before returning to normal paddling position.

Teaching Cues

- Encourage participants to use nose plugs and goggles during this exercise. Water in the sinuses degrades the learning experience.
- If participants are tentative, the first attempt can be made while placing one hand on the bow of the rescue kayak. This helps to prevent some of the disorientation.
- Emphasize that good execution of bow-rescue skills will accelerate learning the kayak roll.

Activity 3: Rolling

Learning to roll a kayak provides a huge boost of confidence to most paddlers. Not only is it cool to roll a kayak, but rolling competence minimizes personal and group risk.

Skill Cues

- When first learning to roll, begin the setup for the roll when you are upright, rotating the torso to the side you will tip toward.
  - Place the paddle alongside the kayak with the blade at the bow flat or preferably with an open face away from the kayak.
  - Tip the kayak over by rolling toward the paddle side (figure 9.10).
  - While underwater, confirm setup by ensuring full paddle extension. Hands are above the surface of the water and bow paddle blade is flat to slap (to check for support), or preferably the

Figure 9.10   The paddler attempts a high brace before completely overturning for a roll.

outside edge of the blade is higher than the edge near the kayak (to prevent the paddle from diving).

- Initiate the sweep stroke with the leading blade skimming the surface while providing necessary support.
- As the blade passes 1:30 to 2:30 of the arc, initiate the hip flick to bring the kayak to its righted position.
- Bring the paddle to high-brace position as the head sweeps along the surface of the water to the deck.
- The head should be the last body part out of the water.
- Some roll progressions have the paddler finishing over the front deck whereas others finish over the back deck. Finishing over the front deck provides added protection for the face.
- Almost all of the roll power comes from the hip flick or the C-to-C movement of the spine and not the paddle.

Teaching Cues

- Swim goggles are helpful and dive masks are even better (to prevent water from going up the nose).
- There are various techniques for teaching the roll; the method listed here is only one of many.
- Full paddle extension, hands above the surface of the water, and the leading edge of the supporting blade being higher than the trailing edge of the supporting blade are essential in the setup.
- Emphasize that almost all of the roll power comes from the hip flick or the C-to-C movement of the spine and not the paddle.
- Some roll progressions have the paddler finishing over the front deck whereas others finish over the back deck. Finishing over the front deck provides added protection for the face and is safer in areas where underwater obstacles are close to the surface.
- Kayaks with high back rests will make it difficult or impossible to finish over the back deck.
- Teaching the progressions to the roll early, even if the skill is not achieved, offers a good means for visualization and mental preparation for future success.

Lesson Closure

It is not expected that participants will achieve the roll in only one lesson. What is important is that participants leave with a clear concept of the progressions and a belief that over time they will be able to achieve the roll. Part of this process may include participants sharing what worked for them and what they saw working for others.

LESSON 4

Paddle Strokes

Overview

This lesson completes and reviews all the basic strokes and edging techniques required to move the sea kayak.

Learning Objectives

- To refine technique of the forward stroke and sweep strokes
- To understand and demonstrate competency of the high and low braces
- To understand and demonstrate an effective draw stroke
- To refine reverse paddling

Activity 1: Review of the Forward and Sweep Strokes

With added time on the water, there is a greater expectation for participants to refine strokes to the point where they can get the greatest effect for the least effort.

Skill Cues

- Refine strokes. Top hands are somewhere between the chin and eyes and are not allowed to drop at the end of each stroke.
- Sweep strokes should be full; the paddle blade should make a full 180-degree arc.

Teaching Cues

- Set up a straight-line course using a few markers or buoys to see if the participants can paddle in a straight line for 30 meters (33 yards) and control the turning tendency of the kayak by using forward sweeps.
- Any negative stroke such as stopping or reverse sweeps should be discouraged at this time. All corrections to the kayak should be positive.
- This review should also involve boat edging to facilitate carving turns and boat control.

Figure 9.11 The low brace.

Figure 9.12 The high brace. In this position, the paddler will capsize without a supplementary hip flick.

Activity 2: Braces

Braces are self-righting strokes that can prevent the kayak from capsizing.

Skill Cues

- The low brace is performed using the non-power face of the blade with the knuckles of each hand pointing down and the paddle shaft remaining as horizontal as possible (figure 9.11).
- Once the tipping motion has been corrected by the brace, the kayak should be righted using the hip flick.
- The high brace is performed using the power face of the blade with the knuckles of each hand pointed up and the paddle shaft remaining as horizontal as possible. Ensure that the elbow is slightly bent to minimize risk of shoulder injury. The hip flick is used to right the kayak (figure 9.12).
- A stroke brace can also be achieved from a power stroke and hip flick.

Teaching Cues

- Ask participants to demonstrate each brace technique.
- Encourage participants to go further only when the stroke techniques are perfected.
- Low and high braces can be taught together or separately—low always first!
- Make sure participants' elbows are slightly bent in the high brace; if they are not, shoulder injury could occur. This is the reason why some beginner courses do not teach the high brace.
- The bow rescue is also a useful recovery when braces have failed.

Activity 3: Draw Stroke

The purpose of the draw stroke is to move the kayak sideways.

Skill Cues

- The paddle shaft should remain as vertical as possible during the stroke (figure 9.13).
- The torso should be twisted sideways in the direction the kayak is moving, and the stroke ends approximately 10 centimeters (4 inches) from the edge of the kayak with an in-water or out-of-water paddle recovery.
- The head and eyes should always point in the direction of motion. Look where you want to go.

Teaching Cues

- For the draw stroke, the upper hand remains in a fixed position and is used as a pivot with the torso turned in the direction of motion and lower arm fully extended to propel water deep under the kayak.
- The recovery starts with a 90-degree snap of the wrist in the lower blade to feather the blade for either an in-water or out-of-water recovery.
- Have participants look where they want to go.
- Participants should be aware that when there is no pressure on the paddle blade or the blade is close to or under the hull, they will likely feel less stable (and at higher risk of capsizing) than during the initial power phase of the stroke.

Figure 9.13 The draw stroke: Stop the draw before the side of the kayak to maintain stability.

Activity 4: Reverse Paddling

Reverse paddling is used to slow, stop, or paddle the kayak in reverse.

Skill Cues

- Use a normal grip on the paddle.
- Reverse paddling is the exact opposite of the forward power stroke, but hands are lower and the paddle is more horizontal.
- Choose high-angle (top hand at eye level) technique for increased power if required.

Teaching Cues

- This is an important skill to learn for many situations (avoiding another boat, surfing a breaking wave, rafting up, and so on).

- Have participants practice by approaching an object (e.g., float, kayak) and then stop or back up.
- Have participants raft all kayaks together without forward strokes.

Lesson Closure

Although this lesson concludes the instructional portion of this unit, it represents the beginning of the learning and refinement process. Participants' skills can be compared to a mechanic's tools—now they take their tools and apply them to improve and further develop their paddling ability.

LESSON 5

Sea Kayak Tour

Overview

Sea kayak touring is the ultimate goal and a highlight experience. To ensure a positive experience in conditions where water is frigid and weather may rapidly change, planning, preparation, and good judgment are essential. The potential consequences of an oversight or accident are extreme. Whether it is a short or extended trip, the planning, preparation, on-water protocols, and decision-making processes are similar for ensuring an enjoyable and memorable trip (figure 9.14).

Figure 9.14 Making a memorable sea kayak tour.

Learning Objectives

- To take part in a sea kayak tour
- To be aware of the sea kayaker's code of ethics

Risk Management

Because of the high risk inherent in this lesson, specific risks and related hazard management strategies are included in each of the activities with the intent that due consideration will be given to each issue in the progression deemed appropriate. All risk management strategies within the activities in this lesson are essential for minimizing risk.

Activity 1: On-Water Sea Kayak Tour

The on-water tour is an opportunity for participants to apply all they have learned in a real-world situation. It is hoped that this tour not only will provide an opportunity to practice what they have learned but also will enrich their lives with memorable moments.

Skill Cues

- Stay together as a group and follow all instructions closely.
- Stay behind the lead kayak, ahead of the sweep kayak, and between the inside and outside kayaks (if used).
- Avoid shoals that may create breaking waves.
- In the event of capsizing, all kayaks not involved raft together while rescue is performed if it's safe to do so. Depending on the conditions, it may be better to have the kayaks point into the wind, hold position, and stay with the rescue. This can be helpful if someone in the rescue needs help or if gear such as a paddle floats away during the rescue.
- Communication is the key to healthy and happy relationships within the group. Participants should communicate concerns to the outdoor leader as they arise.
- Know your position at all times.

Teaching Cues

- The sea state may vary significantly from current wind and atmospheric conditions. Consider both current and possible future conditions when making decisions.
- In the event of reduced visibility, lightning, or other conditions unsuitable for the group's skills, put ashore.
- If tides are a factor, know their schedule, amplitude, and consequences (currents). Tide tables will provide this information.
- Avoid risks and stay as close to shore as possible; rough seas may dictate moving offshore to avoid reflective waves.
- If crossing a shipping lane, do so quickly and by the shortest possible route.
- It is important to notify the person who has the route plan of your safe arrival. This will avoid costly and unnecessary searches by search-and-rescue organizations.

Activity 2: Sea Kayaker's Code of Ethics

The sea kayaker's code of ethics should be the guiding principles for all sea kayaking individuals and groups.

Skill Cues

- You are the best person to ensure your safety. Plan your trips carefully.
- Remain courteous at all times and respect other users. Offer assistance to anyone who appears to be in trouble.
- Find out about and follow applicable regulations. Respect private property.
- Avoid abrupt changes in direction. They can disturb wildlife and may surprise other boaters on the water.

- Never camp on islands that are smaller than 60 meters (66 yards) in diameter or home to colonies of birds and seals. On land, avoid nesting areas and seal haul-outs.
- Never go within 200 meters (219 yards) of wild animals.
- Cut noise and speed near animals. Never circle or chase them.
- Move away if you see signs of nervousness or panic in wild animals.
- Never wash anything directly in a river or lake. Do all washing (dishes, clothing, and yourself) on land using biodegradable soap. This ensures that the ground will fulfill its role as a filter.
- Use a camp stove rather than an open fire for preparing meals.
- Pack out all your garbage and make sure you don't leave any trace of your passage behind.
- Share and encourage adherence of this code with others.

Teaching Cues

- Share and encourage adherence of this code with others.
- Reward participants who adhere to the code.

Lesson Closure

- It is important to notify the person who has the route plan (e.g., principal, camp director, administrator) of your safe arrival. This will avoid costly and unnecessary searches by search-and-rescue organizations.
- Consider hosting a slideshow, posting pictures on the organization Web site, or creating poster displays of the tour.
- Emphasize to participants that an additional sea kayaking course is recommended before venturing out on their own.

References and Resources

Dillon, P.S., and J. Oyen. 2008. *Kayaking.* Champaign, IL: Human Kinetics.

Redmond, K., and D. Murphy. 2003. *A guide to sea kayaking in Newfoundland and Labrador.* Halifax, NS: Nimbus.

Nordic Skiing

▼ Sean Dwyer ▼

When I am on my skis
and they are running
good on the snow, I
get a thrill from gliding
effortlessly with the
push of my poles and
the kick of my skis. I
accept the struggle
of climbing the hills
to reap the benefits
of an exhilarating and
challenging ride down
the other side.

— Aubrey Sanders, Corner Brook,
Newfoundland and Labrador

Nordic or cross-country skiing is an activity well recognized for the development and maintenance of cardiorespiratory fitness. The benefits of Nordic skiing include

- conditioning of leg muscles through the skiing action and development of the triceps muscles in the arms through the motion of poling, and
- strengthening of the core muscles as a result of the flexing of the hips in double poling and kick double poling.

In recent decades there has been an evolution in the technology of Nordic ski equipment. The quality of the equipment directly affects participants' ability to learn new skills and achieve success. Without success, participants can be unmotivated to learn and enjoy Nordic skiing. Success equals fun.

Modern technology, such as the step-in binding system that has replaced the three-pin binding, affords participants much more control and balance. Ski boots are cut higher, providing superior comfort and ankle support, and they have better channels in the soles that work integrally with new binding systems. Contoured handles on ski poles with easily adjustable straps have replaced bamboo poles with unadjustable straps, allowing skiers to use the poles more for propulsion than for balance.

Nordic skiing, commonly referred to as *cross-country skiing,* is perhaps best experienced on managed, well-groomed trails. Restricted access (memberships or fees) to such areas should not discourage outdoor leaders from offering skiing to participants. Proximity or time factors may or may not make a trip to a ski park possible. Sport fields are great areas to ski given their absence of obstructions such as branches and stumps that would be found in wooded areas. With as little as 10 to 20 centimeters (4-8 inches) of snow, participants can enjoy cross-country skiing. Large amounts of snow can actually prove to be a disadvantage if not firmly packed. The weight of the skier can force skis to sink in the snow, reducing the amount of glide when performing classic technique, and skate skiing can be difficult due to the heavy snow load on the skis, making recovery difficult.

Nordic skiing offers a variety of skills that can be both exciting and challenging. Classic skiing is great for beginners because the motion initially is similar to walking. Increasing the amount of glide comes with practice and moves the skier from a walk to a skiing motion. Coupled with classic ski technique are the kick double pole and double pole. These techniques allow the skier to navigate rises and falls in the landscape. Occasionally, skiers must employ the skills of ascending and descending hills and may feel a refreshing sense of freedom and accomplishment after climbing a hill and then letting the skis run down the other side.

With the right attitude and sense of adventure, Nordic skiing can provide participants with a fantastic outdoor experience that is beneficial to their health and well-being and that they can enjoy throughout their lives.

Equipment

Group Equipment

- 1 set of cross-country ski boots, skis, and poles for each participant
- 1 bottle of glide enhancer for waxless skis
- Group first aid kit

Personal Equipment

- Outdoor clothing to suit the weather conditions (hat, gloves, windproof pants and jacket)
- Layers of clothing for easy temperature regulation (no cotton; clothing should wick moisture from the body)
- Sunglasses (optional)
- Sunscreen (optional)
- Lip balm (optional)

Equipment Care and Maintenance

- Ski equipment should be inspected seasonally to maintain proper working condition and to ensure the safety of participants.
- Skiers should avoid tracking across roadways and parking lots; grit and abrasives from the surface will damage the base of the skis.
- Ski poles should not be used to bear the weight of the skier in preventing a fall because they can easily break.
- Store skis and poles in the designated area in an orderly fashion to reduce wear and tear on equipment and allow easy access for the next user.

Site Selection

- A cross-country ski park will provide the best conditions for skiing.
- A flat plot of land such as a sport field is ideal for teaching Nordic skiing if access to a ski park is not possible.
- Hills with gentle slopes will afford opportunities to teach the skills of ascending and descending.
- Frozen ponds and lakes should be avoided unless local regulations for safe ice thickness are observed.
- Streams and brooks entering a pond or lake are unsafe for skiing at any time throughout the skiing season.

Social Skills and Etiquette

- Do not ski over the tips or tails of another person's skis.
- Be extra careful with the sharp tips of ski poles.
- Help skiers up if they are having difficulty returning to their feet.
- No roughing about or throwing snow.
- When skiing through deep snow, take turns breaking the trail (skiing in the lead) to share the energy burden.
- When skiing on a groomed ski trail, the slower skier heeds the call of "Track" from a faster skier by stepping to the side of the tracks to allow the faster skier to pass.

Risk Management

- Hills pose an element of risk for beginning skiers.
- Extra care should be taken to guard against skiers going straight down the hill because cross-country skis do not afford the support of downhill ski boots and bindings and dangerous falls are imminent.
- The outdoor leader should carry the first aid kit.
- Participants must maintain an adequate distance (6-8 meters, 7-8 yards, or 3-5 body lengths) between each other to prevent the trailing skier from being struck with a ski pole.
- Frozen ponds and lakes should be avoided unless local regulations for safe ice thickness are observed.

- Avoid areas of known moving water such as where streams or brooks enter ponds or lakes. These areas are unsafe areas for skiing at any time throughout the skiing season!

Unit Organization

When presenting the skills of Nordic skiing, the outdoor leader needs to recognize individual differences. There may be experienced skiers, but less-skilled skiers or beginners will most likely make up the largest demographic of the group. Use skilled skiers to assist with the instruction and encouragement of beginner skiers. Demonstrating often and providing feedback and group skill corrections will allow participants to have a rest and catch their breath. This is especially important for beginners, whose unrefined technique requires more energy to achieve and maintain a glide.

The lessons in this unit outline a progression that takes participants from getting properly fitted and getting used to the feel of the skis to achieving and maintaining balance. Falling down and getting up are the first skill cues provided in order to help curb feelings of frustration and helplessness. The skills of turning and changing directions will help participants navigate from place to place and organize them for the skiing skills to come. From there, skiers learn the skills of Nordic skiing as listed in the lessons.

Lesson Plans

Lesson 1: Fitting Participants for Nordic Ski Gear. This beginning lesson highlights some quick, commonsense tips on how to get participants outfitted for Nordic skiing. Having participants properly fitted with suitable skiing equipment is an essential start to this unit. Participants will enjoy greater success if they are comfortable with their gear. Organization also means that participants can efficiently obtain their gear in subsequent lessons.

Lesson 2: Introductory Skills and Classic Ski Technique (Diagonal Stride). Before the instruction of skiing skills, participants should feel comfortable on skis, be able to get up after falling, and be able to turn around and change direction. The most natural style for Nordic skiing is the classic or diagonal stride. This style is the best to begin with because most participants can get along even with a basic skill level and continue to fine-tune their skills throughout the unit.

Lesson 3: Classic Ski Technique (Diagonal Stride). Building on the previous lesson, participants will continue working on the introductory skills of the classic stride and receive further progressions to help improve their comfort level and skiing skills. Use of body weight and posture to assist in the grip and glide phases of the classic stride is emphasized throughout this lesson.

Lesson 4: Double Pole and Kick Double Pole. In this lesson, participants will experience further aspects of the classic stride as they understand how the skills of double pole and kick double pole can assist with skiing effectiveness. The flow from technique to technique is introduced in this lesson as participants are instructed on how to link the classic stride, kick double pole, and double pole.

Lesson 5: Putting It All Together. On a Nordic ski trail, the terrain is the main determinant of the skill to be used. In this lesson, participants will be guided over varying terrains to illustrate how to shift between the gears of classic skiing. If participants can draw upon their experience and practice from previous lessons, they should be able to navigate the terrain in an efficient manner.

Lesson 6: Endurance Ski Using Classic Ski Technique. To fully appreciate the fitness demands of Nordic skiing and how to use the various skill sets, participants partake in an endurance ski. Safety guidelines should be clearly communicated because the possibility of participants not being under direct supervision is more likely.

Lesson 7: Ascending and Descending Hills. In this lesson, participants will gain a further appreciation of how to negotiate more extreme terrain. Safety is a priority in this lesson because the level of risk is elevated. Using the edges of the skis effectively is important in climbing, traversing, and descending slopes to ensure that safety is not compromised.

Lesson 8: Skate Skiing—Two-Skate Technique. Skate skiing is a much more recent form of skiing than classic skiing. Participants will enjoy success much more if they have suitable equipment and the area is flat and groomed, making it more conducive to skate skiing. This lesson focuses on the more common style of skate skiing, the two-skate technique.

Lesson 9: Skate Skiing—One-Skate Technique and Skate Turning. This lesson builds on the introduction to skate skiing. Extra involvement of the arms requires participants to have a higher level of proficiency to perform the one-skate technique. Once balance is refined, participants can practice turning while skate skiing to complete the skill set.

Lesson 10: Relay Race, Obstacle Course, or Ski Tour. This final lesson presents three options for bringing closure to the unit: a relay race, an obstacle course, or a ski tour. The choice will depend on the ability and motivation of the group. Participant enjoyment and success should be given priority in making this decision.

Terminology

- **camber**—Upward curve in the middle of a ski; used to raise the grip zone off the snow when gliding and to cause the grip zone to contact the snow when pushing weight on the ski.
- **double pole**—Skiing technique whereby both poles are used for propulsion; the skier reaches forward with both poles, plants them in the snow, and pulls while flexing at the hips with knees fairly straight.
- **edging**—Hill-climbing technique whereby the skis remain parallel and the hill is climbed by stepping sideways beginning with the uphill ski.
- **fish scales**—Pattern of grips in the middle zone on the bottom of the ski that grips the snow during the push phase of the classic ski technique.
- **glide zone**—Smooth zone on the tip and tail of the bottom of the ski that allows the ski to glide on the snow.
- **grip zone**—Middle zone on the bottom of the ski that has fish scales or that can be waxed with grip wax to provide grip during the push phase of the classic stride.
- **herringboning**—Method of ascending a hill whereby the tips of the skis are pointed outward and the poles are planted behind for support and balance.
- **kick double pole**—Skiing technique whereby the skier performs the double pole followed by alternating kicks with each ski each time the poles are recovered to perform another double pole.

- **kick-turn**—Method of turning whereby one ski is lifted and turned opposite the planted ski, followed by swinging the planted ski around so that the skis are again parallel.
- **one-skate technique**—Skiing technique whereby one poling action is performed with both poles during every second skiing stride.
- **step-turn**—Method of turning that involves stepping in a circular pattern, keeping the tails of the skis together, and moving the tips apart and together.
- **track**—Communication between skiers that requests a slower skier to move to the side and allow a faster skier to use the track to pass.
- **traversing**—Method of hill climbing where the skier skis up and across a hill by pointing the tips of the skis uphill on a slight angle.
- **tuck**—Skiing technique where the skier places the poles in the armpits and bends at the hips and knees to carry speed down a hill.
- **two-skate technique**—Skiing technique whereby one poling action is performed with both poles during every skiing stride.
- **wedge (snowplow)**—Method of descending a hill under control by placing the poles in a tuck position while bringing the tips of the skis together and the tails apart; a slight inward tilt of the skis causes the inside edge of the ski to grip into the snow.

LESSON 1

Fitting Participants for Nordic Ski Gear

Overview

The activities in this lesson are designed to get the participants fitted with their gear. When equipment works well and fits well, there will be a better likelihood that people will use the equipment properly and safely, which will lead to a positive experience. Participants need to be properly fitted for ski equipment to have success with skiing and to avoid injury during a fall.

Poles should be long enough to provide propulsion but not so long that they strain the arms during a fall if the tip stays dug into the snow. Skis should be at the right length to allow the participant to maintain control while skiing and provide the appropriate amount of grip in the camber of the ski. Skis that are too short or that have a soft flex will cause the camber to flatten for a heavier skier even while trying to glide. This will cause too much resistance and reduce the amount of glide. Companies are developing skis that are shorter than traditional skis but have a stiffer camber. The length allows for easier control of the ski while the stiffer camber allows for use by a heavier skier since the ski does not flatten as easily.

Learning Objectives

- To learn proper fitting of cross-country skiing equipment (boots, poles, skis)
- To learn features of skiing equipment and how to use the equipment effectively and safely
- To record skiing equipment on a record sheet

Risk Management

- While moving skis and poles about during fitting, it is crucial that participants keep the tips of poles and skis under control to avoid contacting other people.
- Skis and poles should be held vertically to avoid such accidents.

Activity 1: Ski Length and Boot Fitting

Properly fitting boots are necessary for many reasons, most of which are obvious. However, another critical aspect of a successful introduction to skiing is the length of the ski itself.

Skill Cues

Ski Length

- The length of the ski for general skiing is approximately head height. This may vary depending on equipment availability.
- Traditionally, classic skis were fitted to the length of the wrist when the hand was extended above the head. This length can prove difficult for beginners; hence, shorter skis may be acceptable to facilitate control for the novice learner.
- Skis that have a stiffer camber should be reserved for heavier skiers. Length may have to vary a bit for these skiers; the amount of camber for glide and grip is more important than length. A longer pair of skis for a tall person will be less effective if the camber does not flex back to the natural curved position while in the glide phase of the ski stride.

Grip Zone of Ski

- This part under the foot grips the snow when all weight is on that ski.
- Uses wax or fish scales that, when pressed into the snow, prevent the ski from slipping back and losing grip.

Glide Zone of Ski

- This part of the ski (bottom) is ahead of and behind the grip zone and glides on snow.
- During the first phase of the glide, the weight isn't fully on the ski and the glide zones (ends of the ski) are predominantly in contact with the snow, allowing a good glide.

Boots

The boots should fit comfortably and allow room for warm socks.

Teaching Cues

- It is useful to do a dry-land session pointing out the parts of the skis, boots, and poles. This helps ensure that participants select the correct equipment.
- Step-in bindings when compatible with the ski boots generally do not require practice fitting. However, participants could practice stepping in and releasing the bindings while indoors so that they are familiar with the system before heading outside in the next session.
- The floor surface should be clean if participants are testing bindings indoors so as to avoid scratching the gliding surfaces of the skis.

Activity 2: Pole Length

A properly fitting pole will help beginner skiers with not only balance but also propulsion when used with the correct stride.

Skill Cues

- For beginners, the length of the poles should be at armpit height.
- When performing maneuvers on hills, a shorter pole is more effective than a longer pole.

Teaching Cues

- Pole length is dependent on a skier's ability. More experienced skiers who are capable of maneuvering longer poles gain more propulsion. Poles that are too short to allow for a full ski stride restrict the skier to more of a walk than a ski.
- Poles can be changed at any time if a skier feels more comfortable with a shorter or longer pole.
- Poles with damaged baskets should not be used because the pole can plunge into the snow and restrict the amount of push. This can also lead to breaking the pole while moving forward and experiencing difficulty in recovering the pole from the snow.

Activity 3: Pole Straps

Once participants understand how to fit the pole, the importance of the straps is discussed. Straps help with arm stability and fixing the hand to the grip.

Skill Cues

- Hands go up through the straps (figure 10.1).
- Hands then naturally hold the grips on the poles (figure 10.2).
- This method allows the hands to pull down on the straps for propulsion and especially to slightly release the grip on the poles to achieve maximum propulsion with follow-through.

Teaching Cues

- Be sure the straps are tight enough to keep the pole in close proximity to the hands to keep up the poling action after release.
- Bending forward at the hips, the arms are extended to the back with the hands open, allowing the poles to dangle in the air.
- If the poles fall to the ground, the straps are too loose.
- If this grip is uncomfortable and tight, the straps need to be loosened slightly.
- The poles should extend back completely in line with the arms.

Lesson Closure

- Once participants have selected their equipment, they should find a location to store their equipment until everyone has found suitable gear. If skis and boots are placed back in the storage area, there is a risk that another person will reserve the equipment. This will cause confusion during the next session and waste valuable time when trying to get outdoors quickly.
- Do not let participants put their equipment back in storage until everyone has been outfitted. The boots and skis should have a number on them, and once the participants

Figure 10.1   The hand goes up through the pole strap.

Figure 10.2   The grip should be natural and relaxed.

have matched equipment, have them record these numbers on the sheet provided (figure 10.3). Each session then just becomes a matter of checking the numbers with names. Before replacing the equipment in the storage area, be sure the boots are tied together and replace the elastic bands on the poles and skis.

Name	CROSS-COUNTRY SKIS		SKI BOOTS	
	Ski #	Description	Boot #	Description
1.				
2.				
3.				
4.				
5.				
6.				
7.				
8.				
9.				
10.				
11.				
12.				
13.				
14.				
15.				
16.				
17.				
18.				
19.				
20.				
21.				
22.				
23.				
24.				
25.				
26.				
27.				
28.				
29.				
30.				

Figure 10.3 Cross-country ski equipment list.

From K. Redmond, A. Foran, and S. Dwyer, 2010, *Quality lesson plans for outdoor education* (Champaign, IL: Human Kinetics).

Introductory Skills and Classic Ski Technique (Diagonal Stride)

Overview

This is the first session on skis, and therefore the main objective is to get participants comfortable with basic skills for falling and the art of getting up! Then participants learn how to change direction; once they are on the skis, this skill will prove essential. The next sensible skill to introduce at this point is a classic ski technique—the diagonal stride.

Learning Objectives

- To learn the skills of falling and getting up safely
- To perform a step-turn to change direction
- To perform a kick-turn to change direction
- To learn introductory aspects of the classic stride
- To demonstrate the use of ski zones to produce propulsion

Risk Management

- When practicing falling and getting up, participants need to ensure adequate spacing between each other to avoid accidental contact with skis and poles.
- Take special note of snow conditions; if the snow is crusty, the impact from falling could be damaging to the wrists and possibly the face.
- If the snow is deep and powdery, getting up may be more challenging.

Activity 1: Falling and Getting Up

Learning to fall is an essential skill. Learning this skill early in the unit will help prevent serious injury. In addition, learning how to get up is key to keeping participants motivated. The longer participants struggle to upright themselves, the more frustrated they may become. At first this may seem humorous, but after a prolonged experience sitting and lying in the snow, energy levels will drop and cold will set in, both of which may undermine the positive nature of the pursuit.

Skill Cues

Falling

There are three methods of falling.

- Sideways
  - Be careful when falling sideways; it is easy to break a ski or damage the wrist or shoulder.
  - Flex the elbow to absorb the fall and decrease the impact to the wrist and shoulder.
- Forward
  - Catch the body on your forearms if possible.
  - Try to avoid this method in crusty snow to prevent injury to the wrists and face.

- Backward
  - This can sometimes be used to slow yourself down.
  - Bend the knees and lean back until the hands and eventually the bum touch the ground.

Getting Up
- Roll onto your back and place skis to the sides of the body.
- Keep the skis together.
- Move your center of gravity over the skis to begin rising to your feet.
- Use the poles for stability, but avoid pushing the body up entirely with the poles to avoid breaking them.
- Leave one hand at the top of the pole and place the other hand on the pole close to the basket (the bottom hand is the side you're getting up on).
- If using the poles becomes problematic, simply position a flat hand on the snow near the bum, push while straightening the legs, and keep body weight close to the base of the skis.
- If the center of gravity is positioned correctly, the pole wrist straps may not have to be removed from the wrist.

Teaching Cues

Of the three methods of falling, it is preferable to have participants fall to the side first because it is least intimidating.

Activity 2: Turning—Step-Turn

This turn allows a skier to change directions. This may be a slight change in direction or it may be a complete 180-degree turn to retreat in the opposite direction. These turns are meant to get participants comfortable controlling their skis so that they can turn to make repeated trials in their practice track. Because these initial lessons should occur on the flat, most beginners can maintain control easily by gliding slowly to a stop followed by step-turn to return in their practice track. Hence the step-turn in this activity is relatively stationary, whereas the moving step-turn, which is used to control direction when skiing with momentum, is introduced in a later lesson.

Skill Cues

- Lean back slightly with the knees bent in a crouched position (body weight is on the heels of the skis).
- Repeatedly pick up one ski at a time and move to the left or to the right (figure 10.4).

a

b

c

d

Figure 10.4 Step-turn.

Teaching Cues

When stationary, this turn is done rhythmically and slowly.

Activity 3: Turning—Kick-Turn

As participants master the turn, they can advance the skill by adding in a kick-turn, which is a 180-degree turn. This skill is useful for returning in the direction just skied. The kick-turn is also useful when ascending and descending hills because the skier maintains a sideways stance on the hill.

Skill Cues

- Pick up the right ski and turn it so that when the ski is replaced to the snow it is facing in the opposite direction of the other ski (figure 10.5, *a-c*).
- The tails of the skis are about 25 centimeters (10 inches) apart.
- The left ski is then picked up and crossed over the heel of the right ski and placed parallel with it (figure 10.5, *d-e*).
- Plant the poles firmly.
- Do not move skis and poles simultaneously.
- When moving the right ski, move the right pole at the same time, leaving the left pole planted and relied upon for balance.

a

b

c   d

e

Figure 10.5   Kick-turn.

Teaching Cues

- Teach and practice this skill on flat or low-slope terrain before moving to steeper slopes.
- Balance is maintained throughout the entire action using poles.
- The kick-turn is a good method for descending steep slopes and reducing speed.

Activity 4: Classic Skiing Form (Diagonal Stride)

Efficient skiing is about form. In this session, participants are simply introduced to the classic ski technique. Once mastered, skiers can advance their ability to navigate and ski with speed, but it starts with the basics.

Skill Cues

- The action of the skis and poles are in opposition, as with a natural walking stride.
- Poles assist with forward propulsion.
- When pushing off with the ski, the body weight is committed to that ski. The skier, therefore, moves along in an up-and-down rhythm.

Teaching Cues

- With all participants standing at the beginning of their individual ski track, ski perpendicular to the group (5-6 meters [5.5-6.5 yards] in front) so that all participants get a good perspective on the elements of the skill.
- If there are participants who are proficient skiers, they could be used to demonstrate skiing techniques.
- These participants could also move about helping other participants with their skiing.

Lesson Closure

- Review the main points of the unit and encourage participants by recognizing their efforts.
- Cross-country skiing can be demanding, especially in the beginning because the body is not relaxed due to the hard work necessary to maintain balance and get propulsion.

LESSON 3

Classic Ski Technique (Diagonal Stride)

Overview

Ask the group, "Who knows how to ski?" Participants will learn to repeat, "Tony knows (toe knee nose)." Then explain, "I will be using this little question to teach and remind you to keep the toe, knee, and nose in line to be sure you commit your weight onto your glide ski. This will allow you to get a better glide and enable a more efficient recovery of the back ski." Efficient skiing is simply determined by effective execution of skill.

Learning Objectives

- To learn safety precautions when using ski poles in close proximity to other skiers
- To make tracks with others for cross-country skiing in a group
- To demonstrate the classic stride
- To use the camber of the ski to provide grip for propulsion
- To receive positive feedback on skiing technique
- To improve skiing technique in response to feedback

Risk Management

If skiers are sharing a track, they need to maintain adequate distance between each other (minimum of two body lengths; increase distance with speed) so that the rear skier can avoid being struck with the sharp tip of a ski pole.

Activity 1: Making Tracks

Someone has to be first, and let's thank the trailblazers. If the skiing sessions are not taking place at a ski park, the area probably won't have groomed ski trails. An option is for you to groom the instructional trail in advance or to allow the group to establish the trail for the session.

Skill Cues

- All participants line up across the skiing area (e.g., field) so that they are facing in the same direction.
- Allow 3 to 4 meters (3-4 yards) between skiers.
- The outdoor leader stands at one end of the line and begins a slow walking motion on skis across the field.
- One at a time, participants also go across the field making their track, resulting in a chain effect.

Teaching Cues

- To lay down a good set of tracks, it is important to keep skiers and their skis as parallel as possible.
- Participants go in a staggered fashion to ensure that all tracks will be laid down as parallel to each other as possible.
- Once across the field, participants perform a step- or kick-turn and follow their track back to the start.

Activity 2: Skill Progressions for Classic Ski Technique

With a good trail beneath them, participants are most likely ready to advance their ski performance.

Skill Cues

- Without poles, participants stand stationary in their individual tracks and follow the actions of the outdoor leader.
- The outdoor leader dips with the knees and swings the arms in opposite directions (mimicking the ski poling action).
- When the knees are straight, the arms are swung away from the body (right arm forward, leaning slightly to the left).

- Upon straightening again, the left arm is extended forward and the right arm is extended back, with a slight body lean to the right.
- The group performs these movements in unison.

Teaching Cues

- Place special emphasis on shifting the weight onto the glide ski. This will take a lot of practice and participants should continue to gain confidence to achieve the weight shift needed to ski more proficiently.
- Progressions for this activity may include the following:
  – Walk two lengths of field using poles for stability and propulsion.
  – Ski two lengths of the field, lengthening the ski action by using the poles more for propulsion (figure 10.6).
  – After skiing each length of field, practice turns (step-turn and kick-turn).

a

b

c

d

Figure 10.6 Classic ski technique. After learning the fundamentals of the classic ski technique, participants can use poles for stability and propulsion.

Activity 3: Provide Key Points as Feedback

Constructive feedback is essential for growth and improvement in a skill.

Skill Cues

- Shift the body weight onto the glide ski.
- Keep the weight ahead over the front foot.

- Grip and glide (keeping the weight on the ski for grip).
- Front leg is straight.
- Back leg is extended.
- Poling action is opposite the front leg action (reach ahead with the pole to form just under a 90-degree angle between arm and pole).

Teaching Cues

- Visit participants individually to correct technique and regularly stop the whole group to point out improvements in technique that are common to many of the participants.
- Highlight beginning skiers who demonstrate efficient technique.
- Demonstrate ease of correct technique compared with effort of poor technique.
- Emphasize going slow with a pause to hold the glide form to emphasize the glide phase.

Lesson Closure

Review and highlight the main points of classic ski technique.

LESSON 4

Double Pole and Kick Double Pole

Overview

This lesson broadens Nordic skiing for many participants by having them experience enhanced skills of cross-country skiing. This lesson will help participants recognize that there are times along a trail when various skills have to be applied to move as effectively as possible.

Learning Objectives

- To learn safety procedures for skiing with other skiers in the same track (sharp pole tips)
- To learn the double pole
- To learn the kick double pole
- To properly set pole straps for correct extension when poling

Risk Management

- If skiers are sharing a track, they need to maintain adequate distance between each other so that the rear skier avoids being struck with the sharp tip of a ski pole.
- This is especially important in this lesson because skiers bend at the hips while double poling, making the eyes more susceptible to impact if skiers are too close to each other.

Activity 1: Double Pole

Learning to use the poles effectively will greatly enhance the glide aspect of cross-country skiing; the key here is timing and position.

Skill Cues

- The pole plant should be ahead of the feet and outside the skis.
- Get a good forward lean with fairly straight legs and a bend at the hips.
- Be sure to use full extension with the poles after the push.

Teaching Cues

- Snow conditions must be good to allow the skis to glide.
- Have participants observe each other in pairs to provide feedback to each other while taking turns executing the skill.

Activity 2: Kick Double Pole

This is an extension of the double pole that must be performed faster than the double pole. It will enable the skier to carry on for a longer time.

Skill Cues

- The timing of the pole and the kick is crucial to success with this technique.
- A slight forward body lean is required.
- Both poles are brought forward simultaneously with a single ski stride.
- Pull with the poles and bring both skis together to a glide.
- Crouch and extend the poles as far behind as possible on the follow-through.
- Rise and extend the poles forward with a lunge of the front leg.
- Each lunge alternates legs.
- Maintain the balance during this action by not kicking the back ski too high.

Teaching Cues

- Demonstrate the full action in front of the participants, who are organized in a line.
- The timing is tricky for many participants, and they should practice this technique in a stationary position first.
- Again demonstrate the actions, this time stationary, and encourage the participants to mimic the actions without digging in the poles.
- Now with movement, participants perform four to five classic strides before attempting the kick double pole.

Lesson Closure

- Encourage participants that they have just completed a series of steps that will prepare them for the next lesson.
- The purpose of the next lesson is to put it all together and practice skiing using all components learned so far.

Putting It All Together

Overview

After participants have experienced the range of skills and had ample time to practice, you can converge the skill sets into a lesson that combines the learned skills. This lesson will give participants a better feel for Nordic skiing.

Learning Objectives

- To review the skills learned earlier in the unit (classic stride, double pole, kick double pole)
- To combine the skills of Nordic skiing
- To learn the four gears of Nordic skiing
- To know when to change gears during the course of skiing

Risk Management

Participants should watch their balance while switching from one technique to another; such transitions can prove tricky for beginning skiers.

Activity 1: Ski for Warm-Up and Review

Allow time to warm up and review skills. This establishes a greater sense of confidence before the group encounters the trail.

Skill Cues

Participants find their ski track and ski continuously for 4 to 5 minutes, practicing each of the three ski techniques learned thus far—classic stride, double pole, and kick double pole.

Teaching Cues

Encourage participants to feel their effort expenditure and to try to determine the time to switch from one technique to another.

Activity 2: Four Gears of Classic Ski Technique

Nordic skiing is similar to driving a car with a manual transmission. You go through the gears in order. To start, you use first gear, the classic stride. Once you have your speed up, kick double pole (second gear). When your speed is up again, change to double pole (third gear). If you approach a slight downhill in the trail, change to fourth gear—tuck!

The terrain largely determines which of the four components is to be implemented. In general, greater speeds mean that a higher gear is the most effective and best maintains balance. Imagine trying to classic ski (diagonal stride) while going quickly down a decline in the trail. If starting on a slight downhill section, the kick double pole may be implemented. Once speed increases, the skier can switch to third gear—double pole.

Skill Cues

Review the following skills. The key performance points of these skills do not change during the skiing sequence.

- First gear—classic (diagonal) stride
- Second gear—kick double pole
- Third gear—double pole
- Fourth gear—tuck position

Teaching Cues

- Demonstrate the four gears in front of the line of participants.
- Question participants about the progression of speed after the demonstration— "What did you notice about my speed throughout that demonstration?"
- Participants should be able to see an increase in speed as you progress through the gears.
- Have participants ski starting at the beginning of the sequence with the classic ski, and about one-third of the way down the track or when the speed feels right, switch to kick double pole (second gear).
- About two-thirds of the way down the track or when the speed feels right, participants should switch to double pole (third gear).
- If this skiing session is being performed on flat terrain, the transition to fourth gear (tuck) will not be very effective because the amount of glide will quickly diminish. Ideally the sequence would end on a slight downhill grade so the tuck could be applied.
- Have all participants start at the same time. Shout out commands to switch to a particular gear in the sequence.
- Participants could experience what it is like to switch to the appropriate gear and feel the awkwardness of switching into the wrong gear.

Lesson Closure

- Review the four gears with participants and address questions regarding how to use this concept while skiing.
- Explain that the next lesson will be an endurance ski where participants will get a fuller appreciation of how to apply these skills so they can endure a longer ski session without many breaks for instruction.

LESSON 6

Endurance Ski Using Classic Ski Technique

Overview

More time on the skis will give participants a better feel for their ability to perform the various skills. Learning to ski and gaining confidence comes with playing in the snow—the participants need to be in the field to appreciate the range of the pursuit.

Learning Objectives

- To apply the skills of Nordic skiing during an endurance ski
- To learn and apply the skill of setting a comfortable and suitable pace
- To seed skiers to avoid slowing the faster skiers
- To learn safety procedures for keeping a large group together on a wilderness trail

Risk Management

- Given that this lesson involves an endurance ski, an extensive warm-up is necessary.
- The duration of the endurance ski will depend on the skiing ability and fitness levels of the participants.
- Ensure that the route is well defined and easily monitored.
- If participants extend to an area that is less monitored, make sure they carry a whistle and travel in groups with a minimum of three per group (in case of an accident, one person stays with the victim and one seeks help).

Activity: Endurance Ski

A local park or ski park that can provide the opportunity to ski a series of laps would be most suitable for an endurance ski. This may be the best approach until the participants are ready for an extended ski along an established trail.

Skill Cues

- Determine a comfortable working pace for an extended ski.
- Practice appropriate ski etiquette (passing and being passed).

Teaching Cues

- Participants may set their own pace—encourage starting slow and maintaining a consistent pace.
- Ask participants to seed themselves so that the faster skiers begin first. Seeding reduces the amount of waiting and passing on the trail when trying to overtake slower skiers.
- Do a ski tour of various routes in the ski park, and then let participants choose a personal route (they are required to ski with at least two other people).
- Take participants on a ski tour of a hiking route.
- Do a ski tour of an area not normally accessible by foot; demonstrate that skiing can easily be a mode of travel for exploration.

Lesson Closure

A cool-down and stretching session should follow this activity to allow participants to lower their heart rates slowly.

LESSON 7

Ascending and Descending Hills

Overview

Because skiers will encounter all types of terrain, it is important to introduce participants to hills and teach them how to safely negotiate hillsides and slopes. With the right approach, hills can be descended safely on cross-country skis.

Learning Objectives

- To learn safety guidelines for ascending and descending hills
- To execute the three methods of ascending hills (traversing, herringboning, edging)
- To learn how to safely descend hills on cross-country skis (moderate-slope descent, wedge or snowplow, and steep-slope descent)
- To learn how to use edges of skis in ascending and descending
- To learn how to ascend hills safely when other participants are present on the hill

Risk Management

- No straight-down descents should be allowed on steep hills.
- Icy and crusty-snow hillsides should be avoided due to the potential for accident and injury. Cross-country skis do not have metal edges like those found on downhill skis, which makes turning and maintaining balance virtually impossible.

Activity 1: Ascending Hills

There are three methods for ascending hills: traversing, herringboning, and edging or sidestepping.

Skill Cues

Traversing

The easiest way to climb a hill on cross-country skis is to essentially eliminate the hill by climbing across the hill (traversing).

- Once tired from going in one direction, a partial kick-turn may be employed to change the uphill ski (this allows the opposite side of the body to rest).
- The skis have to be turned to their edges to be able to dig into the hill.
- Basically, the skier performs the classic stride across and up the hill.
- In the kick-turn, keep both poles planted behind and be careful when stepping to the opposite ski.

Herringboning

- Herringboning involves forming the skis in a *V* with the poles planted behind the skis, stepping up the hill (figure 10.7).

Figure 10.7 Herringboning up a hill.

- The angle of the skis provides the grip and helps prevent the skis from slipping backward.
- The poles stay planted behind the skis at all times because they are used extensively for pushing.
- This can be one of the most tiring methods of hill climbing.
- The skier has to climb the hill on the inside edges of the skis.
- The steeper the hill, the closer the angle of the skis will be to 180 degrees.

Edging or Sidestepping

- Tilt the skis so the edges facing into the hill are the ones being used (figure 10.8).
- Lift the top ski first.
- Pull with the top pole while pushing with the bottom pole.
- This is a slow system of climbing but is somewhat less tiring.

Teaching Cues

Figure 10.8   Edging up a hill.

Traversing

- The most effective angle will depend on snow conditions, ski grip, and slope.
- Inform participants that trying to traverse at too steep of an angle will result in a lot of slipping backward.

Herringboning

- Participants should not step too far with each step so as to avoid losing balance.
- Poles should be kept just far enough behind the skis to avoid being stepped on.
- This method is one of the fastest for ascending short hills.
- Placing the poles between the skis is ineffective for executing this skill.

Edging or Sidestepping

Steps should not be too far apart; this becomes tiring and may lead to overbalancing.

Activity 2: Descending Hills

There are three methods for descending hills: the moderate-slope descent, the wedge or snowplow, and the steep-slope descent.

Skill Cues

Moderate-Slope Descent

- Keep the feet about shoulder width apart and bend the knees slightly.
- Weight goes directly over the feet so there is a feeling of support.
- Tuck the poles safely into the armpits with the baskets extended back and slightly down.

Wedge or Snowplow

- The tips of the skis are pointed toward each other (figure 10.9).
- The heels are pressed to the sides so that the tails of the skis separate.
- The knees should be flexed to provide balance.
- The poles are tucked loosely under the arms at the sides, not out in front.

Figure 10.9   Snowplow.

Steep-Slope Descent

The hill will be descended by zigzagging across the hill to avoid any buildup of speed. For the beginner, wedge or snowplow turns work well to control speed.

- When skiing across the hill to stop or slow down, begin to ski up the hill on a slight uphill angle.
- At this point, assume the skier has skied across the hill going to the right (the right ski will be the uphill ski).
- Turn into the hill with the chest facing uphill.
- Place the right ski pole below the left ski while turning to the right to bring the chest into the hill.
- Plant both poles firmly about two and a half shoulder widths apart.
- Pick up the right ski and perform a kick-turn to the right.
- Push down on the right pole as the ski is brought around.
- Finish the kick-turn by pressing down on the left pole and bringing the left ski around to face the same direction as the right ski.
- The skier is now ready to continue skiing across the hill in the opposite direction.

Teaching Cues

Moderate-Slope Descent
- Emphasize "Tony knows," as in the toe, knee, and nose form a perpendicular line from the ski to maintain balance; hence the steeper the slope, the more forward the body will appear.
- If the hill is relatively steep, unhook the poles from the wrists.
- Balance is the key.

Wedge or Snowplow
- The greater the separation of the tails, the greater the resistance and the slower the skier moves down the hill.
- Designate a location on the hillside where you would expect participants to be able to come to a full stop.

Steep-Slope Descent
- Make sure participants allow plenty of space to avoid crowding at turning points.
- Once confidence has been established, the skier may wish to descend the hill using step-turns or the snowplow (wedge) instead of kick-turns.
- Using either of these skills will make the progression down the hill more continuous.
- Design a short circuit on the side and base of the hill. This short ski course should require participants to use the skills of ascending and descending hills, classic ski techniques, and changing direction.

Lesson Closure

Review safety considerations for ascending and descending hills.

Skate Skiing—Two-Skate Technique

Overview

Skate skiing has become popular in the past 20 years. The equipment for skate skiing differs greatly from traditional ski equipment. The skis are much shorter with less camber and less curve on the tips. The base of the ski does not have fish scales because the edge of the ski is used to push off instead of doing a backward kick as in classic skiing. The boots are higher, providing more ankle support, and they often have a hinge design between the upper and lower boot to allow some ankle flexion.

Learning Objectives

- To recognize suitable snow conditions for skate skiing
- To learn about specialized equipment for skate skiing versus classic skiing
- To learn to use the inside edges of skis for propulsion
- To employ the 3, 1, 3, 1 rhythm for the two-skate technique
- To learn the importance of weight shifting

Risk Management

- The ski area should have snow that is packed fairly well.
- The skis are pointed diagonally to skate ski, and deep snow would make ski recovery difficult.
- Ski tips would certainly hook in the deep snow, causing participants to fall forward.

Activity 1: Two-Skate Technique—Ski Action

The two-skate technique involves double poling during every second push action. The skier employs a 3, 1, 3, 1 rhythm. For example, the right ski and both poles (3) contact the ground and provide a ski push and double pole simultaneously. The skier then transfers body weight to the left ski only (1) while recovering both poles for the next phase of the skate ski. The sequence then repeats.

Skill Cues

- After pushing with the right leg, the skier has to transfer weight directly over the left ski as it glides across the snow.
- The toe, knee, and nose are in line to ensure that the weight transfer is complete.
- It is important to complete each leg push equally.
- The ski being recovered should be held parallel to the ground.

Teaching Cues

- The timing to change legs comes just as the glide begins to decline.
- At this point, transfer weight to the other ski by pushing off with the glide ski.
- Introduce the technique by performing a stationary action of lifting the skis to feel the weight shift and align toe, knee, and nose.

- Slowly advance forward to skate for short distances without poles.
- Increase glide by using the arms to swing to the sides (as with speed skating) to help provide momentum; this drill encourages participants to get their weight over the glide ski.
- If the recovery ski is not parallel to the ground, the tip or tail may drag on the ground.
- This technique involves a work phase while poling and ski pushing and a rest phase while pushing with only the single ski.

Activity 2: Two-Skate Technique—Pole Action

Effective use of pole action assists the skier with balance and provides extra momentum.

Skill Cues

- While completing the pole push, there is a slight flex at the hips.
- After the pole push is complete, the hands relax on the pole grips and allow the poles to lay idle in the hands.
- Plant the poles naturally and stand slightly erect.
- The poles are recovered smoothly and effortlessly as the ski glide diminishes.
- The poles are planted to begin the sequence again.

Teaching Cues

- The pole action after the push is the same as with the classic ski technique; the hands should release the poles to get the longest push possible.
- Perform a stationary action of lifting skis and poling.
- Perform the full action of skate skiing.

Lesson Closure

Reinforce the 3, 1, 3, 1 rhythm of the two-skate technique.

LESSON 9

Skate Skiing—One-Skate Technique and Skate Turning

Overview

The one-skate technique is a version of the two-skate technique that requires greater skill to perform.

Learning Objectives

- To maintain the extra balance required for the one-skate technique
- To recognize when to use the one-skate technique versus the two-skate technique

- To employ proper weight shifting from ski to ski
- To make adjustments in skiing and poling to complete turns while skate skiing
- To perform the skate ski technique and skate turns over a small course

Risk Management

- The one-skate technique requires more balance than the two-skate technique.
- Participants need to start slowly and be careful to maintain balance while practicing the skill.

Activity 1: One-Skate Technique

The one-skate technique involves a double-pole action with each ski push. This technique is used to increase acceleration or to maintain speed on slight inclines in the trail.

Skill Cues

- Complete each leg push equally.
- The toe, knee, and nose are lined up to ensure weight transfer.
- The ski being recovered should be held parallel to the ground.

Teaching Cues

- Start slow to ensure adequate balance while practicing double poling with each ski push.
- This technique requires more balance than the two-skate technique because the arms need to be recovered for the extra pole push.

Activity 2: Skate Turning

Turning while skate skiing involves a slight modification in the push of the skis.

Skill Cues

- Turning to the left involves increasing the angle of the left ski while decreasing the angle of the right ski, accompanied with a pronounced push-off with the right ski to steer to the left.
- The poles assist with the turning action.

Teaching Cues

- Ski a large rectangle in both directions to practice turning while skate skiing.
- Ski 20 meters (22 yards), do a 360-degree skate turn left, continue on for 20 meters (22 yards), and do a 360-degree ski turn right.
- Ski 60 to 80 meters (66-87 yards), completing partial alternating left and right skate turns every 15 meters (16 yards) to form a zigzag pattern.

Lesson Closure

Review the difference between the one-skate and two-skate techniques and the components necessary to successfully complete each skill of skate skiing.

Relay Race, Obstacle Course, or Ski Tour

Overview

You can opt to do one or all three of the suggested activities in this lesson. Experienced groups may appreciate an obstacle course, or athletic groups may opt to experience a relay race. Most groups would likely value the opportunity for a ski tour exploring the scenic wonders of the woods during winter.

Learning Objectives

- To complete one of the three options (relay race, obstacle course, or ski tour)
- To maintain technique when completing a challenging outing
- To maintain safety when racing and skiing among other skiers
- To work with partners to develop a strategy for the relay race
- To experience the beauty of the winter wilderness during a ski tour
- To recognize the importance of pace
- To recognize the importance of lead and sweep skiers to keep the group together
- To properly employ skiing techniques over varying terrain

Risk Management

- Technique is often jeopardized when racing.
- Participants need to maintain good technique to avoid falling and possibly injuring themselves or damaging ski equipment.
- When racing in close proximity to other participants, the sharp tips of poles need to be kept under control and avoided by trailing skiers.

Activity 1: Relay Race

The format of the relay race depends on the terrain. The first setup for the relay race should be fairly simple to enable all participants to experience success; with success comes enjoyment and motivation. Keep the focus on personal best—improving individual ability—and having fun in competition.

Skill Cues

- Teams of four are organized in typical relay fashion around an oval track.
- First skier skis one lap with the classic ski.
- Second skier skis half a lap with the classic ski, half a lap with the kick double pole.
- Third skier skis half a lap with the classic ski, half a lap with the double pole.
- Fourth skier skis one lap with the skate-skiing technique.

Teaching Cues

- Each group of participants can decide which leg of the relay race they will ski.

- Have groups come up with names for their teams to add excitement and motivation for the teams to perform their best during the races.

Activity 2: Obstacle Course

An obstacle course can provide great challenge and excitement.

Skill Cues

- An obstacle course should be designed to use natural features such as small slopes or trees. You can also use cones, if necessary.
- Creativity will make the obstacle course both interesting and challenging.
- Map out the route participants should follow through the obstacle course. Make sure participants understand the route.

Teaching Cues

- Design an obstacle course that matches the ability level of the group.
- A course that is too difficult will decrease motivation.
- Participants could be organized as in the relay race described previously.

Activity 3: Ski Tour

Getting outdoors is the benefit of learning how to ski. The skills from the unit will afford participants the wonderful opportunity to explore natural settings during a beautiful time of year—winter. These basic skills will allow participants to explore the mysteries of a winter woodland.

Skill Cues

- Take a ski tour 2 to 15 kilometers (1-9 miles) from your program site or in your area.
- Take personal responsibility for navigation, knowing your route, and where you are at all times relative to your route.
- Note specific features, landmarks, and highlights and share with others in the group.
- Look out for the safety, comfort, and enjoyment of other skiers in your group.
- Take turns being the lead and sweep skiers.

Teaching Cues

- Put slower skiers in the lead as pace setters.
- Assign navigational responsibilities and rotate as appropriate.
- If traveling in a large group, break the group into pods with pod leaders.
- Ensure that all skiers stay between the lead and sweep skiers.
- Ensure that the lead skier is knowledgeable of the route.
- Assign navigational responsibilities and rotate as appropriate.
- Carry extra moleskin, a first aid kit, and other guide supplies.
- Consider having a snowmobile follow the group for emergency services if traveling in a wilderness area.
- A viable option is taking a ski tour in a local ski park or wilderness area.

Lesson Closure

Highlight the skills that the participants have learned and point out how they were able to complete the lesson activities with these skills.

References and Resources

Cook, C. 1997. *Essential guide to cross-country skiing and snowshoeing in the United States.* New York: H. Holt.

Gullion, L. 1993. *Nordic skiing: Steps to success.* Champaign, IL: Human Kinetics.

Linnamo, V., P.V. Komi, and E. Muller. 2007. *Science and nordic skiing.* Oxford, England: Meyer and Meyer Sport.

Snowshoeing

▼ Sean Dwyer ▼

Who says I can't hike my favorite trail in winter? Winter adventures are the best! Winter snow is no reason to stay out of the woods; rather a real good reason to wear some funky shoes that will allow me to explore year round.

– Dave Hubley, physical education specialist

Snowshoeing is a great way to experience the outdoors in winter. The amount of snow and varying snow conditions determine the nature of the experience. Deep snow makes progress challenging, and icy conditions can be treacherous depending on the type of snowshoes worn.

Snowshoeing is an intimate affair, providing the ability to admire and fully absorb the beauty of the natural surroundings. Sightings in nature are more common and more vivid when snowshoeing. This perspective is unique to snowshoeing for reasons that are best left to each person to discover.

The physical health benefits of snowshoeing include cardiorespiratory conditioning and the development of lower-body musculoskeletal tissue, namely the hip flexors. Some hill-climbing techniques and the optional use of ski poles improve muscular strength and endurance of the upper body.

Originally, snowshoes were made of wood and laced with natural rawhide. The bindings consisted of leather straps and a buckling system (figure 11.1).

Today, traditional snowshoes made with heavy wire frames and laced with nylon lacing offer a different experience but more versatility over the wooden predecessor (figure 11.2).

Technology has advanced the snowshoe to a specialized piece of outdoor equipment.

Modern technology has introduced snowshoes that are manufactured from aluminum tubing and decking made of synthetic materials. Harnesses have evolved greatly and now provide much more control and dependability than rawhide, rubber, or string bindings. Another feature of modern snowshoes is their crampon-like sole that makes travel over ice much more secure.

The cost of modern snowshoes is much more than that of traditional snowshoes. Expect to pay CDN$150 to CDN$400 for an advanced pair. Some areas may have local craftspeople who make snowshoes at reasonable prices.

Equipment

Group Equipment

- 1 pair of snowshoes for each participant
- 1 pair of ski poles for each participant (optional)
- Small first aid kit
- Small repair kit, including extra webbing, buckles, and duct tape

Figure 11.1 Traditional wooden snowshoes.

Figure 11.2 Modern aluminum snowshoes.

Personal Equipment

- Waterproof, breathable clothing suitable for weather conditions (easily layered because snowshoeing is a high-output activity)
- Gaiters (optional)
- Sunglasses (optional)
- Sunscreen (optional)
- Lip balm (optional)

Equipment Care and Maintenance

- Snowshoes should not be worn across roadways or rocky outcrops because lacings and decks can become scuffed and worn.
- When walking across obstacles, take care not to stress the frame of the snowshoe and cause damage.

Site Selection

- Snowshoeing is most exciting and enjoyable in a wooded setting.
- Walking among snow-laden trees is a tranquil experience.
- Terrain variations also add to the excitement when participants experience uphill and downhill areas.
- Avalanche-prone slopes or sites should be avoided.

Social Skills and Etiquette

- Participants should gain an appreciation of the environment and refrain from harmful activities such as cracking off tree branches while walking.
- Small trees and shrubs should not be stepped on.
- Participants should take care of each other by not going ahead or falling behind and by being available to lend assistance if someone gets caught up in an obstacle or takes a fall.

Risk Management

- Safety is a requirement when selecting a site for snowshoeing.
- Waterways should be avoided because banks tend to be sloped and icy and snowshoes may slip and cause participants to fall into the water. A snowshoe attached to the foot would make getting free from the ice and current difficult.

- Walking near the treetops of small evergreen trees is dangerous because tree branches collect snow and form air pockets. Participants on snowshoes can easily sink among the branches and twist a knee or scrape a leg with a sharp stick or small stump.
- Avoid avalanche-prone slopes and chutes such as valleys, gorges, or gulches that naturally funnel avalanche debris.

Unit Organization

This unit includes core snowshoeing skills and safety skills while emphasizing the value of snowshoeing as a fitness activity and a lifelong pursuit.

Lesson Plans

Lesson 1: Equipment Selection and Walking Technique. This lesson addresses commonly unknown aspects of snowshoeing. Many people assume that snowshoeing is simple, but technology has increased the need for adequate instruction before setting out on an adventure. Proper walking technique requires a slight adjustment to regular walking posture and stepping.

Lesson 2: Recognizing Hazards, Managing Hazards, and Finding Routes. Proper walking technique can greatly assist participants with navigating hazards on the trail. Obstacles such as air pockets formed by snow-covered trees and fallen trees require good judgment, balance, and agility. Participants will also gain experience navigating through varying terrains to make good route-planning decisions.

Lesson 3: Hill Ascending and Descending Techniques. In this lesson, participants will gain experience and enjoy the adventure associated with ascending and descending hills on snowshoes. The terrain largely determines the techniques to be used, and therefore various options to practice and employ these skills are presented.

Lesson 4: Running in Snowshoes. The thrill of snowshoeing can be enhanced when participants sense the freedom of running on snowshoes. This freedom, however, can be interrupted if participants do not pay full attention to lifting their snowshoes out of the snow. Setting up a relay race or obstacle course enables participants to use their skills while cooperating in a competitive but lighthearted event with their peers.

Lesson 5: Snowshoe Walk Through a Nature Area. The liveliness and beauty of winter woodlands, river valleys, and barrens are the focus of this lesson as participants experience nature while on snowshoes. Snowshoeing can be a quiet and calming activity that affords the opportunity to look around while moving about. Exploration is exciting on snowshoes because nearly all areas can be navigated using the skills learned in this unit. Participants may be lucky enough to see wildlife and scenery that most people never get a chance to experience.

Terminology

- **avalanche**—Occurs when the snow on a hillside becomes unstable and suddenly slides downward.
- **bindings**—A system of straps that keep the foot in place on top of the snowshoe.
- **chute**—A narrow channel on a hillside that might indicate a small waterway.
- **cornice**—An overhang of snow over a hillside or ledge that can break off and possibly lead to an avalanche.
- **crampons**—Metal projections that provide grip on the underside of a snowshoe.
- **decking**—The flat platform of a snowshoe that provides flotation on top of the snow.
- **drift lines**—The edge of a snow drift that may overhang and break off or give way if stepped upon with snowshoes.
- **edging**—Method of hill climbing where a series of sideways steps are taken up a hill leading with the top snowshoe. This method does not work well on icy slopes.
- **gait**—Style of walking or stepping.
- **groping**—Method of hill climbing where there is bending at the waist, the hands are used to claw up the hill, and the toes of the snowshoes are pointed outward.
- **gulch**—A small, narrow valley usually formed by the eroding action of water.
- **herringbone step**—Hill-climbing method that involves walking up a hill with the toes of the snowshoes turned outward.
- **kick-turn**—Method of turning that involves rotating the right snowshoe clockwise to end up facing the opposite direction of the left, followed by swinging the left hip clockwise so that both snowshoes are parallel.
- **natural rawhide**—Natural leather product that is laced together to form the decking for traditional snowshoes.
- **snow reading**—The ability to read and recognize snow conditions to be able to decide the easiest and safest routes.
- **step-turn**—Series of small steps with the tips of the snowshoes keeping the tails together, allowing the person to turn in a circle.
- **toeing out**—Method of hill climbing where the toe is pushed forward through the bottom of a traditional snowshoe and plunged into the hillside to act as a cleat for grip.
- **traverse**—Method of hill climbing that involves walking upward and across a hillside. This method does not work well on icy slopes without using crampons.

Equipment Selection and Walking Technique

Overview

At first glance, it may seem that little skill is needed to snowshoe: You simply strap the device onto your boot and walk. However, not all snowshoe equipment is equal in design and use. Although the beauty in snowshoeing is its simplicity, certain considerations need to be followed to make this pursuit successful.

Learning Objectives

- To know what it means to be prepared with the proper clothing and footwear
- To know how to put on snowshoes and make any necessary adjustments
- To ensure proper stance and progression when learning to walk in snowshoes
- To walk in deep snow and break trails with snowshoes
- To perform a step-turn and a kick-turn on snowshoes to change direction
- To use ski poles to assist with walking and turning

Risk Management

- Some light walking and stretching of the hip flexors should be done because the lifting motion can be demanding, especially in deep snow.
- Steps should be small at first; it is easy to lose balance if a snowshoe gets caught in heavy snow or crust.

Activity 1: Fitting the Snowshoes

A quick glance would not reveal that there is a left and a right snowshoe. The buckling system will determine this alignment; buckles on the wrong side of the foot will cause frustration because they have a tendency to catch onto leg material, tripping participants.

Skill Cues

- Be sure shoes are placed on the correct feet so that the buckles are on the outside of the feet.
- If using traditional snowshoes, the toes of the boots should not go too far forward; otherwise they might hook under the crossbar of the snowshoe.

Teaching Cues

- Most winter boots provide a good fit in snowshoe bindings.
- Modern snowshoes have bindings with toe stops that prevent the toe from going ahead too far, especially on hill descents.

Activity 2: Walking on Snowshoes

Walking in snowshoes involves walking as naturally as possible with just enough compensation in stance to prevent one snowshoe from impeding the other.

Figure 11.3 A slight side-to-side sway makes walking in snowshoes easier.

Skill Cues

- Widen the stance just enough to avoid stepping on the other snowshoe.
- When stepping, the heel of the shoe should touch the snow first; the heel of the snowshoe should drag slightly when the knee is lifted (figure 11.3).
- If in deep snow, a slight press and pause at the end of each step allows the snow to compact under the snowshoe, providing more stability.
- Traditional snowshoes tend to be wider and require a side-to-side motion while walking in order to have one snowshoe clear the other; modern snowshoes are narrower and require less side-to-side motion.

Teaching Cues

- When breaking a trail, keep steps a little shorter and keep the tips from being loaded with snow.
- Slightly sway the body from side to side with each step if necessary to help relieve hip stress.
- If the heel of the snowshoe lifts high or flicks up with each step, the back of the pants will be covered with snow, which may lead to wetness and discomfort.
- Modern snowshoes are sleek and narrow, which allows for greater stability in balance for women, people with short walking strides, and children.
- Not only does the lightweight material make the activity more accessible to many age groups, but the design also allows their shoeing stride to be more natural.

Activity 3: Turning on Snowshoes

Once participants have grasped the shuffling gait for snowshoeing, the next skill set is turning and keeping balanced on the snow. There are two turns for this activity: the step-turn and kick-turn.

Skill Cues

Step-Turn

The step-turn involves stepping to the side one foot at a time to either change direction while walking or completely turn around.

- If turning right, the right shoe is used first.
- Take short steps until the turn is achieved.
- The tail of the shoe covers little distance and the toes move the most.

Kick-Turn

The kick-turn involves turning 180 degrees.

- If turning right, lift the right snowshoe and turn it clockwise so that the tip is next to the tail of the left snowshoe.

- Picking up the left shoe, pivot the hips right so the left shoe is once again facing the same direction as the right snowshoe.

Teaching Cues

Step-Turn

Once balance is achieved, sharp turns can be mastered.

Kick-Turn

- Ski poles can help with balance while executing the kick-turn (figure 11.4).
- The kick-turn is used when a quick turn and change of direction is required.

Lesson Closure

- Review the techniques of walking and turning covered in this lesson.
- Emphasize the natural motion necessary for ease of walking while on snowshoes, as well as how snow conditions might affect walking.

Figure 11.4   Using ski poles for balance while turning.

LESSON 2

Recognizing Hazards, Managing Hazards, and Finding Routes

Overview

In this lesson, you will guide participants through a natural area and point out hazards that are present. Buried treetops, fallen trees, and snow conditions are all safety concerns. Participants need to be able to recognize hazards and know how to avoid or deal with them. Route finding is integral to recognizing and dealing with hazards in the wilderness.

Learning Objectives

- To understand the importance of staying together as a group in the wilderness
- To observe hazards pointed out by the outdoor leader
- To learn to recognize hazards such as buried trees, fallen trees, and varying snow conditions
- To gain experience in finding routes and dealing with hazards

Risk Management

With obstacles in the snow such as fallen trees, stumps, and small, snow-covered bushes and trees, participants must proceed with caution while walking.

Activity 1: Guided Walk in Wooded Area

The skill of snowshoeing allows participants to access natural areas otherwise not accessible during the winter months. Accumulated snow makes a wooded hike extremely challenging due to participants sinking up to their knees or deeper in snow. The shoes allow them to enter into the woods off main trails and plowed roads and appreciate the winter landscape.

Figure 11.5 Be aware of potential dangers under the surface of the snow.

Skill Cues

- Step slowly and with caution.
- When crossing a fallen tree, do not step on it with the tip or tail of the snowshoes; this will stress the snowshoe and probably cause it to break.
- If a fallen tree must be negotiated, it is best to step on the tree with the section of snowshoe that is under the boot so that the foot steps on the tree.

Teaching Cues

- Inform participants of the types of obstacles they might face while walking through the woods (figure 11.5).
- Lead participants through a wooded area and point out obstacles.

Activity 2: Snow Reading on a Guided Walk

The ability to read the snow and understand snow terrain is essential when deciding on the best routes to hike. This activity is yet another form of natural literacy—snow reading.

Skill Cues

- Recognize drift lines and cornices, and avoid steeply drifted slopes and cornices.
- In mountainous areas, measure approximate slopes. Avoid 30- to 45-degree slopes, gulches, and chutes because of the probability of avalanche.
- Identify where water runs under snow. Avoid such areas, and if they must be traversed, rope off (establish a roped boundary that must not be crossed) for traversing.
- Participants use ski poles to probe and identify snow-covered hazards such as treetops that prop up a thin layer of snow.

Teaching Cues

- Inform participants of the features, hazards, and hazard management strategies they might face while snowshoeing.

- Lead participants through various terrain and point out features, hazards, and hazard management strategies.

Activity 3: Route Finding

Snowshoes allow participants to carve out their own path through the woods. There is no need for groomed snow trails or open walking trails, so participants need a sense of snow reading, energy to explore, and navigational awareness.

Skill Cues

- Steps should be short and planted firmly into the snow to ensure solid footing before committing body weight and stepping forward.
- If carrying ski poles, use them to probe the snow of the intended path.

Teaching Cues

- Lead participants to an area where they can explore by making their own tracks.
- The site must allow you to easily direct participants toward a common meeting spot such as a trail or an open field.
- Participants are not allowed to wander on their own during this activity but must stay close and move with the group toward a common area.
- You should be familiar with any hazards in the area and participant activity proximal to such hazards.
- Have the group follow the leader, allowing participants to guide the group through the woods.
- Switch roles often to allow each participant to have a turn as the leader.

Lesson Closure

- When participants are back together in the meeting area, discuss the obstacles they faced.
- Inform participants that in the next lesson they will experience ascending and descending hills.
- Ask if any participants encountered hills in this activity and inquire as to how they negotiated them.

LESSON 3

Hill Ascending and Descending Techniques

Overview

Metal claws on the underside of the snowshoe beneath the binding assist greatly in hill climbing. The claws are especially effective in packed or crusty snow. Descending hills with claws can help prevent the slipping that can occur with traditional snowshoes, which happen to be more effective when gliding down a hillside (figure 11.6).

a　　　　　　　　　　　　　　　　　　　　*b*

Figure 11.6　Ascending and descending hills on snowshoes is challenging and exhilarating.

Learning Objectives

- To learn several techniques for safely ascending and descending hills
- To understand how to use traditional and modern snowshoes for ascending and descending hills
- To learn safety considerations when venturing around steep slopes on snowshoes

Risk Management

- Steep hills require caution, especially when descending.
- Any steep hills used for practice should be short hills and not mountainous slopes. Hills should be short enough to ensure there is no risk of avalanche.
- Participants need to keep their body weight leaning slightly back. If they lose their balance, they will fall harmlessly backward instead of falling forward, where they might face-plant or tumble uncontrollably.
- You should be familiar with the area of the hillside to know if any dangerous obstacles exist beneath the snow.

Activity 1: Hill Ascending

Going up a hill in snowshoes is not as easy as it looks. The more modern shoes have serrated clamps around the toe position that help bite into the snow for traction. However, maintaining momentum and working against gravity to get up the slope still requires a few techniques.

Skill Cues

Gentle Slope

Until the ability to ascend is mastered, begin on smaller hills. Climb small slopes with shortened steps.

Moderate Slope

As participants become more accomplished, move to a steeper slope to challenge their skills.

- Herringbone step:
  – Widen the stance slightly and turn the toes outward to provide a wider base of support.
  – Walk regularly while keeping the snowshoes in this position and with a slight forward lean.
- Edging:
  – Step with the lead foot (the uphill foot) and press into the snow to achieve a base for support; bring the second foot up just below the lead foot and also press it into the snow.
  – When the lead leg gets tired, switch by performing a kick-turn on the hillside.
- Zigzag: Walk back and forth up and across the hill using the skills of edging and turning.
- Turning: The kick-turn is employed with the uphill leg first to prevent sliding down the hill.

Steep Slope

For accomplished snowshoers and to give participants a fuller experience of ascending with snowshoes, move to steeper inclines.

- Groping (figure 11.7):
  – Bend at the knees and waist until the hands are on the ground between the snowshoes.
  – Turn the toes of the snowshoes out in a herringbone position.
  – Dig the hands into the snow to assist in getting up the hill.

a   *b*

Figure 11.7   Using the hands to assist in ascending a steep slope.

- Toeing out:
  – If using traditional snowshoes, loosen the bindings on the shoes so the toes can go out through the toe hole.
  – The snowshoes are walking straight up the hill with the toes poking through and sticking into the snowbank.
  – Use the hands in the same manner as groping if necessary.

- Snowshoe removal:
  - Snowshoes with tails can be used as poles.
  - The tail of the snowshoe must be firmly positioned in the snow before applying weight to the shoe.
  - Before lifting the snowshoe out of the snow to move ahead, be sure the body weight is directly over the top of the snowshoe.
  - Make small advances without overextending the reach.

Teaching Cues

Gentle Slope

The planted foot may slip backward and cause a fall if the stride is too long.

Moderate Slope

- The herringbone cannot be used for long because it is tiring on the hips.
- Poles can be an asset for the edging technique, which is best performed with a narrow snowshoe.
- With the zigzag technique, the steepness of the climb is decreased while the distance to travel is increased.

Steep Slope

- Locate an area with a variety of slopes to practice these techniques.
- Toeing out is for traditional snowshoeing; modern snowshoes have claws that perform in this way.
- When using the snowshoe as a pole, overextending the reach will force the body to work too hard and may break the snowshoe.
- Deep, powdery snow will be difficult to climb and require a lot of energy but can be a lot of fun to descend; crusty or hard-packed snow will be easier to climb as long as the necessary traction can be attained (figure 11.8).
- A further discussion of safety and snow conditions is a good extension to this lesson.
- Visit various hills and question participants about safety considerations at each location.
- Snow conditions also affect the ability to navigate hillsides.

Figure 11.8 Use short steps when walking upright up a hill to reduce fatigue and backward slipping.

Activity 2: Hill Descending

Depending on the slope of the hill, one of the following techniques may be used to safely descend. Use the same progression as in ascending.

Skill Cues

Gentle Slope

Lean backward slightly so the body weight falls toward the tail of the snowshoe (figure 11.9).

Moderate Slope

- In very deep snow, tie a piece of rope around the top of each snowshoe and grasp the cord with the corresponding hand.

• While moving down the hill, pull the shoe slightly by tugging on the cord.

Steep Slope

• Bend your knees to a full squat position and sit back to the tails of the snowshoes.
• Do not let the bum touch the snow or the snowshoes.
• Try to keep the feet at least shoulder width apart.
• Be careful not to let the snowshoes cross over one another.
• Place the arms out to the side with the hands touching the snow; the arms are used for balance and steering.
• If you fall forward, tuck the head quickly and go into a forward roll; do not slide.

a   *b*

Figure 11.9   Lean back slightly to avoid falling forward while descending.

Teaching Cues

Gentle Slope

• Short, quick steps are recommended to avoid tripping in deep snow.
• Short steps should be used to pack deep snow or push excess snow down the hillside.

Moderate Slope

Pulling on the cord prevents the toe of the snowshoe from going under the snow crust and causing a forward fall.

Steep Slope

• A slightly upturned shoe is a definite advantage.
• Traditional snowshoes with tails allow for great sliding action.
• Modern snowshoes with claws will not allow a sliding motion.

Lesson Closure

• Review safety considerations for ascending and descending hills.
• Advise participants that hills should only be attempted if success is guaranteed, and overhangs should be avoided due to the risk of an avalanche.
• If they are unsure, participants should track around the hill.

LESSON 4

Running in Snowshoes

Overview

A fun way to challenge participants who have become accomplished in the skill sets from the first three lessons is to set up a small obstacle course and allow speed and technique efficiency to come to the forefront.

Learning Objectives

- To learn how to run in snowshoes
- To experience varying depths of snow while running in snowshoes
- To participate in obstacle courses and relay races while running in snowshoes
- To practice teamwork during obstacle courses and relay races

Equipment

6 to 8 pylons

Risk Management

- The progression should be slow to avoid certain falls from striding too fast without the skill of recovering snowshoes from the snow.
- Snow with a layer of crust makes running particularly difficult because the tip of the snowshoe can hook and cause a stumble or fall.

Figure 11.10 Arm swing greatly assists with running in snowshoes.

Activity 1: Running in Snowshoes

Running in snowshoes is not just walking. Participants must exact efficient movements to refine their technique, allowing the speed of the stride to maximize the distance of the gait. An important lesson for participants to discover is how snow quality affects speed. How far participants sink is balanced with how high they can lift the shoe and how fast they can extend their running gait.

Skill Cues

- The action of the arms should be emphasized to encourage the legs to stride fully (figure 11.10).
- The height of the knee lift depends on the depth of the snow; deep snow requires a higher knee lift to clear the surface.
- To be efficient, the knee lift should be just high enough to clear the surface of the snow.
- The heel should strike first, as with regular running.

Teaching Cues

- First attempts at running should be on well-packed surfaces to avoid hooking in deep snow.
- Striding should be as natural as running on dry land.
- Deep-snow running can be fun but strenuous.

Activity 2: Relay Races and Obstacle Courses

A little competition can be beneficial as long as you prioritize teamwork, fair play, and a sporting attitude steeped in fun. This type of competition can allow participants to push themselves a bit further and dig a bit deeper to get their shoes out of the snow quicker.

Skill Cues

Participants will walk, jog, or run the course using the skills covered throughout the unit such as turning, hill work, and edging.

Teaching Cues

- If available, use natural features such as fences, trees, and hills.
- The available terrain and obstacles will largely determine the challenge of the course.
- The skill and fitness levels of the participants need to be considered when developing the course.
- Create teams large enough to allow participants to rest between legs of the race but small enough to prevent waiting too long in line.
- Design an orienteering course around the area and provide pairs with a map to complete the course.
- Participants will easily see the tracks of each other and the course setter; to remedy this, the course setter should approach control marker sites through the least obvious routes and make lots of extra tracks to confuse participants.
- Assign each group a different order in which they have to complete the course and send them off all at once.
- The many sets of tracks will soon place all teams on an even playing field.

Lesson Closure

- Lead a class discussion of the highlights experienced during the races.
- Participants will have stories to share about how they almost fell but didn't, or how fast they were able to scramble up a steep hill.
- Sharing is a valuable way to summarize many activities, especially where some adventure is involved.

LESSON 5

Snowshoe Walk Through a Nature Area

Overview

The final lesson demonstrates the biggest benefit of snowshoeing: the winter landscape witnessed by few. Winter offers many natural wonders and beautiful experiences that go untapped because many of us have forgotten the value of the fourth season. Getting outside during the winter months can do wonders not only for physical health but for a more positive mental attitude toward winter. Snowshoeing allows us to get out there and enjoy what nature has to offer and to discover that the world is still active during the snowy months.

Learning Objectives

- To experience the adventure and beauty of a winter walk on snowshoes
- To learn the importance of remaining together as a group for safety
- To demonstrate the importance of a route plan
- To understand the importance of a buddy system and keeping track of all participants
- To experience local wildlife and how animals might cope in the winter season
- To share experiences of the outing with other group members

Risk Management

Ensuring that all group members stay together is crucial when touring an area. Participants who stray from the group could become injured and be far from assistance. Also ensure that every participant is properly dressed for the environmental conditions. The outdoor leader should pack extra gear (hats, gloves, fleece) just in case.

Activity: Nature Walk

Nature can be found in more than established parks; a patch of woods in the winter will suffice. If parkland is accessible, that is a logical choice, but there are many winter treasures right in our own wooded backyards (figure 11.11).

Skill Cues

Using a combination of map, compass, GPS, stride length, direction, and distances, participants collect data on the trail and develop a route map.

Teaching Cues

- You should be familiar with the area and plan a route before heading out on the trail.
- If traveling far, leave a route plan with a responsible person who knows the area.
- Assign one participant to be at the front and one at the end of the group to ensure that participants stay together during the walk.
- The leader can change regularly to share the burden of breaking the trail.

Figure 11.11 Venturing through a natural area highlights the beauty of snowshoeing.

- Establish a buddy system so that partners are responsible for helping each other with any troubles and to ensure that the group stays together.
- Perform a headcount before embarking on the walk so that you can make regular checks to ensure all are present.
- A roll-call system could be put in place to have participants call out assigned numbers or their names.
- Obtain a pamphlet or book of local wildlife and see if participants can spot any animals during the tour.
- Tracks in the snow can also be used as clues about the types of animals that inhabit the area during the winter.
- Other signs of wildlife could be noted, such as cones picked apart by squirrels, burrows used by rabbits, or droppings from deer, moose, weasels, or other animals.

Lesson Closure

- Ensure that all participants are present and have safely returned from the outing.
- Discuss highlights after the walk is over and give each pair the opportunity to provide input.

References and Resources

Cook, C. 1997. *Essential guide to cross-country skiing and snowshoeing in the United States.* New York: H. Holt.

Jensen, C.R. 1977. *Winter touring: Cross-country skiing and snowshoeing.* Minneapolis: Burgess.

Savignano, P. 2000. *Basic essentials: Snowshoeing.* Guilford, CT: Falcon.

Archery

▼ Sean Dwyer ▼

> You're only as good as your worst shot.
> – Anonymous

Courtesy of Sean Dwyer.

The discovery of the first stone arrowheads in Africa indicates that the bow and arrow were invented there as early as 50,000 BC. First used for hunting, the bow and arrow became the weapon of choice for armies throughout the world by 2,000 BC. Today, the bow and arrow are used for recreational target shooting and hunting worldwide. Archery is even the national sport of Bhutan.

Success in archery is dependent on bringing so many tiny details together. Archery emphasizes skills using hand–eye coordination, focus, controlled breathing, consistency, and accuracy. Concentration and focus are needed to perform skills successfully. Good archers have control of their mind and equipment while beginners have fleeting success and are often very inconsistent in hitting their targets. From a beginner's perspective, even if they hit the target, they might have done everything wrong. Archery takes a lot of practice!

Equipment

Arrows

Many arrows are available. Advanced archers will likely choose more expensive arrows such as carbon because they are fast and provide greater accuracy and consistency. Wooden arrows are relatively inexpensive but are more susceptible to breakage and fly less consistently. Fiberglass arrows are more durable but not to the degree of aluminum and carbon arrows. Aluminum and carbon arrows are more expensive but are durable and will last a long time in an educational setting. Aluminum and carbon arrows can be easily sized for length, unlike wooden arrows, which come with a factory-clamped point.

Considering all advantages and disadvantages, aluminum and carbon are the best choices for an educational setting given the durability and quality, which will enable participants to have greater success and fun with the activity. The cost is fairly high, but in time a class set can be accumulated and will provide a better archery experience.

When compiling a class set of arrows, it is advisable to have a variety of lengths to accommodate different draw lengths (figure 12.1). With high school participants, the most common draw lengths are between 71 and 76 centimeters (28 and 30 inches), but expect to accommodate draw

Figure 12.1 Display of assorted arrows. Arrows on the left are wooden; arrows on the right are aluminum.

lengths as low as 61 centimeters (24 inches) and as high as 81 centimeters (32 inches). It is advisable to have five arrows in each set, with several sets of the most common 71-centimeter (28-inch) draw lengths. Having five arrows allows participants to shoot three arrows per round and still have two arrows in reserve for breakages.

Bows

Several bows are available, including straight limb, recurve, and compound (figure 12.2). Fiberglass straight-limb and recurve bows are relatively inexpensive and are commonly used by educational institutions. Recurve bows produce more arrow speed than straight-limb bows because recurve bows have additional curves at the tips that bend toward the back of the bow. When the bow is drawn, the curves straighten and store more energy. Compound bows work a pulley or cam system that store a lot of energy. The advantage of the compound is that the pulley system allows the archer to easily hold the string at the full draw position. The pulleys are designed so that the draw weight is greatest at about mid-draw. This means that on release, the arrow starts slowly but quickly increases in speed. With recurve and straight-limb bows, drawing weight increases as the archer draws the string back to the anchor position.

Figure 12.2   A rack of compound bows.

Bows with a lighter draw weight are easier for beginners to hold and provide the best chance of success at holding proper anchoring positions. The flight of the arrow (trajectory) will not be as level, but as the archer becomes more familiar with shooting and gains strength, a bow with a greater draw weight can be used. As a general rule, shorter bows are more suitable for archers with shorter draw lengths, whereas archers with a longer draw length need a longer bow. A participant with a long draw length will experience a great deal of awkwardness using a short bow.

Protective Equipment: Arm Guards and Finger Tabs

An arm guard protects the elbow and forearm of the bow arm from the bowstring after release. A full-length arm guard (three straps) is most suitable for nervous shooters or beginners, who are more likely to hit their inner forearms with the string. With experience, shooters learn how to properly position the bow arm and thereby avoid hitting the inner forearm with the string. A short arm guard (two straps) is satisfactory for shooters who have learned to roll the elbow out of the way of the string. The narrow end of

the arm guard is positioned toward the wrist with straps secured snugly to avoid shifting and bunching of the arm guard.

The finger tab has two main purposes: to protect the fingers from the friction of the string and to provide a smooth release of the string from the fingers, allowing the arrow to fly truer from the bow with fewer wobbles and deviations. The smooth side of the finger tab should contact the string. Finger tabs provide a more universal fit than archery gloves in a large group; however, they are not suited for both right and left hands. More right-handed finger tabs are generally needed than left within a typical group.

Group Equipment

- 1 bow for every two participants, 9- to 13.5-kilogram (20- to 30-pound) draw weight
- 5 arrows of an appropriate length for each participant (several extra sets will be required to ensure compatibility)
- 1 finger tab (left or right) and 1 arm guard for each participant
- 10 to 12 archery butts and stands
- 2 archery nets (open-weave nylon mesh)
- 3 to 4 bow stands

Personal Equipment

- Comfortable footwear that is nonslip and provides good stability
- Short-sleeved shirt that fits snugly and does not have buttons or pockets on the front
- Hair elastic to tie back long hair
- Quiver or arrow basket to hold arrows while shooting

Equipment Care and Maintenance

- All equipment must be in good repair.
- Bows and arrows should be properly stored during the shooting session, with all bows placed on the stands when not in use and arrows in quivers or baskets (not laid flat on the ground).
- Serious injury could result if damaged arrows are used.
- Damaged arrows (nock missing or broken, tip damaged or missing, shaft bent) should not be fired and should be put aside for repair.
- Bowstrings should not be used if any of the strands are broken or chafed.
- All arrows should be inspected for deficiencies by the shooter before each round of shooting.

- Depending on the type of stand used to support the butt, arrows may penetrate the butt, strike the stand behind the butt, and damage the arrow.

Site Selection

An established archery range would be the safest site to shoot while in the outdoors. However, most areas do not have archery ranges, and if they do, the ranges may be located too far away. Sport fields are possible sites, but you must exercise great caution because the background needs to be absolutely free of risk from the arrows. In residential areas, sport fields may not be an option given the close proximity of houses, playgrounds, and public parks. An arrow can travel a great distance either in the air or by skipping across the grass or a roadway. No matter the site selected, a mesh backstop is recommended for beginner to intermediate archers (figure 12.3).

Depending on local regulations, it may be illegal to hold archery sessions outdoors unless in a certified archery range. It is advisable to check with the local firearms or wildlife office for regulations. Depending on local regulations, the classification of bows may require a permit to transport bows and other archery equipment to an archery range or to use them in the outdoors. If an accident were to occur in an outdoor setting, where there are many variables to control, the outdoor leader may be vulnerable to a legal case involving negligence. If unsure, take the activities inside where it is much easier to control these variables.

The group demographic will help determine whether or not an archery lesson will be offered indoors or outdoors. In the outdoors, this unit may not be suitable for a regular physical education class with a range of abilities and motivation. Safety may be compromised because this situation could lead to fooling around and unsafe behavior. In contrast, in a camp setting, the outdoors would be ideal for this unit. The participants' intentions would be appropriate and they would be there for their own enjoyment and experience.

Social Skills and Etiquette

- Do not talk to or distract others while they are shooting.
- Follow all shooting regulations as outlined by the outdoor leader.
- Do not make any sudden or loud noises; shooters may mistake them for commands from the outdoor leader.

Figure 12.3 A typical outdoor archery range.

- Do not remove any arrows from the butt or target until all scoring is done (if shooting in tournament format with scoring targets).

Risk Management

- Archery is a potentially dangerous activity given the nature and velocity of the arrows; however, when participants understand safety regulations, equipment selection, and shooting regulations and procedures, archery is a safe and enjoyable physical activity.
- To ensure the safety of all, there must be a zero-tolerance policy for participants who do not follow safety and shooting procedures. If a participant persists in not adhering to the conditions for safety, the instructor should remove their privilege to participate until the participant demonstrates the ability to responsibly practice the lesson.
- Once fitted for equipment, participants must use only that equipment throughout the unit. Using arrows that are measured and fitted for another participant is especially dangerous.
- All participants (including the outdoor leader and range marshal) must stay at or behind the shooting line when shooters are at the line.
- Follow all safety regulations, procedures, and etiquette.

Unit Organization

This archery unit is designed in a progressive manner. Safety regulations, shooting regulations and procedures, eye dominance, and equipment selection are covered first to ensure that participants fully understand the necessity of these components before shooting. Fooling around, pulling pranks, or being noisy are unacceptable behaviors on an archery range.

Once participants are fully prepared with procedures and guidelines, they are ready for instruction on shooting technique. There are many fun games and alternatives to regular tournament shooting that can capture the interest of beginning shooters. The advantage of these games and activities is that they require proper shooting technique and aiming procedures.

Lesson Plans

Lesson 1: Getting Ready. The first lesson is the most important in this unit. As the outdoor leader, you will need to ensure that participants are prepared for archery and realize that shooting cannot commence until all aspects of this lesson are learned. The key aspect of this lesson is obviously safety. Safety is sought through clear communication of safety and shooting regulations, determination of eye dominance, and selection of equipment.

Lesson 2: Shooting Technique. In this lesson, participants begin shooting. Once they have learned and understood the safety and shooting regulations, they can learn the mechanics of loading the arrow on the bow (nocking), drawing the string to the proper anchor point, and releasing the arrow. The underlying theme is safety at all times for all participants. Participants must understand that these shooting techniques are not only for the purpose of safety but also to ensure that they have success.

Lesson 3: Aiming. Aiming is the ultimate means by which the archer hits the target. Shooting with the use of sights and aiming aids will not be covered in this archery unit. Most beginning archers will be using a bare bow to learn the activity. Two aiming methods are introduced: instinctive and point of reference.

Lesson 4: Shooting Technique—Feedback and Self-Correction. This lesson is an extension of the previous lesson. As the outdoor leader, you should review the shooting techniques and then circulate among the group and offer corrections and feedback where necessary. Participants should begin to self-correct and improve their shooting on their own. To assist with this process, encourage participants to use a buddy system to discuss good points and make suggestions for improvement.

Lesson 5: Tournament Target Shooting. The most common shooting in archery uses tournament target faces. Participants will learn how to properly score and record their results with tournament target faces. The scoring circles on the targets provide instant feedback on the location of the arrow. Flaws in shooting technique are still to be detected by the shooter and corrected throughout successive rounds. Shooting target faces is not limited to one lesson; you can choose to repeat this lesson several times. In a club setting, this lesson will be a mainstay.

Lesson 6: Archery Games. This lesson also can be extended to cover several sessions. The suggested games in this lesson are meant to capture the enthusiasm of participants, who have a chance to put their skills to the test with some fun challenges and friendly competition.

Terminology

- **anchoring**—Setting the bowstring against the chin, lips, and nose for shooting consistency and safety.
- **archery butt**—A backstop for arrows, usually mounted on a stand that can be made from many types of materials.
- **archery net**—A safety device constructed of durable mesh strung in the air behind the archery butts to catch stray arrows.
- **arm guard**—A flat safety device strapped to the inside of the forearm on the bow hand to protect the arm from the bowstring upon release.
- **compound bow**—A stiff-limbed bow that uses cables and pulleys as a levering system to bend the limbs of the bow; the levering system allows for an easier draw weight with more stored energy and faster arrow speed.
- **creeping**—Allowing the draw hand to follow the arrow upon release, which negatively affects the flight of the arrow.
- **drawing**—Pulling the string to the anchoring position.
- **dry fire**—Releasing the bowstring without an arrow. This can cause major damage to the limbs of the bow and should not be done under any circumstances.
- **dynamic release**—Bringing the draw hand straight back beside the head after releasing the arrow; reserved for advanced archers because beginners may mistakenly overdraw the arrow.
- **eye dominance**—The preference of receiving stimuli in one eye over the other.
- **finger tab**—A device usually made of leather that protects the fingers from the bowstring upon release.
- **fletch**—Natural feather or plastic fins that are attached to the arrow to stabilize flight.

- **hen fletch**—Two fletches of the same color that are oriented toward the bow when nocking an arrow.
- **indicator (cock) fletch**—A fletch of a different color than the hen fletches; oriented away from the bow when nocking an arrow.
- **instinctive aiming**—Method of aiming where the dominant eye focuses on a point and the body naturally adjusts to hit the intended target.
- **nock**—A plastic end point that is used to clip the arrow to the string.
- **nocking**—Loading an arrow on a bowstring using the nock.
- **nocking point**—A small metal device that is clipped to the bowstring to ensure that the arrow is nocked in the proper location.
- **plucking**—Allowing the draw hand to leave the anchor position to the side, which causes an uneven lateral flight of the arrow.
- **point-of-release aiming**—Method of aiming whereby the archer focuses the tip of the arrow on a point in the foreground of the archery butt. The archer adjusts this point in response to each arrow location on the target.
- **quiver**—Holder for carrying arrows, usually hung from the side.
- **recurve bow**—A popular style of bow with top and bottom limbs that curve away from the archer.
- **static release**—Keeping the draw hand in the anchor position upon release of the arrow; the release is achieved by a quick release of the fingers only.
- **straight-limb bow**—An inexpensive bow with straight limbs that is harder to draw because the energy increases dramatically (stacks) as the string is drawn; recurve and compound bows are easier to draw but still provide significant stored energy.
- **trajectory**—The curved flight of an arrow while it travels through the air.

Getting Ready

Overview

The first lesson in this unit is designed to prepare participants for shooting archery. Understanding the four sections of this lesson will enable participants to be safe archers and maximize their success.

Whether or not participants shoot during this first lesson will depend on the amount of time available and the progress that can be made with the group while going through all components of the lesson. This session should not be done in a classroom. The entire shooting range should be set up so that participants can see how all routines and procedures are to be followed.

Learning Objectives

- To know and understand the importance of safety regulations for the archery range
- To determine eye dominance
- To understand the safety aspect of determining eye dominance
- To understand shooting regulations and procedures for safe and effective archery sessions
- To understand selection of equipment (arrows, bow)
- To understand selection of safety equipment (finger tab, arm guard)

Risk Management

- When participants are measuring arrows for length, it is vital to have control of the arrow tips.
- Given that the arrows are held horizontally at head height, watch out for striking another participant in the face with the sharp arrow tip.

Activity 1: Safety Regulations

The focus of this lesson is safety. In order for the outdoor leader to achieve this, they must be able to clearly communicate the safety procedures expected of all participants. Furthermore, safety is not automatic—practice is required to support the developing attitude on the archery range. As the outdoor leader, you will need to ensure that participants are mentally and practically prepared before any shooting elements of future lessons commence. Safe and successful archery experiences depend on consistent, clear, and practiced techniques. A common practice in teaching safety is to build the discussion of regulations around shooting tips, determination of eye dominance, and selection of equipment.

Skill Cues

The following safety procedures are not suggestions or options; they are mandatory for safe and enjoyable shooting.

- All shooters need to take responsibility to ensure the safety of themselves and others.
- Be alert at all times.

- Obey all starting and stopping signals.
- Straddle the shooting line evenly.
- Never stand farther away from or closer to the target than others.
- Do not shoot over or past others.
- Do not nock an arrow until you have checked the range.
- Do not shoot an arrow until commands are given to do so.
- After shooting all three arrows, step back from the shooting line.
- Replace the bow on the bow stand and stay behind the bow stand until all arrows are fired. At the outdoor leader's command, all shooters go to the targets (butts).
- Safely draw arrows and wait at the targets until told to return to the firing line.
- Repeat the same procedure for each round.
- Always check the range *before* nocking an arrow.
- Wear all appropriate protective equipment.
- Wear comfortable but appropriate clothing and shoes.
- Avoid pins, buttons, watches, jewelry, and loose-fitting or long sleeves that could hook a bowstring.
- Tie back long hair.
- Never point an arrow in a bow at anyone.
- Never nock an arrow until shooting line is straddled.
- Never retrieve arrows while others are shooting.
- If an arrow falls out of the bow and past the shooting line, it is considered fired unless the arrow can be retrieved using a sweeping motion with a foot.
- Never turn away from the shooting line while an arrow is nocked.
- Do not talk to other archers while shooting.
- Respect all equipment.
- Never dry fire a bow (releasing the string without a nocked arrow).

Teaching Cues

- Safety is paramount in archery.
- Participants need to be familiar with all of these regulations and understand the possible deadly consequences if they choose not to follow them.
- The list of safety regulations in this activity may not be all inclusive, but it provides the key points to abide by when shooting.
- Post the list on sturdy Bristol board. Select one or two of the regulations and have one or two participants explain the importance of the regulations to the rest of the group.
- Be sure all equipment and backstops will stop the arrows.

Activity 2: Determining Eye Dominance

Eye dominance determines which hand will hold the bow and which eye will be used to aim while shooting. In most cases, a right-handed person will be right-eye dominant and will hold the bow with the left hand, and a left-handed person will be left-eye dominant and will hold the bow with the right hand. In cases where handedness does not match eye dominance, the shooter should side with eye dominance. Some people cannot detect the dominant eye and should go with their preference.

Following are three common methods for determining eye dominance. Draw on at least two of these techniques to accommodate the uniqueness of each of participant—one method never seems to work for all learners. Having a couple of options allows each participant to experiment in discovering their eye dominance. This is important because if they are not experiencing success after making their initial choice, reassessing eye dominance via an alternative method may reveal a misinterpretation due to confusion.

Skill Cues

Method 1

Form a triangle by touching the tips of the index fingers and the tips of the thumbs of the left and right hands. Make a smaller triangle, if necessary, by sliding and overlapping the hands toward each other (figure 12.4). Hold both arms out at full length. Pick an object in the distance and look at it through the triangle. Close the left eye. Is the object is still in view? If it is, the right eye is dominant. To double-check, repeat the procedure, but this time close the right eye. If the object shifts out of the line of vision, it confirms that the right eye is dominant. The reverse will occur for left-eye dominance.

Method 2

Some beginners and younger children have difficulty with method 1. A slight variation makes it much easier to determine eye dominance. Place the hands as described in method 1. Look at an object in the distance through the triangle formed by the index fingers and thumbs. Slowly bend the elbows and bring the hands toward the face, keeping the object in sight the entire time. The hands should go directly to the eye that is dominant.

Method 3

Hold the right arm out in front of the body and point at an object in the distance with the index finger (figure 12.5). Hold the arm steady and close the left eye. If the finger remains pointing at the object, the right eye is dominant. To double-check, repeat the procedure, but this time close the right eye. If the finger seems to jump to the right of the object, it confirms that the right eye is dominant. The reverse will occur for left-eye dominance.

Teaching Cues

- Inform participants that eye dominance is important to shoot successfully and safely.
- Incorrectly established eye dominance means that arrows can be shot too far to the left or right and frustrate the shooter.
- With correct eye dominance, arrows that shoot to the left or right are a different problem, but at least one correction option is off the list.

Figure 12.4   Method 1 for determining eye dominance.

Figure 12.5   Method 3 for determining eye dominance.

Activity 3: Equipment Selection

With the dominant eye established, the archer needs to be able to identify the proper bow and the length of arrow that is best suited for their draw weight. This must occur before the archer begins to shoot arrows.

Skill Cues

Arrows

Arrows of the proper length must be selected. Arrows that are too long will not fly correctly, but most importantly, arrows that are too short can fall behind the bow rest and puncture the bow hand or smash off on the face of the bow when released.

Arrow length is determined by draw length, which can be measured using a long ruler, but arrows themselves can be measured by participants:

- Select an arrow.
- Stand with heels, back, and head touching a wall or fence.
- Place the nock of the arrow on the chin.
- Slide both hands evenly along the arrow shaft until the elbows are fully extended.
- The shoulders should remain on the wall in a relaxed position and should not extend forward to increase the reach on the arrow shaft.
- To ensure an adequate length, the tip of the arrow should extend 5 to 8 centimeters (2-3 inches) beyond the fingertips.

Bows

- Participants select a bow of the appropriate length and draw weight.
- If using compound bows participants are to select the correct right- or left-handed bow.
- Participants with a longer draw length require a longer bow.
- The draw weight should be light at first to ensure proper execution of technique.

Protective Equipment

Each participant requires an arm guard and a finger tab.

- Arm guards:
  - The narrow end of the arm guard is positioned toward the wrist.
  - Straps must be snug to avoid shifting and bunching of the arm guard (figure 12.6).
- Finger tabs:
  - The finger tab is designed so that the index finger is above the nock of the arrow and the nocking point of the string while the middle and ring fingers are below.
  - With the palm of the dominant hand (right hand, if right-eye dominant), position the finger tab with the smooth side facing toward the body.

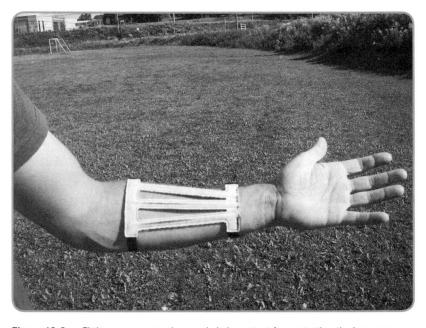

Figure 12.6 Fitting an arm guard properly is important for protecting the bow arm.
Courtesy of Sean Dwyer.

  - Slide the tab so that the middle finger fits fully through the hole; then fold the finger tab flat onto the fingers.

Teaching Cues

Arrows

- Arrange participants along one area (wall or fence) to measure their arrows; this will avoid accidental contact with arrow tips while measuring the arrows.
- Once participants have determined that an arrow is of the appropriate length, they should retrieve the remaining arrows from the arrow rack to avoid having another person choose the same arrows.
- Record either the number of the arrows or the position of the arrows on the rack to avoid confusion in subsequent lessons and to prevent participants from taking others' arrows.

Bows

If the number of bows is limited, participants should be paired by bow length with one shooter shooting in round 1 while the other shoots in round 2.

Protective Equipment

- Check each arm guard to makes sure the fit is snug and that the protection is facing the right way—on the inside of the arm.
- Make sure the guard is not too tight.

Lesson Closure

- Ensure that participants know the purpose of equipment and how to properly fit it.
- Reinforce these points to help participants select equipment for the next session when they prepare to shoot.

Activity 4: Safe Shooting Procedures and Archer Stance

Shooting safely requires a consistent, easy-to-follow routine. The outdoor leader has to have the routine practiced so that when demonstrated to the participants it flows together in a sensible sequential order. There is no room for misunderstandings—showing one thing and saying something else to participants causes confusion and mistakes that could compromise safety. The following activity keeps the procedure simple and user friendly and is aimed at maximizing safety.

Skill Cues

The following shooting procedures are not suggestions or options; they should be a mandatory practice to ensure safe and enjoyable shooting.

- The archer will select a compound bow based on eye dominance.
- Each archer will select three arrows.
- The archer goes to the shooting line and places three arrows in the arrow basket or arrow stand (quill).
- The archer straddles the shooting line.
- The archer needs to be positioned sideways, bow hand extended down range.
- Archer stance should be shoulder width apart.
- The archer should be able to comfortably reach up with the drawing hand and touch the bowstring.
- The archer steps back from the shooting line and places the bow on the bow stand.
- Once back behind the firing line, the entire shooting procedure begins again with the next group of archers.

Teaching Cues

- You must have complete control of this shooting procedure.
- This procedure should be clearly communicated and practiced to ensure adherence.
- Participants who do not follow every step of the procedures are putting others at risk.
- Disobedient participants should be declined shooting privileges—safety first!
- Check the stance of each archer and ensure that they have the correct bow for their eye preference.
- Have archers recite the safety procedure list as a review.
- Introduce the shooting commands to prepare them for the next step when they fire their arrows.

• Make sure archers do not pull back on the bowstring with their draw hand—prevent a dry fire.

Lesson Closure

• In groups of two, have archer pairs create a list of the safe shooting procedures.
• Assign one procedure to each paring and have them explain the importance of the step.
• Have participants identify potential hazards if one of the steps is skipped in the safe shooting procedures.

LESSON 2
Shooting Technique

Overview

Participants need to know how to
• properly nock an arrow,
• draw the bowstring to an anchor point, and
• release the string.

These steps are taught for success in archery but are equally important for safety.

Learning Objectives

• To learn proper shooting techniques
• To nock an arrow with fletches oriented properly
• To draw the bowstring with correct body posture
• To anchor the bow hand and string
• To understand safety concerning drawing and anchoring
• To release the arrow safely
• To learn how to remove arrows from an archery butt

Risk Management

• The steps involved in shooting need to be taught and demonstrated so that all participants can see and understand each step.
• This process should not be rushed and should only progress as quickly as participants are able to recognize the significance of each step.
• Saying, "Nobody can shoot until this is understood," will help make participants focus and be more likely to follow the steps.
• When drawing the arrow, participants are not to wrap the index finger of the bow hand around the arrow to keep it on the arrow rest; fletches will slice the finger as the arrow travels through to the target.

Activity 1: Nocking the Arrow

Nocking is loading the arrow on the bowstring (figure 12.7).

Skill Cues

- The arrow is placed on the bow rest; some bows have two bow rests to allow for right- and left-handed shooters.
- When gripping the bow, lay the arrow on the same side of the bow as the knuckles of the bow hand.
- The arrow is properly nocked when the indicator fletch points away from the side of the bow.
- The indicator fletch is often a different color than the hen fletches and is perpendicular to the slot in the nock.
- The hen fletches lie relatively flat in relation to the side of the bow and will slide with little interference past the side of the bow upon release.
- With fletches oriented, pull the arrow toward the string and snap the nock into place below the nocking point.

Teaching Cues

- Demonstrate the procedure for nocking an arrow at the shooting line.
- You must model good behavior and not swing the bow toward the participants during this demonstration.
- Keep the bow and the arrow pointing down range.
- If you are right-eye dominant, participants should be situated at or behind the shooting line to the right of you.

Figure 12.7   Nocking an arrow.
Courtesy of Sean Dwyer.

Activity 2: Drawing the Bowstring

Drawing the bowstring means pulling the string back to the anchor position in preparation for releasing the arrow. At this stage, the nock of the arrow is snapped into place on the string immediately below the nocking point.

Skill Cues

- The slot in the finger tab accepts the nock of the arrow with the index finger above and the next two fingers below the nock.
- The draw hand should be kept in an extended position and not allowed to close in on the string; only the first joints in the three draw fingers should bend.
- The bow hand should hold the grip firmly enough to have control, but if it holds too tightly, the bow will snap to the side upon release and affect the arrow flight.

Figure 12.8   Drawing the bowstring.
Courtesy of Sean Dwyer.

- The bow arm should be held out level and extended, and the elbow should be cocked outward, slightly allowing enough space for the bowstring to snap past the forearm (figure 12.8).
- The stance should be perpendicular to the shooting line so that the chest and back of each archer are facing—the archers should either be seeing their neighbor's face or back, according to their right- or left-hand grip.
- Pull the string back toward the face to the desired anchor position (to be covered in the next activity)—attempt full draw weight.

- The shoulder and back muscles should help with the draw because relying only on the arm can be tiring. Squeezing the shoulder blades helps tremendously.
- Final bow check: The bow arm should be positioned so that the shoulder is rotated inward, elbow cocked outward, causing the elbow to turn out and away from the path of the string.
- Return the bowstring without firing by easing the bowstring back to the original position, relieving the pressure of the draw weight.

Teaching Cues

- The fingers used with the finger tab should not squeeze the nock; the nock is clipped into the string, so it will not fall off.
- Squeezing the nock with these fingers usually causes the arrow to swing away from the arrow rest during the drawing phase.
- The thumb should not contact the nock at all because it will push the arrow off the string during the draw.
- The elbow of the drawing arm should remain at least level or a little higher throughout the entire drawing motion.
- Dropping the elbow of the draw arm will almost always cause the arrow to fall off the rest.
- If the nock is too big for the string, simply pinch the nock together with the fingers or the teeth and it should clip in just fine.
- The thumb should be tucked in or kept up depending on the type of anchor being used.
- Do not allow the archer to dry fire when returning the bowstring to the original position.

Activity 3: Anchoring

There are many anchoring methods, and the use of each depends on the type of shooting being performed. Some hunters and compound shooters use a trigger release, which removes the imperfections of a finger-tab release and increases accuracy.

Anchoring is a key component in the safe administration of an archery unit. For beginners, anchoring can be challenging if clear cues and pointers are not used. Anchoring can be a large determinant of safety because many beginners draw the arrow too far and risk catching the side of the face with the string. Even more dangerous, if the arrow tip is drawn behind the arrow rest, it is not guided properly and could be released into the bow hand or into the face of the bow, which will likely cause it to buckle and break in front of the participant's face.

Skill Cues

- The knuckle of the index finger is drawn back under the chin and slides under the jaw bone.
- The string is drawn to the face so that it intersects the chin, lips, and nose.
- The head should be in an upright position; it should not lean forward or to the side to meet the string.
- Squeezing the shoulder blades together will assist in getting the string to anchor firmly.

Teaching Cues

- This method of anchoring prevents overdrawing because the arrow cannot be drawn any farther than the chin, lips, and nose.

- If a participant draws beyond the face, it is easy to detect and correct; this method gives an unambiguous skill cue as to the draw location of the string.
- Drawing to the same location every time an arrow is fired will increase the consistency of shooting because all arrows will be projected with a similar force. This should lead to greater success for participants (figure 12.9).
- Aiming can be achieved when all arrows are fired consistently.
- If a different anchor location is used each time, aiming will be a gamble and success will be more fluke than intentional.
- The method of anchoring described here is suited to the method of measuring arrows as described in lesson 1; therefore, arrows that are anchored correctly will not be over-drawn in the bow.
- The archer can practice anchoring using pieces of string cut to fit their draw weight.

Figure 12.9 Anchor the bowstring so that it intersects the chin, lips, and nose.
Courtesy of Sean Dwyer.

Activity 4: Releasing the Arrow—Shooting

When the archer is comfortable in stance (with the bowstring situated in the finger grooves and ready to pull back with the draw hand), is anchored, and has the bow arm positioned down range with the elbow out, the archer is then ready to begin releasing arrows. The next set of techniques to help with accuracy is breathing and timing when sighting the target. There are two skill versions for the outdoor leader: Method A will focus on guiding the archer, and method B will guide the outdoor leader in running an archery course.

Skill Cues

Method A

- The draw hand should be kept in the anchor position when the string is released (called *static release;* see figure 12.10). This is a point mainly for beginners; more advanced archers may choose to bring the draw hand back after the release (referred to as *dynamic release*).
- To release the string, the fingers should extend simultaneously and quickly so that they are pointed toward the target; the fingers flick forward.
- The bow hand should be kept stationary for a 2-second count after the arrow is released. This helps beginners avoid the tendency

Figure 12.10 Releasing the arrow in the static-release position.
Courtesy of Sean Dwyer.

to drop the bow before the arrow is fully past the arrow rest and helps prevent any lateral motions that can send the arrow to the left or right.

- The string should slide smoothly from the finger tab without interference from the fingers.
- Creeping (following the string with the draw hand after release) should be avoided; it will affect the flight and reduce the speed of the arrow.
- Plucking should also be avoided during the release. In plucking, the draw hand leaves the anchor position by moving out to the side and away from the face.

Method B

The following shooting procedures are for the big picture when running an archery course for multiple participants. The following are not suggestions or options; they are mandatory for safe and enjoyable shooting.

- The archer selects a compound bow based on eye dominance.
- Each archer will select three arrows.
- To begin round 1, the archer goes to the shooting line and places three arrows in the pylon or arrow stand (quill).
- The archer straddles the shooting line.
- When all shooters are properly situated, the outdoor leader tells shooters to begin firing.
- Each shooter continues firing until all three arrows are fired.
- Once three arrows are fired, the shooters step back from the shooting line and place the bow on the bow stand.
- After all shooters from round 1 have finished and have replaced their bows on the bow stand, they step back behind the stands.
- The second round of shooters goes to the shooting line with their bows and place their arrows in the pylon or stand.
- Upon the outdoor leader's command, the second round of shooters begins firing.
- As shooters finish firing three arrows, they replace their bows on the bow stands.
- When all arrows are fired, all bows are replaced on the bow stands, and all archers are away from the shooting line, the outdoor leader gives the command for archers to proceed to the butts and retrieve the arrows.
- Shooters pull their own arrows from the archery butt, one shooter at a time.
- When all arrows are drawn, the outdoor leader gives the command to return behind the firing line; the entire group moves together throughout this procedure.
- Once back behind the firing line, the entire shooting procedure begins again.

Teaching Cues

- You must have complete control of this shooting procedure.
- This procedure should be clearly communicated and practiced to ensure adherence.
- Participants who do not follow every step of the procedures are putting others at risk.
- Disobedient participants should be declined shooting privileges—safety first!
- Check the stance and release of each participant.

Activity 5: Drawing Arrows From the Archery Butt

After each archer has released a set of arrows, each participant has returned their bows to the rack, and all are standing on the firing line, the outdoor leader can give the all clear signal. This signal allows archers to move down range to the targets to retrieve their arrows. The practice is not to simply grab and go—rather, they should safely extract arrows as to not cause harm to other archers and to prevent breaking the arrow shaft (which is easily done!).

Skill Cues

- Locate the arrow closest and highest to the archer.
- Place the palm of one hand against the archery butt so the arrow is between the index finger and the thumb.
- Place the other hand over the arrow shaft as close to the butt as possible so both hands are touching and then grasp the arrow.
- Gently pull (no twisting) the arrow from the butt.
- Keep a closed palm over the arrow points and keep arrows at waist height.

Teaching Cues

- Be sure no one is standing close behind when an arrow is being pulled.
- Emphasize that archers should not draw another archer's arrows unless requested.
- Archers must keep two hands on the arrows: one palm over the points and the other hand at midshaft (figure 12.11).
- Archers must walk back to the quill location and carefully and gently return the arrows for the next round.

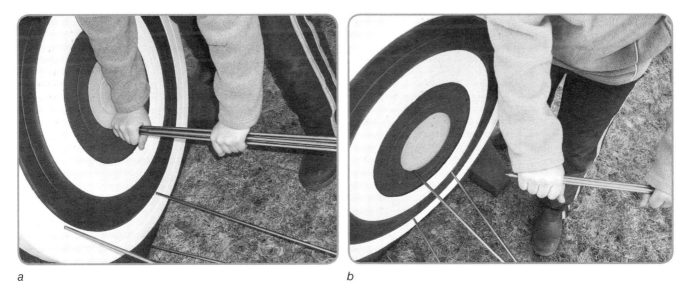

a   b

Figure 12.11   Safely removing arrows from the archery butt.

Lesson Closure

- The steps described in these activities should be constantly reinforced and repeated throughout the lesson.
- A summary of the steps at the end will encourage participants to check their learning.
- You may wish to quiz the participants during the review by asking "What step comes next?" or "Why is it important to do this step?" to check their understanding.

LESSON 3

Aiming

Overview

Aiming in archery is an enormous topic. Some archers prefer advanced equipment such as sights and other aiming gadgets. Many beginners and traditionalists, on the other hand, shoot bare bow without sighting aids. The activities presented in this lesson do not deal with sights and focus instead on instinctive and point-of-reference aiming—natural sighting.

Learning Objectives

- To understand the concepts of instinctive and point-of-reference aiming
- To allow the dominant eye to focus on the target and guide the body to aim at the target
- To use arrow locations as feedback to make adjustments when shooting other arrows
- To anchor properly and consistently in order to control variables and adjust aiming with a consistent draw length
- To control breathing for more consistent aiming

Equipment

Cardboard or paper circles of various sizes

Risk Management

- Participants should use common sense when aiming and be aware of other archers and progression of procedures provided by the outdoor leader at all times.
- If participants see someone aiming too high or too low, they should quietly alert that person or the outdoor leader immediately.

Activity 1: Instinctive Aiming

This is a skill that comes with practice, and compounding the complexity are timing and the feel. The best way to describe how to get this skill is by feeling the natural sight line. Some archers will easily find their way and comment after they release their arrows that it just felt right and that they knew they were on target as they released their draw hands. The outdoor leader can best assist by keeping the practice sessions positive and fun and not allowing frustration to be the teacher.

Skill Cues

- Instinctive aiming involves focusing the dominant eye on the target and anchoring long enough to allow the body to naturally adjust to the focal point.
- Archers at this point should be able to go through the stages of shooting stance, nocking the arrow, setting the bow arm, drawing the bowstring to the anchor position, sighting the target, controlling their breathing, and instinctually deciding on the timing for release when the sighting is aligned.

Teaching Cues

- To practice instinctive aiming, attach various sizes of cardboard or paper circles to the archery butt; participants choose the circle they wish to shoot.
- Following all shooting techniques to the best of their ability, participants take note of where the arrows hit and use this feedback in the next round to try to gain more accuracy.
- Allow ample practice time, because precision shooting is best supported by the feel, as the participant perfects the technique to the best of her ability.

Activity 2: Point-of-Reference Aiming

A simple way to express this skill in sighting is to see your mark. This requires the archer to know where the sighting location is in relation to where they want the arrow to end up on the target.

Skill Cues

- *Point of reference* refers to focusing the tip of the arrow on a spot in the foreground to aim consistently.
- The tip of the arrow will not be focused on the target because the shooter does not look down the length of the arrow—the sighting location is relative to the target.
- The nock of the arrow is anchored at chin level and can lead an archer to shoot well over the target if the tip is aimed at the target.
- The level or height of the shot is harder to judge with point-of-reference aiming, based on the trajectory of the arrow's flight path.
- Participants must proceed slowly through the shooting procedures to make corrections.

Teaching Cues

- This type of aiming can be practiced in the same way as instinctive aiming (activity 1).
- This type of aiming will be more challenging for beginners, especially as the distance from the target increases.

Lesson Closure

- Encourage participants to take a relaxed approach to shooting regardless of the type of aiming they choose.
- Feedback is important in aiming; participants need to take note of where they aimed the last shot and where the arrow actually landed.
- Using this information, participants make the necessary adjustments. Shooting technique is critical to ensure consistency, because without consistent technique, aiming will be difficult.
- When all arrows consistently land within a circle formed by the index fingers and thumbs of both hands, the shooter demonstrates natural aiming skills.
- Arrows that are scattered over the target face make diagnosing errors much more difficult.
- If arrows are tightly grouped but off target, it is much easier for the participant to make adjustments.

LESSON 4

Shooting Technique—Feedback and Self-Correction

Overview

In this lesson, help participants by providing feedback on technique, including corrections and tips for improvement. The aim is to have participants learn to diagnose their own shooting errors. When participants can detect their own errors, they have truly learned the technique and have gained body awareness—the feel.

Learning Objectives

- To receive feedback on archery technique and make adjustments
- To learn to detect errors and make adjustments
- To conference with a partner to assist with detecting errors and making necessary adjustments

Equipment

10 to 12 target faces, 60 centimeters (24 inches)

Risk Management

- There will be some communication between partners. You must create an atmosphere where partners can converse about technique without creating too many distractions.
- Shooters must never turn from the line while shooting to communicate with their partners. This is especially important if an arrow is nocked.
- Conferences between partners should occur after the shooter is behind the bow stand.

Activity: Partner Conferencing

Target faces can be used for this session; the scoring circles will provide good feedback on the location of the arrows. Larger targets such as a 60-centimeter (24-inch) target face are recommended because they will provide more success than a 40-centimeter (16-inch) target face.

Skill Cues

- Participants shoot in pairs, with one partner observing the other while he shoots.
- The shooter fires all three arrows without interruption.
- The observer should note positive points (via discussion after the round) and some points that need improvement (via immediate corrective feedback discussed before the next arrow).

Teaching Cues

- After the round, partners meet behind the bow stands and have a conference; they share information and take these points to the next round, trying to maintain good technique and improve those items that were highlighted by their partner.
- Provide participants with a checklist of archery techniques to guide them in this task (figure 12.12).
- Allow participants to state what they think, because this information is just as important as the observer's points. This should be a supportive conversation that builds on the positives to help guide the next round.
- Move about behind the shooters and provide feedback and corrections, especially when safety is jeopardized.

Shooting phase	Key skill techniques	Common error results
Nocking the arrow	– Arrow on knuckle side of bow. – Indicator fletch points away from bow rest. – Nock clipped on string below nocking point.	– Arrow will wobble sideways through the air if indicator fletch strikes side of bow. – Arrow will aim downward if nocked above nocking point.
Drawing the bowstring	– Stance should be perpendicular to shooting line. – Index finger is placed above nocking point and nock of arrow. – Bow hand maintains a relaxed grip. – Draw hand does not close on or clinch the string. – Elbow of bow arm must be rotated out of the way of the string. – Draw arm must have elbow held level or higher.	– String will contact arm if bow hand is gripping tightly. – Arrow will fall off arrow rest if fingers clinch string, stance is not perpendicular, or draw elbow is not held high. – Elbow will be struck with string if elbow is not rotated.
Anchoring	– Knuckle of index finger is drawn under the jaw bone. – String touches and intersects the nose, lips, and chin. – Head should be held upright. – Squeeze shoulder blades to maintain a full draw and anchor.	– Arrow will lose velocity if full draw is not achieved. – Aiming will be jeopardized if anchoring position is not held long enough to properly aim. – Drawing too far could cause serious injury to the shooter.
Aiming	Focus on target with dominant eye and let body naturally adjust by moving bow arm.	Failure to aim by releasing arrow too fast after anchoring or failure to anchor, which does not allow for proper aiming.
Releasing the arrow	– Draw hand stays in anchor position while releasing the arrow. – Fingers flick forward to release arrow. – Avoid creeping or plucking. – Maintain position of bow hand until arrow has been released.	– Reduced velocity on arrow if creeping occurs. – Arrow will have affected flight if archer plucks the string upon release. – Arrow flight will be affected if bow hand is dropped too early or is moved to the side.

Figure 12.12 Checklist of key archery techniques.

From K. Redmond, A. Foran, and S. Dwyer, 2010, *Quality lesson plans for outdoor education* (Champaign, IL: Human Kinetics).

Lesson Closure

- Review the process of working with a partner to help improve shooting technique.
- Highlight that the intention of this process is to lead participants to be more reflective about their own performance.
- Self-corrections are necessary in archery to avoid forming bad habits.

LESSON 5

Tournament Target Shooting

Overview

Traditional tournament target faces consist of five zones of concentric circles decreasing in point value from the center to the outside (yellow, red, blue, black, and white). Each of these zones consists of two circles, with a point for each circle. The center circle (yellow) is worth 10 points, the second yellow circle is worth 9 points, the first red circle is worth 8 points, and so on until the outside white circle, which is worth 1 point. Any arrow that lands outside the 1-point circle or misses the target face or butt is scored as a zero. Participants apply their shooting and aiming skills to a tournament situation by shooting traditional target faces.

Learning Objectives

- To learn to score with target faces in a tournament setting
- To apply shooting and aiming skills in a tournament
- To score arrows properly with tournament target faces
- To learn procedure and precautions for pulling arrows from the archery butt
- To reinforce the concept of pausing after anchoring to ensure correct aiming

Equipment

10 to 12 target faces, 60 centimeters (24 inches)

Risk Management

- Participants will be scoring arrows together and should be careful during the scoring procedure because arrows must be left in the butt until all arrows are scored.
- Caution should be exercised when pulling arrows from the butt to ensure that no one is standing close enough to get hit with an arrow.

Activity: Tournament Targets

Participants proceed to the targets once instructed by the outdoor leader. Partners score all arrows for each other. Arrows are scored where they land in the target face and are not to be touched or pulled until all arrows are scored. Arrows touching a line are scored as the higher point value.

Skill Cues

- The tournament format in archery consists of 10 rounds for each participant.
- Participants shoot three arrows per round.
- Participants shoot in pairs to witness and score arrows in each end.

Teaching Cues

- Encourage participants to keep their shooting relaxed and to pause when aiming before releasing the arrow.
- Participants should use feedback from each arrow to make aiming adjustments for the next arrow.

Lesson Closure

Participants review their score sheets with partners to check their performance and detect any trends in their shooting.

- Did shooting improve at any point and if so, why?
- Did shooting results decrease?
- Was tiredness a factor?
- Did attention to technique affect shooting?

LESSON 6

Archery Games

Overview

This lesson introduces fun games that require proper shooting regulations and procedures. The purpose is to capture the enthusiasm of participants and provide a fun experience. Any of these games can be offered as part of a session to reinforce shooting and aiming techniques or as a full lesson to provide plenty of recreation time.

Learning Objectives

- To apply shooting and aiming procedures to fun archery games
- To cooperate with a partner when playing archery games
- To maintain safety by observing all shooting regulations

Equipment

- Target faces for Tic-Tac-Toe and Archery Darts
- Balloons
- Sticky notes
- Permanent markers
- String
- Clothespins

Risk Management

- Excitement with the games can lead to carelessness in a class setting more so than with an archery club.
- Turning away from the shooting lines with an arrow nocked is of particular concern as participants get excited and turn to their friends for reassurance and to check if they saw that shot.
- Encourage participants to remain responsible while shooting.

Activity 1: Tic-Tac-Toe

Target faces for Tic-Tac-Toe are available commercially but are simple to make. Using chart paper and heavy (thick tip) permanent marker, the outdoor leader can simply chart out a Tic-Tac-Toe grid.

Skill Cues

- Pairs of participants playing the game stand on the shooting line next to each other.
- Specify which partner will represent *X* and which will represent *O.*
- Participants shoot arrows in turn, attempting to align their three arrows either in line or diagonally as with standard Tic-Tac-Toe play.

Teaching Cues

- Skilled shooters may win a game in one end whereas beginners may take two or more ends to complete a game.
- To continue a game over several rounds, place a sticky note marked either *X* or *O* on the appropriate space to claim that spot for the next round when shooters try to shoot vacant areas and complete the game.
- Participants may choose new partners as games are completed.

Activity 2: Archery Darts

Archery Darts is based on the popular recreational game of darts. Commercially available target faces allow shooters to take aim and play popular dart games.

Skill Cues

Participants partner with one another to play.

Teaching Cues

- With beginners, it is recommended that shooters deduct points immediately and enforce the rule of needing to hit a double score as proficiency increases. The double score zone is the outer ring of the target face.
- Starting and ending games in darts usually involve having to hit a double score.

Activity 3: Balloon Breaking

Breaking a balloon with an arrow is exciting and can increase participants' interest in archery. Group settings accentuate this experience as several balloons are popped within a short time.

Skill Cues

- Follow all shooting and aiming procedures.
- Attach a string to a clothespin to quickly attach the balloons to the archery butt after each round.
- As participants break balloons, they are responsible for blowing them up and replacing them when they retrieve their arrows.

Teaching Cues

- Caution needs to be exercised; participants are not allowed to shoot more laterally than the neighboring butt.
- Dangerous deflections can occur if arrows are shot at a wide angle.
- Participants must unnock their arrow, walk to the new location, straddle the line, renock the arrow, and resume shooting.
- Attach one or more balloons to each archery butt.
- Participants shoot in one or more rounds depending on the size of the group.
- You may either save unbroken balloons for the next round or allow participants with arrows remaining to shoot balloons on other archery butts.
- Write numbers or messages on small pieces of paper and place them inside the balloons. This number or message could be a prize claim ticket, or it could be a command that allows a participant to shoot an extra arrow or some other privilege.

Lesson Closure

- Count the total number of broken balloons to begin a friendly competition between groups.
- Discuss safety and how it may have been jeopardized during this shooting session.

References and Resources

Axford, R. 1996. *Archery anatomy: An introduction to techniques for improved performance.* London: Souvenir Press.

Haywood, K. 2005. *Archery.* 3rd ed. Champaign, IL: Human Kinetics.

Ruis, S., and C. Stevenson. 2003. *Precision archery.* Champaign, IL: Human Kinetics.

Fly Casting and Fly Fishing

▼ Len Rich and Kevin Redmond ▼

No life is so happy
and so pleasant as
the life of the well-
govern'd angler.
– Izaak Walton

Fly fishing is a recreational pastime in which the angler simulates the actions of the insect life of a watershed in order to attract fish to an artificial fly. It is quite different from using a spin-cast rod. In the latter, the lure or bait acts as a weight and pulls the line from the reel as it is cast. In fly fishing, however, the opposite is true. The fly line is cast as the weight, and the artificial fly, which is attached to a nearly weightless and invisible leader, follows the weight of the fly line.

Fly fishing is the only accepted method of pursuing some species (e.g., Atlantic salmon) in many parts of the world (due to local regulations geared toward preserving fish stocks). It is used to attract fish in both freshwater and saltwater environs by simulating natural food sources of the fish. People fly fish for many reasons, including personal enjoyment, relaxation, physical activity, being one with nature, and the thrill of playing a fish that they have fooled with a human-made insect.

Equipment

Group Equipment

For the first lesson, Fly-O teaching rods and yarn are best. If the Fly-O rods are not available, the top half of a fly rod may be substituted. For all other lessons, it is ideal for each participant to have access to a set of equipment including a fly rod and a fly reel equipped with backing and fly line. An alternative is to divide the group into pairs, with one set of equipment shared between two people.

- 1 91-centimeter (3-foot) Fly-O teaching fly rod per participant (If these are not available, 1 section of a regular 3-meter (9-foot) fly rod may be used.)
- 1 fly rod and reel equipped with fly line, backing, leader, and tippet per participant
- Leaders, tippet, and artificial fly selection available as teaching aids
- Lengths of rope or twine to practice knots used in fly fishing
- Nail clippers for trimming monofilament when tying knots
- 5 meters (16 feet) of knitting yarn per rod
- Marker to mark on yarn
- Dry-fly oil (for dry flies only)
- Pliers for crimping barbs on hooks

Personal Equipment

Depending on the weather and water conditions, all or some of the following may be desirable:

- Hat
- Polarized sunglasses
- Sunscreen
- Insect repellent
- Rainwear
- Waders
- Nail clippers
- Participants' own rod, reel, and flies when available

Equipment Care and Maintenance

It is important that participants know the equipment components and their functions to help in the assembly of fly-fishing gear. Careful attention must be given to assembly of the equipment to ensure proper alignment and attachment of the components, thus reducing risk of damage to equipment and maximizing ease of casting and playing fish.

- Insect repellent should be kept away from all fishing gear because most repellents break down fishing line, leader, and even rods. This can lead to malfunction and breakage, especially when under pressure, as in playing a fish.
- Reels should be greased on a regular basis according to usage.
- Keep sand, dirt, and grime off the rod and reel. In case of soilage, clean parts immediately, especially sand in the reel.
- To protect fishing line, apply line dressing when required.
- Keep the rod and reel away from sand.
- When a rod is not in use, it should be stood up or stored vertically.
- If participants bring their own equipment, you should inspect it before they use it.

Site Selection

Initial fly-fishing activities can be taught in any open space, but an attractive border of trees, foliage, or water sets the stage best for this unit. Sites should also be selected for the absence of wind for all the casting lessons to enhance learning and success. It is suitable for the first lesson using shortened rods with yarn to be taught and practiced indoors, as the yarn will not cast outdoors in wind. Later lessons that include actual fishing activities are best done in an area where fish are plentiful, even if the fish are small. This provides more opportunity for practice to reinforce concepts taught throughout the unit.

The ideal setting would be outdoors in a cleared area near a body of moving water where there is adequate space for learning to cast. A secondary choice would be a gymnasium with a high ceiling and smooth floor. Lesson 1 is suited to a gymnasium-type area indoors or out, but as noted it is essential that there be no wind present for activities in lesson 1.

Social Skills and Etiquette

Fly-fishing etiquette is a combination of respect and common sense:

- Never crowd another fisher.
- Be friendly to other fishers.
- Respect the environment.
- Respect the fish—only keep what you intend to eat.
- When releasing fish, revive the fish before release and use accepted hook-and-release protocols.

Risk Management

- Artificial flies are tied on sharp steel hooks that may be accidentally embedded in parts of the body. The barb of the hook should be flattened or removed to facilitate easy and painless removal should such an incident occur.
- Fly rods are not to be laid flat on the ground where they can be stepped on and broken.
- Fly reels must be kept away from dirt and sand, which can damage internal workings.
- Care must be taken to maintain a clear area behind participants when casting.
- It is recommended that participants wear safety glasses or sunglasses (for eye protection) throughout the learning stages of casting.
- Rod-piece ends and tips should be kept away from eye level.
- Where possible, rod-piece ends should be covered or held in hand when not in use.

Unit Organization

Fly fishing requires patience and precision. The introductory lesson in this unit is designed to develop precision and technique. This first lesson features modified equipment and stands on its own as an introduction to casting. It also has the flexibility to serve as a rainy-day activity in a gymnasium or a similar space. Furthermore, the first lesson can serve as a hook for participants because they are immediately involved in casting. It is possible to skip this lesson and move directly to lesson 2 with the real equipment, but this would make for a slower start to the unit because real fly-fishing equipment requires significant setup and preparation activities.

For novices, seeing and hooking fish is often their measure of success and is important in developing their confidence. For many mature fishers, their most pleasurable experience is often the company of others and being outdoors and on the water. The sooner beginners develop the mature mindset, the more successful and pleasurable their fly-fishing forays will be.

Lesson Plans

Lesson 1: Yarn Casting Progressions. This first lesson is a quick-start guide to fly casting. Using modified 91-centimeter (3-foot) Fly-O fly rods (or rod sections) and yarn (to simulate fly line), a series of basic casting activities focus on how to cast with precision and technique. This lesson is an abbreviated version of Joan Wulff's casting progressions and is used with permission. It is recommended that those who find this lesson valuable consider her resources noted at the end of this unit.

Lesson 2: Fly-Fishing Equipment and Assembly. This lesson introduces fly-fishing equipment parts and functions followed by assembling the rod, attaching the reel, and threading the fly line through the eyes of the rod. Each aspect of this lesson is important in the proper functioning of the fishing gear in later lessons.

Lesson 3: Attaching the Leader. There are a variety of methods for attaching the leader to the fly line. This lesson presents the three most common methods: the nail knot, the needle knot, and the loop-to-loop connection.

Lesson 4: Attaching the Tippet and Fly. Attaching a tippet to the leader minimizes the disturbance on the water when the fly lands at the conclusion of a cast. Although a tippet is not mandatory, in some situations it is essential for success. In this lesson, participants practice attaching a tippet to the leader and attaching a fly to the tippet.

Lesson 5: Casting the Fly Rod. This lesson introduces the four steps in casting the fly rod: the lift, stop and load, forward or power cast, and drop and release. Casting the fly to where the fish lie is an integral component of fly fishing.

Lesson 6: Applying Fly-Fishing Principles. A wide variety of flies may be used for fly fishing, some of which are cast differently. This lesson introduces casting techniques for the floating fly, nymph fly, wet fly, and streamer. These casting techniques are followed with hooking and playing, landing, and retaining fish.

Lesson 7: Live-Release Fishing. Live-release fishing is exercised by sport fishers throughout the world and contributes to maintaining fish stocks. This lesson shows participants how to adjust fishing tackle to facilitate the release of fish, how to humanely play the fish and remove the hook, and how to revive and release the fish. Live-release fishing should be reinforced from the beginning of the unit if possible.

Terminology

- **adult**—The winged stage of aquatic insect life.
- **backcast**—The backward-direction portion of the casting motion.
- **backing**—Usually a braided Dacron line that adds length to the casting line and is used when fighting larger fish such as salmon, steelhead, and some saltwater species.
- **blood (barrel) knot**—The most widely used knot for tying together two pieces of monofilament line with similar diameters.
- **breaking strength**—Effort required to break a strand of unknotted monofilament or braided line, usually stated in kilograms or pounds such as 4.5-kilogram (10-pound) test.
- **caddis**—One of the three aquatic insects imitated in freshwater habitats.
- **casting arc**—The path that the fly rod follows during a complete cast, usually related to the face of a clock, as in 10:00 to 2:00.
- **dead drift**—Where the fly travels at the same pace as the current; used for dry-fly and nymph fishing.
- **double taper (DT)**—A fly-line design where both ends of the line are tapered; better suited for short casting.
- **drag**—Resistance (usually adjustable) applied to the reel spool that prevents the reel from turning faster than the line leaving the spool.
- **dry fly**—Any fly fished upon the surface of the water and normally appearing inactive as it moves with the current; dry flies usually imitate the adult stage of aquatic insect life.
- **dry-fly floatant**—Chemical preparation applied to a dry fly to waterproof the fly and aid flotation.
- **eyes (eyelets)**—Loops on the rod through which line passes; eyelets keep the line close to the rod so tension on the line is transferred to the rod.
- **false cast**—Casting the line without touching the water; normally used to adjust line length, change direction, or dry fly.
- **ferrule**—The end piece of a rod section that attaches one rod section to another. A male ferrule is inserted into a female ferrule to create a solid join.
- **floating fly line**—A fly line where the entire line floats.
- **fly casting**—Normal method of presenting a fly to a target when fly fishing.
- **fly line**—The casting line used when fly fishing.
- **fly reel**—Holds the fly line and backing and is used when playing fish.
- **fly rod**—Fishing rod designed to cast a fly line and play fish. Although rod lengths vary, the most common lengths are between 213 and 274 centimeters (7 and 9 feet).
- **forceps**—Hand-operated tool used to remove flies from the jaws of a hooked fish.
- **forward cast**—Forward-direction portion of the casting motion.
- **graphite**—The most common rod material that offers the best weight, strength, and flex ratio.
- **hook**—Curved, sharp object upon which the fly is tied and is attached to the leader.
- **leader**—Monofilament line between the fly line and the fly.
- **loading the rod**—Describes the bend put on the rod by the weight of the line as it travels through the air when casting.
- **mayfly**—The most imitated aquatic insect commonly found in cold or cool freshwater environments.
- **mending line**—Adjusting line position after laying down a cast to achieve a drag-free float.
- **monofilament**—Clear, supple nylon filament used in fly-fishing leader.
- **nail knot**—Knot used to attach a leader or butt section of monofilament to the fly line or to attach the backing to the fly line; can be tied with a small-diameter tube, nail, matchstick, or twig.

- **open loop**—Describes what the fly line looks like as it travels through the air during a poor cast; normally caused by a wide casting arc.
- **pickup and lay-down**—A cast using only a single backcast and no false cast.
- **playing the fish**—The act of allowing the fish to swim in an effort to get the fish fatigued enough that the fish can be landed easily while still maintaining control of the fish.
- **presentation**—The art of putting the fly on the water.
- **reel seat**—Mechanism that holds the reel to the rod.
- **retrieve**—Bringing the fly back toward the caster after the cast is made.
- **rod flex**—The degree to which the rod bends in the acceleration phase of the casting motion.
- **roll cast**—Cast that does not require a backcast.
- **setting the hook**—Pulling the rod back to seat the hook in the flesh of the fish.
- **spool**—The part of the fly reel that holds fly line (and backing) and revolves.
- **stripping line**—Retrieving line by pulling it in through the fingers; sometimes used to describe pulling line out from the reel to extend cast length.
- **surgeon's knot**—Knot used to tie together two lengths of monofilament that are different diameters.

- **tippet**—The smallest-diameter section of a tapered leader where the fly is attached.
- **turnover**—Describes how the fly line and leader straighten out at the completion of the cast.
- **unloading the rod**—Straightening of the rod as casting energy is transferred from the rod back to the fly line.
- **vest**—A vest worn by the fisher that includes fly-fishing paraphernalia normally found in a tackle box.
- **waders**—High-topped waterproof boots that may include boots or require wading shoes.
- **wading shoes**—Shoes or boots made to be worn over stocking-foot waders.
- **weight forward (WF)**—A fly line that carries most of its weight in the forward section of the line, making it easier for casting.
- **wet fly**—A traditional style of fly tied with swept-back hackle and a backward sweeping wing that is normally fished with the fly running against the current.
- **wet-fly swing**—Typical wet-fly presentation where the fly is cast diagonally downstream followed by the fly swinging toward the shore, imitating mayflies, emerging caddis, and small fish swimming across the current.
- **wind knot**—An overhand knot in the leader caused by poor casting and sometimes wind, significantly reducing the breaking strength of the leader.

LESSON 1

Yarn Casting Progressions

Overview

When casting with yarn, the power, timing, and stroke length of the cast are all comparable to fly line. The length ratio of yarn to real fly line is approximately 1 to 4 or 1 to 5 (depending on the weight of yarn and line used); hence, a 184-centimeter (6-foot) yarn cast is equivalent to a 213- to 274-centimeter (24- to 30-foot) fly-line cast. For best learning, this lesson should be done in an area with still air (since yarn will not cast in wind) using a 91-centimeter (3-foot) fly rod with brightly colored yarn. This lesson is suited to an indoor space.

Lesson 1 is adapted from the Atlantic Salmon Federation Fly-Casting module from Magic on the River, originally created by the Joan Wulff Casting program.

Learning Objectives

- To demonstrate understanding of casting methods and terms
- To demonstrate casting yarn, making different shapes with the whole arm such that the rod tip leads and the line follows the rod tip
- To demonstrate casting yarn 180 degrees
- To demonstrate overhead casting for accuracy
- To demonstrate casting on different planes
- To become familiar with terms *backcast, forward cast,* and *rod hand*

Activity 1: Threading Knitting Yarn Through the Rod Eyes

Threading the knitting yarn through the rod eyes is the first step in the setup for this lesson.

Skill Cues

- Open the spool of yarn, taking approximately 457 centimeters (15 feet) of yarn.
- Beginning at the handle end of the rod, push the loop through each eye, carefully threading it through all eyes until exiting from the rod tip.
- Ensure that no eyes were missed while threading the line.
- Once the yarn is through all the eyes, tie an overhand knot near the tip of the yarn to simulate the fly.

Teaching Cues

- Participants should rest the butt end of the rod on a clean surface.
- Double-check each participant to ensure the line has passed through each eye.
- Threading with a small loop is preferable to attempting to push the leader through the eyes, if space permits. If using the Fly-O rods, it's best to thread them without a loop in the yarn, because the eyes are too small to easily allow a loop of yarn through.
- Explain the value of using yarn in learning to cast: It requires less space, and it gets participants casting sooner with power, timing, and stroke length all being comparable to fly line.

Activity 2: Marking the Yarn

Marking the yarn provides appropriate progressions. Once the yarn is threaded and marked, participants are ready for the next activity. If the yarn is already marked, the markings should be highlighted to participants before moving on to activity 3.

Skill Cues

- From the tip of the yarn (knot simulating the fly), mark the yarn at 183-, 244-, 305-, and 366-centimeter (6-, 8-, 10-, and 12-foot) intervals with a dark-colored marker.
- Ensure marks are a different color from the yarn, making them clear and visible.

Teaching Cues

Provide template markings going from zero to 183-, 244-, 305-, and 366-centimeter (6-, 8-, 10-, and 12-foot) intervals so participants can mark their own yarn, or provide the marked yarn and skip this activity.

Activity 3: Casting Setup and Rod Grip

The casting setup establishes the line length for the participants' first casting progressions.

Skill Cues

- Set the 183-centimeter (6-foot) mark at the tip of the rod.
- Hold the yarn between the rod handle and palm of the dominant hand that is holding the rod.
- Position the thumb of the dominant hand on top of the rod (figure 13.1).

Teaching Cues

- Provide a quick demonstration and then have participants repeat.
- Check all participants to ensure their setups are correct before moving on.

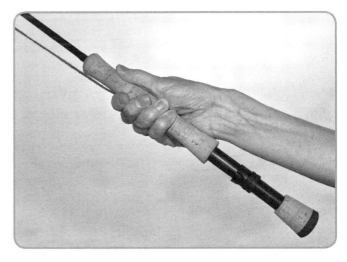

Figure 13.1   The thumb is aligned with the rod to add force in the finish of the cast.

Activity 4: Getting Comfortable With Rod and Line

Using a short line, participants are introduced to a variety of simplified casting patterns to aid their understanding of the relationship between rod, line, and casting mechanics. Here participants receive immediate visual feedback (i.e., "If I do this, then this will happen").

Skill Cues

- Make sure the 183-centimeter (6-foot) mark is at the tip of the rod.
- With wrist straight (but not stiff) and elbow bent and close to the body, use the whole arm to make large, counterclockwise circles about 122 centimeters (4 feet) in diameter.
- Wherever the rod tip leads, the line will follow.
- Take a full 2 seconds for each circle, ensuring motion is continuous.
- Keep the line moving without hesitation.

- Follow the movement with your eyes.
- Try making figure eights, ovals, or your name with the rod tip without letting the line hesitate or tangle.

Teaching Cues

- Demonstrate large circles without hesitation and have participants count "One thousand one, one thousand two" during the demonstration.
- Emphasize performing movement without line hesitation.
- Encourage participants to count as they make their circles.
- Reinforce making the shape with the rod tip and letting the line follow.

Activity 5: Introduction to Horizontal Casting

Casting uses all three parts of the arm: the hand, forearm, and upper arm. Learning basic principles on a horizontal plane allows casters to see the forward cast and the backcast and make any necessary adjustments immediately to refine casting technique.

Skill Cues

- Start with the elbow close to your body, hand extended forward, rotating the palm 90 degrees so the palm is facing up (to the sky).
- Using your forearm and hand with a loose shoulder, make side-to-side motions in front of your body, keeping the line parallel to the ground.
- Movement of the rod handle should not exceed 30 centimeters (1 foot) for the 183 centimeters (6 feet) of yarn.
- Stop the casting stroke abruptly in each direction, watching the line unroll completely.
- On the backcast, there should be no hinging of the wrist; on the forward cast, the wrist will hinge forward to finish with the forefinger pointing toward the intended target.
- When the line is fully unrolled but before it hits the floor, start the next stroke.
- Waiting for the line to unroll sets the timing for casting.
- Perform five false casts (backcast and forward cast combine to make one false cast) and at the end of the fifth cast, let the line unroll completely, laying the line on the floor. The line should finish straight and unwrinkled on the floor if done correctly.

Teaching Cues

- Begin with a demonstration.
- Pay special attention to 30-centimeter (1-foot) rod-tip movement, making sure the forearm is the primary mover with some upper arm movement.
- When casting, the elbow should move and not hinge. Movement of the elbow allows the full arm and body to contribute to casting power and efficiency.
- The casting movement can also be monitored by the outdoor leader holding a yardstick in front of the person casting, just under their casting hand. The objective for the person casting is to keep their casting thumb just above and in line with the yardstick throughout each horizontal cast.
- Encourage participants to watch the loops unroll fully before initiating the next casting stroke.
- If performing the five false casts, ensure everything is kept straight and level.
- On the backcast, participants need only to squeeze the rod butt to stop the cast.
- On the forward cast, add the force of the forefinger in a pushing motion as it is squeezed to a stop; this gives the unrolling line added speed and direction.
- Introduce this type of casting as *false casting*.

Activity 6: Horizontal Casting With Targets

This activity provides immediate feedback to participants and plenty of opportunity for them to understand what they have to change to improve their casting. Casters start from a kneeling or sitting position with the rod tip in between targets (e.g., books, paper plates) 183 centimeters (6 feet) to the right and left of the rod tip and the end of the line on the left target (for right-handed casters) (figure 13.2).

Skill Cues

- Start from a kneeling or sitting position with the rod tip in between targets (e.g., books, plates) 183 centimeters (6 feet) to the right and left of the rod tip and the end of the line on the left target (for right-handed casters).
- Slide the line off the target and accelerate to a quick stop (with a total stroke length or hand movement of only 30 centimeters [1 foot]), allowing the line to unroll fully with the tip landing in the target. This is the backcast.
- Repeat going forward for the forward cast, stopping after each cast.
- The shoulder, forearm, and casting hand all move as one; there is no hinging of the wrist on the backcast, but there is wrist motion at the end of the forward cast.
- On the forward cast, the forefinger should finish pointing at the target.
- The goal is to have line unroll to the targets without any sagging in the unrolling loops.
- Practice until you can cast with precision without looking at the backcast.

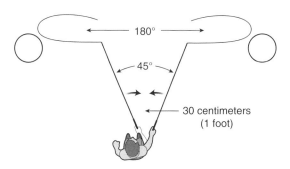

Figure 13.2 Unrolling the line 180 degrees to hit the targets.

Teaching Cues

- Begin with a demonstration and description of the activity.
- Participants should work on this activity until they know how far and fast they should move the rod to get the desired results.
- Too large or small of a casting arc is the most common cause of inaccuracy, but speed and power of hand movement can also affect where line finishes.
- Be sure the shoulder, forearm, and hand move as one; there should be no hinging at the wrist on the backcast.
- On the forward cast, the forefinger should finish pointing at the target.
- As precision improves, progress to making five false casts over the targets and finish laying the line in the target.
- Horizontal casting is often used in small streams where bushes and obstacles limit vertical casting.
- If the line tip is landing below the target, the casting stroke is too long and the casting arc is too large.
- If the line tip is landing above the target, the casting arc is too small.

Activity 7: Vertical Casting

Once horizontal casting is mastered, the casting plane may be changed to a vertical rod, applying the same principles as learned in activity 4 (page 399).

Skill Cues

- Begin with the palm of the casting hand facing up and cast horizontally as in activity 4, gradually changing the plane a few centimeters at a time, moving toward vertical as comfort and precision dictate.

- The shoulder, forearm, and casting hand all move as one, with no hinging of the wrist on the backcast.
- Once the cast is vertical, make the backcast high and the forward cast low, unrolling the line about 30 centimeters (1 foot) above the target.
- Progress to picking the line up off the floor and then laying it back on the target without false casting.
- Alternate between false casting and picking the line up and laying it down.

Teaching Cues

- Ensure that as the cast becomes vertical, the casting motion changes from back and forth to up and down; take the forefinger to your forehead on the backcast, and end up with the forefinger pointing to the target on the forward cast.
- Alternate between false casting and picking the line up and laying it down.
- If participants are having accuracy problems, have them keep the rod in the vertical plane between their eyes.

Activity 8: Casting on Different Planes

Casting on different planes combines all the skills of the last three activities to demonstrate the fisher's ability to adjust the cast to the task.

Skill Cues

- Shorten the line to 122 centimeters (4 feet).
- Cast to different objects at different heights and planes so the fly touches the target with each false cast.

Teaching Cues

- Your demonstration should include objects at a variety of heights and angles that require horizontal, vertical, and diagonal casts.
- With this length of line, challenge participants to be accurate within 2.5 centimeters (1 inch) of the target.
- Once participants are competent with 122 centimeters (4 feet) of line, move to 183 centimeters (6 feet) of line.

Activity 9: Lengthening the Cast

This activity repeats the skills of activities 6, 7, and 8 with a longer line. For this activity, casting 244 centimeters (8 feet) of yarn is the equivalent of casting 10 to 12 meters (32-40 feet) of regular line.

Skill Cues

- Lengthen the line to 244 centimeters (8 feet).
- Repeat activities for horizontal casting, vertical casting, and casting on different planes.
- The added length requires a slightly longer stroke (about 61 centimeters [2 feet]), a little more power, and a longer waiting time for the line to unroll.
- If power is limited when casting longer lengths, put the casting foot back and shift weight back and forth with the cast for supplementary stroke length and power.

Teaching Cues

- Demonstrate longer-length casting, emphasizing slightly longer stroke (about 61 centimeters [2 feet]), a little more power than at 183 centimeters (6 feet), and a longer waiting time for the line to unroll.
- Once mastery is achieved at this length, move to 305-centimeter (10-foot) length (12- to 15-meter [40- to 50-foot] cast length equivalent) and 366-centimeter (12-foot) length (15- to 18-meter [48- to 60-foot] cast length equivalent).

Lesson Closure

The value of practicing fly-casting techniques in this lesson cannot be underestimated. Through these activities, fly casting can be learned and practiced with minimum cost, in a small area, away from water, and even throughout the winter, leading to significant improvement the following fishing season. The activities in this lesson are invaluable to the novice and expert fisher alike.

LESSON 2

Fly-Fishing Equipment and Assembly

Overview

Participants must know the fly-fishing equipment components and functions to help in the assembly of fly-fishing gear. Careful attention to assembly of the fly-fishing equipment ensures proper alignment and attachment of the components, thus reducing the risk of damage to equipment and maximizing the ease of casting and playing fish.

Learning Objectives

- To understand the function of the following parts: rod, rod label, reel, line, backing, leader, fly, false fly, eye or eyelet, and ferrule
- To assemble rod and reel, ensuring the reel matches the user's dominant hand
- To understand that disassembly of a rod and reel is the exact opposite process of assembling a rod and reel
- To thread line through the eyes of the rod

Activity 1: Identifying Equipment Components

Being able to identify equipment components is essential to understanding instructions. This activity also lays the foundation for those that wish to window shop or purchase their own fly fishing equipment at some time in the future.

Skill Cues

Participants should know the following pieces of equipment and their functions (figure 13.3):

- **Rods** may be constructed in two-piece, three-piece, four-piece, or five-piece sections that are joined by a ferrule that has a male and female end. They also

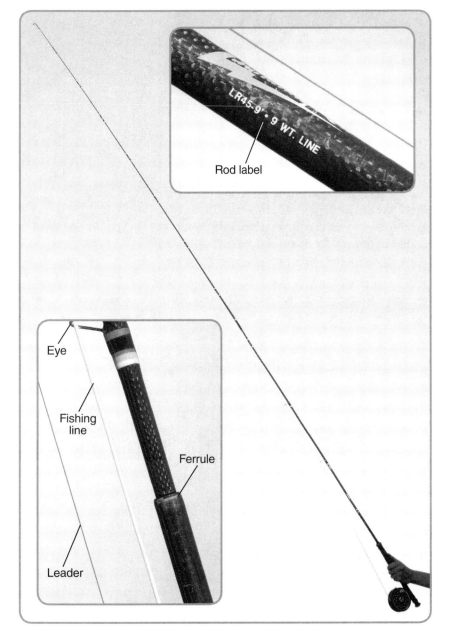

Figure 13.3 Fly rod and components: (inset top) The rod label indicates that this is a 9-foot (275-centimeter) pole requiring a 9-weight line; (inset bottom) a closer look at the ferrule and eye.

come in various lengths (normal range is 244-274 centimeters [8-9 feet]) and degrees of stiffness, or resistance.

- The **rod label** is a label just above the handle that identifies the actual weight of the rod, its length, and its amount of stiffness. The label also indicates what weight of fly line to use for maximum performance.

- **Reels** are simple devices that normally include a spool to hold fly line and backing and that are equipped with a braking device called a *drag.* They come in various sizes that identify their capacity for holding a certain length of fly line and the thin running line called *backing.*

- The weight of the **line** should match the rod. Look for the line-weight number on the rod label and ensure the line weight matches.

- **Backing** is a thin-diameter running line, usually of 9-kilogram (20-pound) test rating, that is attached to the reel first and then connected to the end of the fly line using a nail knot. This running line permits a fish to run farther distances than the limitation of the fly line. A small reel may contain as few as 50 meters (55 yards) of backing, whereas a large reel may contain 200 meters (219 yards) or more.

- **Leader** is a clear length of monofilament, about 274 to 366 centimeters (9-12 feet) long, that is attached to the end of the fly line. It is usually tapered from a large to small diameter, with the large end attached to the fly line using a knot or loop-to-loop connection. The smaller end will be attached to a tippet.

- A **tippet** is a short length (61-91 centimeters [2-3 feet]) of clear monofilament material that will be tied between the leader and the artificial fly.

- **Flies** are hooks that have materials attached, such as hair, feathers, tinsel, and wool, to simulate an insect. Flies come in numerous sizes and shapes according to a formula known as a *pattern* and may be designed to sink or float.

- A **false fly** is used in casting practice. It is often a small piece of high-visibility wool or other material that is attached to the tippet to simulate the size of an artificial fly.

Teaching Cues

- Provide participants (individuals or groups) with a list of equipment to collect from the storage or display area.
- Identify each piece of equipment in order of use, beginning with the rod and proceeding to the reel, backing, line, leader, tippet, and fly.
- Identify any safety concerns associated with each piece of equipment, such as ensuring that the rod tip is not caught in a tree or closing door and that the reel is kept away from dirt.
- Review equipment parts and functions by questioning participants so they can name the basic equipment parts and their use.

Activity 2: Assembling the Rod

If fly rods are stored fully assembled, this activity may be passed over until later or completed at this point. If rods are stored disassembled, this activity must be done to proceed to further activities. Note that skipping this activity completely is not an option as participants should know how to assemble and disassemble a fly rod.

Skill Cues

- Understand the terms *eye* (also referred to as *eyelet*) and *ferrule.*
- Connect the sections by aligning the eyes of the rod.
- Carefully but firmly push the sections together.
- When attaching rod sections, keep hands close to the ferrules to avoid strain and possible breakage.
- When the rod is assembled, check alignment of both your own rod and those of fellow participants by looking from handle to tip to ensure all eyes are in a straight line.
- Reinforce vertical rod assembly and positioning to avoid personal injury or damage.
- To lubricate the ferrule sections, rub the male end on the crease between the side of your nose and cheekbone before inserting it into the female end. This will facilitate disassembly later.
- Disassemble the rod using reverse steps of rod assembly.

Teaching Cues

- Depending on the number of sections, have participants begin at the handle (butt) section and attach sections according to diameter of the ferrule and rod section.
- Inform participants that the handle section may have to be turned again once the reel is attached to ensure proper alignment of the reel with the eyes.
- Remind participants that hands should be close to the ferrule when pressing together.
- Have participants check their own rod and those of adjacent participants to ensure alignment.
- Have participants disassemble the rod using reverse steps of rod assembly.

Activity 3: Attaching the Reel

This activity introduces the fly-fishing reel. Attaching the reel properly ensures it will stay on the rod and will be seated appropriately, making it easy for the fisher to control the release and retraction of line (figure 13.4). The physical weight of the reel should balance the weight of the fly rod at a point toward the front of the rod handle. Reels are designed for either right-handed or left-handed retrieves and usually may be converted easily.

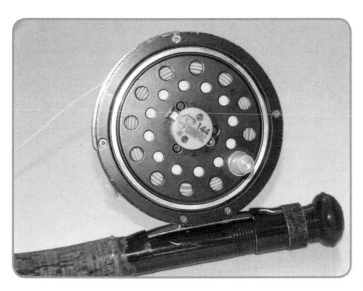

Figure 13.4 Fly-fishing reel attached to the rod. Note the ears of the reel secured by adjustable slots in the handle.

Skill Cues

- The fly rod has a specific place to attach the reel, often an indentation or slot located on the reel seat, which is located on the bottom (or butt end) of the rod below the handle.
- Locate the site and insert an ear of the reel securely into the slot just below the handle.
- Slide the locking rings on the reel seat over the other ear and turn to tighten.
- Ensure that the reel is firmly attached.
- Check to see that the drag is set so there is resistance as the fly line comes off the reel.
- Conversion from left-handed to right-handed retrieve requires complete removal of the fly line and backing, changing the direction according to the manufacturer's instructions, and then reattaching so the handle is facing the right side of the reel and there is no resistance as the fly line is retrieved.
- Disassemble the reel using reverse steps of reel assembly.

Teaching Cues

- Divide participants into pairs or groups according to left- or right-handed reels.
- Get right-handed reel users started and then spend time with the left-handed users. If possible, teach a couple of left-handed users before doing this activity with the whole group so that the left-handed users taught in advance may assist other left-handed users in the group and speed up the process.
- Have students disassemble the reel from the rod using reverse steps of reel assembly.

Activity 4: Threading the Fly Line Through the Eyes

Fly line is thick, usually constructed of a fabric core coated with a smooth coating of flexible plastic or other derivative. Fly lines have various shapes in which parts of the line are thicker than others.

- A level line has one diameter throughout its length and is designated as *L*.
- A double-tapered line is thin at both ends but thick in the center section and is designated as *DT*.
- A weight-forward line has the thick section in the first 20 to 30 percent of its length and is designated as *WF*.

Fly lines are also designed to float or sink, or for the forward section to sink. A floating line is designated as *F*, a sinking line as *S*, and a sinking tip as *ST*. They are also measured in physical weight in grams and conform to a formula developed by the American Fishing Tackle Manufacturers Association (AFTMA) to ensure that they will match the stiffness of the fly rod and result in quality performance.

Skill Cues

- Pull about 366 centimeters (12 feet) of fly line from the reel.
- Form a small loop in the fly line toward the tip.
- Beginning at the handle, push the loop through each eye, carefully threading it through all eyes until exiting from the rod tip.

- Ensure that no eyes were missed while threading the line.
- In the disassembly of the rod and reel, the line that was threaded through the eyes should be returned to the reel. Keep a slight pressure on the line by lightly squeezing the line close to the reel with your nonreeling hand as the line enters the reel. This action prevents the line from knotting up in the reel.

Teaching Cues

- Participants may rest the reel and butt end of the rod on a clean or clear surface such as a table, clean rock, or grass.
- Double-check each participant to ensure the line has passed through each eye.
- Threading with a small loop is preferable (where possible) to attempting to push the leader through the eyes.
- In the disassembling process, check the line in the reel to ensure it is not knotted. If the line is knotted, pull the line out of the reel and reel the line in, maintaining tension on the line as noted in the skill cues.

Lesson Closure

Ensure that the rod sections are firmly joined, that the reel is securely fastened to the reel seat, that the line pulls from the reel with some resistance (but has none while reeling in), that the fly line matches the rod, and that the line is threaded through each eye. At the completion of this lesson, participants should be familiar enough to assemble the fly fishing outfit, making it ready for lesson 3. If the leader is attached, disassemble the rod, reel, and line so it can be properly stored.

LESSON 3

Attaching the Leader

Overview

The leader is a length of monofilament that tapers from a thick end that attaches to the fly line to a smaller end that attaches to a tippet. Several knots may be used to achieve this attachment. For this lesson, we will focus on the nail knot and the needle knot. Another method is the loop-to-loop connection.

When teaching this lesson, you have a choice: Teach it all or teach only what is relevant to getting started. Although preferable, it is not essential to know all the knots in this lesson in order to get participants' gear outfitted; hence you may choose just one knot that best suits the equipment and participants' abilities and interest. By the end of this lesson, participants should be completely comfortable attaching leader to a fly line using at least one of the methods from this lesson. If you choose to cover only one knot, it is recommended that you explain and demonstrate the alternate methods.

Learning Objectives

To be familiar with three common methods for attaching the leader to the fly line: the nail knot, the needle knot, and the loop-to-loop connection

Activity 1: Equipment Selection

Participants need to know how to attach a leader to the fly line using a nail knot, needle knot, or loop-to-loop connection. The first step in tying these knots is knowing what is required and selecting the equipment.

Skill Cues

- Identify equipment to be used in this activity: a 274-centimeter (9-foot) length of tapered leader material, a nail, a needle, and a loop-to-loop connection (if available).
- Select equipment to be used for each knot.

Teaching Cues

Lay out equipment for each knot.

Activity 2: Tying the Nail Knot

The nail knot is commonly used to attach backing to fly line and leader to fly line. It is a strong knot that should be learned by anyone who practices fly fishing. This knot is so named because a nail is commonly used to tie it. Use a curved blood-knot tool that includes a needle eye to further simplify and speed the tying process.

Skill Cues

This description of tying a nail knot is for a right-handed tier with the fly line on the right and leader extending to the left.

- Hold the leader at the end of the fly line with the leader overlapping the fly line approximately 15 centimeters (6 inches) up the line.
- Hold the nail in position at the end of the fly line where the leader overlaps with the fly line. The head of the nail should extend beyond the fly line.
- With the leader, construct 6 to 10 concentric circles sequentially from right to left without a bight (see figure 13.5a).
- Push the end of the leader (used in making circles) to the right through the middle of all the circles.
- While holding the line, leader, and nail in place, gently pull on both leader lines (left and right of circles) to take slack out of the circles made by the leader (see figure 13.5b).
- Slowly remove the nail (to the left).
- Once again while holding the line and leader, gently pull on both leader lines (left and right of circles) to take slack out of the circles made by the leader; then pull the leader ends to tighten the nail knot on the line.
- Cut tag ends close to the knot (see figure 13.5c).

Teaching Cues

- Illustrate the nail knot using a large rope and wooden dowel as props.
- Participants work in pairs or groups under your direction, practicing on the props until they clearly understand how the knots are tied.

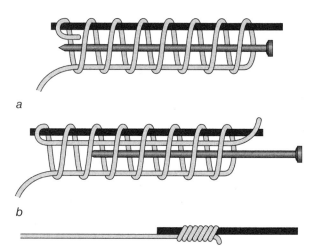

a

b

c

Figure 13.5 Steps for tying the nail knot.

- Inspect each knot for correctness.
- Pull on the leader and fly line to ensure it is firmly attached.
- Explain about trimming the ends of the finished knot with clippers.

Activity 3: Tying the Needle Knot

The needle knot is created using a sewing needle and is used to connect the leader butt to the fly line. It is a simple yet effective method that eliminates bulk at the connection. This knot cannot be tied to fly lines with a solid or monofilament core. In this activity, participants will tie a needle knot using a large-eyed needle and leader material.

Skill Cues

- Prepare the leader butt by cutting it at a slant to make a point.
- Insert a needle into the end of the fly line and out of the side, as shown in figure 13.6*a*. (Rotate the needle to ease its passage through the fly-line core.)
- Keep the fly line folded back as you withdraw the needle and insert the leader butt, threading 20 centimeters (8 inches) out of the side of the line (figure 13.6*b*).
- Wrap four or five turns loosely around the fly line (figure 13.6*c*).
- Fold the end of the leader back to create loop A.
- Fold the leader a second time to create loop B (figure 13.6*d*).
- Hold loop B alongside the end of the fly line where the final knot is to be and unwind the five turns, covering loop B with each turn.
- While preventing the turns from uncoiling, pull on both free ends of the nylon.
- Finally, push turns closely together, tighten fully, and trim off the loose end of the leader butt (figure 13.6*e*).

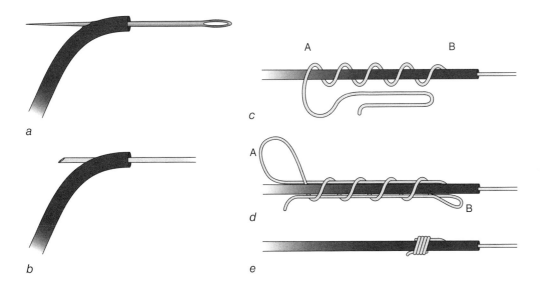

Figure 13.6   Steps for tying the needle knot.

Adapted, by permission, from Pat O'Reilly at First Nature (www.firstnature.com).

Teaching Cues

- Inspect each knot for correctness.
- Pull on the leader and fly line to ensure it is firmly attached.
- Explain about trimming the end of the finished knot with clippers.

Risk Management

- Breakage may occur when the knot is tied incorrectly, resulting in loss of the material and possibly a fish.
- A needle is used to attach the leader. Care must be taken in pushing the needle into the tip of the fly line to avoid puncturing a finger.

Activity 4: Tying the Loop-to-Loop Connection

Many fly-line manufacturers now offer a loop on the end of the fly line to accommodate a looped butt on the leader material. Though simple to tie, this connection may interrupt the smooth transfer of energy from fly line to leader from an effect known as *elbowing*.

Skill Cues

- Tie a double overhand loop in one or both lines to be joined, as required (i.e., factory line may be already looped) (figure 13.7*a*).
- Pass one loop through the other (figure 13.7*b*).
- Thread the hook end of the line through the inner loop (figure 13.7*c*).
- Continue to feed this complete line (including the overhand knot) through the loop.
- Pull knots tight.
- This is the loop-to-loop connection (figure 13.7*d*).

Teaching Cues

Check each participant to ensure the connection has been made.

Figure 13.7 Steps for tying the loop to loop connection.

Lesson Closure

Review the knots with the participants to ensure they know the nail knot, the needle knot, and the loop-to-loop connection.

LESSON 4

Attaching the Tippet and Fly

Overview

Proper knots are required to attach the tippet to the leader and the fly to the tippet. This lesson teaches the water knot and the tucked half blood knot.

Learning Objectives

- To attach the tippet to the leader using a water knot
- To attach a fly to the tippet using a tucked half blood knot

Risk Management

Improper knot connections cause knots to break or slip when strain is placed on the fly-fishing equipment, such as when a fish is played.

Activity 1: Attaching the Tippet

The water knot is used for joining lengths of nylon monofilament.

Skill Cues

- Lay the two lengths of nylon alongside one another with the long end of the finer nylon to your right (to your left if you are left-handed) (figure 13.8a).
- Wet the overlapping sections so that they cling together, and then form a large loop (figure 13.8b).
- Bring the longer end of the tippet nylon and the short end of the heavier nylon over and through the back of the loop, as in an overhand knot. Do not pull tight, but repeat step 3, making sure both ends pass through the loop (figure 13.8c).
- Pull on all four ends to close the knot (figure 13.8d).
- Use your thumbnails to push the turns close together as you pull on the main line and tippet.
- Trim off unwanted ends.

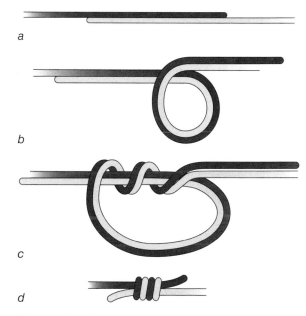

Figure 13.8 Steps for tying the water knot.

Teaching Cues

- Use two lengths of different-colored rope to illustrate the method of tying the water knot.
- Divide participants into pairs or groups to learn this knot using ropes.
- Participants tie the knot using the leader and tippet materials.
- Saliva may be used if necessary as a lubricant to help materials slide together.
- Participants clip off the ends of the knots with clippers.

Activity 2: Attaching the Fly

To attach the fly to the tippet, use the tucked half blood knot.

Skill Cues

- Thread the leader tippet through the eye of the hook, leaving at least 10 centimeters (4 inches) of spare material to complete the knot (figure 13.9a).
- Wrap the loose end of the tippet around the leader five times (figure 13.9, b-c).
- Bring the loose end of the tippet over to the hook and insert it through the loop of nylon you have now made in front of the eye of the hook.
- Bring the loose end back up and pass it through the new loop you created in step 3 (figure 13.9d).

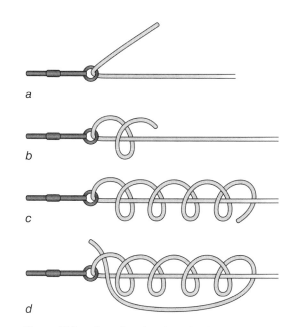

Figure 13.9 Steps for tying the tucked half blood knot.

Adapted, by permission, from Pat O'Reilly at First Nature (www.firstnature.com).

- Pull the knot down slowly, using a thumbnail to bring the turns close behind the eye. Do not pull tight yet.
- Spit on the knot to lubricate it.
- Tighten the knot by pulling on the leader with the hook bend secured on the ring of your scissors. Jiggle to fully tighten the knot.
- Trim off the spare end.

Teaching Cues

- Using a length of rope and a large metal device to simulate a hook (which may be constructed by bending a coat hanger into the shape of a hook), illustrate the proper method of tying the tucked half blood knot.
- Describe the advantages of each knot for securing the fly to the tippet.
- Divide participants into pairs or groups to practice tying the knot.
- Ensure that each participant has a clear understanding of how to tie the knot.
- Ensure participants are aware that if the loose end of the tippet is not around the leader at least five times, the knot is subject to unravel under pressure.

Lesson Closure

- Review the knots and reasons for tying them.
- Review the benefits of each knot.
- Test each connection for strength.

LESSON 5

Casting the Fly Rod

Overview

Casting the fly line involves four simple steps: (1) the lift, (2) the stop and load, (3) the forward cast, and (4) the drop and release. This lesson will introduce the processes involved in each step.

Learning Objectives

- To cast the fly rod, connecting the four stages of casting
- To practice casting to improve accuracy and fluidity

Risk Management

- Participants must maintain a safe distance from each other to avoid accidental crossing of lines during the lesson.
- Participants should ensure there are no obstacles behind them to tangle the line on the backcast.
- Participants will cast on a surface such as grass, wooden floor, or water (preferred) to minimize friction and resistance to lifting the line from the surface.
- Flies should have all metal surfaces removed from the bend, point, and barb, or a practice hook consisting of a piece of bright wool or cloth should be substituted.

Activity 1: Lift

The purpose of the lift phase is to retrieve the line off the water in front of the fisher.

Skill Cues

- Pull approximately 9 to 11 meters (30-35 feet) of fly line from the reel and ensure it is extended straight out in front of you.
- Hold the rod out in front of you, pointing the tip down toward the ground.
- Ensure all loose or slack line has been retrieved.
- Holding the fly line against the handle with an index finger to maintain a firm hold and prevent the line from slipping, tilt the rod slightly away from your body, rapidly and forcefully lift the rod to a vertical position, and abruptly stop at that position (figure 13.10).
- If performed correctly, the line will lift from the surface and loop behind you.

Figure 13.10　Casting, step 1: the lift.

Teaching Cues

- Inspect each hook or practice hook to ensure there are no sharp edges.
- There should be no slack or loops in the line prior to the lift.
- Ensure that participants tilt the rod slightly away from their body before the lift.
- Ensure the rod is pointed at the ground before the lift.
- Repeat this action until everyone has mastered this activity.
- The natural tendency is to push the rod back further than vertical; ensure that each participant stops at vertical or just beyond at 1 o'clock.

Activity 2: Stop and Load

In this activity, participants will learn to stop the rod at the vertical position, hesitate as the line loops behind, feel the pressure against the rod, and anticipate the forward (or power) cast.

Figure 13.11　Casting, step 2: the stop and load.

Skill Cues

- Practice the lift until the line flows behind in a loop.
- Feel the weight of the line as it reaches the end of the loop, also known as the *load* or loading of the rod (figure 13.11).

• As this occurs, mentally prepare for the forward cast.

Teaching Cues

• Ensure that each participant has grasped the meaning of the lift, the stop, the hesitation, and the loading of the rod.
• Illustrate the actions of the lift and stop while explaining the load placed on the rod by the weight of the fly line looping behind.
• Another illustration is answering a telephone, where the receiver is lifted from the base (the lift), brought up to the ear to hear the caller's voice (the stop), and placed back on the receiver (the forward cast).

Activity 3: Forward or Power Cast

In this activity, once the line loops behind the caster and loads the rod, the rod is forcefully directed forward from the vertical or 1-o'clock position, stopping at 10 o'clock as the line loops forward and unwinds.

Skill Cues

• Feel the load of the fly line as it loops behind before beginning the forward cast.
• Use the power and length of the fly rod on the forward cast (figure 13.12).
• Practice the lift, the stop and load, and the forward cast as three connected steps in a smooth action.
• Consistently stop at vertical on the lift and stop the power or casting stroke at the 10-o'clock position.

Figure 13.12 Casting, step 3: the power cast.

- Divide into pairs and assist each other by observing casting and offering assistance or bringing problems to the outdoor leader's attention.

Teaching Cues

- Illustrate the motions involved in the lift, the stop and load, and the forward or power cast as three smooth steps.
- Make sure everyone understands the concept by providing one-on-one assistance as the participants practice these steps.

Activity 4: Drop and Release

In this final step, the rod will slowly drop as the loop of the line extends outward in front of the caster, lowering the rod tip from 10 o'clock to point directly at the fly at the tip.

Skill Cues

- Stop the rod at the 10-o'clock position on the forward cast as the line loops outward until the leader loops out, carrying the fly with it.
- Slowly lower the rod until it points at the fly. The line should be fully extended in a straight line in front of you if the sequence has been performed correctly (figure 13.13).
- Practice all four steps until the action is smooth and unimpeded.

Teaching Cues

- Illustrate the drop-and-release portion of the cast.
- Assist participants who are having trouble with this step.
- Explain the actions taking place as energy is transmitted from the fly rod to the fly line as a result of the casting steps.

Figure 13.13   Casting, step 4: the drop and release.

- Evaluate the skill of each participant and separate those who have a good grasp of the techniques from those who are still having trouble.
- Allow the skilled participants to practice by themselves while you focus on the participants having difficulties. You can use either one-on-one teaching sessions with each person or hold a group session if there is a large number.

Lesson Closure

- Have participants illustrate their knowledge of the casting technique.
- Participants requiring more time should be mentored by skilled participants or the outdoor leader until the lesson has been completed.

LESSON 6

Applying Fly-Fishing Principles

Overview

Fly fishing is a method of casting a fly line with an artificial fly created from a steel hook. The fly may simulate an insect upon which fish are feeding, or it may follow a formula (pattern) that has been used for centuries to pursue species such as Atlantic salmon that do not feed in the freshwater environment.

Flies are generally categorized as wet, dry, streamers, or nymphs (figure 13.14). Each has a specific purpose in attracting fish.

a   b

c   d

Figure 13.14 Four types of flies: *(a)* streamer, *(b)* dry, *(c)* nymph, and *(d)* wet.

- Streamer flies are elongated and simulate minnows. Touch is used to feel the fish.
- Dry flies float on the surface and imitate floating insects. Vision is used to observe when a fish has taken the fly.
- Nymphs simulate a stage of insect life and are weighted to bounce along the bottom. Vision is used to observe when a fish has taken the fly.
- Wet flies sink beneath the surface film. Touch is used to feel the fish.

Learning Objectives

- To apply proper casting technique for floating flies
- To apply proper casting technique for nymph flies
- To apply proper casting technique for wet flies and streamers
- To apply proper technique for hooking, landing, and retaining fish
- To apply proper technique for playing fish

Risk Management

- Participants will be using real hooks that have sharp points and barbs. Ensure that each hook has the barb removed or pinched down for easy removal in the event the hook is accidentally embedded in a part of the body.
- Ensure that there is adequate space between participants as they cast to avoid accidentally striking or hooking each other.

Activity 1: Casting the Floating Fly

In this activity, participants will learn the technique for casting the floating fly. Activity will take place while standing on the riverbank of a stream with flowing water.

Skill Cues

- Attach a floating (dry) fly using the knots learned in lesson 4.
- Cast the fly line at an angle of 90 degrees upstream.
- Watch the fly float downward on the current with no tension on the fly line.
- Ensure that the rod tip is down and pointed at the fly as it makes its circuit.
- When the line straightens, lift the rod as in lesson 5 and cast the fly line upstream on the forward cast, repeating the entire sequence.
- Make sure there is clear space behind with no obstructions for the backcast.
- This technique is called the *dead float*.

Teaching Cues

- Provide extra space between casters.
- Monitor participants and remind those who move their body to stay square, or torso facing the fly as it floats downriver.

Activity 2: Casting the Wet Fly and Streamer

In this activity, participants will learn the technique for casting the wet (sinking) fly and streamer fly. The activity will take place while standing on the bank of a stream with flowing water.

Skill Cues

- Cast the wet fly and streamer across the current with the fly line and fly landing downstream from your position at a 45-degree angle.

- Ensure that the rod tip is down and pointed at the fly as it makes its circuit.
- Watch as the fly line straightens; then lift the rod as in lesson 5 and cast the fly line across the stream again, repeating the entire sequence.
- Ensure that the rod tip is down and pointed at the fly as it makes its circuit.
- This technique is called the *standard wet-fly cast.*

Teaching Cues

- Beginner fishers or those not yet skilled in hooking fish may wish to hold the rod at 90 degrees to the riverbank as the fly swings in. With this strategy, the fish is more likely to hook itself.
- Encourage fishers to maintain constant eye contact with their fly to monitor fish interest and activity.

Activity 3: Casting the Nymph Fly

In this activity, participants will learn to cast a nymph fly. This technique differs from the previous two activities in that the fly is cast upstream and permitted to sink to the bottom as the current carries it. A small, bright piece of floating material known as a *strike indicator* is connected to the leader several centimeters above the fly, depending on depth of the water. It is designed to suspend the nymph fly just off the bottom and, when disturbed, to indicate to that a fish has taken the fly. The activity will take place at the same location as activities 1 and 2.

Skill Cues

- Attach a strike indicator to the leader material.
  - The strike indicator should be positioned far enough from the nymph to allow the nymph to fish as deep as possible without the hook getting caught on the bottom.
  - Some strike indicators have a small ring (similar to the eye on a fish hook). The ring should be tied onto the leader in the desired position before the nymph is tied on, using a simple overhand knot or double figure-eight knot.

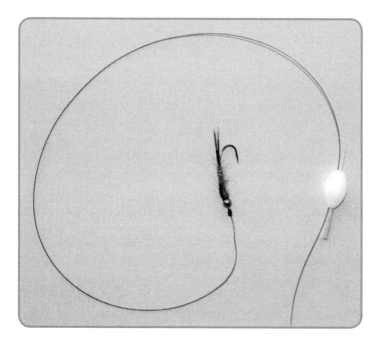

  - Other strike indicators (such as the one shown in figure 13.15) have a hole that allows them to be threaded onto the leader before tying onto the nymph. These strike indicators can be secured to the leader using a short stick (similar to a toothpick), which is used to wedge the leader against the inside of the strike indicator. The advantage of this system is that it allows for easy adjustment of the distance between the nymph and the strike indicator without untying the nymph from the leader. Simply remove the stick, slide the strike indicator to the new position, and replace the stick.
  - There are biodegradable putties available in vibrant colors that are designed specifically for use as strike indicators. These are applied by pinching a small ball onto the leader where required, and they can be removed and used again. A great advantage of this system is that you can decide for yourself how big the strike indicator should be. If you have a very heavy nymph that causes the

Figure 13.15 A threaded strike indicator.

strike indicator to sink, you can increase the buoyancy of the indicator by adding more putty.

- Cast the fly line upstream and focus on the strike indicator as it floats downstream on the current.

Teaching Cues

- Divide the group into pairs and assist participants in attaching the strike indicator.
- Ensure that each participant has an opportunity to learn this technique.
- Work one on one with participants who are having difficulty.
- Allow participants with prowess to move to another area and continue practicing while you work with participants who are having problems.
- Be cognizant of safety considerations with separate participants by monitoring frequently.

Activity 4: Hooking and Playing a Fish

In this activity, much depends on cooperation by fish in the stream or watershed. Participants should learn to react to either visual or touch indications when a fish accepts (or takes) the fly. The rod tip should remain pointed down, as learned in activity 4 of lesson 5 (page 415), and any slack line is retrieved before the line is lifted from the water, as in activity 1 of lesson 5 (page 413).

When a fish strikes, the first reaction is to immediately and strongly lift the rod tip. This is called *setting the hook*. From this point onward, the fisher will maintain the rod in a nearly vertical position and maintain tension on the fly line by retrieving line to the reel. Large fish must be allowed to run, which will allow line to escape from the reel. A *fish run* is when the fish swims vigorously upstream, downstream, or toward the bottom in an effort to escape, and the desired effect for the fisher is to tire or fatigue the fish before attempting to land the fish. Drag set on the reel should be strong enough to maintain tension on the fly line but not so strong that the leader, tippet, or knots will exceed their limitations and break. Participants must ensure that they maintain tension on the fish by not allowing any slack line to develop. If held high, the rod is designed to be flexible and absorb sudden shocks, such as fish jumping from the water or suddenly twisting.

Skill Cues

- Apply knowledge from lesson 5 to the fishing experience.
- React to visual or tactile sense as the fly is taken by a fish.
- Raise the rod tip to set the hook.
- React to visual or touch senses as the fly is taken by a fish.
- Apply the following principles when playing the fish:
  - Hold the fly rod vertically (figure 13.16).
  - Use the rod tip to guide the fish while keeping the rod tip vertical. Point the rod tip to the shore or in the desired direction you would like the fish to go.
  - Maintain tension on the fly line by retrieving any slack line as quickly as possible, either by reeling the line in or by shifting your body position away from the fish to make the line tight.
  - Ensure the drag on the reel is set to an appropriate resistance that allows line to be stripped from the reel as the fish runs (swims away from the fisher). There should not be so much resistance that the fish cannot run. Appropiate drag should make it harder for the fish to run but not stop it from running, and therefore the drag will contribute to fatiguing the fish as it is being played.

Figure 13.16 When hooking a fish, keep the rod upright to maintain strain on the fish.

  – Play the fish with a series of run-and-reel sequences intended to tire the fish and make it ready for landing. The *run* part of this sequence is when the fish swims vigorously upstream, downstream, or toward the bottom in an effort to escape, and the desired effect is for the fisher to tire or fatigue the fish before attempting to land the fish. The *reel* portion of the run-and-reel sequence is when the fisher quickly reels in any slack line (as the fish runs or stops a run) to maintain tension on the line at all times.
  – Note that if it is intended that the fish will be released, then playing time should be short; if it is intended that the fish will be kept, playing the fish longer is acceptable.

Teaching Cues

• Review and explain the content of this activity by demonstration if fish are plentiful and predictable enough to make this possible. If a demonstration with fish is not possible, have a leader or participant hold the line with a gloved hand or hold a soft object such as a sock or foam fish that is tied to the end of the line. Note: If a person is used to simulate a fish, the hook should be removed from the line.
• Show the flexibility of the rod by holding it in the vertical position and having a participant pull and jerk on the fly line.
• Illustrate how to apply tension to the reel by adjusting drag.
• Explain the concept of letting the fish run if necessary.
• Ensure that each participant has an opportunity to learn this technique.
• Work one on one with participants who are having difficulty.
• Allow participants with prowess to move to another area and continue practicing while working with people who are having problems.
• Be cognizant of safety considerations with separate participants by monitoring frequently.

Activity 5: Landing and Retaining Fish

In this activity, participants will learn to safely land the fish if it is being retained for food purposes. If releasing fish, proceed directly to lesson 7.

Skill Cues

- Play the fish to shore using the fly rod and reel. To guide the fish, keep the rod upright and point the rod tip in the direction you want the fish to go. Lead the fish with the tip of the rod. As the fish fatigues, reel the fish in proximally to your intended landing area (i.e., where you want to land the fish). A pool of water without obstacles and a low sloped beach is preferred.
- Guide the fish (using the techniques described) to a landing net or your hand.
- Remove the fish away from the water's edge and remove the barbless hook.
- If retaining the fish, dispatch it humanely with impact or knife blade applied to the top of the head.

Teaching Cues

- Demonstrate how to play a fish to the shore.
- Explain and identify an acceptable landing area that is free of obstacles, allowing the fish to be landed without damage from contact with rough rocks and stones.
- Teach participants to net the fish in deeper water (figure 13.17) or grip the fish just ahead of the tail with a gloved hand.
- Demonstrate how to remove the hook by holding the eye of the hook and pushing the hook in the opposite direction of the hook tip until the hook is free.
- Demonstrate how to humanely dispatch the fish with a rock or a heavy instrument known as a *priest* by a swift blow to the head.
- Explain the concept of conservation and the importance of hook and release to the health of fish resources.
- Explain that a photo will record the moment forever, whereas a dead fish is soon forgotten.
- A fish must be supported by a hand beneath the stomach and the other gripping the tail for a photograph, and it must be held in the water as much as possible if it is planned for release (as described in lesson 7).
- Participants continue casting and fishing. When one of the participants is successful in attracting a fish to the fly, assemble the rest of the group to watch the procedure, commenting and correcting as the fish is played, landed, and released.

Figure 13.17 Net used to land a fish.

Lesson Closure

- Review the purpose and casting technique for the following flies: wet, dry, streamers, and nymphs.
  - Streamer flies are elongated and simulate minnows. Touch is used to feel the fish.
  - Dry flies float on the surface and imitate floating insects. Vision is used to observe when a fish has taken the fly.
  - Nymphs simulate a stage of insect life and are weighted to bounce along the bottom. Vision is used to observe when a fish has taken the fly.
  - Wet flies sink beneath the surface film. Touch is used to feel the fish.
- Review proper technique for hooking, playing, landing, and retaining fish.

LESSON 7

Live-Release Fishing

Overview

Whether or not anglers should play fish and then release them back to the wild is a valid question. Traditionally, fishing has provided a valuable food source. With dwindling fish stocks worldwide, an increase in recreational fishery has led to greater emphasis on live release to the wild to help preserve healthy fish stocks. The thrill of playing a prize fish while conserving the fish stock has become a motivating factor for live release by a growing number of anglers today.

Learning Objectives

- To crimp the barb on a hook
- To understand the value of barbless hooks in preserving fish stocks
- To know how to humanely play a fish for conditions and recognize how water conditions affect the process
- To learn how to remove hooks from fish for live release
- To learn how to humanely revive and release a fish

Activity 1: Knowing the Fishing Area

The better a fisher knows a fishing area, the greater the probability of success.

Skill Cues

- Consult with local experts on water levels and conditions that are healthy and those that jeopardize fish stocks.
- Log water temperatures, water levels, and water conditions of local areas over a fishing season.
- Know what affects fish in your area; for example, sea-run Atlantic salmon in freshwater rivers are stressed by high water temperatures and low water levels, which should affect how a fish behaves on the end of the line.

Teaching Cues

- Consult with local experts and organizations to get a sense of local fish stocks, stats, and conditions.
- Have participants research and identify three to five promising fishing spots in your area.
- Part of your practice fishing could be extended to include one or some of these areas.

Activity 2: Adjusting Fishing Tackle to Facilitate Release

If you are planning on releasing fish, your fishing tackle should be adjusted before you start fishing to facilitate the eventual release of the fish. The barbless hook makes hook removal quick and easy.

Skill Cues

- Use a barbless hook or crimp to flatten the barb of the hook.
- In water conditions that stress fish, use a hook that is cracked off or cut the hook just behind the barb. This will hook the fish enough for short play and then facilitate a long-line (hands-off) release of the fish.

Teaching Cues

- Demonstrate removal of barbed and barbless hooks from a piece of rag or clothing.
- Have participants crimp or flatten barbs on a hook with pliers.
- Have participants try to remove barbed and barbless hooks from rags or clothing.
- Discuss the value of barbless hooks for live-release fishing.

Activity 3: Playing the Fish

For most fishers, the two main pleasures are hooking and playing fish. Hooking the fish is the act of the fish taking the fly and the fisher setting the hook. Once this is complete, the struggle of the fish to escape combined with the fisher's effort to bring the fish in is referred to as *playing the fish*. Hence, playing the fish occurs from the time the fish is hooked to the time the fish is landed.

Skill Cues

- Keep the rod tip up.
- Point the top of the rod (upstream or downstream) in the direction you want to bring the fish (figure 13.18).
- Limit fish runs according to fish and water conditions. Fresh fish in cold, high water can withstand longer runs.
- If possible, keep fish in a pool.
- Poorer water conditions (e.g., warm, low water) dictate much shorter time playing fish.
- Avoid playing the fish to complete exhaustion; severe exhaustion reduces the odds of survival.
- Bring the fish quickly to quiet water and within reach to remove the hook.

Figure 13.18 Fish jumping as it is being played.

Teaching Cues

- Demonstrate how to play a fish to the shore.
- Group members fish, and when one person hooks a fish, all lines come in while you talk the fisher through the playing process while the others watch.
- In the absence of fish, this activity can be simulated by a partner holding the end of the line (using a gloved hand holding line without hooks or loops).
- Teach participants to net the fish or grip it without damage by ensuring it does not contact rough rocks and stones on the shore.

Activity 4: Removing the Hook

Once the fish is retrieved to the intended landing area, the hook should be removed quickly and gently to minimize stress to the fish.

Skill Cues

- Leave the fish in water.
- Handle the fish gently without squeezing.
- Carefully remove the hook with pliers or thumb and forefinger or cut the leader near the hook, sparing the fish further trauma.

Teaching Cues

- Cut a sponge to simulate a fish and practice removing hooks from the sponge; the sponge provides an effective indicator of pressure being applied to fish.
- Demonstrate how to keep fish in the water while removing the hook.

Activity 5: Reviving and Releasing the Fish

Reviving the fish appropriately is essential to the fish's survival, and releasing the fish often provides as much pleasure to the fisher as it does to the fish.

Skill Cues

- A fish that fights for its life will likely need help to recover.
- Hold the fish underwater in a natural position facing the current.
- If the water is lacking current, create conditions where water passes over the gills of the fish; this may mean moving the fish forward and repeating the process to keep water passing over the gills.
- Handle the fish as little as possible, keeping it in the water.
- Photograph the fish in the water (if desired).
- Recognize when the fish is ready to be released, giving it enough time to recover so it can swim away on its own.
- When the fish is recovered, release it.

Teaching Cues

- Allow participants to continue casting and fishing. When one of the participants is successful in attracting a fish to the fly, assemble the rest of the group to watch the procedure, commenting and correcting as the fish is played, landed, and released.
- For video of Atlantic salmon live release, visit http://asf.ca/live_release.php.
- Explain the concept of conservation and the importance of hook and release to preserving fish stocks so that others experience the pleasure of hooking the same fish, maintaining the health of the fish resources while still enjoying the experience.
- Explain that a photo will record the moment forever, whereas a dead fish is soon forgotten.
- A fish must be supported by a hand beneath the stomach and the other gripping the tail for a photograph, and it must be held in the water as much as possible (figure 13.19).
- Demonstrate how to hold the fish with its head into the current while it recovers strength from the exertion of being played.

Figure 13.19 One hand holds the fish by the tail while the other hand supports the underbelly of the fish.

- Explain how to recognize when the fish has regained strength by its activity level (when the fish is breathing easily on its own and appears anxious to get away) and how to let it go back into the stream.

Lesson Closure

- This lesson has the power to change one person at a time, and once this change is made, it lasts a lifetime. Individual commitments are more likely to positively influence others as they see and share the benefits of live-release fishing and conservation of fish stocks.
- Every person who feels the power of saving a life is likely to become an advocate for live-release and preservation of fish species.
- The emotional responses to personal empowerment activities in this lesson are likely to affect personal values, appreciation for natural habitat, and a quest for finding balance in life.
- Review the importance of hook-and-release fishing; if practiced properly, it ensures a future for generations of fishers to follow.

References and Resources

Lord, M., D. Talleur, and D. Whitlock. 2006. *The L.L. Bean ultimate book of fly fishing.* Guilford, CT: Lyons Press.

Paine, A.B. 1993. *The tent dwellers.* Halifax, NS: Nimbus Classics.

Illustrations of knots are based on illustrations at www.first-nature.com.

Lesson 1 of this unit was adapted from the Atlantic Salmon Federation Fly-Casting module from Magic on the River, originally created by the Joan Wulff Casting program. For Fly-O rods or Joan Wulff's casting video or book, please contact Royal Wulff Products, HCR 1 Box 70, Lew Beach, NY 12758; 800-328-3638.

About the Editors

Kevin Redmond, MPE, is a physical education teacher at Gonzaga High School in St. John's, Newfoundland and Labrador, Canada. He served as national chairperson for Paddle Canada's Technical and Program Development committees and was the second person in Canada to be awarded Master Canoe Instructor as advanced instructor trainer in the disciplines of lakewater canoeing, whitewater canoeing, and canoe tripping.

Redmond, who has taught physical education and outdoor activities for 30 years at the community, K-12, and university levels, was awarded the National Award of Merit for his contribution to canoeing in Canada. He has worked in the camp system as a counselor, aquatics director, program director, and camp director. He also was a lead contributor in physical education curriculum development that introduced mandatory outdoor curriculum components in Newfoundland and Labrador. Redmond is an award-winning photographer and has completed work for various tourism agencies, such as Parks Canada, and adventure gear manufacturers throughout North America. In his spare time, Redmond enjoys photography, skiing, and salmon fishing.

He can be reached at kevinredmond8@gmail.com.

Andrew Foran, PhD, is an associate professor and chair of the teacher education program at St. Francis Xavier University in Antigonish, Nova Scotia. Dr. Foran is a wilderness and remote first aid instructor trainer for the Canadian Red Cross, an instructor of the National Archery in the Schools program, and a certified canoe tripping instructor and canoe flatwater and advanced tandem and solo instructor with Paddle Canada. He has taught outdoor education leadership modules for Nova Scotia Outdoor Leadership Development and has received numerous grants to develop curriculum related to outdoor pursuits and leadership.

Dr. Foran is a frequent lecturer and workshop presenter, having presented on a variety of outdoor and wilderness topics. He has developed curriculum for outdoor pursuits, leadership, and wilderness and remote first aid and has numerous publications to his credit. He conducts research in how the outdoors is experienced by adults and children. In his leisure time, he enjoys canoe tripping, geocaching, and leading backpacking expeditions.

About the Contributors

Sean Dwyer is a physical education teacher with Western School District in Newfoundland and Labrador, Canada. He completed a physical education degree at Memorial University of Newfoundland and completed a master's degree at the University of Alberta. He is a member of the Provincial Curriculum Committee for Physical Education. Sean worked closely with Kevin Redmond, among others, to introduce mandatory outdoor adventure components to the provincial curriculum. He currently runs a successful outdoor pursuits club at his school in which students are involved in caving, hiking, night hikes, orienteering, winter camping, snowshoeing, geocaching, and camping. In 2005, he won the Physical Education Teacher of the Year award for the Western School District. In his spare time, he enjoys camping, backpacking, and woodworking.

Justin Barlow is a physical education teacher who has been involved in outdoor education since 2001. He received a bachelor of arts in physical education, specializing in outdoor pursuits, from the Augustana Faculty of the University of Alberta in 2007 and graduated from St. Francis Xavier in 2009. He has had the opportunity to both contribute and lead various outdoor trips during his time at Augustana as a student leader and as a camp counselor during his summers.

David Chorney, PhD, is an assistant professor in the Faculty of Education, Department of Secondary Education at the University of Alberta,

Edmonton, Canada. His active research program focuses on teacher education and physical education, curriculum theorizing in physical education, and technology integration within the field of physical education. Hired as an assistant professor in 2003 by the University of Lethbridge in Lethbridge, Alberta, and receiving numerous teaching and research awards as a new emerging scholar, Dr. Chorney accepted a position as an assistant professor with the University of Alberta in July of 2007. His scholarly work as a researcher and teacher educator of physical education teacher education (PETE) is nationally and provincially recognized. In 2002, he was recognized by the Canadian Association for Health, Physical Education, Recreation and Dance as a Canadian Young Professional Award winner.

Zacchari Crouse, MEd, CTRS, has worked over the past 10 years as a recreation therapist and wilderness therapist in both Canada and the United States. Recently he completed his master of education thesis research on the experiences of adolescents with substance use and mental health issues in a recreation therapy program. He is an avid rock climber and has pursued his passion for paddle sports all over the world: whitewater kayaking throughout Canada, the United States, Mexico, and Uganda; circumnavigating the island of Cape Breton in an open canoe; and circumnavigating the island of Newfoundland in a sea kayak. He is also a sea kayak and canoe instructor. He currently lives in Halifax, Nova Scotia.

Blair Doyle has an active outdoor background, having hiked, biked, climbed, parachuted, kayaked, and canoed most of Atlantic Canada. Being from the watery world of the east coast, running rivers led him to teaching paddling and underwater to become a PADI divemaster since 1985. Currently he is a sea kayak, river kayak, and canoe instructor with the National Paddle Canada program. He continues to serve in various roles, such as treasurer and vice president with Paddle Canada, and has been on the board of Canoe Kayak NS since 2003, now serving as president. As a first aid/CPR and emergency medical responder master instructor trainer with the Nova Scotia Region of the Red Cross, he was responsible for implementation of the now nationalized Wilderness Remote First Aid Program in Atlantic Canada in 1996. He has been involved in ground search and rescue since 1988 and is currently search director with Halifax Regional SAR. As an active responder and former training officer with HRSAR, he continues to teach all aspects of wilderness practices, including the National Association for SAR (NASAR) Managing the Lost Person Incident course to numerous federal and provincial authorities. He is also an advanced care paramedic in Nova Scotia. He has a strong drive to "keep it real" for the learner, thereby bridging the gap between actual and perceived capabilities in the wilderness. With an experiential approach to wilderness wisdom, he currently uses his consulting and training business to impart his energy and passion to several organizations, government agencies, and individuals.

Mark Dykeman is recognized as one of the pioneers of kayaking in Newfoundland and Labrador. He brings with him a strong background of moving-water skills and many years of experience tripping in places such as northern Labrador. His paddling skill is matched only by his teaching ability and his love of being on the water. Mark is a level 2 instructor in whitewater kayaking and a level 2 instructor in sea kayaking with Paddle Canada.

Kathlyn Harpman grew up in rural Nova Scotia exploring and enjoying the outdoors. She received a kinesiology degree from Acadia University, placing a focus on children and healthy, active living. She received her bachelor of education from St. Francis Xavier with a major in physical education, focusing on introducing outdoor education to the public school system in Nova Scotia. During her studies, she provided students with the chance to participate in outdoor education programs such as Active Outdoor Living (AOL), teaching them to explore and care for the natural environment and the opportunities it provides. She has built on those experiences by teaching in Iceland and continuing her passion for the outdoors through a variety of activities.

Debra Kraiker is an educator, author, international lecturer, and avid outdoor enthusiast who has been sharing her love for nature with others for over 30 years. A graduate of the University of Guelph, she works with troubled youth to help them develop their skills and their confidence. With her husband, Rolf, she has written a popular guide book, *Cradle to Canoe,* to help others safely introduce children to the outdoors. Co-owner of a small paddling school, Blazing Paddles, Debra enjoys helping clients discover the fine art of paddling and camping skills. Together the Kraiker family has ventured across North America on canoeing expeditions. They love to share these adventures and skills as guest lecturers at some of the largest paddling symposiums across North America.

Rolf Kraiker has been passionate about sharing his love for the outdoors with others for over 35 years. As an avid nature photographer and cinematographer, he soon discovered that fine-tuned technical skills in paddling and outdoor

camping were essential for his success. A former technical advisor for the Canadian Recreational Canoeing Association, Rolf and his wife run a family-operated paddling school located in Central Ontario and are coauthors of *Cradle to Canoe,* a popular guide for parents wishing to venture outdoors with young campers. Rolf is a popular lecturer at some of the largest paddling symposiums across North America. His films have aired as part of popular nature series on the Discovery and Family channels, and his photographs and stories appear in a number of magazines, such as *Canoe and Kayak, KANAWA,* and *Nature Canada.* The Kraiker family has traveled extensively by canoe across North America and elsewhere, including expeditions in the Canadian and Scandinavian Arctic.

Dr. T.A. Loeffler brings 20 years of expertise leading people through significant life-changing experiences to every facet of her work. As a professor of outdoor recreation at Memorial University of Newfoundland, she has developed a reputation for excellence in experiential education because her students are more likely to be outside chasing icebergs than sitting in a classroom. She has received international and national recognition for her innovative teaching. In June of 2008, she was awarded a prestigious 3M National Teaching Fellowship. In 2007, she received the Karl Rohnke Creativity Award from the Association of Experiential Education (AEE). In 2006, *The Globe and Mail* named her "a class act," and she received the Association of Atlantic Universities Distinguished Teaching Award. The Canadian Association for the Advancement of Women in Sport named her to their 2006 Top Twenty Most Influential Women in Canadian Sport and Physical Activity list. Additionally, she received the Memorial University President's Award for Distinguished Teaching in 2005, and the AEE named her the Outstanding Experiential Teacher of the Year in 1999.

Tara Marshall moved to Nova Scotia from North Lake, New Brunswick, to pursue a career in the fisheries field. In 1999, she completed her bachelor's degree in biology from Dalhousie University and began working for the Department of Fisheries on lobsters and groundfish. Since 2002, she has been with the Nova Scotia Department of Fisheries and Aquaculture, where she promotes and develops recreational sportfishery. Tara designed, implemented, and teaches Nova Scotia's L2F (Learn to Fish) program and is an instructor and member of BOW (Becoming an Outdoors-Woman) Nova Scotia, teaching a variety of fishing classes.

Matthew Ngo, BSc, BEd,

is a teacher in science and mathematics in Nova Scotia. He completed his undergraduate studies at Dalhousie University in 2007 and graduated from teacher education at St. Francis Xavier University in 2009. He was first introduced into meteorology during his undergraduate studies, where he was fascinated by the relationships between human lifestyle and the environment—most notably in global warming and climate change. Recently, he has worked on projects such as the Making Tracks program with the Ecology Action Center and is currently teaching secondary school students in Nova Scotia.

Darlene Thomasina Pidgeon has been an avid rock climber since 2001 and has traveled around the globe for climbing, including Europe, Australia, Asia, and the Americas. She is near completion of a degree in biology, but

her studies keep getting postponed by climbing adventures and motherhood. She plans to pursue a degree in naturopathic medicine when the timing is right. She is the first Canadian female to boulder V10, V11, and V12, and she has placed first in numerous national and international climbing competitions. She currently resides in Squamish, British Columbia, with her daughter Cedar, where she works as a birth and postpartum doula and climbs on a regular basis. They continue to escape the winters for the dry sunny rock of the south.

Len Rich (1938–2009) enjoyed the great outdoors of Canada for more than four decades. Regarded by many as an expert in the areas of freshwater and saltwater angling, fly fishing, fly tying, archery, and hunting, he shared his expertise and experience with others through words and photographs. An award-winning writer, he was recognized by the New England Outdoor Writers Association and the Outdoor Writers of Canada (OWC) for his books and articles, and in 1991 he received the coveted Canada Recreational Fisheries Award for "writing that influenced a generation of recreational fishers." In 2007, he was selected to receive the OWC's Jack Davis Mentorship Award for his work with up-and-coming writers. He wrote hundreds of feature articles appearing in numerous outdoor and travel magazines and authored seven books, most in the area of his greatest passion, fly fishing.

Amanda Stanec, PhD, served as an assistant professor of physical education at St. Francis Xavier University, Nova Scotia, from 2006 to

2009. Currently, she is teaching preK-5 physical education at Red Hill Elementary School in Albemarle County, Virginia. She cherishes the outdoors because she is a mountain biker, XTERRA triathlon competitor, snowboarder, 70.3 Ironman finisher, paddler, yogi, and marathoner. She enjoys being active in both the Blue Ridge of Virginia and in her native home of Antigonish County, Nova Scotia. This time is best spent when her husband, Jim, and her nephews and nieces accompany her.

Janel Swain has been involved in outdoor education since being a part of a high school outdoor education and experiential learning course in 1997. She is a wilderness and remote first aid instructor trainer with the Canadian Red Cross and helped to write the program materials for the Red Cross in her position as the senior technical advisor. She has an honors degree in advanced biology from Dalhousie University (Halifax, Nova Scotia) and a bachelor of education from the University of Ottawa (Ottawa, Ontario). During her university studies, she completed Project WILD educator training, a Canadian Wildlife Federation program teaching conservation education. She is currently an A-EMCA paramedic and lives in Ontario.

How to Use the CD-ROM

The *Quality Lesson Plans for Outdoor Education* CD-ROM contains units 1 through 13 (which are also in the book), plus units 14 through 21 (which are only on the disc). All units are provided as PDF files, so you can easily search for and print the lessons and activities you need.

You can use this CD-ROM on either a Windows-based PC or a Macintosh computer.

System Requirements

Windows

- IBM PC compatible with Pentium processor
- Windows 98/2000/XP/Vista
- Adobe Reader 8.0
- 4x CD-ROM drive

Macintosh

- Power Mac recommended
- System 10.4 or higher
- Adobe Reader
- 4x CD-ROM drive

User Instructions

Windows

1. Insert the *Quality Lesson Plans for Outdoor Education* CD-ROM. (Note: The CD-ROM must be present in the drive at all times.)
2. Select the "My Computer" icon from the desktop.
3. Select the CD-ROM drive.
4. Open the file you wish to view. See the "00Start.pdf" file for a list of the contents.

Macintosh

1. Insert the *Quality Lesson Plans for Outdoor Education* CD-ROM. (Note: The CD-ROM must be present in the drive at all times.)
2. Double-click the CD icon located on the desktop.
3. Open the file you wish to view. See the "00Start" file for a list of the contents.

For customer support, contact Technical Support:

Phone: 217-351-5076 Monday through Friday (excluding holidays) between 7:00 a.m. and 7:00 p.m. (CST).

Fax: 217-351-2674

E-mail: support@hkusa.com